RELATIONAL DATABASES

RELATIONAL DATABASES

Chao-Chih Yang

North Texas State University

Prentice-Hall
Englewood Cliffs, N. J. 07632

Editorial/production supervision
and interior design: Tracey L. Orbine
Cover design: Ben Santora
Manufacturing buyer: Gordon Osbourne

Printed in the United States of America

10 9 8 7 6 5 4 3 2 1

ISBN 0-13-771858-6 025

Prentice-Hall International (UK) Limited, *London*
Prentice-Hall of Australia Pty. Limited, *Sydney*
Prentice-Hall Canada Inc., *Toronto*
Prentice-Hall Hispanoamericana, S.A., *Mexico*
Prentice-Hall of India Private Limited, *New Delhi*
Prentice-Hall of Japan, Inc., *Tokyo*
Prentice-Hall of Southeast Asia Pte. Ltd., *Singapore*
Editora Prentice-Hall do Brasil, Ltda., *Rio de Janeiro*
Whitehall Books Limited, *Wellington, New Zealand*

This book is dedicated to my deceased parents
SHENG-YI YANG and PEI-WEN WU YANG
with whom I have never met again since 1948.

CONTENTS

FOREWORD xiii

PREFACE xv

0 A REVIEW OF MATHEMATICAL CONCEPTS 1

0.1   Introduction   1

0.2   Set Theory   1

     0.2.1   basic concepts 1

     0.2.2   set operations 2

0.3   Functions and Relations   3

     0.3.1   functions 3

     0.3.2   relations 4

0.4   Propositional Logic   4

     0.4.1   atoms and formulas 4

     0.4.2   interpretations of formulas 5

     0.4.3   equivalence between formulas 5

     0.4.4   normal forms 6

     0.4.5   logical consequence 6

0.5   First-Order Logic   7

     0.5.1   predicates 7

     0.5.2   quantification 7

     0.5.3   formulas 8

     0.5.4   interpretations of formulas 8

     0.5.5   normal form 9

0.6   Graph Theory   10

     0.6.1   undirected and directed graphs 10

     0.6.2   hypergraphs 11

0.7   NP-Complete and Np-Hard Problems 11

1   THE RELATIONAL MODEL OF DATABASES 12
1.1   Introduction 12
1.2   Attributes and Domains 13
1.3   Tuples 16
1.4   Relations and Databases and Their Schemes 19
1.5   Constraints 22
1.6   The Relational Model of Databases 28
        Exercises 29

2   THE RELATIONAL ALGEBRA 31
2.1   Introduction 31
2.2   Algebraic Operations 32
        2.2.1   union-compatibility 32
        2.2.2   renaming 33
        2.2.3   union 35
        2.2.4   difference 36
        2.2.5   complex product 37
        2.2.6   projection 39
        2.2.7   selection 40
2.3   Additional Algebraic Operations 42
        2.3.1   intersection 42
        2.3.2   theta-join 43
        2.3.3   natural join 44
        2.3.4   quotient or division 45
2.4   The Relational Algebra 46
        Exercises 47

3   THE RELATIONAL PREDICATE CALCULUS 49
3.1   Introduction 49
3.2   Tuple Relational Calculus 49
        3.2.1   formulas 50
        3.2.2   legal formulas 53
        3.2.3   tuple calculus expressions 56
        3.2.4   safe tuple calculus expressions and their
                 interpretations 58
*3.3 Reduction of Relational Algebra to Tuple
        Calculus 68
3.4   Domain Relational Calculus 69
*3.5 Reduction of Tuple Calculus to Domain
        Calculus 72

*3.6   Reduction of Domain Calculus to Relational
        Algebra 72
        Exercises 78

4   FUNCTIONAL DEPENDENCIES 80
    4.1   Introduction 80
    4.2   Functional Dependencies 80
    4.3   Logical Equivalence 81
    4.4   Independent Inference Rules for Functional
           Dependencies 83
    4.5   Other Inference Rules for Functional
           Dependencies 84
    4.6   Closure of a Set of Functional Dependencies 87
    *4.7   Soundness and Completeness of Inference Rules 91
    *4.8   Keys and Superkeys 93
    4.9   Coverings of a Set of Functional Dependencies 94
    4.10   Graphical Representations of Functional
           Dependencies 97
           Exercises 113

5   MULTIVALUED DEPENDENCIES 115
    5.1   Introduction 115
    5.2   Multivalued Dependencies 115
    5.3   Logical Equivalence 116
    5.4   Independent Inference Rules for Multivalued
           Dependencies 120
    5.5   Other Inference Rules for Multivalued
           Dependencies 122
    5.6   Inference Rules for Functional and Multivalued
           Dependencies 124
    5.7   Dependency Basis 125
    *5.8   Embedded Multivalued Dependencies 127
    *5.9   Conflict-Free Virtual Keys 128
    5.10   Final Remarks on Logical Equivalence 130
           Exercises 130

6   JOIN DEPENDENCIES 132
    6.1   Introduction 132
    6.2   Join Dependencies 132
    6.3   Testing of Losslessness 136
    6.4   An Existence Theorem 139
    6.5   The Membership Problem for Full Join
           Dependencies 140
    *6.6   Inference Rules for Join Dependencies 141
           Exercises 143

7   NORMALIZATION 145

7.1   Introduction 145
7.2   First Normal Form 145
7.3   Second Normal Form 146
7.4   Third Normal Form 150
7.5   Elementary Key Normal Form 155
7.6   A Synthesis Algorithm Based on FD-Graphs 157
    7.6.1   *an algorithm for finding a nonredundant graph covering 158*
    7.6.2   *an algorithm for finding a minimal graph covering 159*
    7.6.3   *an algorithm for finding an LR-minimal graph covering 163*
    7.6.4   *finding a database scheme 167*
7.7   Boyce-Codd Normal Form 169
*7.8   Relationships Among 3NF, EKNF, and BCNF Relation Schemes 171
7.9   Fourth Normal Form 172
7.10   Project-Join Normal Form 174
7.11   Horizontal Normalization 179
7.12   Final Remarks on Normalization 180
    Exercises 181

8   QUERY LANGUAGES AND DATA BASE MANAGEMENT SYSTEMS 000

8.1   Introduction 183
8.2   ISBL and PRTV 183
    8.2.1   *introduction 183*
    8.2.2   *objects, attributes, and named variables 184*
    8.2.3   *operations 185*
    *8.2.4   *user extensions 187*
    *8.2.5   *other features of PRTV 188*
    8.2.6   *query processing 188*
8.3   QUEL and INGRES 190
    8.3.1   *introduction 190*
    8.3.2   *QUEL 190*
    8.3.3   *INGRES 194*
    *8.3.4   *EQUEL 195*
    8.3.5   *creating or destroying a database 195*
    8.3.6   *entering or leaving INGRES environment 196*
    8.3.7   *creating a relation scheme 196*
    8.3.8   *creating or destroying a relation 197*
    8.3.9   *displaying and saving a relation 199*
    8.3.10   *printing or resetting the query buffer 200*
    8.3.11   *storage structures 200*

    8.3.12   secondary indexes 202
    8.3.13   system relations 203
    8.3.14   editing the work space 204
    8.3.15   query processing 206
8.4   Query by Example and QBE DBMS 210
    8.4.1   introduction 210
    8.4.2   entering QBE environment 210
    8.4.3   defining a data table 210
    8.4.4   command and condition boxes 214
    8.4.5   single table processing 215
    8.4.6   multiple table processing 218
    8.4.7   aggregates 225
    8.4.8   renaming 226
    8.4.9   deleting a relation scheme 226
8.5   PROLOG and PROLOG DBMS 226
    8.5.1   introduction 226
    8.5.2   clausal form of logic and Horn clauses 227
    8.5.3   UNIX and PROLOG environments 228
    8.5.4   correspondence of terminology and notation 228
    8.5.5   scripting a session 229
    8.5.6   textfiles and indexfiles 229
    8.5.7   knowledge representations 230
    8.5.8   initialization and maintenance of system
            relations 230
    8.5.9   creating a relation 232
    8.5.10 query processing 234
    8.5.11 updating and deleting tuples 242
    Exercises 243

APPENDIX: AN EXTENSION OF PROLOG
WITH A DATABASE OPTION 247
BIBLIOGRAPHY 251
INDEX 259

FOREWORD

Many areas of knowledge begin as art and only later become scientific. The immaturity of such an area can be measured by the extent to which it is still an art, demanding intuition and experimentation in applying myriad rules of thumb, each rule with only a narrow scope. As the field matures, these features fade and are replaced by a relatively small number of powerful rules that can be applied systematically.

When I taught database systems in the mid-1970s, it was clear that the field was still very much an art (some would say witchcraft!). There were, for example, the three competing models (relational, network and hierarchical), although even then it seemed likely that the relational model provided the underlying foundation, and the other to had the nature of *ad hoc* implementations.

At that time the relational model had already demonstrated a number of elegant aspects, particularly the opportunity to apply relational algebra or calculus. On the other hand, the model had fairly clear shortcomings in the area of normalization of relations. The student who actually tried to design a relational database quickly outran the then existing theory and had to fall back (with some disappointment) on intuition and experiment.

In the decade since then, much progress has been made. In particular, an algorithm has been developed for refining relations into their "elementary key normal form." This is a major step toward the systematic design of relational databases and confirms the long-suspected superiority of the relational model: the two competing models are not so helpful in providing systematic methods of database design.

The time, therefore, seems right for a fresh presentation of the fundamentals (as we now know them) of database, a presentation that will strip away unnecessary embellishments to reveal the stark beauty of the underlying structure. This is the purpose of the present book by Dr. Chao-Chih Yang.

Like Julius Caesar's Gaul, the body of the book is divided into three parts. Part I, consisting of chapters 1, 2, and 3, provides the fundamentals of the relational model, including the relational algebra and calculus. The second part (chapters 4–7) addresses database design issues, particularly dependencies and normalization. Part III, which is chapter 8, covers four implementations of the principles developed in the earlier chapters. The presentation of INGRES is particularly thorough, and coverage of QBE is also extensive. PROLOG, a logic programming language that has been used to implement relational database systems, is included because of its promise for the future. Dr. Yang's examples in INGRES, QBE, and PROLOG have all been verified on actual systems at UAB.

A one-semester database fundamentals course for undergraduate seniors or first-year graduate students could be supported by this book. Parts I and II would be covered in class, probably omitting those sections marked with an asterisk. Each chapter in the body of the book has exercises, which students are strongly encouraged to work through. Part III could be assigned to students as supplementary material to be tackled on their own initiative, depending on the actual database systems accessible to them (for example, INGRES and PROLOG are available to students in the UAB Computer and Information Sciences Department).

Mathematics is the language of science, and in emphasizing the *science* of database systems, this book is unabashedly mathematical. Dr. Yang has helped the reader by providing a mathematical review in the preliminary chapter, by simplifying and unifying the notation, and by providing many examples. The reward for the reader who masters this material should be that fundamental theoretical truths, stated precisely in mathematical terms, are durable; the corresponding knowledge should therefore depreciate rather slowly.

However, I would not want to leave you thinking that mastery of this book will reduce database to a dull subject in which the designer mechanistically turns the crank, and the answer emerges. Refining relations beyond their elementary key normal form is still an art. Applying database in demanding situations will always push the outer limits of our knowledge. Perception and creativity will always be vital characteristics of the database professional.

In short, there is still truth in the old saying that a database designer must be able to walk on water; Dr. Yang's book helps by mending most of the holes in the shoes.

Anthony Barnard
Dean, UAB Graduate School

PREFACE

This book is developed from notes I originally wrote for a graduate course in database systems at the University of Alabama at Birmingham (UAB). The course covered primarily the first seven chapters concerning the theory of relational databases. The manuscript is revised and further extended by including the query languages ISBL, QUEL, Query-by-Example (QBE) and PROLOG and their supporting database management systems to provide a mix of principles and practice in one volume. I hope that the book will be not only a textbook on relational databases for seniors and first-year graduate students but also a useful reference for practitioners and researchers working in this area.

I am grateful to Dr. Moshe M. Zloof of IBM for permission to use his department store database scheme in the examples throughout the book. I am grateful for the encouragement I received from Dr. Warren T. Jones and Dr. Kevin Reilly, and to Dr. Susan Dean who served as technical reader for the entire manuscript and also offered much advice.

Two classes at UAB used the draft of the first seven chapters and made many helpful suggestions. In particular, my students Richard O. Nord found typographical errors, Ted Reynold tested QBE examples, and Akram Salah provided help with PROLOG. Balanjaninath Edupuganty and Tina Liu each typed a couple of chapters.

My wife, Yu-Hua, and daughter, Hsiao-Pei, have been encouraging and forbearing throughout the past two years.

Finally, use of the support facilities of the Department of Computer and Information Sciences at UAB including UNIX's word processor and spell program, INGRES, PROLOG, and the Versatek printer, is greatly appreciated.

Chao-Chih Yang
North Texas State University

chapter 0

A REVIEW
OF MATHEMATICAL
CONCEPTS

0.1 INTRODUCTION

In this chapter, we review some relevant mathematical concepts that are the basic tools for defining the relational model of databases in this book. In particular, we review set theory, relations, functions, propositional logic, first-order logic, and graph theory. This chapter defines many important notions that will be referenced in subsequent chapters, and is not necessarily a prerequisite of this book.

0.2 SET THEORY

0.2.1 Basic Concepts

A collection of distinct objects is called a *set* or *family* and is represented by a pair of braces ({ }) enclosing its objects separated by commas. A set consisting of no objects is called the *empty set,* represented by the symbol ϕ. A collection of (not necessarily distinct) objects is called a *multiset* and is represented by a pair of square brackets ([ ]) enclosing its objects separated by commas. In this section, we review only concepts concerning sets.

An object of a set is called an *element* or a *member* of the set. If e is an element of a set S, then we say that e *belongs to* S or e is *in* S, denoted by $e \in S$. On the other hand, if e does not belong to S or e is not in S, then we denote that $e \notin S$. The *cardinality* or *cardinal number* of a set S, denoted by $|S|$, is the number of elements in S. A set is *finite* or *infinite* if its cardinality is also. A set of cardinality 1 is known as a *singleton set.*

A set S_1 is *equal* to a set S_2, denoted by $S_1 = S_2$, if S_1 and S_2 consist of the same elements. A set S_1 is a *(proper) subset* of a set S_2, S_1 is *(properly) contained* or *included* in S_2, or S_2 *(properly) contains* or *includes* S_1, written as $(S_1 \subset S_2)$ $S_1 \subseteq S_2$ if each element of S_1 is also an element of S_2. When S_1 is a subset of S_2, we also say that S_2 is a *superset* of S_1. A set is a subset of itself and is also a superset of itself. By means of the inclusion relationship between S_1 and S_2, $S_1 = S_2$ is equivalent to $S_1 \subseteq S_2$ and $S_2 \subseteq S_1$.

The *power set* of a finite set S, denoted by P(S), is the set consisting of all subsets of S (including S itself and the empty set, ø), i.e.,

$$P(S) = \{S_j \mid S_j \subseteq S, j = 1, 2, \ldots, 2^{|S|}\}.$$

0.2.2 Set Operations

The *union* of two sets S_1 and S_2, written as $S_1 \cup S_2$, is the set consisting of all elements in S_1 or S_2 (or both), i.e.,

$$S_1 \cup S_2 = \{e \mid e \in S_1 \text{ or } e \in S_2\}. \tag{0.1a}$$

The union of S_1 and S_2 has the property that it contains both S_1 and S_2.

The *intersection* of two sets S_1 and S_2, written as $S_1 \cap S_2$, is the set consisting of all elements in both S_1 and S_2, i.e.,

$$S_1 \cap S_2 = \{e \mid e \in S_1 \text{ and } e \in S_2\}.$$

The intersection of S_1 and S_2 has the property that it is contained in both S_1 and S_2. The sets S_1 and S_2 are called *disjoint* or *mutually exclusive* if their intersection is the empty set, ø. A family of sets is called *mutually disjoint* if every two distinct sets in the family are disjoint.

The *difference* of a set S_1 and a set S_2, written as $S_1 - S_2$, is the set consisting of all elements that are in S_1 but not in S_2, i.e.,

$$S_1 - S_2 = \{e \mid e \in S_1 \text{ and } e \notin S_2\}.$$

If S_2 is a subset of S_1, then the difference of S_1 and S_2 is called the *complement* of S_2 relative to S_1. If S_1 is understood, then the complement of S_2 (relative to S_1) can be written as $\sim S_2$, i.e.,

$$\sim S_2 = \{e \mid e \in (S_1 - S_2) \text{ and } S_2 \subseteq S_1\}.$$

The *complex product* of two sets S_1 and S_2, written as $S_1 * S_2$, is the set consisting of all strings a b of a in S_1 and b in S_2 where a and b are concatenated, i.e.,

$$S_1 * S_2 = \{a\,b \mid a \in S_1 \text{ and } b \in S_2\}. \tag{0.2a}$$

Note that the binary concatenation operator between a and b is omitted, and a and b are separated by at least one blank.

The *Cartesian product* of two sets S_1 and S_2, written as $S_1 \times S_2$, is the set consisting of all ordered pairs (a,b) of a in S_1 and b in S_2, i.e.,

$$S_1 \times S_2 = \{(a,b) \mid a \in S_1 \text{ and } b \in S_2\}. \tag{0.3a}$$

The binary operations of intersection, union, and complex product are associative and can be naturally extended to k-ary operations represented by prefixed notation as follows:

$$\cap(S_1, \ldots, S_k) = \{e \mid e \in S_1 \text{ and } \cdots \text{ and } e \in S_k\}.$$

$$\cup(S_1, \ldots, S_k) = \{e \mid e \in S_1 \text{ or } \cdots \text{ or } e \in S_k\}. \qquad (0.1b)$$

$$*(S_1, \ldots, S_k) = \{e_1 \cdots e_k \mid e_j \in S_j, 1 \le j \le k\}. \qquad (0.2b)$$

In (0.2b), each element $e_1 e_2 \cdots e_k$ is called a *string* whose *length* is k, the number of concatenated objects of the string.

The binary operation of Cartesian product is not associative, i.e., $(S_1 \times S_2) \times S_3 = \{((a,b), c)\}$ and $S_1 \times (S_2 \times S_3) = \{(a, (b, c))\}$ where a, b, and c are, respectively, in S_1, S_2, and S_3. The k-ary Cartesian product cannot be naturally extended from the binary version but it can be defined as

$$\times(S_1, \ldots, S_k) = \{(e_1, \ldots, e_k) \mid e_j \in S_j, 1 \le j \le k\}. \qquad (0.3b)$$

In (0.3b), each element $(e_1, e_2, \ldots, e_k)$ is called a *k-tuple* (or simply *tuple*) whose *arity* is k, the number of objects in the tuple. If $S_1 = \cdots = S_k = S$, then the k-ary Cartesian product of (0.3b) is written as S^k for short.

0.3 FUNCTIONS AND RELATIONS

0.3.1 Functions

Let S and S_j for each j, $1 \le j \le n$, be sets of objects. A *function* with *n arguments* f: $\times(S_1, \ldots, S_n) \to S$ (i.e., mapping from the Cartesian product $\times(S_1, \ldots, S_n)$ to the set S) is a subset of the Cartesian product $\times(S_1, \ldots, S_n, S)$ such that for any two tuples $(a_1, \ldots, a_n, a_{n+1})$ and $(b_1, \ldots, b_n, b_{n+1})$ if we have $a_j = b_j$ for each j, $1 \le j \le n$, then we must have $a_{n+1} = b_{n+1}$ (or equivalently, if we have $a_{n+1} \ne b_{n+1}$, then we must have $a_j \ne b_j$ for some j, $1 \le j \le n$), i.e.,

$$f = \{(a_1, \ldots, a_n, a_{n+1}) \mid (a_1, \ldots, a_n) \in \times(S_1, \ldots, S_n) \text{ has a unique } a_{n+1} \text{ in } S\}.$$

A function with n arguments is also called an *n-place* or *n-ary function*. A function is also called a *map*. If $(a_1, \ldots, a_{n+1})$ is in f, then the last element a_{n+1} is called the *value* of f for the tuple $(a_1, \ldots, a_n)$ of arguments or the *image* of the tuple $(a_1, \ldots, a_n)$ of arguments under f. If there exists no a_{n+1} such that $(a_1, \ldots, a_{n+1})$ is in f, then the value of f for the tuple $(a_1, \ldots, a_n)$ or the image of the tuple $(a_1, \ldots, a_n)$ under f is undefined (this implies a partial function as will be defined).

The *domain* of a function f is the set

$$D_f = \{(a_1, \ldots, a_n) \mid (a_1, \ldots, a_{n+1}) \in f \text{ for some } a_{n+1} \in S\}. \qquad (0.4)$$

The domain of f is a subset of the Cartesian product $\times(S_1 \ldots, S_n)$. A *restriction* f' of a function f is a map if the domain of f' is a proper subset of D_f. A restriction of f may use the same name f. The *range* of f is the set

$$R_f = \{a_{n+1} \mid (a_1, \ldots, a_{n+1}) \in f \text{ for some } (a_1, \ldots, a_n) \in D_f\}.$$

The range of f is a subset of the set S. The set S is called the *co-domain* of f (i.e., a superset of the range R_f).

A function f: $\times(S_1, \ldots, S_n) \to S$ maps from its domain D_f *onto* its co-domain S if $R_f = S$, and f maps from its domain D_f *into* its co-domain S if $R_f \subset S$. A function f: $\times (S_1, \ldots, S_n) \to S$ is a *partial function* if the domain of f is a proper subset of the Cartesian product of $S_1, \ldots, S_{n-1}$, and S_n (i.e., $D_f \subset \times(S_1, \ldots, S_n)$). In this case, the image of each tuple in the difference of $\times(S_1, \ldots, S_n)$ and D_f under f is undefined.

A function f is *one-to-one* if, for any two different elements $(a_1, \ldots, a_{n+1})$ and $(b_1, \ldots, b_{n+1})$ in f, it is not the case that $a_{n+1} = b_{n+1}$, and is *many-to-one* otherwise. A one-to-one and onto function f is usually known as a *one-to-one correspondence*. If a function f is a one-to-one correspondence, then the *inverse* of f, denoted by f^{-1}, exists such that the *composition* of f and f^{-1}, denoted by $f \ o \ f^{-1}$, is identical to the composition $f^{-1} \ o \ f$ where both compositions define the *identity function* I, i.e., $I = f \ o \ f^{-1} = f^{-1} \ o \ f$, and the symbol "*o*" stands for "composition."

0.3.2 Relations

A *relation* with *n arguments* between $\times(S_1, \ldots, S_{n-1})$ and S is a subset of the Cartesian product $\times(S_1, \ldots, S_{n-1}, S)$. A relation with n arguments is also called an *n-place* or n-ary relation. Hence, a relation with n arguments is a generalization of a function with n-1 arguments. If a relation is one-to-one or many-to-one, then it is also a function. If a relation is one-to-many or many-to-many, then it is not a function.

Of particular interest, is a *binary relation* r on a set S (i.e., between S and S). Relation r is *reflexive* if (e, e) is in r for each e in S and is not reflexive otherwise. Relation r is *non-reflexive* if (e, e) is not in r for each e in S. Relation r is *symmetric* if, whenever (e_1, e_2) is in r, (e_2, e_1) is also in r and is not symmetric otherwise. Relation r is *asymmetric* if, whenever (e_1, e_2) is in r, (e_2, e_1) is not in r. Relation r is *antisymmetric* if both (e_1, e_2) and (e_2, e_1) in r imply that $e_1 = e_2$. Relation r is *transitive* if, whenever both (e_1, e_2) and (e_2, e_3) are in r, (e_1, e_3) is also in r and is not transitive otherwise. Relation r is an *equivalence relation* on S if it is reflexive, symmetric, and transitive.

A *partition* on a set S is a set of some subsets of S such that the union of the subsets is equal to S, and every two distinct subsets are disjoint. An equivalence relation on a set S defines a partition on S whose elements are called *equivalence classes*.

0.4 PROPOSITIONAL LOGIC

0.4.1 Atoms and Formulas

In the propositional logic, we use five logical operators or connectives: $^-$ ("logical not" or "negation"), $\cdot$ ("logical and" or "conjunction"), $+$ ("logical or" or "disjunction"), $\Rightarrow$ ("implication" or "if-then"), and $\equiv$ ("equivalence" or "if and only if" (abbreviated as iff)).

A declarative sentence that is either true or false (and cannot be simultaneously true and false) is called a *proposition*. The symbols that are used to denote propositions are informally called *atomic formulas* (or simply *atoms*). We can use the five logical operators to construct compound propositions from propositions. Informally speaking, an expression that represents a proposition or a compound proposition is called a *well-formed formula* (or simply *formula*). *Formulas* in the propositional logic are defined recursively as follows.

(1) An atom is a formula.

(2) If F is a formula, then $(\overline{F})$ is a formula.

(3) If F and G are formulas, then $(F \cdot G)$, $(F + G)$, $(F \Rightarrow G)$, and $(F \equiv G)$ are formulas.

(4) Nothing else is a formula.

We can omit the use of parentheses by assigning the following order of precedence to the logical operators $^{-}$, $\cdot$, $+$, $\Rightarrow$, and $\equiv$ from the highest order of precedence to the lowest.

The formula $\overline{F}$, called the *negation* of F, is true if F is false, and is false otherwise. The formula $F \cdot G$, called the *conjunction* of F and G, is true if F and G are both true, and is false otherwise. The formula $F + G$, called the *disjunction* of F and G, is true if at least one of F and G is true, and is false otherwise. The formula $F \Rightarrow G$, read as "F implies G" or "if F then G", is false if F is true and G is false, and is true otherwise. The formula $F \equiv G$, read as "F is equivalent to G" or "F iff G" is true whenever F and G have the same truth value (either true or false), and is false otherwise.

0.4.2 Interpretations of Formulas

Given a formula F, let $A_1, \ldots, A_{n-1}$, and A_n be the atoms occurring in F. An *interpretation* of F is an assignment of truth values to $A_1, \ldots, A_{n-1}$, and A_n in which each A_j, for $1 \leq j \leq n$, is assigned either true or false. Since there are 2^n possible ways of assigning truth values to n atoms, there are 2^n interpretations of F. A formula F is said to be true under an interpretation if F is evaluated to true in the interpretation and is said to be false otherwise. A formula is said to be *valid* or a *tautology* if it is true under all its interpretations and is said to be *invalid* otherwise. A formula is said to be *inconsistent* or a *contradiction* if it is false under all its interpretations and is said to be *consistent* otherwise. If a formula is valid, then it is consistent, but the converse is not true. Similarly, if a formula is inconsistent, then it is invalid, but the converse is not true. For example, the formula F $\Rightarrow \overline{F}$ is invalid since it is not a tautology, yet it is consistent since it is not a contradiction. If a formula F is true under an interpretation M, then we say that M *satisfies* F, or F is *satisfied* by M. On the other hand, if a formula F is false under an interpretation M, then we say that M *falsifies* F, or F is *falsified* by M.

0.4.3 Equivalence Between Formulas

Two formulas F and G are *equivalent* or F is *equivalent* to G, written as $F \equiv G$, if the truth values of F and G are the same under each interpretation. For example, the following equivalences are very useful to simplify formulas.

$$F \Rightarrow G \equiv \overline{F} + G. \tag{0.5}$$

$$(F \equiv G) \equiv \overline{F} \cdot \overline{G} + F \cdot G. \tag{0.6}$$

In (0.6), use of parentheses for enclosing $F \equiv G$ can be omitted since the direction of scanning a formula for evaluation of its value is conventionally from the left to the right.

Let $\mathbf{F}$ be a contradiction, $\mathbf{T}$ be a tautology, and G and H be formulas. The following equivalences are very useful to handle functional and multivalued dependencies in chapters 4 and 5.

$$G + \mathbf{F} \equiv G. \tag{0.7a}$$

$$G + \mathbf{T} \equiv \mathbf{T}. \tag{0.8a}$$

$$G + \overline{G} \equiv \mathbf{T}. \tag{0.9a}$$

$$\overline{\mathbf{T}} \equiv \mathbf{F} \text{ (DeMorgan's law).} \tag{0.10a}$$

$$G + \overline{G} \cdot H \equiv G + H. \tag{0.11a}$$

$$\overline{G + H} \equiv \overline{G} \cdot \overline{H} \text{ (DeMorgan's law).} \tag{0.12a}$$

By the principle of duality, we have more useful equivalences:

$$G \cdot \mathbf{T} \equiv G. \tag{0.7b}$$

$$G \cdot \mathbf{F} \equiv \mathbf{F}. \tag{0.8b}$$

$$G \cdot \overline{G} \equiv \mathbf{F}. \tag{0.9b}$$

$$\overline{\mathbf{F}} \equiv \mathbf{T} \text{ (DeMorgan's law).} \tag{0.10b}$$

$$G \cdot (\overline{G} + H) \equiv G \cdot H. \tag{0.11b}$$

$$\overline{G \cdot H} \equiv \overline{G} + \overline{H} \text{ (DeMorgan's law).} \tag{0.12b}$$

In addition, the equivalence

$$(F + G) \cdot (F + H) \equiv F + G \cdot H \tag{0.13}$$

is also very useful to produce simplified formulas. When two formulas are equivalent, the more complicated formula can be replaced by its equivalent counterpart for achieving a simplification or even a minimization.

0.4.4 Normal Forms

An atom or the negation of an atom (referred to as a *negated atom*) is called a *literal*. A formula F is in a *conjunctive normal form* if F is the conjunction of subformulas F_1 through F_k where each subformula F_j, for $1 \leqslant j \leqslant k$, is the disjunction of some literals. A formula F is in a *disjunctive normal form* if F is the disjunction of subformulas F_1 through F_k where each subformula F_j, for $1 \leqslant j \leqslant k$, is the conjunction of some literals.

0.4.5 Logical Consequence

Given formulas $F_1, \ldots, F_n$, and G, G is said to be a *logical consequence* of $F_1, \ldots, F_{n-1}$, and F_n; or $F_1, \ldots, F_{n-1}$, and F_n *logically imply* G, if for any interpretation in which the formula $F_1 . \ldots . F_n$ is true, G is also true.

In the propositional logic, there is an important theorem that is very useful in relational database theory. This theorem states that ''given formulas $F_1, \ldots, F_n$, and G, G is a logical consequence of $F_1, \ldots, F_{n-1}$, and F_n if the formula $F_1 \cdot \ldots \cdot F_n \Rightarrow G$ is valid.'' By (0.5) and (0.12b), the formula $F_1 \cdot \ldots \cdot F_n \Rightarrow G$ is equivalent to $\overline{F}_1 + \cdots + \overline{F}_n + G$. If $F_1, \ldots, F_n$, and G are atoms, then $\overline{F}_1 + \ldots + \overline{F}_n + G$ (with only one unnegated atom) is called a *Horn clause*. The formula $\overline{F}_1 + \ldots + \overline{F}_n$ without any unnegated atoms is also a Horn clause.

0.5 FIRST-ORDER LOGIC

0.5.1 Predicates

The first-order logic has three more logical notions: terms, predicates, and quantifiers. *Terms* are defined recursively as follows.

(1) A constant, such as a numeric constant or nonnumeric symbol (character string is an example), is a term.

(2) A variable is a term.

(3) If f is an n-place function symbol and $t_1, \ldots, t_{n-1}$, and t_n are terms, then $f(t_1, \ldots, t_n)$ is a term.

(4) Nothing else is a term.

An *n-place predicate* is an n-place function from $\times(S_1, \ldots, S_n)$ to {true, false} where ''true'' and ''false'' are truth values. An n-place predicate is also called an *n-ary predicate*. Formally, an atom in the first-order logic is defined as follows: if p is an n-place predicate symbol and $t_1, \ldots, t_{n-1}$, and t_n are terms then $p(t_1, \ldots, t_n)$ is an *atom*. There are four types of symbols that can be used to construct an atom: constants, variables, function symbols, and predicate symbols.

0.5.2 Quantification

In a programming language, when a procedure P contains internally a procedure Q and there is an identifier x occuring in Q, x is a *local variable* in Q if x is declared in Q and is otherwise a *global variable* in Q. A variable x occurring in a formula F, being free or bound in F, is, respectively, analogous to a global or local variable in a programming language.

The universally quantified variable is $(\forall x)$, read as ''for all x,'' ''for each x,'' or ''for every x.'' The existentially quantified variable is $(\exists x)$, read as ''there exists an x,'' ''for some x,'' or ''for at least one x.'' The symbols $\forall$ and $\exists$ are called, respectively, the *universal* and *existential quantifiers*.

Let G(x) be a formula where x is a free variable (i.e., x is not quantified in G). The *scope* of Q in $\{\forall, \exists\}$ occurring in a formula $F := (Qx)G(x)$ is the subformula G(x) to which Q is applied where the symbol := means "is defined as." In this formula F, the first occurrence of x located to the right side of Q is bound in F, and every other occurrence of x located in the scope G(x) is free in G since x is not quantified in G but becomes bound in F. Similarly, if y for y $\neq$ x is also a free variable in G, then y occurs *free* in both G(x,y) and F(y) where F(y) := (Qx)G(x,y). A variable can be both free and bound in a formula. For example, the variable y in the formula ($\forall$x)G(x,y) · ($\exists$y)H(y) is free in ($\forall$x)G(x, y) but is bound in ($\exists$y)H(y). Thus, a variable in a formula is *free* or *bound* in the formula if at least one of its occurrences is free or bound in the formula.

0.5.3 Formulas

Well-formed formulas (or simply *formulas*) in the first-order logic are defined recursively as follows.

(1) An atom is a formula.
(2) If F and G are formulas, then ($\bar{F}$), (F · G), (F + G), (F $\Rightarrow$ G), and (F $\equiv$ G) are formulas.
(3) If F is a formula and x is a free variable in F, then ($\forall$x)F(x) and ($\exists$x)F(x) are formulas.
(4) Nothing else is a formula.

In a formula, parentheses may be omitted by following the same order of precedence as in the propositional logic. In addition, both quantifiers have the same order of precedence, which is higher than that of the logical operator "negation."

A formula is called *closed* if all variables in it are quantified and is called *open* otherwise. As will be seen in the following section, a closed or an open formula can or cannot be readily interpreted respectively.

0.5.4 Interpretations of Formulas

An *interpretation* of a formula F in the first-order logic consists of a nonempty domain D of values and an assignment of values to each constant, function symbol, and predicate symbol occurring in F as follows.

(1) To each constant, the constant itself is an element in D.
(2) To each n-place function symbol, we assign a value in D mapped from D^n.
(3) To each n-place predicate symbol, we assign a truth value (either true or false) mapped from D^n.

For each interpretation of a formula over a given domain D, the formula is *evaluated* to either true or false according to the following rules.

(1) Each of the formulas ($\bar{F}$), (F · G), (F + G), (F $\Rightarrow$ G), and (F $\equiv$ G) is evaluated to either true or false as shown in section 0.4.1.

(2) $(\forall x)F(x)$ is evaluated to true if F is evaluated to true for all elements in the underlying domain, and to false otherwise.

(3) $(\exists x)F(x)$ is evaluated to true if F is evaluated to true for some element in the underlying domain, and to false otherwise.

A closed formula can be readily interpreted. However, an open formula cannot be interpreted unless all free variables occurring in the formula are instantiated by values in the underlying domain.

All other concepts, such as validity, inconsistency, and logical consequence defined in section 0.4 of the propositional logic, can be applied analogously here. The following two equivalences are particularly useful in chapter 3.

$$\overline{(\forall x)F(x)} \equiv (\exists x)\overline{F(x)}. \tag{0.14a}$$

$$\overline{(\exists x)F(x)} \equiv (\forall x)\overline{F(x)}. \tag{0.14b}$$

0.5.5 Normal Form

In the first-order logic, a formula can be represented by a *prenex normal form*. A formula F in the first-order logic is in a prenex normal form if F is of the form $(Q_1 x_1) \ldots (Q_k x_k)$ $G(x_1, \ldots, x_k)$ where every $(Q_j x_j)$, for $1 \le j \le k$, is either $(\forall x_j)$ or $(\exists x_j)$, and G is a formula containing no quantifiers. Given a formula, we can transform it into a prenex normal form by using some of the following equivalences together with those shown in (0.14a) and (0.14b). Let $F(x)$ and $H(x)$ be formulas containing the free variable x, and let G be a formula that does not contain x. Let Q be a quantifier. Then we have the following equivalences:

$$(Qx)F(x) + G \equiv (Qx)(F(x) + G).$$
$$(Qx)F(x) \cdot G \equiv (Qx)(F(x) \cdot G).$$

$$(\forall x)F(x) \cdot (\forall x)H(x) \equiv (\forall x)(F(x) \cdot H(x)). \tag{0.15a}$$

$$(\exists x)F(x) + (\exists x)H(x) \equiv (\exists x)(F(x) + H(x)). \tag{0.15b}$$

Note that the following two inequivalences are not similar to (0.15a) and (0.15b):

$$(\forall x)F(x) + (\forall x)H(x) \not\equiv (\forall x)(F(x) + H(x)).$$
$$(\exists x)F(x) \cdot (\exists x)H(x) \not\equiv (\exists x)(F(x) \cdot H(x)).$$

The formulas on both sides of $\not\equiv$ are not equivalent.

Let Q_1, Q_2, Q_3, and Q_4 be either $\forall$ or $\exists$, and assume that the variable y does not occur in $F(x)$. Then we have two additional equivalences.

$$(Q_1 x)F(x) + (Q_2 x)H(x) \equiv (Q_1 x)(Q_2 y)(F(x) + H(y)).$$
$$(Q_3 x)F(x) \cdot (Q_4 x)H(x) \equiv (Q_3 x)(Q_4 y)(F(x) \cdot H(y)).$$

Note that if $Q_1 = Q_2 = \exists$, then we do not have to rename x's in $(Q_2 x)H(x)$ since we can use (0.15b) directly. Similarly, if $Q_3 = Q_4 = \forall$, then we do not have to rename x's in $(Q_4 x)H(x)$ since we can use (0.15a) directly.

0.6 GRAPH THEORY

0.6.1 Undirected and Directed Graphs

An *undirected graph* G is a pair (V, E) where V is a finite, nonempty set of elements called *vertices* or *nodes* and E is a finite multiset of unordered pairs of vertices called *edges*. The word *multiset* in the definition allows the existence of multiple edges. If E is a set of unordered pairs of vertices, then G is called a *simple undirected graph*. We use the set notation {u, v} to represent an edge in an undirected graph and call an edge {u, u} a *self-loop* where u and v are vertices. An edge {u, v} is said to be *incident to* vertices u and v. The *degree* of a vertex v in an undirected graph is two times the number of self-loops incident to v plus the number of other edges incident to v.

A *directed graph* G is a pair (V, A) where V is a finite, nonempty set of elements called *vertices* or *nodes* and A is a finite multiset of ordered pairs of vertices called *arcs*. If A is a set of ordered pairs of vertices, then G is called a *simple directed graph*. A (simple) directed graph is also called a (simple) *digraph*. We use an ordered pair (u, v) in the Cartesian product V × V to represent an arc that is *incident from* u and *incident to* v. We call an arc (u, u) in V × V a *self-loop* (i.e., incident from u and incident to u). The *in-degree* of a vertex v is the number of arcs incident to v. The *out-degree* of v is the number of arcs incident from v. The *degree* of v is the in-degree of v plus the out-degree of v.

Given an undirected or a directed graph G, a *vertex-sequence* in G is a finite sequence of vertices $v_1, \ldots, v_k$ for each v_j in V, $1 \le j \le k$, such that each pair of consecutive vertices in the sequence defines an edge or arc in G. Such a vertex-sequence induces an *edge-* or *arc-sequence*. The *length* of an edge- or arc-sequence in G is the number of edges or arcs in the sequence. The first and last vertices in a vertex-sequence are, respectively, called the *initial* and *final vertices*. An edge- (arc-) or a vertex-sequence in which all the edges (or arcs) are distinct is called a *trail*. If in addition, all vertices in a trail are distinct, except possibly the initial and final vertices, then the trail is called a *path*. A trail or path is *closed* if its final vertex coincides with its initial vertex and is *open* otherwise. A closed path composed of at least one arc or edge is called a *cycle*. A graph is called *acyclic* if the graph contains no cycles, and is called *cyclic* otherwise. Note that a cycle in a simple undirected or directed graph without any self-loops must have at least three edges or two arcs respectively. A cycle consisting of all vertices in a graph is called *Hamiltonian*.

An undirected graph is said to be *connected* or a directed graph is said to be *strongly connected* if, given any pair of distinct vertices u and v in the graph, there is a path from u to v. A directed graph is said to be *connected* if its associated undirected graph, obtained by ignoring the directions of all its arcs, is connected. A graph is *disconnected* if it is not connected. Each maximally connected subgraph is called a *component*. Thus, a connected graph is also a component, and a graph with more than one component is disconnected. A vertex v of a graph G is called an *articulation point* if the removal of v (and all of its connecting edges or arcs) increases the number of components of G. Similarly, a minimal set of vertices of G is called an *articulation set* if the removal of all vertices in the set increases the number of components of G.

A *forest* is defined to be a graph that contains no cycles. A connected forest is called a *tree*. A tree having only a single vertex is called a *degenerate tree* or an *isolated vertex*. Let T be a graph with n vertices. Then the following statements are equivalent.

(1) T is a tree.
(2) T has n − 1 edges and is acyclic.
(3) Every two distinct vertices of T are connected by exactly one path.
(4) T is acyclic, but the addition of any new edge creates exactly one cycle.

Two vertices u and v are *adjacent* if there is an edge or arc connecting u and v, and are *independent* otherwise. A vertex v is not adjacent to itself unless there is a self-loop incident to v.

A *rooted tree* is a tree in which a specific vertex is the root, and all vertices adjacent to the root are the roots of its subtrees. Each vertex of degree one (except the root in the case of a rooted tree) in a tree is called a *leaf*.

0.6.2 Hypergraphs

A *hypergraph* H is a pair (V, E) where V is a finite, nonempty set of elements called *vertices* or *nodes* and E is a finite set of some subsets of V called *hyperedges*. The empty subset of V is called the *empty hyperedge*. Let H = (V, E) be a hypergraph, and let u and v be vertices in V. A *path* between u and v is a hyperedge-sequence $e_1, \ldots, e_k$, for k = 1, 2, . . . , such that u is in e_1, v is in e_k, and the intersection of any two consecutive hyperedges in the sequence is nonempty. We also say that this hyperedge-sequence is a path between e_1 and e_k.

In a hypergraph H = (V, E), a vertex is connected to itself, and two distinct vertices are *connected* if there is a path between them. A hyperedge is connected to itself, and two distinct hyperedges are *connected* if there is a path between them. A set of hyperedges is *connected* if there is a path between every two distinct hyperedges in the set. A *component* of H is a maximally connected set of hyperedges. Hypergraph connectivity is an equivalence relation on E.

The *Graham-reduction* of a hypergraph is accomplished by applying the following rules in any order.

(1) Eliminate a node that appears in only one hyperedge.
(2) Eliminate a hyperedge that is a subset of another hyperedge.

Then a hypergraph is *acyclic* if it Graham-reduces to one empty hyperedge.

0.7 NP-COMPLETE AND NP-HARD PROBLEMS

It is well known that the satisfiability problem is NP-complete [Coo71] and is also NP-hard. NP-completeness implies NP-hardness; but the converse may not be true. Each NP-hard problem cannot be solved by an algorithm with a polynomial time complexity when the classes of P and NP are not equal. The reader can refer to [Gar79] for more detail.

chapter 1

THE RELATIONAL MODEL
OF DATABASES

1.1 INTRODUCTION

We introduce an architecture of a database management system (abbreviated as DBMS) that seems to fit a large number of DBMSs reasonably well and is in agreement with the proposal made by the ANSI/SPARC Study Group on DBMSs [Tsi78].

The architecture is divided into three levels as follows:

(1) Conceptual level—This level is referred to as the *conceptual* or *logical database*. It is located between the other two levels. It consists of the abstract representation of the database (i.e., independent from the physical implementation).

(2) Internal level—This lowest level is referred to as the *physical* or *internal database* that is the implementation of the logical database. It is concerned with data types, record formats, storage structures, and access methods. It represents the database as actually stored and retrieved.

(3) External level—This highest level is referred to as the *external database*. It is concerned with the views created from the logical database by users. Each view consists of some portion of the logical database.

A DBMS is a software system that manages the three levels and other necessary interfaces.

A model of databases, conventionally known as a *data model,* is primarily used for modeling a logical database that is the most important part in the design of a DBMS. There are many data models proposed and available in the literature [Fry76, Lie82, Sib76, Tsi82], such as the entity-relationship model [Che76], the network model [CODASYL71,

Tay76], the hierarchical model [Tsi76, IBM78b], etc. Among these is the relational model conceived by pioneer Codd in 1970 [Cha76a, Cod70, Cod72a, Cod72b, Cod79], which is introduced in this chapter.

In addition to freedom from the frustrations of having to deal with the clutter of the details of storage structures and access methods from the user interface, the relational model has other important advantages: it is simple and has a sound theoretical foundation. Simplicity is achieved since the user is presented with simple and consistent tabular relations. The model is mathematically rigorous because it rests on the well-developed mathematical theory of relations and the first-order logic [Gal84]. Because this model is of a strong theoretical foundation, the design and evaluation of relational databases can be accomplished by systematic methods based on abstractions, which enable us to concentrate on general approaches, to reduce complexities, and to aid understanding.

This model has also provided an architectural focus for the design of databases and some general purpose DBMSs, such as INGRES[Sto76], SYSTEM R [Ast76, Ast80, Bla81], PROLOG]Bru80, Clo81], among others [Cod79].

This chapter covers the basic terminology and notation of relational databases and the structural aspects that a relational DBMS supports. This chapter also includes the basic concepts, such as relationships among attributes, keys, universal relations, and database hypergraphs.

1.2 ATTRIBUTES AND DOMAINS

In the file management system of an operating system, the familiar term *field* refers to the smallest item of data that has meaning in the real world. This item has a specific data type, such as integer, floating point number, or character string and needs a number of bytes of storage space to be specified. This item has also a name. Thus, a field is the smallest typed and named item of data. In a relational database, each relation is represented by a table. Each column of a tabular relation corresponds to a field.

Definition 1.1:   The *universe* of a relational database, denoted by U, is a finite, nonempty set of elements $A_1, \ldots, A_{n-1}$, and A_n called attribute names or simply, *attributes,* i.e.,

$$U = \{A_1, \ldots, A_n\}. \tag{1.1a}$$

The *domain* or *value-set* of an attribute A_j for $j = 1, \ldots, n$, written as $DOM(A_j)$, is a finite set of the values of A_j, which must be of the same data type. A domain is *simple* if all its elements are atomic (i.e., nondecomposable by the underlying DBMS). The domain of a subset U_j of U, denoted by $DOM(U_j)$, is the union of the domains of all attributes in U_j, i.e.,

$$DOM(U_j) = \bigcup_{A_K \in U_j} DOM(A_k)$$

where $DOM(\emptyset) = \emptyset$ if $U_j = \emptyset$ and $\emptyset$ is the empty set. Note that the word domain used in this definition follows only the convention adopted in this area and is not in the same sense as the domain of a function as defined by (0.4) in chapter 0. By this consideration, the term *value set* might be better than "domain." Note also that although the types of the values in a simple domain must be identical, the elements in $DOM(U_j)$ are not restricted to be of the same type since U_j may contain attributes with different domains.

In a relational database, each relation is represented by a table. Attributes are simply the symbols used to differentiate and label the columns of the table denoting a relation. Thus, a field or column name is also an attribute. All attributes occurring in a table must be distinct and included in the universe U. Attributes are global in a relational database in the sense that an attribute occurring in any two distinct tables of a relational database must mean the same thing, i.e., a field having values with the same data type when a relation is implemented. Hence, any table of a relational database must involve only a nonempty subset of U. Attributes should be time-invariant in the sense that their values should be more or less time-independent. For example, a personnel database having AGE as an attribute to indicate the ages of employees would have different AGE-values for any employee from year to year, whereas the values of the attribute DATEOFBIRTH for each employee would have the property of time-independence, and the current age of an employee would be easily computed from the date of birth of the employee and the value of the current year. Use of DATEOFBIRTH rather than AGE as an attribute is a better choice.

By convention, the set-oriented universe U of (1.1a) and a subset $X = \{A_{i_1}, \ldots, A_{i_k}\}$, for some $k \geq 1$, of U (i.e., each A_{i_j} is in U for $j = 1, \ldots, k$ and $1 \leq k \leq n$) are represented by strings, i.e.,

$$U = A_1 \cdots A_n, \tag{1.1b}$$

and

$$X = A_{i_1} \cdots A_{j_k}. \tag{1.2}$$

In (1.1b) and (1.2), every two consecutive attributes separated by at least one blank are concatenated, and the operator for the binary operation "concatenation" is omitted. Note that since $1 \leq k \leq n$, X is a nonempty subset of U and since $|U| = n$, the number of nonempty subsets of U is $2^n - 1$ (the empty subset of U is the empty set $\emptyset$). Thus, X of (1.2) can be viewed as a variable that can assume at most $2^n - 1$ values where each value is a string of k distinct attributes. Note also that although a string can generally have duplicated elements, the strings of U and X cannot have duplicates since U and X are both sets of attributes.

By means of the string representation, we can use the simpler notation $A_j \subseteq U$, rather than $\{A_j\} \subseteq U$, to stand for "A_j is a subset of U." The union of two subsets Y and Z of U is conventionally represented by the symbol Y Z where Y and Z are separated by at least one blank, and the operator for the binary operation "union" is omitted. Note that the symbol Y Z is only a shorthand of $Y \cup Z$. Note also that the subsets Y and Z are not restricted to be nonempty since $\emptyset Z = Z$, $Y \emptyset = Y$, and $\emptyset \emptyset = \emptyset$.

The *complement* of a subset Y (relative to U) is denoted by ~Y, i.e.,

$$\sim Y = U - Y. \tag{1.3a}$$

If Y = ø in (1.3a), then we have the special case

$$\sim\! ø = U, \tag{1.3b}$$

and if Y = U in (1.3a), then we have another special case

$$\sim U = ø.(\tag{1.3c}$$

For a tabular relation having i rows and j columns, the relation has i × j entries. Each entry is filled by a value from a simple domain. Although all attributes in the universe U must be distinct, the domains of these attributes are not necessarily mutually disjoint. For example, a manager is also an employee (or a subpart is also a part), which implies that the domains of the attributes MANAGER and EMPLOYEE (or SUBPART and PART) are not disjoint. In other words, MANAGER and EMPLOYEE (or SUBPART and PART) can be defined on the same domain.

For the purpose of avoiding the occurrence of an infinite relation, each domain is necessarily kept finite. This is the reason why each domain is defined as a finite set of values in definition 1.1. Although attributes are time-invariant, an insertion into, an update of, or a deletion from any table of a relational database yields a different table, which implies a different relational database. The set of all values of an attribute A_j in U actually occurring in a current relational database db, denoted by $ADOM(A_j)$, is called the *active domain* of A_j relative to db. As will be seen in subsequent chapters, active domains are useful to define the complement of a relation as being finite or even not too large, and to increase the processing speed of some queries. However, when a query involves an expression containing a value that is not in any active domain, the provision of active domains is not sufficient to evaluate the expression. In this case, we need another concept known as *extended active domains* that will be introduced in chapter 3.

Example 1.1:[1]

A part of a department store database proposed by Zloof [Zlo74] consists of four tabular relations named as EMP, SALES, SUPPLY, and TYPE.

The first table representing the relation EMP stores the name, salary, manager, and department of each employee. It has four attributes: NAME, SALARY, MGR, and DEPT. The SALES tabular relation lists the items sold by various departments. It has two attributes: DEPT and ITEM. The SUPPLY tabular relation specifies the items supplied by various suppliers. It has two attributes: ITEM and SUPPLIER. The TYPE tabular relation describes the items by their colors and sizes. It involves three attributes: ITEM, COLOR, and SIZE.

The entries of each such table are filled by the (atomic) values taken from the (simple) domains of its attributes. The attribute DEPT in the tabular relations EMP and SALES must be the same field and so must be the attribute ITEM in the tabular relations

---

[1]Some of the material that appears in the examples throughout this text has been taken from M. M. Zloof, ''Query By Example,'' *IBM Research RC 4917 RC 4917 (#21862),* July 2, 1974, p. 4.

named SALES, SUPPLY, and TYPE. The eight attributes occurring in the four tables constitute the universal set of attributes, i.e.,

$$U = \text{NAME SALARY MGR DEPT ITEM SUPPLIER COLOR SIZE}$$

where the eight attributes from left to right correspond respectively to A_1 through A_8 in (1.1b). In the table denoting the relation SALES, the subset DEPT ITEM of U is a value of string variable X where DEPT and ITEM correspond respectively to A_{i_1} and A_{i_2} in (1.2), which in turn correspond respectively to A_4 and A_5 in (1.1b).

The domain of the attribute NAME consists of possible names and must contain the active domain of NAME, which includes only those names of the employees currently working in the department store. In this database, the top level manager may not be recorded as an employee in EMP since he/she does not have a manager or does not belong to a department. Thus, his/her name may not be in the active domain of NAME, but is in the domain of NAME. However, he/she must have a salary. How can we store his/her information in the database, or should we ignore it? The domain of SALARY may involve a set of positive integers. Since the set of positive integers is infinite, each SALARY-value cannot exceed the maximum value so that DOM(SALARY) can be maintained finite. The other domains and active domains can be similarly defined. In this database, some employees are also managers, so the domains and active domains of NAME and MGR are not disjoint.

1.3 TUPLES

In the file management system of an operating system, a set of related fields treated as a single unit for storage and retrieval is known as a *record*. A record has a specific format since its fields have specific data types. The rows in a tabular relation correspond to records and are conventionally called *tuples* in relational databases. However, the definition of these tuples is not the same as that of the tuples in mathematics referred to as *mathematical tuples* as defined in (0.3b) of chapter 0.

Definition 1.2: Let X be a nonempty subset of the universe U (as defined in (1.2)). Let DOM(X) be the domain of X (as defined in definition 1.1). Let $\mu : X \rightarrow$ DOM(X) be a function such that

$$\mu = \{(A_{i_1}, a_1), \ldots, (A_{i_k}, a_k)\}. \tag{1.4a}$$

Each A_{i_j} for $1 \leq j \leq k$ is an attribute in X and an *argument* of μ. Each a_j for $1 \leq j \leq k$ is a value in $DOM(A_{i_j})$ and the *value* of μ for A_{i_j} or the *image* of A_{i_j} under μ, denoted by $\mu(A_{i_j}) = a_j$. This 1-place function μ is called a *tuple over X*. Consider a restriction of μ. Let $Y = B_1 \cdots B_v$ be a nonempty proper subset of X. The *Y-value* of μ, conventionally represented by $\mu[Y]$, is

$$\mu[Y] = \{(B_p, b_p) \mid b_p = \mu(B_p) = \mu(A_{i_q}), 1 \leq p \leq v \text{ and } q \in \{1, \ldots, k\}\}. \tag{1.5a}$$

When $Y = A_{i_j}$ for any j in $\{1, 2, \ldots, k\}$, the A_{i_j} *value* of μ is $\mu[A_{i_j}]$. This value is also called the A_{i_j}-*component* of μ.

In this definition, we defined

$$\mu(A_{i_j}) = \mu[A_{i_j}] = a_j$$

for $a_j \in DOM(A_{i_j})$. We will not differentiate the symbols $\mu(A)$ and $\mu[A]$ for any A in U. In (1.4a), μ is represented by a set of its (argument, value) pairs. Since μ is represented by a set, the ordering of its elements is insignificant. However, the ordering of the elements in any mathematical tuple (such as $(a_1, \ldots, a_k)$) belonging to the Cartesian product $\times(DOM(A_{i_1}), \ldots, DOM(A_{i_k}))$ is significant. Hence, a tuple defined in definition 1.2 is obviously not a mathematical tuple.

By this definition, a tuple μ over X is a function whose domain is the set X, whose co-domain is the set $DOM(X)$, and whose range is a subset of $DOM(X)$. By definition, Y and A_{i_j} are nonempty proper subsets of X, Y-value and A_{i_j}-value of μ are both restrictions of μ such that their domains are proper subsets of X, and their co domains and ranges are proper subsets of $DOM(X)$. Since X and Y are nonempty and A_{i_j} is a single attribute (or a singleton set), $\mu[\emptyset]$ or $\mu(\emptyset)$ is never defined where $\emptyset$ is the empty set.

For the convenience of representation, we might alternatively denote μ and $\mu[Y]$ as

$$\mu = \begin{bmatrix} A_{i_1} & \cdots & A_{i_k} \\ a_1 & \cdots & a_k \end{bmatrix} \tag{1.4b}$$

or

$$\mu = <a_1 \cdots a_k \mid A_{i_1} \cdots A_{i_k}>, \tag{1.4c}$$

and

$$\mu[Y] = \begin{bmatrix} B_1 & \cdots & B_v \\ b_1 & \cdots & b_v \end{bmatrix} \tag{1.5b}$$

or

$$\mu[Y] = <b_1 \cdots b_v \mid B_1 \cdots B_v>. \tag{1.5c}$$

When the columns of the tabular relations corresponding to X and Y are labeled by the attributes in X and Y, the orderings of the column names follow, respectively, the same orderings of the attributes in the strings X and Y. Once these orderings are definite and understood, the representations of μ and $\mu[Y]$ can be further simplified as follows:

$$\mu = a_1 \cdots a_k \tag{1.4d}$$

and

$$\mu[Y] = b_1 \cdots b_v. \tag{1.5d}$$

By using (1.4d) and (1.5d), we are able not only to represent a set of attributes by a string but also to denote a set of attribute-values by a string. Once the column ordering of a table is specified as indicated by the corresponding attribute-string, the attributes in the original string and the attribute-values of each tuple over this attribute-string are accordingly ordered. When the columns or attributes of a table are permuted, the attribute-values of each tuple in the original table are accordingly permuted. Although the string representations of each original tuple and its permuted tuple are no longer the same, the data contents of both tuples are still identical so that we can consider them as the same tuple. Thus, when Z is permuted from Y, the original table labeled by the attributes in Y and the new table labeled by the attributes in Z denote the same relation.

By the string representation of a tuple μ over X as shown in (1.4d), we can view μ as an element in the complex product of $DOM(A_{i_1})$, . . . , $DOM(A_{i_k - 1})$, and DOM (A_{i_k}), i.e.,

$$*(DOM(A_{i_1}), \ldots, DOM(A_{i_k})) = \{a_1 \cdots a_k \mid a_j \in DOM(A_{i_j}), j = 1, 2, \ldots, k\}. \quad (1.6a)$$

This complex product is written as TUP(X) which consists of all possible tuples over X, i.e.,

$$TUP(X) = *(DOM(A_{i_1}), \ldots, DOM(A_{i_k})). \quad (1.6b)$$

If we do not follow definition 1.2 and define a tuple μ over X as an element of the Cartesian product of $DOM(A_{i_j})$, . . . , $DOM(A_{i_k - 1})$, and $DOM(A_{i_k})$, then tuple μ is a mathematical tuple. Consider the binary version, since the elements of the Cartesian product of a set of j-tuples (i.e., $\{(a_1, \ldots, a_j)\}$) and a set of k-tuples (i.e., $\{(b_1, \ldots, b_k)\}$) are ordered pairs each of which has an j-tuple as its first element and an k-tuple as its second element (i.e., $((a_1, \ldots, a_j), (b_1, \ldots, b_k))$), they are obviously not (j + k)-tuples (i.e., $(a_1, \ldots, a_j, b_1, \ldots, b_k)$). However, the elements of the complex product of a set of strings with length j (i.e., $\{a_1 \cdots a_j\}$) and a set of strings with length k (i.e., $\{b_1 \cdots b_k\}$) are also strings whose lengths are j + k (i.e., $a_1 \cdots a_j b_1 \cdots b_k$). Hence, it would be more rigorous to adopt complex product rather than Cartesian product in this aspect.

Example 1.2:

Let $DOM(A) = \{a, b, c\}$ and $DOM(B) = \{2, 1\}$. Then the Cartesian product of DOM(A) and DOM(B) is

$$\times(DOM(A), DOM(B)) = \{(a, 2), (a, 1), (b, 2), (b, 1), (c, 2), (c, 1)\},$$

which consists of six ordered-pairs. The complex product of DOM(A) and DOM(B) is

$$TUP(A \ B) = \{a\ 2, a\ 1, b\ 2, b\ 1, c\ 2, c\ 1\},$$

which consists of six strings of length two.

As shown in (1.4b) and (1.4c), a tuple μ over X has two parts: the attribute-string $A_{i_1} \cdots A_{i_k}$ is time-invariant, whereas the value-string $a_1 \cdots a_k$ is time-varying. We consider the time-invariant part as the *scheme* for μ, denoted by $sch(\mu) = X$. After defining the scheme for a tuple, the terminology *tuple μ over X* and *tuple μ with scheme X* will be used interchangeably.

For notational convenience, a tuple with name μ and scheme X can be denoted by combining its name and scheme as $\mu(X)$ such that

$$\mu(X) = \mu(A_{i_1}) \; \mu(A_{i_2}) \; \cdots \; \mu(A_{i_k}) \qquad\qquad (1.4e)$$

where $\mu(X)$ is the shorthand of the string on the right side of $=$ in (1.4e). We can view $\mu(X)$ as a tuple variable over X and each $\mu(A_{i_j})$ for $1 \leqslant j \leqslant k$ as a domain variable with scheme A_{i_j}. When $\mu(X)$ has constants forming its value-string such as $c_1 \cdots c_k$ and all these constants $c_1, \ldots, c_{k-1}$, and c_k belong to DOM(X), we call it a *constant tuple* over X.

Example 1.3:

In the tabular relation EMP, there are constant tuples over X = NAME SALARY MGR DEPT, which are the values of the following tuple variable:

$$\mu(X) = \mu(NAME) \; \mu(SALARY) \; \mu(MGR) \; \mu(DEPT)$$

where $\mu(NAME)$ is the NAME-component of μ, and so forth. For example, a constant tuple in EMP is of the form ''YANG 30000 JONES COMPUTER'' indicating that YANG is an employee in the COMPUTER department managed by JONES and has an annual salary of \$30,000. Consider Y = NAME MGR. The tuple (variable) is $\mu[Y] = \mu(NAME) \; \mu(MGR)$. The constant tuple with scheme Y derived from the constant tuple ''YANG 30000 JONES COMPUTER'' in EMP is ''YANG JONES.''

1.4 RELATIONS AND DATABASES AND THEIR SCHEMES

Relations and relational databases in a relational database management system correspond respectively to files and sets of files in a file management system. A tabular relation of data is not a relation in mathematics (referred to as a *mathematical relation*) as defined in section 0.3.2 of chapter 0 since a mathematical relation is a subset of a Cartesian product, whereas a relation in a relational database is a subset of a complex product.

Definition 1.3:   Let U_j be a nonempty subset of the universe U. A *relation* r_j over U_j of a relational database is defined on $TUP(U_j)$ if it is a set of tuples with scheme U_j. The *arity* of relation r_j is equal to the cardinaltity of U_j. A *relational database* (or simply *database*) denoted by db, is a set of relations $r_1, \ldots, r_{m-1}$, and r_m (i.e., db = $\{r_1, \ldots, r_m\}$) such that r_j is a relation over U_j for each j, $1 \leqslant j \leqslant m$. The set U_j is defined to be the *scheme* for relation r_j, denoted by $sch(r_j) = U_j$. The set Db, of the relation schemes $U_1, \ldots, U_{m-1}$, and U_m for relations $r_1, \ldots, r_{m-1}$, and r_m respectively such that the union of $U_1, \ldots, U_{m-1}$, and U_m is equal to U, is called the *scheme* for the database db (i.e., Db = $\{U_1, \ldots, U_m\}$).

Note that a relation scheme is also called an *intention,* and a relation is also called an *extension* or *instance.* By the tabular representation, the skeleton of a table is an intention, and the set of tuples filled into the table constitutes an extension. A relation scheme U_j and a databases scheme Db are both time-invariant, whereas a relation r_j and a database db are both time-varying. After an update, an insertion, or a deletion is performed, a new relation and a new database are yielded, whereas their corresponding schemes are not changed.

Example 1.4:

> In the department store database scheme, EMP is a named relation or a relation with name EMP. Its relation scheme is NAME SALARY MGR DEPT. The department store database is the set {EMP, SALES, SUPPLY, TYPE} consisting of four relations, and its scheme is the set {NAME SALARY MGR DEPT, DEPT ITEM, ITEM SUPPLIER, ITEM COLOR SIZE} consisting of four relation schemes. The tabular representation for the relation EMP with scheme NAME SALARY MGR DEPT is shown in table 1-1.

In this table, EMP is the relation name, NAME, SALARY, MGR, and DEPT are the attributes in the relation scheme to label the columns, and YANG 30000 JONES COMPUTER is so far the only tuple filled into the relation. Other tuples are omitted here and remain to be added (see table 8-13 in chapter 8).

A set consisting of no tuples is also a relation by definition 1.3, and is known as the *empty relation*, represented by the symbol Φ. When tuples over U_j are represented by attribute-value strings, a relation consisting of some such tuples is a subset of $TUP(U_j)$, i.e., the complex product of the domains of all attributes in U_j. Since $TUP(U_j)$, is a subset of itself, $TUP(U_j)$ is also a relation over U_j.

A *relation over* U_j and a *relation with scheme* U_j will be used interchangeably. This relation is a set of tuples over U_j where each such tuple is a function from U_j to $DOM(U_j)$ as defined in definition 1.2. If each individual domain constituting $DOM(U_j)$ is simple, such a relation has a tabular representation with the following properties.

(1) There is no duplication of column names since these names are the attributes in the set U_j.

(2) There is no duplication of rows since r_j is a set of tuples and a tuple is filled into a row.

(3) Row order is insignificant since r_j is a set of rows.

(4) Column order is insignificant since all columns of r_j are identified by distinct attributes in U_j. When columns are permuted for any reason, the attribute values in each row are also accordingly permuted. A permuted relation (yielded by a column permutation) and the original relation are considered the same.

(5) All attribute-values of r_j are atomic since the domains are simple.

Extensions, instances, tables, relations, and files can be used interchangeably; rows, tuples, and records can be so used; and columns, attributes, fields, and components (meaning tuple-components) can be so used. However, we will use relations, tuples, and attributes to be interchangeable with tables, rows, and columns, respectively.

The relations that are defined independently from other relations in a database are called *base relations*. Any relation that can be completely derived from some base relations is called a *derived relation* or *view*. Base relations are designed by a database admin-

TABLE 1-1 RELATION EMP

EMP	Name	Salary	Mgr	Dept
	YANG	30000	JONES	COMPUTER

istrator (abbreviated as DBA), whereas views are defined by ordinary users. In this book, we will concentrate on the design of the base relations of a logical database.

Relations over specific sets of attributes do not need to be named, since they are distinguishable and uniquely identifiable by their schemes. Thus, we might have *unnamed relations*. For an unnamed relation with scheme U_j, we simply use its scheme U_j to denote it. Relation names are created primarily as convenient shorthands to avoid having to list the column names all the time. When a relation over U_j is named as r_j, it is sufficient to use its name, r_j, for references. A relation with name r_j and scheme U_j can be denoted by combining its name and scheme as $r_j(U_j)$. A relation consisting of only constant tuples is known as a *constant relation*.

In the remark preceding section 1.3, we raised a question regarding a tuple with unknown components. For example, the top level manager does not have a manager and/or does not belong to a department. The inclusion of such types of tuples in a relation forces the admission of *null values,* or simply, *nulls.* Nulls exist (do not belong to DOM(U)) but mean that "values are at present unknown," "properties are inapplicable," or "no information is available" [Atz84, Cod79, Gal84, Lip79, Vas79, Zan82b]. For another instance, an unmarried employee cannot be omitted from a relation containing the attribute SPOUSE. An unmarried employee must be represented by a row containing a null SPOUSE-value. Because of this possible existence of nulls, previous definitions involving domains should be modified to allow some nulls in those domains [Bis83].

Example 1.5:

> In the database scheme as shown in example 1.1, there are four named base relations EMP, SALES, SUPPLY, and TYPE which have arities 4, 2, 2, and 3, respectively. The unnamed relation over Y = NAME MGR as derived from the base relation EMP in example 1.3 is a view created by a user using an operation called "projection" (definition 2.6).

In the theory of relational databases, there is a controversial issue [Ken81, Fag82, Ull83, Mai83a] concerning the existence and uniqueness problems of the universal relation assumption. To describe formally a/the universal relation, the notions of projection and join (definition 2.10) are required. Since these notions will be defined in chapter 2, we are not ready to formally introduce the universal relation assumption. Informally speaking, given a relation r(U), r(U) is the universal relation over U if each relation $r_j(U_j)$ for $1 \le j \le m$ forming the underlying database is derived from r(U) by a "projection" operation which retains only those columns in U_j and eliminates any duplicated tuples; and the data contents of r(U) can be exactly recovered from its projected relations $r_1(U_1)$ through $r_m(U_m)$ by combining their tuples based on a "join" operation. On the other hand, if each relation $r_j(U_j)$ for $1 \le j \le m$ in the underlying database is given, can we find a relation r(U) such that each given relation $r_j(U_j)$ is a projected relation of r(U)? This is the existence problem. If such a relation r(U) exists, is this relation unique? This is the uniqueness problem. In addition, even if such a relation r(U) exists and can be found, is it equal to the data contents obtained by joining the given relations $r_j(U_j)$ for each j, $1 \le j \le m$? We will answer these important questions in chapter 2. Note that the complex product TUP(U) is not necessarily the/a universal relation over U, although each relation over U must be a subset of TUP(U) since universal relations are determined not only by projections and joins but also by the losslessness of a join (definition 6.3). The reader is encouraged to solve exercise 1.1(d) and (e) and exercise 1.4(b) and (c) concerning the existence and uniqueness problems of the universal relation assumption.

1.5 CONSTRAINTS

In addition to the constraints imposed on attributes, domains, tuples, and relations as described in previous sections, there are many other constraints. These constraints can be classified into two major types as follows.

(1) One type of constraint specifies the characteristics of an attribute (including its domain) independent of any other attributes in a database. For instance, all SALARY-values in the relation EMP should be greater than zero and also upper bounded by a specific value indicating the maximum salary. As another example, the date of birth of any employee cannot be dated back as long as a century or as short as several years. These are related to the semantics of the values in domains.

(2) The other type of constraint specifies a relationship among several attributes (i.e., a relation among several domains of attributes) in a database. This type of constraints is related to the structure of a database. In the EMP relation, if a manager is also an employee but some employees are not managers, then DOM(NAME) contains DOM(MGR). This inclusion relationship implies a subset dependency [Sag82]. If each employee earns one salary, has one immediate manager, and belongs to one department, then the NAME-values can uniquely identify all tuples in the EMP relation. In other words, the relationship between NAME and any other attribute in EMP is a (many-to-one) function, since more than one employee may have the same salary (many-to-one) and may belong to the same department (many-to-one). These constraints are called *functional dependencies* in general and *key dependencies* in particular. Functional and key dependencies will be discussed in detail in chapter 4. Other data dependencies such as multivalued and join dependencies that are useful in database design will be covered in chapters 5 and 6, respectively.

In addition, if the home address, home telephone number, office location, and spouse of each employee are all unique, then the corresponding attributes and also the attribute DATEOFBIRTH might be added to the relation scheme for EMP. In this case, if some employee is only a temporary worker without an office or is still single, then the value of the attribute OFFICE or SPOUSE can be filled by a null. Suppose that the underlying database needs to include the children of each employee. Can we simply add the attribute CHILD to the relation scheme for EMP? The solution depends on the relationship between NAME and CHILD. If an employee has at most one child, the relationship is a function from DOM(NAME) to DOM(CHILD) so that CHILD can be added to EMP. In this case, a child can have more than one father or mother (natural, adopted, step, or whatever) who is an employee in the department store. On the other hand, if some employee has more than one child, then the relationship between NAME and CHILD becomes a mathematical relation between DOM(NAME) and DOM(CHILD) so that CHILD cannot be included in EMP because the structure of data dependencies is no longer the same. In the relation scheme SALES(DEPT ITEM), can we add the attribute LOC indicating the locations of the departments? Similarly, if we want to add the attributes PRICE and QTY indicating the prices and quantities of items in the underlying database, how can we handle them? To answer these questions, we need first to examine the relationships among the relevant attributes.

Definition 1.4:   Let U be the universe of attributes, a nonempty subset U_j of U be a relation scheme, and K be a nonempty subset of U_j. The set K of attributes is a *candidate key* (or simply, a *key*) for the relation scheme U_j or for a relation with scheme U_j if it has the following time-independent properties.

(1) A relation with scheme U_j does not have the same K-value for any two distinct tuples in the relation.

(2) If any attribute is deleted from K, then property (1) is lost.

Property (1) enables the K-values of a relation to uniquely identify all tuples in the relation. If the relation is stored in an associative or content-addressable storage in a database machine (abbreviated as DBM) [Hsi83], then use of a K-value with the uniqueness property (1) for retrieving a tuple stored in the DBM would exactly match the tuple (including this K-value as its component(s)). However, achieving the uniqueness property can also be accomplished if K properly contains a key. In this case, the attributes in K are sufficient to achieve the goal, but some of them are not necessarily required and can be deleted without violating uniqueness. On the other hand, if K is only a proper subset of a key, then use of such a K-value for retrieval would simultaneously match all those tuples, which include the K-value as their components. Property (2) assures that a key K contains only those attributes that are necessary and sufficient to achieve the uniqueness property. In other words, a K-value always provides an exact extent of information, no more and no less, to retrieve a unique tuple from its relation. Obviously, the empty set cannot be a key for a relation consisting of at least two tuples. This is why a key defined in definition 1.4 is a nonempty subset of attributes.

With each relation is associated a set of (candidate) keys from which one is chosen as the *primary key* for the relation or its scheme. When K is a key for a relation scheme U_j, the relationship between K and U_j is a function from TUP(K) to TUP(U_j) constituting an important dependency called a *key dependency*.

Definition 1.5:   A primary key for a relation is called *simple* if it consists of only one attribute and is called *compound* otherwise. For a given database, a domain on which a simple primary key is defined is called a *primary domain* of the database. Note that not all attributes of a compound primary key need be defined on primary domains, although a simple primary key must be defined on a primary domain.

All insertions into, updates of, and deletions from base relations are constrained by the following rules known as the *insert-update-delete rules* [Cod79].

(1) A primary key for a base relation cannot have a null component.

(2) If an attribute A of a compound primary key for a relation r_j is defined on a primary domain, then there must always exist a base relation r_k having a simple primary key B such that each A-value in r_j occurs as a B-value in r_k.

Since the primary key for a base relation is used to uniquely identify all tuples of the relation stored in the physical database, each component of a key-value cannot be null because the extent of information provided by the corresponding key value is not sufficient for storage and retrieval with the uniqueness property. In rule (2), the attribute A in a compound primary key for a relation r_j and the attribute B that is the simple primary key for a base relation r_k must define on either a common domain or two compatible domains so that each A-value occurring in r_j can also occur in r_k as a B-value. Two domains are compatible if their values can be identically characterized.

Example 1.6:

Let a database scheme consist of two relation schemes, namely: DEPT LOC and DEPT STOCK QTY where DEPT, LOC, STOCK, and QTY are the attributes denoting the department, location of department, stock, and quantity of stock respectively. Suppose that DEPT is the simple primary key for the first relation scheme, and DEPT STOCK is the compound primary key for the second relation scheme. Then DOM(DEPT) is the primary domain. By rule (1), DEPT-values and STOCK-values cannot be nulls. Only QTY and LOC can have null values. By rule (2), each DEPT-value occurring in relation INVENTORY(DEPT STOCK QTY) must also occur in relation DEPARTMENT(DEPT LOC). Then the connection between each DEPT-value and its corresponding LOC-value is always available in the underlying database. On the other hand, if it happens to be the case in which some DEPT-value is stored the first time in relation INVENTORY but is not added to relation DEPARTMENT, then the corresponding LOC-value is not stored in the base relation DEPARTMENT. Consequently, the underlying database is not adequate. Rule (2) attempts to enforce the essential constraint for avoiding this kind of trouble.

Example 1.7:

The four relation schemes for EMP, SALES, SUPPLY, and TYPE have respectively based their candidate keys on a number of assumptions.

(1) In EMP(NAME SALARY MGR DEPT), if the relationship between NAME and each attribute in the set {SALARY, MGR, DEPT} is a function from DOM(NAME) to each one in {DOM(SALARY), DOM(MGR), DOM(DEPT)}, then there is a key dependency between the candidate key NAME and the relation scheme NAME SALARY MGR DEPT. The primary key for EMP is NAME, and DOM(NAME) is a primary domain for the department store database.

(2) In SALES(DEPT ITEM) and SUPPLY(ITEM SUPPLIER), since each department generally sells and each supplier generally supplies at least one item, and similarly, each item is usually sold by at least one department and supplied by at least one supplier, the relationships be-

tween DEPT and ITEM and between ITEM and SUPPLIER are both mathematical relations between DOM(DEPT) and DOM(ITEM) and between DOM(ITEM) and DOM(SUPPLIER). Consequently, the primary key for either relation must contain both of its attributes. This key is known as an *all-key* and is compound.

(3) In TYPE(ITEM COLOR SIZE), each item may have different colors and/or sizes; several items may have the same color and/or size, and so forth. It is very unlikely that its key can be simple. We can assume that the primary key for TYPE is compound.

In this example, DOM(NAME) is the primary domain, and the compound primary keys for SALES, SUPPLY, and TYPE are not defined on this primary domain.

By rule (1), the attributes of the four primary keys cannot have nulls. Since the three compound primary keys are not defined on the primary domain DOM(NAME), there is no way to demonstrate rule (2) by this example.

Suppose that some assumptions made in (1) of example 1.7 are modified such that some employee can work in more than one department but still have one salary. Then some employee may have more than one immediate manager. Consequently, the relationships between NAME and DEPT and between NAME and MGR are no longer functions and become mathematical relations.

However, the relationship between NAME and SALARY is still a function. In addition, if some department has comanagers and several departments can share a manager, then the relationship between DEPT and MGR is also a mathematical relation. The three mathematical relations and the one function just described imply that the primary key for EMP is no longer the simple primary key NAME but becomes the compound primary key NAME DEPT MGR. However, the function from DOM(NAME) to DOM(SALARY) assures that the NAME-values can still uniquely identify all SALARY-values.

If all four attributes NAME, SALARY, MGR, and DEPT are retained in the single table EMP, then anomalies may be caused by insertion, deletion, or update. These anomalies will be discussed in chapter 7, which covers the design of databases by normalization. For example, update anomalies may arise since the repetition of some values of NAME and SALARY existing in EMP can lead to an inconsistency if arbitrary updates on individual tuples are permitted.

To avoid any such anomaly, the relation scheme for EMP under the assumption just made should be split into two subrelations by an operation called projection. These subrelations are EMP_1 with scheme NAME SALARY and EMP_2 with scheme NAME DEPT MGR. The singleton set containing the underscored attribute NAME is the simple primary key for EMP_1 that defines the primary domain DOM(NAME). The set of the underscored attributes NAME, DEPT, and MGR is the compound primary key for EMP_2 that is defined on the primary domain DOM(NAME). By rule (2), each NAME-value occurring in EMP_2 must also occur in EMP_1. This example demonstrates that an adequate relation scheme previously proposed may have anomalies when the constraints among its domains are generalized from functions to mathematical relations. Based on the modified constraints, the original relation scheme can be split into subrelation schemes for improvements. Splitting a relation scheme is called *vertical normalization,* which will be introduced in chapter 7.

Contrary to vertical normalization, we consider adding attributes to a relation scheme. Can we add the attribute LOC to SALES(DEPT ITEM)? If each department has a unique location, then it might be better to create a new relation scheme DEPT LOC, otherwise the tuples in SALESLOC(DEPT ITEM LOC) may have excesively duplicated DEPT-values and LOC-values since each department can have only one LOC-value but may sell a number of items.

Can we add the attribute PRICE to the department store database indicating the prices of items? Does PRICE depend only on the types or specifications of items including colors and sizes? If each ITEM-COLOR-SIZE-value has a unique PRICE-value, then we can add PRICE to TYPE. Does PRICE mean the prices of items supplied by various suppliers? In this case, the same type of item may have different prices because it may be supplied by various suppliers. Consequently, PRICE cannot simply be added to TYPE in which SUPPLIER is not included, or to SUPPLY in which COLOR and SIZE are not included. Does PRICE mean the prices of items sold by different departments? In this case, if the sale price of each type of item is unique within the underlying department store, then we can simply add PRICE to TYPE.

How can we handle the attribute QTY, indicating the quantities of items supplied, sold, or on hand? There is no simple solution.

To design a good database, we may need to collect enough practical data; to choose appropriate attributes and their domains; to propose relation schemes; to find data dependencies, particularly the key dependency for each relation scheme; to reduce redundancies; and to eliminate anomalies caused by insertion, deletion, and updates, among others. During the initial state, entity-relationship diagrams established in the entity-relationship data model proposed by Chen [Che76] provide valuable aids to solve a part of this problem.

As already seen in previous sections, each tuple or relation has a specific set of attributes as its scheme, and a database has a specific set of subsets of attributes as its scheme. A tuple, relation, or database also has a specific set of constraints. A minimum set of attributes, known as a key for a relation, is one of the most basic and important constraints. Thus, defining a relation scheme only by a set of attributes is not sufficient. A set of data dependencies is another essential part of the definition.

Definition 1.6: Let U be the universe of attributes and U_j be a nonempty subset of U. Let C_j be a set of data dependencies on U_j such that $ATTR(C_j) \subseteq U_j$ where $ATTR(C_j)$ is the set of all attributes occurring in C_j. Let $TUP(U_j)$ be the complex product of the domains of the attributes in U_j. We define $SAT(U_j)$ to be the set of all relations over U_j where each relation is a subset of $TUP(U_j)$. We define $SAT(C_j)$ to be the subset of $SAT(U_j)$ such that each relation in $SAT(C_j)$ satisfies every data dependency in C_j.

By this definition, a relation scheme U_j constrained by a set C_j of data dependencies on U_j should be represented by R_j where $R_j = (U_j, C_j)$. Similarly, a database scheme Db, defined in definition 1.3, should be accordingly modified as $Db = \{R_1, \ldots, R_m\}$.

Note that a relation $r_j(U_j)$ is in $SAT(U_j)$. If K is a key for $r_j(U_j)$, then the key K and the set U_j of attributes constitute a key dependency in C_j. Let this key dependency be denoted by $K \rightarrow U_j$. Then we have $C_j = \{K \rightarrow U_j\}$, $R_j = (U_j, \{K \rightarrow U_j\})$, and $r_j(R_j) \in$ SAT($\{K \rightarrow U_j\}$).

Given TUP(U_j) and C_j on U_j, relations in SAT(C_j) with the maximum number of tuples are not necessarily unique. Because of this nonuniqueness problem, we cannot define TUP(C_j) as the maximal set of tuples over U_j satisfying each data dependency in C_j. Exercise 1.2 provides an example to demonstrate this nonuniqueness problem.

Example 1.8:

> The complex product TUP(A B) = {a 2, a 1, b 2, b 1, c 2, c 1} (defined on DOM(A) = {a, b, c} and DOM(B) = { 2,1}) and the empty relation Φ(A B) are relations in SAT(A B). Each nonempty proper subset of TUP(A B) consisting of j tuples for j = 1, 2, . . . , or 5 is also a relation in SAT(A B). Thus, SAT(A B) for DOM(A) = {a, b, c} and DOM(B) = {2, 1} consists of sixty-four relations over A B since there are 1, 6, 15, 20, 15, 6, and 1 relations over A B with cardinalities 0, 1, 2, 3, 4, 5, and 6, respectively. The complex product TUP(A B), represented by a set of tuples, has the tabular form as shown in table 1-2.

Suppose that each A-value cannot be equal to b, and the only B-value is 1 in any relation over A B constituting the set C of constraints imposed on data. Then the set of attributes occurring in both constraints consists of A and B; i.e., ATTR(C) = {A, B}, and SAT(C) consists of only four relations in SAT(A B); i.e.,

$$\text{SAT}(C) = \{\Phi(A\ B), \{a\ 1\}, \{c\ 1\}, \{a\ 1, c\ 1\}\}.$$

This example is used only to illustrate the concepts defined in definition 1.6 and may not have any practical significance. In practical applications, an attribute whose domain consists of only a very limited number of values needs not be included in a database scheme. We can define separate relation schemes dedicated to those values. More specifically, the EMP relation scheme needs not to include the attribute SEX since we can define two relation schemes, one dedicating to male employees and the other to female employees. There are many similar occasions in which the same approach can be followed. This is the reason to have another decomposition of relation schemes, known as *horizontal normalization*, which will be discussed in chapter 7.

A database scheme can be graphically represented by a hypergraph [Bee81a, Bee81c, Mai81a, Fag81b, Sac82, Fag83b]. The attributes are represented by vertices. Each relation scheme is represented by a hyperedge. In drawing a hypergraph, vertices or nodes are labeled by the attributes in U, and each hyperedge is represented by a closed curve enclosing the attributes of a relation scheme.

TABLE 1-2 RELATION TUP(A B)

TUP(A B)	A	B
	a	2
	a	1
	b	2
	b	1
	c	2
	c	1

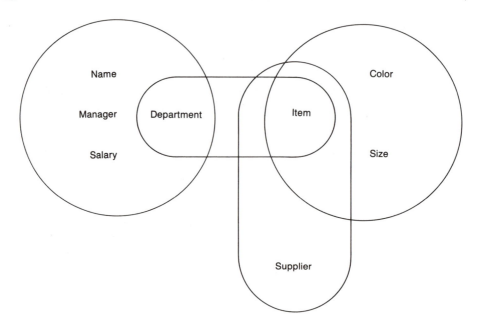

Figure 1-1   The hypergraph for the department store database scheme

Example 1.9:

In the department store database, the hypergraph of the database scheme is shown in Fig. 1-1. This small hypergraph is obviously acyclic. Note that acyclic database schemes possess several desirable properties, whereas cyclic database schemes are undesired [Bee81a, Bee81c, Fag83b]. To decide whether a hypergraph is acyclic or not, the Graham-reduction of a hypergraph in section 0.6.2 of chapter 0 can be followed.

In addition to hypergraphs for database schemes, decomposition trees [Zan82] are useful in verticle normalization. In addition to entity-relationship diagrams, there are other graphical methods to represent a relation scheme, such as CAZ-graphs (combined ACOVER and ZCOVER) [Zan82]. To design a database scheme based on functional dependencies (abbreviated as FD), FD-graphs are particularly important to provide a synthesis algorithm. FD-graphs [Aus83, Yan85] will be introduced in chapter 4 and used in chapter 7 in the design of better databases.

1.6 THE RELATIONAL MODEL OF DATABASES

We summarize the materials presented in this chapter by establishing a formal definition of the relational model of databases based on the work of Codd [Cod79].

Definition 1.7:   Let U_j be a subset of the universe U of attributes and C_j be a set of data dependencies on U_j for each j, $1 \leq j \leq m$ and $U = U_1 \cdots U_m$. The *relational model of databases* consists of

(1) a set of time-varying tabular relations $r_1, \ldots, r_{m-1}$, and r_m with time-invariant schemes $R_1, \ldots, R_{m-1}$, and R_m where each $R_j = (U_j, C_j)$, $1 \leq j \leq m$.

(2) the insert-update-delete rules, and

(3) a data sublanguage at least as powerful as the relational algebra (this will be described in chapter 2 in detail).

Closely associated with the relational model are various normalization concepts, which are semantic in nature (being time-invariant properties of time-varying relations). Examples of such concepts are functional dependencies in chapter 4, multivalued dependencies in chapter 5, lossless natural joins in chapter 6, and various normal forms in chapter 7. All of these important concepts will be introduced in greater detail. In addition, Codd [Cod79] proposed various extensions to the relational model of databases in an attempt to capture more meaning.

EXERCISES

1.1 Let $U = A B C D$, $DOM(A) = \{0, 1\}$, $DOM(B) = \{a, b\}$, $DOM(C) = \{3, 4\}$, and $DOM(D) = \{c, d\}$.

    (a) Find the complex product TUP(A B C D).

    (b) Find the Cartesian product $\times$(DOM(A), DOM(B), DOM(C), DOM(D)).

    (c) If the relationship between A and B is a one-to-one function from DOM(A) to DOM(B), then find the number of relations over A B C D satisfying this constraint.

    (d) Suppose that a relation over A B is $r_1 = \{0\,a,\ 1\,b\}$ and a relation over A C D is $r_2 = \{0\,3\,c,\ 0\,4\,d,\ 1\,3\,d,\ 1\,4\,c\}$. Does there exist a unique universal relation over A B C D in a database consisting of both relations r_1 and r_2? Find it if one exists. Otherwise, explain why such a universal relation does not exist.

    (e) Suppose that the given relations in a database are $r_1 = \{0\,a,\ 1\,b\}$ and $r_3 = \{0\,3\,c,\ 0\,4\,d,\ 0\,3\,d\}$. Find a unique universal relation over A B C D if one exists, find all of them if there are more than one, or explain why if such a universal relation does not exist.

1.2 Let $U = A B$, $DOM(A) = \{0,1\}$, and $DOM(B) = \{a, b\}$. Suppose that there is a function from DOM(A) to DOM(B) such that any tuples with the same A-value must have the same B-value. Let this function be denoted by the data dependency c: $A \rightarrow B$.

    (a) Find SAT(A B) (that consists of sixteen relations with scheme A B).

    (b) Find SAT($\{c\}$) (that consists of nine relations with scheme A B, each of which satisfies the data dependency c).

    (c) Discuss why we cannot define a unique TUP($\{c\}$) as the maximal set of tuples with scheme A B satisfying the data dependency c.

1.3 Draw a hypergraph to represent the database scheme {DEPT LOC, DEPT STOCK QTY}. Is this database scheme acyclic?

1.4 Let the relation schemes be DEPT LOC and DEPT STOCK QTY.

    (a) Under what relationships between DEPT and LOC and between DEPT STOCK and QTY are the keys for the given relation schemes, respectively, DEPT and DEPT STOCK?

    (b) Show that the universal relation over DEPT LOC STOCK QTY exists if each DEPT-value occurs in both relations DEPARTMENT(DEPT LOC) and INVENTORY(DEPT STOCK QTY).

(c) Show that a universal relation over DEPT LOC STOCK QTY does not exist if some DEPT-value occurs in only one of the relations DEPARTMENT and INVENTORY.

1.5 What are the differences between a tuple (defined in definition 1.2) and a mathematical tuple, and between a (tabular) relation and a mathematical relation?

1.6 In the relation scheme EMP(NAME SALARY MGR DEPT), if the relationship from DEPT to MGR is also a function from DOM(DEPT) to DOM(MGR) in addition to the functions from DOM(NAME) to DOM(SALARY) and from DOM(NAME) to DOM(DEPT), then there are redundant DEPT-MGR-values. How can we improve the database scheme by reducing the redundant values to the minimal possible extent?

chapter 2

THE RELATIONAL ALGEBRA

2.1 INTRODUCTION

This chapter is a continuation of chapter 1 in discussing the third aspect of the relational model of databases, i.e., the relational algebra.

Query languages for relational databases can be divided into two broad classes:

(1) algebraic languages such as ISBL (Information System Base Language), which will be introduced in section 8.2 of chapter 8 and

(2) predicate calculus languages.

Languages in class (2) can have two versions known as the *tuple* and the *domain relational calculus*. As will be included in sections 8.3 and 8.4 of chapter 8, QUEL (QUEry Language) and QBE (Query-By-Example) are, respectively, a tuple-based and domain-oriented query language.

This chapter covers only the relational algebra, excluding null values. The algebra has a much simpler structure. This feature could be useful in supporting theoretical work, such as providing an inductive proof. Chapter 3 will cover the relational predicate calculus. The calculus allows queries to be expressed more naturally. This feature could be useful, not only for end user purposes, but also to make language specifications by translations to the calculus simpler [Klu82a].

2.2 ALGEBRAIC OPERATIONS

There are six basic operators that serve to define the relational algebra. Three of them are operators for the binary operations: union, complex product, and difference. The other three are the operators for the unary operations: projection, selection, and renaming.

A unary operation in the relational algebra requires a single operand that is a relation. Many such operations can be viewed as 1-place functions. A binary operation in the relational algebra requires two operands that are also relations. Many such operations are binary functions. The union operation is not a function, as will be explained in section 2.2.3.

Although it is sufficient to represent a named relation by its name, we have used and will still use the notation r(R) to denote the relation with name r and scheme R for the sole purpose of description convenience. In this chapter, two relation schemes R and S are said to be equal; (written as R = S) if they consist of the same attributes. However, their string representations are not necessarily identical because their elements may not be arranged in the same ordering.

2.2.1. Union-compatibility

The binary operations of union, difference, and intersection on relations of a database require that their operand relations must be compatible in their schemes. This compatibility is defined in the following.

Definition 2.1:   Two relations r(R) and s(S) in a database are *union-compatible* and so are the two schemes R and S if there exists a one-to-one correspondence (i.e., one-to-one and onto function) f between R and S such that $DOM(A_j) = DOM(B_k)$ for $B_k = f(A_j)$ and $A_j = f^{-1}(B_k)$, A_j in R, and B_k in S where f^{-1} is the inverse of f.

Example 2.1:

> For the department store database, relations SALES(DEPT ITEM) and TYPE(ITEM COLOR SIZE) are obviously not union-compatible. Relations SALES(DEPT ITEM) and SUPPLY(ITEM SUPPLIER), shown in tables 2-1 and 2-2, can be considered union-compatible if DEPT and SUPPLIER are both defined on the same domain (i.e., their values are of the same data type, such as character string with identical maximum length). However, their active domains are still different since some department may not be a supplier or vice versa.

Suppose that this database does not have the EMP relation but has two other relations, say EMP$_3$(NAME1 SALARY MGR DEPT) and EMP$_4$(NAME2 SALARY MGR DEPT) where NAME1 denotes the names of those employees who are currently not managers and NAME2 denotes the names of those managers (excluding the top level manager) who are also employees. Although the active domains of NAME1 and NAME2 relative to the underlying database may not be equal, they can be defined on the same domain, or their domains can be assumed to be equal so that they are union-compatible. As a special case, if two relations have the same scheme, then they are union-compatible. The union compatibility has the properties of reflexivity, symmetry, and transitivity.

TABLE 2-1 RELATION SALES

SALES	DEPT	ITEM
	COMPUTER	CALCULATOR
	COMPUTER	MICRO
	COMPUTER	PRINTER
	COMPUTER	TERMINAL
	DP	MICRO
	DP	PRINTER
	DP	TERMINAL
	PHOTO	CAMERA
	PHOTO	FILM
	VIDEO	RECORDER
	VIDEO	TV

TABLE 2-2 RELATION SUPPLY

SUPPLY	ITEM	SUPPLIER
	CALCULATOR	HP
	CALCULATOR	TI
	CAMERA	KODAK
	FILM	KODAK
	MICRO	HP
	MICRO	IBM
	PRINTER	IBM
	RECORDER	ZENITH
	TERMINAL	IBM
	TERMINAL	ZENITH
	TV	ZENITH

2.2.2 Renaming

When two relations r(R) and s(S) with R $\neq$ S (in the sense of having different but compatible attributes) are union-compatible, although there is a one-to-one correspondence between the schemes R and S, a renaming operation is needed to rename the different attributes in either R $-$ S or S $-$ R.

Definition 2.2:   Let s(S) be a relation. Let X = $A_{i_1} A_{i_2} \cdots A_{i_k}$ be a subset of S, and let Y = $B_1 B_2 \cdots B_k$ such that each B_j is not in S, and DOM(B_j) = DOM(A_{i_j}) for each j, 1 $\leq$ j $\leq$ k. The *subset renaming* (or simply *renaming*) of X to Y in s(S), written as $\delta_{X \leftarrow Y}(s(S))$, or simply $\delta_{X \leftarrow Y}(s)$ when S is understood, is the relation s over R = (S $-$ X) $\cup$ Y such that the columns $A_{i_1}, \ldots, A_{i_{k-1}}$, and A_{i_k} in the given relation s(S) are, respectively, renamed to $B_1, \ldots, B_{k-1}$, and B_k, i.e.,

$$\delta_{X \leftarrow Y}(s(S)) = \{v \mid \mu \in s(S), v[S - X] = \mu[S - X], \text{ and}$$
$$v[B_j] = \mu[A_{i_j}], 1 \leq j \leq k\}. \tag{2.1a}$$

The renaming of X to Y is simply accomplished by the one-to-one correspondence f between Y and X such that $f(B_j) = A_{i_j}$ for each j, $1 \leq j \leq k$, i.e., each column name A_{i_j} of the given tabular relation s(S) is changed to the new name B_j to yield the table s(R). Note that relation s(R) is considered the same as s(S), so we use the same relation name s. The columns of s(R) do not necessarily follow the same ordering of the attributes in the string (S - X) Y. Hence, we use the set-oriented notation (S - X) $\cup$ Y in definition 2.2. Rearranging or permuting columns of a table is not done in (2.1a) but it can be easily accomplished by an operation called *projection* which will be defined in definition 2.6.

Example 2.2:

As assumed in example 2.1, if DOM(NAME1) = DOM(NAME2) for the assumed relations EMP_3(NAME1 SALARY MGR DEPT) and EMP_4(NAME2 SALARY MGR DEPT), we can rename NAME2 to NAME1 (or vice-versa), i.e.,

$$\delta_{NAME2 \leftarrow NAME1}(EMP_4) = EMP_4(NAME1 \ SALARY \ MGR \ DEPT)$$

where s = EMP_4, S = NAME2 SALARY MGR DEPT, X = A_{i_j} = NAME2, Y = B_1 = NAME1, v[NAME1] = μ[NAME2], and v[SALARY MGR DEPT] = μ[SALARY MGR DEPT] for each pair of tuples v in the renamed relation and μ in the original relation. The renaming operation is accomplished by searching the NAME2-column in the original table and then by changing the name to NAME1.

By definition 2.2 when k = 1, a subset renaming becomes a single-attribute renaming. Since A_{i_j} is in S, and B_1 is not in S, A_{i_j} and B_1 are distinct. Consequently, there is no such case in which an attribute is renamed by itself, i.e., $\delta_{A \leftarrow A}(s(S))$ never happens. Similarly, when k > 1, since X is a subset of S and Y is not a subset of S, X and Y are disjoint. Then a subset renaming can be always written as a sequence of single-attribute renamings, i.e.,

$$\delta_{A_{i_1} \cdots A_{i_k} \leftarrow B_1 \cdots B_k}(s(S)) = \delta_{A_{i_k} \leftarrow B_k}(\cdots (\delta_{A_{i_1} \leftarrow B_1}(s(S))) \cdots). \quad (2.1b)$$

The subset renaming shown in (2.1b) is achieved by k sequential operations, i.e., the column named by A_{i_1}, in the original table is first searched, and its name is changed to B_1, A_{i_2} is then similarly renamed to B_2, and so on, until A_{i_k} is finally renamed to B_k. In this case, parallel or simultaneous renamings of A_{i_j} to B_j for all j, $1 \leq j \leq k$ can also accomplished under a multiprocessing environment, i.e., the subset renaming $\delta_{X \leftarrow Y}(s(S))$ can be written as

$$\delta_{X \leftarrow Y}(s(S)) = \{\delta_{A_{i_j} \leftarrow B_j}(s(S)) \mid 1 \leq j \leq k\} \quad (2.1c)$$

where each single-attribute renaming in the set of (2.1c) can be assigned to an individual processor if k processors of a computer system are available. On the other hand, if X and Y are not disjoint, then only parallel renaming of X to Y is feasible. For example, if X = $A_1 A_2$, Y = $A_2 A_1$, and (2.1a) is used, then the temporary table has two columns named by A_2 after the first renaming of A_1 to A_2 is executed. How can this nonuniqueness problem be resolved? The case illustrated by this example is in fact a permutation problem, i.e., to permute $A_1 A_2$ into $A_2 A_1$. This permutation can be easily resolved by "projection.'' To avoid the occurrence of this possible case, the set Y of attributes for renaming X in S is required not to be in S as described in definition 2.2.

The renaming operation can be viewed as an identity function in the sense that the original relation s(S) and the renamed relation s(R) = (S - Y) ∪ Y are considered as the same relation. However, between S and R, there must be a one-to-one correspondence based on their compatible attributes, and this correspondence can be restricted to X and Y.

2.2.3 Union

Unlike the union of two arbitrary sets of objects as shown in (0.1a) of chapter 0, the union of two relations needs an additional constraint on the operand relations, i.e., they must be union-compatible.

Definition 2.3:   The *union* of two union-compatible relations r(R) and s(S), written as r ∪ s, is the relation over R consisting of each tuple belonging to r or s (or both), i.e.,

$$r \cup s = \{\mu \mid \mu \in r \text{ or } \mu \in s\} \text{ if } R = S, \qquad (2.2a)$$

and

$$r \cup s = \{\mu \mid \mu \in r(R) \text{ or } \mu \in \delta_X \leftarrow _Y(s(S))\} \text{ if } R \neq S \qquad (2.2b)$$

where each attribute in X of S but not in R (i.e., $X \subseteq S - R$) is renamed to a relevant attribute in Y of R but not in S (i.e., $Y \subseteq R - S$) such that f(Y) = X under a one-to-one correspondence f: R → S (f: Y → X is a restriction of f: R → S) where f(Y) is a shorthand of $f(B_1) \cdots f(B_k)$ for $Y = B_1 \cdots B_k$.

Note that if R = S, then (2.2a) is similar to (0.1a) in chapter 0. In this case, the strings of R and S may not be identical (in their orderings). Consequently, a permutation, but not a renaming, is needed to permute the columns of the table s(S) based on the one-to-one correspondence f between R and S. This consideration can be ignored to define a union operation here since relations s(S) and s(R) are considered the same no matter how their columns are arranged. However, this consideration should be implemented when a union operation is executed. In other words, the binding time in this aspect is not in the definition time but is postponed to the implementation moment. In QBE and PROLOG DBMSs, which will be introduced in chapter 8, the columns of a table are declared by their position numbers. If R ≠ S, then there is a renaming of X to Y where the attributes in X and Y must be arranged in certain orderings based on a one-to-one correspondence f between R and S since A_{i_j} in X can be renamed only to B_j where $f(B_j) = A_{i_j}$. This consideration will be demonstrated in subsequent examples.

Example 2.3:

Let r(A B C) = {a b 3, d f 3, e g 1} and s(D E F) = {a b 5, d f 3} where r and s are represented by sets of tuples rather than tables for the purpose of description convenience. Since the values of A, B, D, and E occur as nonnumeric letters, and those of C and F occur as integers, we might assume that $DOM(A) = DOM(B) = DOM(D) = DOM(E)$ and $DOM(C) = DOM(F)$. Then there is a one-to-one correspondence $f_1 = \{(A, D), (B, E), (C, F)\}$. In this example, we can view $Y = A\ B\ C$ and $X = D\ E\ F$ because $f_1(R) = S$ where the symbol $f_1(R)$ is the shorthand of $f_1(A)\ f_1(B)\ f_1(C)$, i.e., $f_1(A\ B\ C) = f_1(A)\ f_1(B)\ f_1(C)$. Thus, we have

$$s(A\ B\ C) = \delta_{D\ E\ F\ \leftarrow\ A\ B\ C}(s(D\ E\ F)) = \{a\ b\ 5,\ d\ f\ 3\}$$

and

$$r \cup s = \{a\ b\ 3,\ d\ f\ 3,\ e\ g\ 1,\ a\ b\ 5\}$$

with scheme $A\ B\ C$. For the other one-to-one correspondence $f_2 = \{(A, E), (B, D), (C,F)\}$, we can view $Y = A\ B\ C$, but $X = E\ D\ F$ (rather than $D\ E\ F$) since $f_2(Y) = E\ D\ F$.

The union operator has two properties. It is commutative, i.e., $r \cup s = s \cup r$ and is also associative, i.e., $(r \cup s) \cup t = r \cup (s \cup t)$ for mutually union-compatible relations r, s, and t. Hence, we can write an unparenthesized expression of unions without ambiguity and extend the binary version of union into the k-ary version of union denoted by the prefixed notation $\cup(r_1, r_2, \ldots, r_k)$ where the relations are mutually union-compatible. The prefixed and infixed unions can be used interchangeably. Since $\cup$ is associative, several prefixed unions can be nested into different levels. For example, $\cup(\cup(r, s), t) = \cup(r, \cup(s, t)) = \cup(r, s, t)$.

Union has two special cases. For any relation $r(R)$, $r \cup \Phi = r$ where Φ is the empty relation. If $r \subseteq s$, then $r \cup s = s$.

Union is a k-ary operation for $k \geqslant 2$; its operator is denoted by prefixed $\cup$, and the union of k mutually union-compatible relations is also a relation. The union operation can be viewed as a mathematical relation between the Cartesian product of k mutually union-compatible relations and the union of these relations such that the images of each argument are equal to the distinct elements of the argument, i.e., the number of images of each argument is at least one and at most k.

2.2.4 Difference

Similar to the union operation, the difference of two relations also needs the union-compatibility condition. However, this condition can be relaxed for defining a generalized difference, which will be discussed.

Definition 2.4:   The *difference* of two union-compatible relations $r(R)$ and $s(S)$, written as $r - s$, is the relation over R consisting of each tuple belonging to r but not to s, i.e.,

$$r - s = \{\mu \mid \mu \in r \text{ and } \mu \notin s\} \text{ if } R = S,$$

and

$$r - s = \{\mu \mid \mu \in r \text{ and } \mu \notin \delta_{X\ \leftarrow\ Y}(s(S))\} \text{ if } R \neq S$$

where $X \subseteq S - R$, $Y \subseteq R - S$, $X = f(Y)$, $Y = f^{-1}(X)$, and f: $Y \to X$ is a restriction of f: $R \to S$ and f^{-1}: $S \to R$.

Example 2.4:

Let r(A B C) = {a b 3, d f 3, e g 1} and s(D E F) = {a b 5, d f 3} be two union-compatible relations based on f_1 = {(A, D), (B, E), (C, F)}. Then we have r $-$ s = {a b 3, e g 1} with scheme A B C and s $-$ r = {a b 5} with scheme D E F.

Difference is a binary operation; its operator is denoted by $-$, and the difference of two union-compatible relations is also a relation. The difference operation is a partial function from r to r $-$ s such that for each argument μ_r in r, the image is μ_r if μ_r is not in s and is undefined otherwise. Thus, the difference r $-$ s is always a subset of r.

The difference operator is not commutative, i.e., r $-$ s $\neq$ s $-$ r as seen from example 2.4. The operator is not associative, i.e., (r $-$ s) $-$ t $\neq$ r $-$ (s $-$ t) since (r $-$ s) $-$ t = r $-$ (s $\cup$ t) for mutually union-compatible relations r, s, and t.

There are three special cases. The first one is $\Phi - r = \Phi$, and the second one is r $-$ $\Phi = r$ for any relation r(R) and the empty relation Φ. The third one is the difference between the relation TUP(U_j) and $r_j(U_j)$ known as the *complement* of $r_j(U_j)$ relative to TUP(U_j) denoted by $\sim r_j$, i.e., $\sim r_j(U_j)$ = TUP(U_j) $-$ $r_j(U_j)$. Recall that TUP(U_j) is the complex product of the domains of the attributes in U_j.

The query language ISBL (Information System Base Languages) [Tod75, Tod76], which is a relational algebraic language, defines the difference r $-$ s as the set of tuples μ in r such that μ does not agree with any one tuple in s on those (common) attributes in the intersection of r and s. This is a generalization of definition 2.4 because the union-compatibility condition is relaxed. This difference will be illustrated in example 2.8.

2.2.5 Complex Product

As discussed in chapter 1, we prefer to use complex products rather than Cartesian products concerning relational databases. In the algebraic-based query langauge ISBL, which will be introduced in chapter 8, the term *full quadratic join* means "complex product."

Definition 2.5:   The *complex product* of two nonempty relations r(R) and s(S), written as r * s, is the set (which is not necessarily a relation) consisting of the string $\mu_r \mu_s$ for each pair of strings (μ_r, μ_s) in the Cartesian produce r $\times$ s, i.e.,

$$r * s = \{\mu \mid \mu = \mu_r \mu_s \text{ and } (\mu_r, \mu_s) \in r \times s\}.$$

Note that the complex product is undefined if either operand relation is the empty relation since a tuple is not defined on the empty set (i.e., the tuple consisting of no attribute-values is not defined in definition 1.2), although the null or empty string is defined in mathematics as the identity (i.e., a string concatenated by the null string on either side is the string itself).

Complex product is a binary operation; its operator is denoted by *, and the complex product of two nonempty relations is not necessarily a relation. A complex product is a relation if it is defined on two operand relations whose schemes are nonempty and disjoint. On the other hand, if the operand relations of a complex product are nonempty but are not disjoint, then the complex product involves a multiset of attributes so that it is not a relation. In this case, we can rename those attributes of S in $R \cap S$ by a set Y consisting of $|R \cap S|$ new attributes, i.e., $\delta_{(R \cap S) \leftarrow Y}(s(S))$ with $A_j \notin R\ S$ for each $A_j \in Y$ to make the new intersection empty, i.e., $R \cap ((S - (R \cap S))\ Y) = \emptyset$ where $\emptyset$ is the empty set. Then the complex product of r(R) and $\delta_{(R \cap S) \leftarrow Y}(s(S))$ with scheme $R \cup (S - (R \cap S)) \cup Y$ is a relation.

Example 2.5:

Let ATUP(X) be the *active complex product* consisting of all possible tuples derived from the active domains of the attributes in X. Assume that the department store database involves only those four departments and eight items as shown in tables 2-1 and 2-2. Then the active complex product of the active domains ADOM(DEPT) and ADOM(ITEM) relative to the underlying database defines ATUP(DEPT ITEM) consisting of thirty-two tuples. These tuples are in the union of SALES(DEPT ITEM) of table 2-1 and the active complement ASALES := $\sim_a$SALES(DEPT ITEM) of table 2-3. The relation ATUP(DEPT ITEM) properly contains the relation SALES(DEPT ITEM). Similarly, the complex product of DOM(DEPT) and DOM(ITEM) defines TUP(DEPT ITEM), which contains ATUP(DEPT ITEM) as a subset.

TABLE 2-3 ASALES(DEPT ITEM)

ASALES	DEPT	ITEM
	COMPUTER	CAMERA
	COMPUTER	FILM
	COMPUTER	RECORDER
	COMPUTER	TV
	DP	CALCULATOR
	DP	CAMERA
	DP	FILM
	DP	RECORDER
	DP	TV
	PHOTO	CALCULATOR
	PHOTO	MICRO
	PHOTO	PRINTER
	PHOTO	RECORDER
	PHOTO	TERMINAL
	PHOTO	TV
	VIDEO	CALCULATOR
	VIDEO	CAMERA
	VIDEO	FILM
	VIDEO	MICRO
	VIDEO	PRINTER
	VIDEO	TERMINAL

There is a one-to-one correspondence between the Cartesian produce r $\times$ s and the complex product r * s such that each ordered pair (μ_r, μ_s) in r $\times$ s corresponds to the string μ_r μ_s in r * s. Since each tuple in a database can be represented by a string as shown in (1.4d) of chapter 1, the only difference between r $\times$ s and r * s is that each element of r $\times$ s is an ordered pair (μ_r, μ_s) of two strings μ_r in r and μ_s in s, whereas each element of r * s is still a string μ_r μ_s. Example 1.2 of chapter 1 provided an illustration.

The complex product operator is not commutative but is associative. Hence, we can extend the binary version to the k-ary version and denote the latter by the prefixed notation *(r_1, r_2, . . . , r_k). Note that if the schemes of the relations r_1, . . . , r_{k-1}, and r_k, are not mutually disjoint, then *(r_1, . . . , r_k) is not a relation because of the presence of duplicated columns. The prefixed and infixed complex products can be used interchangeably. The prefixed complex products can be nested into different levels. For example, *(*(r, s), t) = *(r, *(s, t)) = *(r, s, t).

2.2.6 Projection

We mentioned the projection of a relation onto a subset of its scheme concerning universal relations in the last paragraph of section 1.4 of chapter 1. But we have not yet introduced a formal definition for projection.

Definition 2.6:   Let U_j be a nonempty subset of U, $r_j(U_j)$ be a relation over U_j, and X be a nonempty subset of U_j. The *projection* of r_j onto X, written as $\pi_X(r_j)$ or $r_j[X]$, is the relation over X consisting of the X-value of each tuple in r_j, i.e.,

$$\pi_X(r_j) = \{\mu[X] \mid X \subseteq U_j \text{ and } \mu \in r_j(U_j)\}. \tag{2.3}$$

Example 2.6:

> The relation EMP[NAME MGR] is the projection of the relation EMP(NAME SALARY MGR DEPT) onto NAME MGR. This projection consists of the NAME-MGR-value of each tuple in EMP without duplicates.

Projection is a unary operation; it is denoted by $\pi_X(r_j)$ or $r_j[X]$, and the projection of a relation is also a relation. Let SAT(U_j) be the set of all relations over U_j, each of which is a subset of the complex product TUP(U_j). Let SAT(X) be similarly defined. The projection operation is the function $\pi_X : \text{SAT}(U_j) \rightarrow \text{SAT}(X)$ such that each argument $r_j(U_j)$ in SAT(U_j) has a unique image $\pi_X(r_j)$ in SAT(X) as defined by (2.3).

There are three special cases:

(1) If X = U_j, then $r_j[U_j] = r_j(U_j)$ (i.e., projection operation is not really performed).
(2) If X = U_k for k $\neq$ j where U_k is permuted from U_j, then $r_j[U_k]$ is obtained by permuting the columns of $r_j(U_j)$ in accordance with U_k. This is the permutation option.
(3) If $r_j(U_j) = \Phi$, then $\Phi[X] = \Phi$.

If $X = \emptyset$, then $r_j[\emptyset]$ is undefined since the scheme of a tuple is required to be nonempty and so is the scheme of a relation. Thus, a projection has at least one column. If the scheme of r_j is U_j, and X properly contains U_j, then $r_j[X]$ is undefined (based on definition 2.6) since the arity of a projection yielded from a relation cannot exceed that of the relation.

Let U_j, X, and Y be subsets of U such that $Y \subseteq X \subseteq U_j$. Let

$$\pi_X : SAT(U_j) \rightarrow SAT(X)$$

and

$$\pi_Y : SAT(X) \rightarrow SAT(Y)$$

be two functions for projections. The *composition* of π_X and π_Y, denoted by $\pi_X \circ \pi_Y$, is

$$\pi_X \circ \pi_Y(r_j) = \pi_Y(\pi_X(r_j)) = \pi_Y(r_j). \tag{2.4}$$

By means of (2.4), we can view π_Y as a function from $SAT(U_j)$ to $SAT(Y)$ and ignore π_X in (2.4). If $X \neq Y$, then X is not a subset of Y because Y is assumed to be a subset of X. Consequently, $\pi_X(\pi_Y(r_j))$ is undefined, or, equivalently, the composition of π_Y and π_X, denoted by $\pi_Y \circ \pi_X$, is undefined. Thus, the composition of π_X and π_Y is equal to that of π_Y and π_X if $X = Y$, i.e.,

$$\pi_Y(\pi_X(r_j)) = \pi_X(\pi_Y(r_j))$$

if $X = Y$.

By definition 2.5, since X is required to be a subset of U_j, no column names in the projection $\pi_X(r_j(U_j))$ are ever renamed. We can generalize this definition to proide the capability of renaming some attributes in X. Let Y be a subset of X, and Z be a set of new column names (i.e., $Z \not\subseteq U_j$) such that $|Z| = |Y|$. The projection $\pi_X(r_j)$ or $r_j[X]$ with renaming, denoted by $\pi_{X \mid Y \leftarrow Z}(r_j)$ or $r_j[X \mid Y \leftarrow Z]$, is the tabular relation whose column names in Y are renamed to the new names in Z. As a special case in which $Y = X$, both symbols can be shortened to $\pi_{X \leftarrow Z}(r_j)$ or $r_j[X \leftarrow Z]$. This generalized projection might be useful to create views by ordinary users and is implemented in the algebraic-based query langauge ISBL.

2.2.7. Selection

To select some special tuples from a relation, we need to specify a certain condition as the criterion for selection. Let a condition for selecting a subset of a relation be denoted by a *formula* F which is defined recursively as follows:

(1) $A_j \vartheta B_k$, $A_j \vartheta c$, and $c \vartheta A_j$ are formulas where A_j and B_k are compatible attributes in U , c is a constant in $DOM(A_j)$, and ϑ is an arithmetic comparison operator in $\{=, \neq, <, \leq, >, \geq\}$. These formulas are all atomic.

(2) If G and H are formulas, then the conjunction $G \cdot H$, the disjunction $G + H$, and the negations $\overline{G}$ and $\overline{H}$ are formulas.

(3) Nothing else is a formula.

Note that the constant c in (1) can be a value evaluated from an expression where the value must have the same data type as that of A_j. This flexibility and capability is implemented in INGRES and QBE DBMSs. Given a relation $r_j(U_j)$, a formula F is *applicable to* r_j if a constant occurring in F is in $DOM(U_j)$, and an attribute occurring in F is in U_j. A relation r_j *satisfies* F or F *holds* in r_j if F is applicable to r_j, and each tuple μ in r_j *satisfies* F in the sense that the formula G obtained by substituting each attribute A_k occurring in F by the A_k-value of μ is evaluated to the truth value true.

Definition 2.7:   The *selection* of a relation $r_j(U_j)$ under a formula F that is applicable to r_j is the subset of r_j, written as $\sigma_F(r_j)$, consisting of all tuples μ of r_j such that each such tuple μ satisfies F, i.e.,

$$\sigma_F(r_j) = \{\mu \mid \mu \in r_j \text{ and } \mu \text{ satisfies } F\}. \tag{2.5}$$

Example 2.7:

Let the formula F_1 be DEPT = "VIDEO", which is an atom defined in (1). Then the selection of SALES under F_1 is

$$\sigma_{F_1}(\text{SALES}) = \{\text{VIDEO RECORDER, VIDEO TV}\}.$$

Selection is a unary operation, it is denoted by $\sigma_F(r_j)$, and a selection of a relation is also a relation. Similar to the projection operation, the selection operation is the function $\sigma_F : SAT(U_j) \rightarrow SAT(U_j)$ such that for each argument $r_j(U_j)$ in $SAT(U_j)$, there is the image $\sigma_F(r_j)$ in $SAT(U_j)$ as defined by (2.5) if F is applicable to r_j and is undefined otherwise.

There are two special cases to consider:

(1) If F is the expression composed of no atoms referred to as the *null formula*, then $\sigma_F(r_j) = r_j$ since there is no constraint imposed on each tuple of r_j for selection.
(2) If $r_j(U_j) = \Phi$, then $\sigma_F(\Phi) = \Phi$ for any formula F since F holds in the empty relation Φ. If F is not applicable to r_j, then $\sigma_F(r_j)$ is undefined.

Let $\sigma_{F_1} : SAT(U_j) \rightarrow SAT(U_j)$, and $\sigma_{F_2} : SAT(U_j) \rightarrow SAT(U_j)$ be two functions for selections. Then the *composition* of σ_{F_1} and σ_{F_2}, denoted by $\sigma_{F_1} \circ \sigma_{F_2}$, is

$$\sigma_{F_1} \circ \sigma_{F_2}(r_j) = \sigma_{F_2}(\sigma_{F_1}(r_j)) = \sigma_{F_1 \cdot F_2}(r_j).$$

Since the "conjunction" or "logical and" . is commutative, we have

$$\sigma_{F_1 \cdot F_2}(r_j) = \sigma_{F_2 \cdot F_1}(r_j)$$

and

$$\sigma_{F_2}(\sigma_{F_1}(r_j)) = \sigma_{F_1}(\sigma_{F_2}(r_j)).$$

In [Cod79] among others, the operations defined by (2.5) with $F := A_j \vartheta B_k$ is called *theta-selection* or *restriction* and is denoted by $r_i[A_j \vartheta B_k]$. When ϑ is the equality =, the theta-selection operation is simply called *selection*. In both cases, F is restricted to be an atomic formula. Definition 2.7 does not differentiate restriction and selection, and the formula F is not restricted to be atomic.

2.3 ADDITIONAL ALGEBRAIC OPERATIONS

In this section, we introduce intersection, various types of joins, and quotient. In addition to the six basic operations just described in section 2.2, there are other useful algebraic operations that can be expressed in terms of basic ones. Furthermore, some concepts defined previously can be also represented in terms of basic ones. To mention a few, the generalized difference defined in ISBL as described in section 2.2.4 can be formulated as illustrated in the following example:

Example 2.8:

Let $r(R)$ = SALES(DEPT ITEM), and $s(S)$ = SUPPLY(ITEM SUPPLIER). Then $R \cap S$ = ITEM. Consider the generalized difference $r(R) - s(S)$ in this case. Since $r[R - (R \cap S)]$ * $s[R \cap S]$ = SALES[DEPT] * SUPPLY[ITEM], this difference can be formulated by

$$r(R) - s(S) = r(R) - r[R - (R \cap S)] * s[R \cap S].$$

Let $r(R)$ be shown above, and $s(S)$ = EMP(NAME SALARY MGR DEPT). Then $R \cap S$ = DEPT. Consider another difference SALES(DEPT ITEM) - EMP(NAME SALARY MGR DEPT). Since $s[R \cap S]$ * $r[R - (R \cap S)]$ = EMP[DEPT] * SALES[ITEM], this difference can be formulated by

$$r(R) - s(S) = r(R) - s[R \cap S] * r[R - (R \cap S)].$$

The active domain $ADOM(A_k)$ of attribute A_k in U relative to the underlying database db can be expressed as

$$ADOM(A_k) = \bigcup_{r_j \in db} r_j[A_K]$$

where r_j is a relation with its scheme containing A_k. For example, $ADOM(DEPT)$ = SALES[DEPT] $\cup$ EMP[DEPT], and $ADOM(ITEM)$ = SALES[ITEM] $\cup$ SUPPLY [ITEM] $\cup$ TYPE[ITEM].

2.3.1. Intersection

Similar to the union of two relations, the intersection operation requires its operand relations to be union-compatible.

Definition 2.8: The *intersection* of two union-compatible relations $r(R)$ and $s(S)$, written as $r \cap s$, is the relation over R consisting of all tuples belonging to both r and s, i.e.,

$$r \cap s = \{\mu \mid \mu \in r \text{ and } \mu \in s\} \text{ if } R = S$$

and

$$r \cap s = \{\mu \mid \mu \in r(R) \text{ and } \mu \in \delta_{X \leftarrow Y}(s(S))\} \text{ if } R \neq S$$

where $X \subseteq S - R$, $Y \subseteq R - S$, $X = f(Y)$, $Y = f^{-1}(X)$, and f: $Y \to X$ is a restriction of f: $R \to S$ and f^{-1}: $S \to R$.

The intersection operation can be expressed in terms of difference as

$$r \cap s = r - (r - s)$$

with scheme R (and s(S) renamed to s(R) if $S \neq R$) or

$$s \cap r = s - (s - r)$$

with scheme S (and r(R) renamed to r(S) if $R \neq S$).

Intersection is a binary operation; its operator is denoted by $\cap$, and the intersection of two union-compatible relations is a relation. The intersection operation can be viewed as a partial function from the Cartesian product $r \times s$ to the intersection $r \cap s$ such that for each argument $(\mu_r, \mu_s) \in r \times s$, the image is μ_r if $\mu_r = \mu_s$ and is undefined otherwise.

Example 2.9:

Let r(A B C) = {a b 3, d f 3, e g 1} and s(D E F) = {a b 5, d f 3} be two relations, and $f_1 = \{(A, D), (B, E), (C, F)\}$ be a one-to-one correspondence between A B C and D E F. Then $r \cap s = \{d f 3\}$ with scheme A B C.

2.3.2 Theta-join

Let ϑ be an arithmetic comparison operator in $\{=, \neq, <, \leq, >, \geq\}$.

Definition 2.9: Let r(R) and s(S) be two relations and $A_j \vartheta B_k$ be a formula applicable to the complex product r * s. The *theta-join* of r(R) and s(S) on the attributes A_j in R and B_k is S, written as $r[A_j \vartheta B_k]s$, is the set (which is not necessarily a relation) consisting of every string (not necessarily a tuple) $\mu_r \mu_s$ for some μ_r in r and some μ_s in s such that $\mu_r(A_j) \vartheta \mu_s(B_k)$ is evaluated to the truth value true, i.e.,

$$r[A_j \vartheta B_k]s = \{\mu_r \mu_s \mid \mu_r \in r, \mu_s \in s, \text{ and } \mu_r(A_j) \vartheta \mu_s(B_k)\}. \qquad (2.6a)$$

Theta-join is a binary operation; it is denoted by the symbol r[F]s where F is an atomic formula, and the theta-join of two relations is not necessarily a relation. When complex produce r * s is a relation, theta-join of (2.6a) is also a relation and can be expressed in terms of complex product and selection as

$$r[A_j \vartheta B_k]s = \sigma_{A_j \vartheta B_k}(r * s). \qquad (2.6b)$$

On the other hand, when r * s is not a relation because of the existence of duplicated columns (including names and values), the right side of = in (2.6b) is undefined as a selection. The theta-join operation can be viewed as a partial function from the complex product r * s to r * s such that for each argument $\mu_r \mu_s$ in r * s, the image is still $\mu_r \mu_s$ if $\mu_r(A_j) \vartheta \mu_s(B_k)$ is evaluated to the truth value true and is undefined otherwise.

In (2.6a) and (2.6b), the formula $A_j \vartheta B_k$ is atomic. We can trivially extend it to the conjunction of atomic formulas applicable to r * s. If the formula is null, then theta-join becomes complex product as a special case. Another special case arises if ϑ is the equality =. In this case, theta-join is called *equi-join*. In the equi-join $r[A_j = B_k]s$, the A_j- and B_k-column entries have identical value for each tuple, and consequently, it is not a relation unless A_j and B_k denote different attributes. Note that $A_j = B_k$ in the equi-join $r[A_j = B_k]s$ does not mean that A_j and B_k are identical but means that the A_j-value of a tuple in relation r and the B_k-value of a tuple in relation s are compared by the equality =. Even if A_j and B_k are distinct compatible attributes, the B_k-values duplicate the A_j-values in the equi-join.

Example 2.10:

The equi-join SALES[ITEM = ITEM]SUPPLY of SALES(DEPT ITEM) and SUPPLY (ITEM SUPPLIER) is not a relation but is a set of sixteen strings of lengths four (what are they?), since there are two ITEM-columns with identical column-entries in the equi-join.

2.3.3 Natural Join

Since an equi-join has identical names and values in at least two columns, we need a mechanism to retain only one of such duplicated columns. This operation can be accomplished by a "natural join."

Definition 2.10: Let r(R) and s(S) be two relations. The *natural join* (or simply *join*) of r and s, written as r |x| s, is the relation with scheme R (S − (R ∩S)) consisting of all tuples such that for each tuple ν in the join, there exists some tuple μ_r in r and some tuple μ_s is s satisfying $\nu[R] = \mu_r$ and $\nu[S] = \mu_s$, i.e.,

$$r \ |x| \ s = \{\nu \mid (\mu_r, \mu_s) \in r \times s, \nu[R] = \mu_r, \text{ and } \nu[S] = \mu_s\}. \qquad (2.7a)$$

When R and S are disjoint, the join of r and s is identical to the complex product of r and s, i.e.,

$$r \ |x| \ s = r * s \quad (\text{if } R \cap S = \emptyset). \qquad (2.7b)$$

When R and S are not disjoint, a join can be expressed in terms of projection, selection, and complex product. Let A_{i_j} for each j, $1 \le j \le k$ and $k = |R \cap S|$, be in the intersection of R and S, i.e., $R \cap S = A_{i_1} A_{i_2} \cdots A_{i_k}$. Let $Y = B_1 B_2 \cdots B_k$ where each B_j for $1 \le j \le k$ is not in R S. Let $r \cdot A_{i_j}$ and $s \cdot B_j$ be, respectively, attributes in R and (S − R ∩ S) Y, then we have the following join of r and s:

$$r \ |x| \ s = \pi_{R(S − (R \cap S))}(\sigma_F(r * \delta_{R \cap S \leftarrow Y}(s(S)))) \qquad (2.7c)$$

where $F = (r \cdot A_{i_1} = s \cdot B_1) \cdot (r \cdot A_{i_2} = s \cdot B_2) \cdot \ldots \cdot (r \cdot A_{i_k} = s \cdot B_k)$, $Y = f^{-1}(R \cap S)$, and $R \cap S = f(Y)$.

There is an important special case. When R = S, r |x| s = r ∩ s since for each string $\mu_r \mu_s$ in r * s, μ_r is in the join if $\mu_r = \mu_s$, i.e., μ_r is in both r and s. This case can be obtained from (2.7c) by setting R ∩ S = S, S − (R ∩ S) = ∅, and R ∅ = R, i.e.,

$$r \ |x| \ s \ = \ \pi_R(\sigma_F(r * \delta_{S \ \leftarrow \ Y}(s(S))))$$

where the right side of $=$ is equal to the intersection of r and s.

Join is a binary operation; its operator is denoted by $|x|$, and the join of two relations is also a relation. The join operator is not commutative but is associative. Hence, we can write r $|x|$ s $|x|$ t and extend the binary version to the m-ary version denoted by the prefixed notation $|x|(r_1, \ldots, r_m)$. The prefixed and infixed joins can be used interchangeably. Since $|x|$ is associative, the prefixed joins can be nested into different levels. For example $|x|(|x|(r, s), t) = |x|(r, |x|(s, t)) = |x|(r, s, t)$.

Example 2.11:

> Let U = A B, ADOM(A) = r_1(A) = {0, 1}, and ADOM(B) = r_2(B) = {a, b}. ATUP(U) = {0 a, 0 b, 1 a, 1 b} is the join of r_1 and r_2, and both r_1 and r_2 are the projections of ATUP(U). Although r_1 and r_2 can be also derived from six proper subsets of ATUP(U), such as {0 a, 1 b}, {0 b, 1 a}, and so forth, each of these proper subsets is not equal to the join of r_1 and r_2 and should be excluded as a universal relation over U. Then the universal relation over U becomes unique. In this example, the relation schemes A and B of the relations r_1 and r_2 are disjoint so that the join of r_1 and r_2 is equal to the complex product of r_1 and r_2.

2.3.4 Quotient or Division

The quotient (or division operator) is the algebraic counterpart of the universal quantifier as introduced in the first-order logic of chapter 0.

Definition 2.11:   Let r(T R) and s(S) be relations such that S and R are union-compatible. The *quotient* or *division* of r by s, denoted by r / s, is the maximal subset of r[T] such that

$$r \ / \ s \ = \ \{\mu \ | \ p_1\} \tag{2.8a}$$

where p_1 is the predicate stating that "for each tuple μ_s is s(S), there exists a tuple μ_r in r(T R) satisfying $\mu_r[T] = \mu$ and $\mu_r[R] = \mu_s$." Note that when S $\neq$ R, we need to rename X ($\subseteq$ S $-$ R) to Y ($\subseteq$ R $-$ S) based on a restriction of a one-to-one correspondence f between R and S (i.e., X = f(Y), and Y = f^{-1}(X)).

A quotient can be expressed in terms of complex product, difference, and projections as follows:

$$r \ / \ s \ = \ \pi_T(r) \ - \ \pi_T((\pi_T(r) * s(R)) \ - \ r) \ \text{if} \ S \ = \ R \tag{2.8b}$$

where s(R) = s(S), and

$$r \ / \ s \ = \ \pi_T(r) \ - \ \pi_T((\pi_T(r) * \delta_{X \ \leftarrow \ Y}(s(S))) \ - \ r) \ \text{if} \ S \ \neq \ R \tag{2.8c}$$

where the renaming is defined in (2.8a) of definition 2.11.

As will be seen in example 2.10, if r[R] is properly contained in s(S) or s(R), then r /s is the empty relation Φ. If S = R = ø where ø is the empty set, then r / s is undefined since s(ø) is undefined.

Let SAT(T R), SAT(S), and SAT(T) be the sets of all relations with schemes T R, S, and T, respectively, where S and R are union-compatible. Then the Cartesian product of SAT(T R) and SAT(S) is the set of all ordered-pairs of relations with schemes T R and S, respectively. The quotient operation is a function from SAT(T R) $\times$ SAT(S) to SAT(T). To compute a quotient, if $|s| > 1$, then we need to examine a subset of r to determine whether a single image is in the quotient, i.e., a unique image is defined if r contains exactly $|s|$ tuples to satisfy the predicate p_1 in (2.8a). The quotient operator is not commutative and is also not associative.

Example 2.12:

In the department store database, find the departments selling all items supplied by IBM (and possibly other items supplied by other suppliers). Let this query be called Q_1. It is very convenient to process this query by a quotient operation as follows:

$$\text{SALES} / \pi_{\text{ITEM}}(\sigma_{\text{SUPPLIER} = \text{``IBM''}}(\text{SUPPLY})),$$

which is equal to the quotient SALES / {MICRO, PRINTER, TERMINAL}. The value of this quotient is {COMPUTER, DP}, where DP stands for the Department of Data Processing. As checked from tables 2.1 and 2.2, IBM supplies three items: MICRO, PRINTER, and TERMINAL; and COMPUTER department sells these items (plus an additional item CALCULATOR supplied by HP or TI), and DP sells exactly the three items.

2.4 THE RELATIONAL ALGEBRA

In previous sections, we defined six basic operations on relations of a database. We can define a complete algebraic query language based on these six basic operations. However, some queries may be very difficult to express if we use only the six basic ones. Hence, it is useful to add other operations, which are defined in terms of some basic operations and which facilitate the expression of some queries.

Let U be the universe of attributes, Dom be the set of the domains of the attributes in U, and dom be a function from U to Dom such that each attribute in U has a unique domain in Dom (and some attributes may share the same domain). Let Db = {U_1, . . . , U_m} be a database scheme over U such that $U_1 \cdots U_m = U$ (in which the union operator $\cup$ between U_j and U_{j+1} for j = 1, . . . , m $-$ 1 is omitted), and each U_j for $1 \le j \le m$ is a subset of U. Let db = {r_1, . . . , r_m} be a database over scheme Db such that each relation r_j for $1 \le j \le m$ has scheme U_j. Let $\Omega = \{=, \ne, <, \le, >, \ge\}$ be a set of arithmetic comparison operators over domains in Dom. Let O be a set of relational operators including at least the six basic ones known as union, complex product, difference, projection, selection, and renaming. Then the *relational algebra* over U, Dom, dom, Db, db, Ω, and O is a 7-tuple **A** = (U, Dom, dom, Db, db, Ω, O). An *algebraic expression* over **A** is any expression that is formed legally from the relations in db and constant relations with the schemes in Db, and using the operators in O.

Definition 2.12:   The *scheme* of an algebraic expression E, denoted by sch(E), is defined recursively as follows:

(1) If E is a constant relation, then sch(E) is the scheme for the constant relation.

(2) If E is relation r_j with scheme U_j, then sch(E) = U_j.

(3) If E is any one of the algebraic expressions $E_1 \cup E_2$, $E_1 \cap E_2$, $E_1 - E_2$, $\sim E_1$, and $\sigma_F(E_1)$ where F is a formula applicable to E_1, then sch(E) = sch(E_1).

(4) If E is $\pi_X(E_1)$, then sch(E) = X.

(5) If E is E_1 / E_2, then sch(E) = sch(E_1) − sch(E_2).

(6) If E is any one of the algebraic expressions $E_1 * E_2$, $E_1[F]E_2$, and $E_1 |x| E_2$ where F = $A_j \vartheta B_k$ for A_j in sch(E_1) and B_k in sch(E_2), then sch(E) = sch(E_1) $\cup$ sch(E_2).

(7) If E is $\delta_{A_{i_1} \cdots A_{i_k} \leftarrow B_1 \cdots B_k}(E_1)$, then sch(E) = (sch($E_1$) − A_{i_1} . . . A_{i_k}) B_1 . . . B_k.

This chapter covers only the relational algebra without involving any nulls. In addition, query languages may require that aggregate operations such as average, maximum, sum, etc., be able to accept arguments with duplicates. A detailed study of the theoretical considerations concerning aggregate operations is included in [Klu82a]. Some aggregate operations are supported in INGRES and QBE DBMSs, which will be introduced in chapter 8.

EXERCISES

2.1 Let r(A B C) = {a b 3, d f 3, e g 1} and s(D E F) = {a b 5, d f 3} be two relations. Under what conditions are r and s union-compatible?

2.2 Suppose that, in definition 2.2, one of the conditions is changed to "each attribute B_j in Y is not an attribute in S − X." Then X and Y are not necessarily disjoint. What would be the consequence of this change with respect to the operations of sequential and parallel renamings?

2.3 For r(A B C) = {a b 3, d f 3, e g 1} and s(D E F) = {a b 5, d f 3}, find r $\cup$ s with respect to f_2 = {(A, E), (B, D), (C, F)}.

2.4 Let r and s be the relations as given in example 2.3. Find r − s and s − r based on f_2 = {(A, E), (B, D), (C, F)}.

2.5 Find SALES[DEPT], SALES[ITEM], SUPPLY[ITEM], and SUPPLY[SUPPLIER] from tables 2.1 and 2.2. Note that a projection is also a relation so that duplicated tuples (except one) should be deleted.

2.6 Let r(R) and s(R) be two relations and X $\subseteq$ R. Let o be an operator in {$\cup$, $\cap$, −}. Prove or disprove π_X(r o s) = π_X(r) o π_X(s) where π stands for "projection."

2.7 Let r(R) and s(R) be two relations and F be a formula applicable to both r and s. Prove or disprove σ_F(r o s) = σ_F(r) o σ_F(s) where o is in {$\cup$, $\cap$, −} and σ stands for "selection."

2.8 Find the join and equi-join of SALES and SUPPLY, i.e., SALES |x| SUPPLY and SALES[ITEM = ITEM]SUPPLY from tables 2.1 and 2.2.

2.9 Let r(A B C) = {a b 3, d f 3, e g 1} and s(D E F) = {a b 5, d f 3}. Suppose that A and D are compatible; so are B and E; and so are C and F.

   (a) Find r(C A B) / $\pi_{A\ B}(\delta_{D\ E\ \leftarrow\ A\ B}(s(D\ E\ F)))$ where r(C A B) is permuted from r(A B C) and δ stands for "renaming."

   (b) Find r(A B C) / $\pi_{c}(\sigma_{c\ =\ 3}(\delta_{D\ E\ F\ \leftarrow\ A\ B\ C}(s(D\ E\ F))))$ where π and σ stands for "projection" and "selection," respectively.

2.10 Let r(T R) and s(S) be two relations, and let S and R be union-compatible. Show that if r[R] is properly contained in s(R) = $\delta_{X\ \leftarrow\ Y}(s(S))$, where X is a subset of S − R to be renamed by Y, which is a subset of R − S based on a one-to-one correspondence f between R and S, then the quotient r(T R) / s(R) is the empty relation Φ(T).

2.11 Let formula F be A_k = "a" for attribute A_k in U_j and A_k-value a in DOM(A_k), and let F be applicable to relation $r_j(U_j)$. Show that the selection $\sigma_F(r_j)$ is a special case of natural join, i.e.,

$$\sigma_F(r_j) = r_j \ |x| \ \{<a \ | \ B>\} \tag{2.9}$$

where B is an attribute not in U_j and is used to rename the scheme A_k of the constant tuple $<a \ | \ A_k>$. Otherwise the right side of (2.9) is not a relation because of the existence of two columns with the same name A_k, and consequently, the left side of (2.9) is also not a relation.

2.12 Show that intersection is a special case of natural join.

chapter 3

THE RELATIONAL PREDICATE CALCULUS

3.1 INTRODUCTION

In chapter 2, we introduced the relational algebra and mentioned that the relational calculus has two versions, the tuple and the domain relational calculus. The term *relational calculus* comes from the first-order logic and does not imply any connection with the "differential and integral calculus" in mathemathics.

In the tuple relational calculus, a tuple variable with scheme X has its values in TUP(X), and any such value is an entire tuple with scheme X. In the domain relational calculus, a domain variable with scheme A has its values in DOM(A), and any such value is only the A-component of a tuple whose scheme contains the attribute A. Both versions of the relational calculus are equivalent in expressive power to the relational algebra. However, the relational algebra induces procedural systems and involves procedural languages. The relational calculus is nonprocedural. Thus, query languages based on the relational calculus tend to be higher level.

3.2 TUPLE RELATIONAL CALCULUS

Similar to the relational algebra, the tuple relational calculus (or simply tuple calculus) also involves a universal set $U = A_1 A_2 \cdots A_n$ of attributes, a set $Dom = \{DOM(A_{i_j}) \mid i_j \in \{1, 2, \cdots, n\}\}$ of the domains of the attributes in U, a function dom from U to Dom, a set $\Omega = \{=, \neq, <, \leq, >, \geq\}$ of arithmetic comparison operators, a database scheme $Db = \{U_j \mid 1 \leq j \leq m\}$ in which each U_j is a subset of U and $U = U_1 \cdots U_m$, and a database $db = \{r_j \mid 1 \leq j \leq m\}$ where each r_j is a relation with scheme U_j. Note that dom is not necessarily a one-to-one function, since some attributes (such as NAME and MGR in EMP) can share a domain or define on the same domain.

Definition 3.1:   The *tuple relational calculus* (or simply *tuple calculus*) is a sextuple, C_t = (U, Dom, dom, Db, db, Ω) where each element of C_t is as defined above.

3.2.1 Formulas

In the tuple calculus, there are four types of basic building blocks of formulas known as *atomic formulas* or simply, atoms.

Definition 3.2:   *Atoms* in the tuple calculus are defined as follows:

(1) Truth values, denoted by true and false, are atoms.

(2) A tuple variable x belonging to a relation $r_j(U_j)$, written as $r_j(x)$, is an atom where r_j is in a database db, and r_j and x have the same scheme U_j.

(3) $x(A_j) \vartheta y(A_k)$ is an atom where x and y are (not necessarily distinct) tuple variables, A_j and A_k are (not necessarily distinct) compatible attributes in U, ϑ is an arithmetic comparison operator in Ω, and $x(A_j)$ and $y(A_k)$ are, respectively, the A_j-component of x and the A_k-component of y.

(4) $c \vartheta x(A)$ and $x(A) \vartheta c$ are atoms where c is a constant in DOM(A), x(A) is the A-component of tuple variable x, and ϑ is in Ω.

Example 3.1:

In the department store database scheme as shown below:

EMP(NAME SALARY MGR DEPT),
SALES(DEPT ITEM),
SUPPLY(ITEM SUPPLIER),
TYPE(ITEM COLOR SIZE),

$$F_1(y) := \text{SUPPLY}(y), \tag{3.1}$$

$$F_2(x) := \text{SALES}(x), \tag{3.2}$$

$$F_3(x, y) := x(\text{ITEM}) = y(\text{ITEM}), \tag{3.3}$$

$$F_4(x, z) := z(\text{DEPT}) = x(\text{DEPT}), \tag{3.4}$$

and

$$F_5(y) := y(\text{SUPPLIER}) = \text{``IBM''} \tag{3.5}$$

are atoms of types (2), (2), (3), (3), and (4) respectively (the right sides of the assignment operator := in (3.1) through (3.5) are atoms, which are denoted by $F_1(y)$ through $F_5(y)$ for the convenience of later references). Attribute-values, such as IBM coming from nonnumeric domains, are set in double quotation marks. However, x(ITEM) $\neq$ y(COLOR) is not an atom since ITEM and COLOR are not compatible. An explanation of why we should have true and false as atoms is postponed until we introduce definition 3.6.

A tuple variable and its occurrences being free or bound in a formula follow exactly the same definitions as defined in section 0.5.2 of chapter 0.

Definition 3.3:   *Formulas,* and *freedom,* and *boundedness* of tuple variables in formulas are defined recursively as follows:

(1) Each atom is a formula. Any tuple variable occurring in an atom is free.

(2) If F is a formula, then the negation of F, denoted by $\overline{F}$, is a formula. Any tuple variable occurring in $\overline{F}$ is free or bound, as it is free or bound in F.

(3) If F and G are formulas, then the conjunction of F and G, denoted by F · G, and the disjunction of F and G, denoted by F + G, are formulas. Any free (or bound) tuple variable occurring in either F or G, or in both F and G is still the same in F · G or F + G. Any tuple variable occurring free in one of them and bound in the other is free and bound in F · G or F + G depending on where it occurs.

(4) If x with scheme R is a free tuple variable occurring in a formula F, then $\forall$x(R)F(x) and $\exists$x(R)F(x) are also formulas, where x is universally and existentially quantified, respectively. The quantified tuple variable x that is originally free in F becomes bound to $\forall$x(R) in $\forall$x(R)F(x) or to $\exists$x(R) in $\exists$x(R)F(x). Any other tuple variable y for y $\neq$ x occurring in F is free or bound in $\forall$x(R)F(x) or $\exists$x(R)F(x), as it is free or bound in F.

(5) Parentheses may be placed around formulas as needed.

(6) Nothing else is a formula.

We assume that the order of precedence is such that all arithmetic comparison operators are of equal and highest precedence, both quantifiers are of equal and lower precedence, and logical operations +, ·, and − follow in increasing order. The symbols ≡ of equivalence and := of assignment are of equal and lowest precedence.

Example 3.2:

The atoms $F_1(y)$ through $F_5(y)$, as shown in (3.1) through (3.5), are formulas by (1) of definition 3.3. The tuple variables x, y, and z occurring in these formulas are free. The negations

$$\overline{F_1(y)} \equiv \overline{SUPPLY(y)} \tag{3.6}$$

and

$$\overline{F_5(y)} \equiv \overline{y(SUPPLIER) \neq ``IBM"} \tag{3.7}$$

are formulas by (2) of definition 3.3. The negated formula $\overline{SUPPLY(y)}$ denotes that y $\notin$ SUPPLY since the formula SUPPLY(y) denotes that y ϵ SUPPLY.

By (3) of definition 3.3, we have formulas

$$F_6(y) := \overline{\overline{F_1(y)} + \overline{F_5(y)}}$$
$$\equiv \text{SUPPLY (y)} + y(\text{SUPPLIER}) \neq \text{``IBM''} \tag{3.8}$$

as obtained by substituting $\overline{F_1(y)}$ and $\overline{F_5(y)}$ from (3.6) and (3.7), respectively; and

$$F_7(x, y) := F_2(x) \cdot F_3(x, y)$$
$$\equiv \text{SALES}(x) \cdot x(\text{ITEM}) = y(\text{ITEM}) \tag{3.9}$$

as obtained by substituting $F_2(x)$ and $F_3(x, y)$ from (3.2) and (3.3), respectively, where the order of precedence of the arithmetic comparison operator = is higher than that of the logical operator "conjunction." By (3) again, we obtain formula

$$F_8(x, y) := \overline{F_6(y)} + F_7(x, y)$$
$$\equiv \overline{\text{SUPPLY(y)}}$$
$$+ y(\text{SUPPLIER}) \neq \text{``IBM''}$$
$$+ (\text{SALES}(x) \cdot x(\text{ITEM}) = y(\text{ITEM})) \tag{3.10}$$

as obtained by substituting $F_6(y)$ and $F_7(x, y)$ from (3.6) and (3.9), respectively. By (3) once more, we have formula

$$F_9(x, y, z) := F_4(x, z) \cdot F_8(x, y)$$
$$\equiv z(\underline{\text{DEPT}} = x(\text{DEPT})$$
$$\cdot(\overline{\text{SUPPLY(y)}}$$
$$+ y(\text{SUPPLIER}) \neq \text{``IBM''}$$
$$+ (\text{SALES}(x) \cdot x(\text{ITEM}) = y(\text{ITEM}))). \tag{3.11a}$$

By (4) of definition of 3.3, we obtain formula

$$F_{10}(x, z) := \forall y(\text{ITEM SUPPLIER})F_9(x, y, z)$$
$$\equiv \forall y(\text{ITEM SUPPLIER})$$
$$(z(\underline{\text{DEPT}}) = x(\text{DEPT})$$
$$\cdot (\overline{\text{SUPPLY(y)}}$$
$$+ y(\text{SUPPLIER}) \neq \text{``IBM''}$$
$$+ (\text{SALES}(x) \cdot x(\text{ITEM}) = y(\text{ITEM})))).$$

By (4) again, we have formula

$$F_{11}(z) := \exists x(\text{DEPT ITEM})F_{10}(x, z)$$
$$\equiv \exists x(\text{DEPT ITEM})\forall y(\text{ITEM SUPPLIER})$$
$$(z(\underline{\text{DEPT}}) = x(\text{DEPT})$$
$$\cdot (\overline{\text{SUPPLY(y)}}$$
$$+ y(\text{SUPPLIER}) \neq \text{``IBM''}$$
$$+ (\text{SALES}(x) \cdot x(\text{ITEM}) = y(\text{ITEM})))). \tag{3.13a}$$

This formula is in a prenex normal form, as defined in section 0.5.5 of chapter 0.

Note that the addition of parentheses by (5) of definition 3.3 may be necessary. The similar unparenthesized formula would have a different meaning.

Example 3.3:

The following formula $\exists x(R)F(x) + G$ is equivalent to $(\exists x(R)F(x)) + G$ since the existential quantifier has a higher order of precedence. By (4) of definition 3.3, the tuple variable x must be free in F. However, the formula $\exists x(R)(F(x) + G(x))$, with the tuple variable x in both F and G being existentially quantified, is not equivalent to $(\exists x(R)F(x)) + G(x)$ with the tuple variable x being existentially quantified only in F.

3.2.2 Legal Formulas

The rules of definition 3.3 can be applied to construct formulas, some of which may have no practical significance. For example,

$$F_{12}(x) := SALES(x) \cdot x(SALARY) \leqslant 10000 \tag{3.14}$$

is a formula by (3) of definition 3.3. However, the first occurrence of x in the right side of := in (3.14) has sch(x) = DEPT ITEM, whereas the second occurrence of x in the same side involves a different attribute SALARY. The conjunction of two formulas involving different sets of attributes is meaningless, and we say that these formulas are not conjunction- or disjunction-compatible. This type of formula must be excluded so that we need to consider only a restricted class of formulas known as *legal formulas*.

Let F be a formula, and x be a free tuple variable occurring in F. We denote the mention set and the scheme of x relative to F by men(x, F) and sch(x, F), respectively. Note that men(x, F) and sch(x, F) are defined only when x occurs free in F. On the other hand, when either a tuple variable y does not occur in a formula F, or y occurs bound in F, men(y, F) and sch(y, F) are both undefined. In addition, when men(x, F) and sch(x, F) are both defined, the former must be a subset of the latter. When sch(x, F) is defined, men(x, F) is also defined; but the converse may not be true.

(1) Each atom is a legal formula. There are four cases to consider.

    (i) If F := true (or false), the mention set and the scheme of any tuple variable x relative to true (or false) are undefined since x does not occur in F.

    (ii) If $F(x) := r_j(x)$ where r_j is a relation with scheme U_j, then

$$men(x, F) = sch(x, F) = U_j$$

    (since x is the free tuple variable occurring in r_j and $sch(x) = sch(r_j) = U_j$).

    (iii) If $F(x, y) := x(A_j) \vartheta y(A_k)$, then

$$men(x, F) = A_j,$$
$$men(y, F) = A_k,$$

and sch(x, F) and sch(y, F) are both undefined. Note that the scheme of w for w = x or w = y relative to F is undefined since only one component $x(A_j)$ or $y(A_k)$ is known from F.

    (iv) Similarly to case (iii), if $F(x) := x(A) \vartheta c$ or $c \vartheta x(A)$, then

$$men(x, F) = A$$

and sch(x, F) is undefined.

(2) If G is a legal formula and $F := \bar{G}$ (or (G)), then F is a legal formula. The mention

set and the scheme of a free tuple variable x relative to F are the same as those relative to G, i.e.,

$$men(x, F) = men(x, G)$$

and

$$sch(x, F) = sch(x, G).$$

(3) If G and H are legal formulas and $F := G \cdot H$ (or $G + H$), then F is a legal formula provided that one of the following conditions is also satisfied for every free tuple variable x occurring in F.

   (i) The schemes sch(x, G) and sch(x, H) are both defined and they are equal, i.e.,

$$sch(x, G) = sch(x, H). \qquad (3.15a)$$

   When (3.15a) holds, F is legal, and

$$sch(x, F) = sch(x, G).$$

   (ii) Only one of the schemes sch(x, G) and sch(x, H) is defined. There are two possible cases.

   (a) Either sch(x, G) and men(x, H) are both defined and they satisfy

$$sch(x, G) \supseteq men(x, H), \qquad (3.15b)$$

   or sch(x, H) and men(x, G) are both defined and they satisfy

$$sch(x, H) \supseteq men(x, G). \qquad (3.15c)$$

   (b) Either sch(x, G) is defined and men(x, H) is undefined, or sch(x, H) is defined and men(x, G) is undefined.

   In this case, F is legal, and

$$sch(x, F) = sch(x, G) \ (or = sch(x, H)).$$

   (iii) The schemes sch(x, G) and sch(x, H) are both undefined. [Note that at least men(x, G) or men(x, H) is defined since x occurs free in F implies that x occurs free in G or H.] In this case, F is legal, and sch(x, F) is undefined.

In each subcase of case (3), men(x, F) is defined as the union of men(x, G) and men(x, H) if they are both defined and otherwise as men(x, G) or men(x, H) depending on which one of them is defined.

(4) If G is a legal formula, x is a free tuple variable in G(x), and $F := \exists x(R)G(x)$ or $\forall x(R)G(x)$, then F is a legal formula provided that the following condition is also satisfied, i.e.,

$$men(x, G) \subseteq sch(x, G) = R \qquad (3.16a)$$

if sch(x, G) defined, or

$$men(x, G) \subseteq R \qquad (3.16b)$$

if sch(x, G) is undefined.

When F is a legal formula, $men(x, F)$ and $sch(x, F)$ are both undefined since x occurs bound in F. In addition,

$$men(w, F) = men(w, G),$$

and

$$sch(w, F) = sch(w, G)$$

for any tuple variable $w \neq x$.

(5) Nothing else is a legal formula.

Example 3.4:

Consider the formula $F_{12}(x)$ as shown in (3.14), i.e.,

$$F_{12}(x) := SALES(x) \cdot x(SALARY) \leq 10000. \tag{3.14}$$

This formula has only one free tuple variable x, with two occurrences on the right side of $:=$. By (1.ii) of definition 3.4, we have

$$men(x, SALES) = sch(x, SALES) = DEPT\ ITEM,$$

since $sch(SALES) = DEPT\ ITEM$. By (1.iv) of definition 3.4, we have

$$men(x, x(SALARY) \leq 10000) = SALARY$$

and $sch(x, x(SALARY) \leq 10000)$ is undefined. By (3.ii) of definition 3.4, (3.15b) is not satisfied, i.e.,

$$sch(x, SALES) \not\supseteq men(x, x(SALARY) \leq 10000),$$

since DEPT ITEM does not contain SALARY. Hence, $F_{12}(x)$ is not a legal formula.

Example 3.5:

Consider the formula $F_{11}(z)$ as shown in (3.13a) in example 3.2, i.e,

$$\begin{aligned}
F_{11}(z) := &\exists x(DEPT\ ITEM)F_{10}(x, z) \\
\equiv &\exists x(DEPT\ ITEM)\forall y(ITEM\ SUPPLIER)) \\
&(z(\underline{DEPT}) = x(DEPT) \\
&\cdot \overline{(SUPPLY(y)} \\
&+ y(SUPPLIER) \neq \text{``IBM''} \\
&+ (SALES(x) \cdot x(ITEM) = y(ITEM)))).
\end{aligned} \tag{3.13a}$$

This formula has three tuple variables x, y, and z. We list their defined mention sets and schemes in the following. The mention sets and the schemes of these variables not listed below are understood to be undefined.

By means of (1.ii) and (2) of definition 3.4, $\overline{F_1(y)} := \overline{SUPPLY(y)}$ is legal, and

$$men(y, \overline{F_1}) = sch(y, \overline{F_1}) = ITEM\ SUPPLIER,$$

since $sch(SUPPLY) = ITEM\ SUPPLIER$. By means of (1.ii) again, $F_2(x) := SALES(x)$ is legal, and

$$men(x, F_2) = sch(x, F_2) = DEPT\ ITEM,$$

since sch(SALES) = DEPT ITEM. By means of (1.iii), $F_3(x, y) := x(ITEM) = y(ITEM)$ is legal, and

$$men(x, F_3) = men(y, F_3) = ITEM.$$

By means of (1.iii) again, $F_4(x, z) := z(DEPT) = x(DEPT)$ is legal, and

$$men(x, F_4) = men(z, F_4) = DEPT.$$

By means of (1.iv) and (2), $\overline{F_5(y)} := y(SUPPLIER) \neq$ "IBM" is legal, and

$$men(y, \overline{F_5}) = SUPPLIER.$$

By means of (3.ii), $F_6(y) := \overline{F_1(y)} + \overline{F_5(y)}$ of (3.8) is legal, and

$$men(y, F_6) = sch(y, F_6) = ITEM\ SUPPLIER.$$

By means of (3.ii), $F_7(x, y) := F_2(x) \cdot F_3(x, y)$ of (3.9) is legal, and

$$men(x, F_7) = sch(x, F_7) = DEPT\ ITEM,$$

and

$$men(y, F_7) = ITEM.$$

By means of (3.ii) again, $F_8(x, y) := F_6(y) + F_7(x, y)$ of (3.10) is legal, and

$$men(x, F_8) = sch(x, F_8) = DEPT\ ITEM,$$

and

$$men(y, F_8) = sch(y, F_8) = ITEM\ SUPPLIER.$$

By means of (3.ii) and (3.iii), $F_9(x, y, z) = F_4(x, z) \cdot F_8(x, y)$ of (3.11a) is legal, and

$$men(x, F_9) = sch(x, F_9) = DEPT\ ITEM,$$
$$men(y, F_9) = sch(y, F_9) = ITEM\ SUPPLIER,$$

and

$$men(z, F_9) = DEPT.$$

By means of (4), $F_{10}(x, z) := \forall y(ITEM\ SUPPLIER)F_9(x, y, z)$ of (3.12a) is legal, and the mention sets and the schemes of x and z relative to $F_{10}(x, z)$ are the same as those relative to $F_9(x, y, z)$. By means of (4) again, $F_{11}(z) := \exists x(DEPT\ ITEM)F_{10}(x, z)$ of (3.13a) is legal, and the mention set and the scheme of z relative to $F_{11}(z)$ are the same as those relative to $F_9(x, y, z)$.

3.2.3. Tuple Calculus Expression

A tuple calculus expression over the tuple calculus is defined in the following.

Definition 3.5:   A *tuple calculus expression* over the tuple calculus C_t has the form

$$\textbf{Et} := \{x(R) \mid F(x)\}$$

where

(1) F is a legal formula relative to $\mathbf{C_t}$.

(2) x is the only free tuple variable in F.

(3) R is a subset of U and is the scheme for x, and

(4) men (x, F) = sch(x, F) = R if sch(x, F) is defined as R, and men$(x, F) \subseteq R$ if sch(x, F) is undefined.

Example 3.6:

In $F_{11}(z)$, as shown in (3.13a), i.e.,

$$
\begin{aligned}
F_{11}(z) := &\ \exists x(\text{DEPT ITEM})\ \forall y(\text{ITEM SUPPLIER}) \\
&\ (z(\text{DEPT}) = x(\text{DEPT}) \\
&\ \cdot (\text{SUPPLY}(y) \\
&\ + y(\text{SUPPLIER}) \ne \text{``IBM''} \\
&\ + (\text{SALES}(x) \cdot x(\text{ITEM}) = y(\text{ITEM})))),
\end{aligned}
\qquad (3.13a)
$$

where z is the only free tuple variable. We have the tuple calculus expression

$$\textbf{Et}_1 := \{z(\text{DEPT}) \mid F_{11}(z)\}.$$

To find the value of a tuple calculus expression, we need to substitute some relevant tuple for each free tuple variable occurring in the underlying formula because an open formula cannot be evaluated.

Definition 3.6:   Let $F(x)$ be a legal formula with the free tuple variable x in a tuple calculus expression $\textbf{Et} := \{x(R) \mid F(x)\}$. Then $F(x)$ with a tuple μ substituted for x, denoted by $F(x \leftarrow \mu)$, is the formula obtained by modifying each atom in F involving a free occurrence of x as follows:

(1) If $F(x) := r(x)$ where $r(x)$ is an atom denoting tuple variable x belonging to relation r (i.e., $x \in r$), then replace $r(x)$ by the atom true if $\mu \in r$, and by the atom false if $\mu \notin r$.

(2) If $F(x) := x(A_j)\ \vartheta\ y(A_k)$ (or $y(A_k)\ \vartheta\ x(A_j)$) where the right side of := is an atom with $x \ne y$, then replace $x(A_j)$ by the constant c where $\mu(A_j) = c$ for some c in DOM(A_j).

(3) If $F(x) := x(A_j)\ \vartheta\ x(A_k)$, then replace the entire atom $x(A_j)\ \vartheta\ x(A_k)$ by the atom true if $c_1\ \vartheta\ c_2$ where $\mu(A_j) = c_1$ for some c_1 in DOM(A_j), and $\mu(A_k) = c_2$ for some c_2 in DOM(A_k), and by the atom false otherwise.

(4) If $F(x) := x(A)\ \vartheta\ c$ or $c\ \vartheta\ x(A)$ where the right side of := is an atom, then replace the entire atom by the atom true if $c_1\ \vartheta\ c$ or $c\ \vartheta\ c_1$ where $\mu(A) = c_1$ for some c_1 in DOM(A), and by the atom false otherwise.

In (2) of this definition, y is not a free tuple variable in F; in (2) and (3), A_j and A_k are compatible attributes based on (3) of definition 3.2; and in (4), c is in DOM(A) based on (4) of definition 3.2. In this definition, we need to use the atom true or false for replacing any other atom. This is why we include true and false as atoms in definition 3.2. It can be shown that, by definition 3.4, $F(x \leftarrow \mu)$ is a legal formula if the formula $F(x)$ is legal.

Example 3.7:

> Consider the legal formula $F_{11}(z)$ as shown in (3.13a), which is open since z is the free tuple variable. We substitute COMPUTER for z(DEPT) where COMPUTER is in the active domain ADOM(DEPT) to obtain

$$F_{11}(z \leftarrow \text{COMPUTER}) \equiv \exists x(\text{DEPT ITEM}) \; \forall y \; (\text{ITEM SUPPLIER})$$
$$(\text{``}\underline{\text{COMPUTER}}\text{''} = x(\text{DEPT})$$
$$\cdot \; (\text{SUPPLY}(y) \tag{3.13b}$$
$$+ \; y(\text{SUPPLIER}) \neq \text{``IBM''}$$
$$+ \; (\text{SALES}(x) \cdot x(\text{ITEM}) = y(\text{ITEM})))),$$

> which becomes a closed formula and can be interpreted.

By applying definition 3.4 to (3.13b), the mention sets and the schemes of x and y relative to $F_{11}(z \leftarrow \text{COMPUTER})$ are both undefined since x and y occur bound in F_{11}, and men(z, $F_{11}(z \leftarrow \text{COMPUTER})$) becomes undefined since z no longer appears in the right side of $\equiv$. This closed formula is still legal.

3.2.4 Safe Tuple Calculus Expressions and Their Interpretations

As discussed in the remark preceding example 1.1 in section 1.2 of chapter 1, a relation determined from TUP(R) is not guaranteed to be finite or may have a very large cardinality if the domain of any attribute in R is not finite or has a very large cardinality. In a tuple calculus expression $\mathbf{Et} := \{x(R) \mid F(x)\}$, if $F(x)$ is $\overline{r(x)}$, $\exists y(S)G$, or $\forall y(S)G$, then the interpretation of $\mathbf{Et}$ involves TUP(R) for $\overline{r(x)}$; or TUP(S) for $\exists y(S)G$, and $\forall y(S)G$. This interpretation is referred to as *unlimited*, since the underlying domains are not limited to active and/or extended active domains. To avoid the occurrence of an infinite or a very large relation, we must base interpretations on underlying active domains that have finite cardinalities. Since some constant symbols occurring in F may not be included in any active domain as discussed in section 1.2 of chapter 1, we need further to extend the active domains to include any constant that occurs in F but is not present in any active domain. This interpretation is referred to as *limited*. By this approach, we can avoid infinite or very large relations so that we have a limited class of tuple calculus expressions being defined as safe.

Definition 3.7:   Let F be a legal formula in a tuple calculus expression $\mathbf{Et} := \{x(R) \mid F(x)\}$, and let A be an attribute occurring in F. The *extended active domain* of A relative to F, denoted by EDOM(A, F), or simply EDOM(A) when F is understood, is the union of the active domain ADOM(A) and the set of constants occurring in F and DOM(A) but not in ADOM(A). For a set R of attributes, we let ETUP(R, F), or simply ETUP(R) when F is understood, be the set of all possible tuples μ with scheme R such that $\mu(A) \in$ EDOM(A, F) for each A in R.

By using EDOM(A, F) and ETUP(R, F), which are always finite, rather than DOM(A) and TUP(R) to interpret a formula F, it is possible to avoid an infinite or a very large relation. We call ETUP an *extended active complex product*.

Example 3.8:

Suppose that DOM(NAME) = DOM(MGR). Let

$$F_{13}(x) := x(NAME) \neq x(MGR) \cdot x(SALARY) \leq 20000.$$

Then we have

$$EDOM(NAME, F_{13}) = EDOM(MGR, F_{13}) = EMP[NAME] \cup EMP[MGR],$$

where EMP[NAME] and EMP[MGR] are the projections from EMP onto NAME and MGR respectively, and

$$EDOM(SALARY, F_{13}) = EMP[SALARY] \cup \{20000\}.$$

Note that the constant 20000 is included in EDOM(SALARY, F_{13}) if it is not included in ADOM(SALARY), the active domain of SALARY.

Definition 3.8: The *limited interpretation* of a closed tuple calculus formula F, denoted by i(F), is defined recursively, as follows, by using only extended active domains relative to F.

(1) The limited interpretation i(F) is true if F is true, and is false otherwise.

(2) If F is $\overline{G}$, then G must be a closed legal formula. The limited interpretation i(F) is false if i(G) is true, and is true otherwise.

(3) If F is G · H or G + H, then both G and H must be closed legal formulas. If F is G · H, then i(F) is true if i(G) and i(H) are both true, and is false otherwise. If F is G + H, then i(F) is false if i(G) and i(H) are both false, and is true otherwise.

(4) If F is $\exists x(R)G$ or $\forall x(R)G$, then G must be a legal formula, and x must be the only free tuple variable occurring in G. If F is $\exists x(R)G$, then i(F) is true if there is at least one tuple μ in ETUP(R, F) such that $i(G(x \leftarrow \mu))$ is true, and is false otherwise. If F is $\forall x(R)G$, then i(F) is true if, for every tuple μ in ETUP(R, F), $i(G(x \leftarrow \mu))$ is true, and is false otherwise.

Definition 3.9: Let **Et** := $\{x(R) \mid F(x)\}$ be a tuple calculus expression over the tuple calculus $\mathbf{C_t}$. The *value* of **Et** on the database db under the limited interpretation of **Et,** denoted by **Et**(db), is the relation with scheme R consisting of those tuples μ in ETUP(R, F) such that each such tuple μ satisfying $i(F(x \leftarrow \mu))$ = true.

By this definition, the limited interpretation of **Et** always yields a finite relation **Et**(db) as the value of **Et** since, given finite relations to start with, ETUP(R, F) is finite for any legal formula F. In addition, the limited interpretation of a quantified formula is more effective, since $i(G(x \leftarrow \mu))$ needs only to be interpreted for, at most, all tuples in ETUP(R, G), which is always a subset of TUP(R).

Example 3.9:

Suppose that we want to process the following query:

Q_1: Find the departments selling all items supplied by IBM and possibly other items supplied by other suppliers. This query was solved in example 2.12 of chapter 2 by algebraic operations called selection, projection, and quotient. The tuple calculus expression corresponding to this query is $\mathbf{Et_1} = \{z(DEPT) \mid F_{11}(z)\}$ where $F_{11}(z)$ is shown in (3.13a). We interpret $\mathbf{Et_1}$ by performing a limited interpretation of the closed tuple calculus formula $F_{11}(z \leftarrow$ COMPUTER) to decide that whether or not COMPUTER is a value of $\mathbf{Et_1}$ where

$$
\begin{aligned}
F_{11}(z \leftarrow \text{COMPUTER}) &\equiv \exists x(\text{DEPT ITEM}) \; \forall y(\text{ITEM SUPPLIER}) \\
&\quad (\text{``}\underline{\text{COMPUTER''}} = x(\text{DEPT}) \\
&\quad \cdot \; \overline{(\text{SUPPLY}(y)} \\
&\quad + \; y(\text{SUPPLIER}) \neq \text{``IBM''} \\
&\quad + \; (\text{SALES}(x) \cdot x(\text{ITEM}) = y(\text{ITEM})))).
\end{aligned}
\tag{3.13b}
$$

To interpret $F_{11}(z \rightarrow$ COMPUTER), we need to substitute relevant tuples for the tuple variables x and y in their corresponding open subformulas. What tuples are relevant for this interpretation?

We first consider what tuples should be involved during the interpretation. Since the scheme of the existentially quantified variable x in F_{11} is DEPT ITEM and so is the mention set of x relative to $F_9(x, y, z \leftarrow$ COMPUTER) in the scope of this existential quantifier, the scheme of the universally quantified variable y in F_{11} is ITEM SUPPLIER and so is the mention set of y relative to $F_9(x, y, z \leftarrow$ COMPUTER) in the scope of this universal quantifier, and F_{11} does not contain any constant that is not in the union of ADOM(DEPT), ADOM(ITEM), and ADOM(SUPPLIER), we need only to consider tuples in ATUP(DEPT ITEM), consisting of thirty-two tuples ($|\text{ADOM(DEPT)}| = 4$ and $|\text{ADOM(ITEM)}| = 8$) as shown in table 3-1 and ATUP(ITEM SUPPLIER), consisting of forty tuples ($|\text{ADOM(ITEM)}| = 8$ and $|\text{ADOM(SUPPLIER)}| = 5$) as shown in table 3-2.

More specifically, since x(DEPT ITEM) (tuple variable x with scheme DEPT ITEM) is existentially quantified, and SALES(x) appears in (3.13b), we involve at most all eleven tuples in SALES(DEPT ITEM) as shown by tuples with numbers 22 through 32 in table 3-1. Since y(ITEM SUPPLIER) is universally quantified, and $\overline{\text{SUPPLY}(y)}$ occurs in (3.13b), we need to consider all forty tuples in table 3-2. In short, we need to examine all forty tuples in table 3-2 together with at least one of the four tuples with DEPT-value COMPUTER (or with tuple numbers 22 through 25) in table 3-1.

We choose arbitrarily any tuple μ_x with DEPT-value COMPUTER, i.e., $\mu_x(\text{DEPT}) =$ "COMPUTER", or with tuple number 22, 23, 24, or 25 from SALES(DEPT ITEM) of table 3-1. Then

$$
F_{11}(z \leftarrow \text{COMPUTER}) := \exists x(\text{DEPT ITEM})F_{10}(x, z \leftarrow \text{COMPUTER})
$$

has the subformula

TABLE 3-1   ATUP(DEPT ITEM)

Tuple number j	DEPT	ITEM	Remark
1	COMPUTER	CAMERA	Not in SALES
2	COMPUTER	FILM	
3	COMPUTER	RECORDER	
4	COMPUTER	TV	
5	DP	CALCULATOR	
6	DP	CAMERA	
7	DP	FILM	
8	DP	RECORDER	
9	DP	TV	
10	PHOTO	CALCULATOR	
11	PHOTO	MICRO	
12	PHOTO	PRINTER	
13	PHOTO	RECORDER	
14	PHOTO	TERMINAL	
15	PHOTO	TV	
16	VIDEO	CALCULATOR	
17	VIDEO	CAMERA	
18	VIDEO	FILM	
19	VIDEO	MICRO	
20	VIDEO	PRINTER	
21	VIDEO	TERMINAL	
22	COMPUTER	CALCULATOR	In SALES
23	COMPUTER	MICRO	
24	COMPUTER	PRINTER	
25	COMPUTER	TERMINAL	
26	DP	MICRO	
27	DP	PRINTER	
28	DP	TERMINAL	
29	PHOTO	CAMERA	
30	PHOTO	FILM	
31	VIDEO	RECORDER	
32	VIDEO	TV	

$$F_{10}(x, z \leftarrow \text{COMPUTER}) := \forall y(\text{ITEM SUPPLIER})$$
$$(\text{``}\underline{\text{COMPUTER''}} = x(\text{DEPT})$$
$$\cdot \overline{(\text{SUPPLY}(y)} \qquad\qquad (3.12b)$$
$$+ y(\text{SUPPLIER}) \neq \text{``IBM''}$$
$$+ (\text{SALES})x) \cdot x(\text{ITEM}) = y(\text{ITEM})))),$$

which is the scope of the existentially quantified formula $F_{11}(z \leftarrow \text{COMPUTER})$. Since $i(\text{``COMPUTER''} = \mu_x(\text{DEPT})) = \text{true}$ and $i(\text{SALES}(\mu_x)) = \text{true}$, we obtain

$$F_{10}(x \leftarrow \mu_x, z \leftarrow \text{COMPUTER}) := \forall y(\text{ITEM SUPPLIER})$$
$$(\text{true}$$
$$\cdot \overline{(\text{SUPPLY}(y)}$$
$$+ y(\text{SUPPLIER}) \neq \text{``IBM''}$$
$$+ (\text{true} \cdot \mu_x(\text{ITEM}) = y(\text{ITEM})))),$$

TABLE 3-2   ATUP(ITEM SUPPLIER)

Tuple number j	ITEM	SUPPLIER	Remark
1	CALCULATOR	IBM	Not in SUPPLY
2	CALCULATOR	KODAK	
3	CALCULATOR	ZENITH	
4	CAMERA	HP	
5	CAMERA	IBM	
6	CAMERA	TI	
7	CAMERA	ZENITH	
8	FILM	HP	
9	FILM	IBM	
10	FILM	TI	
11	FILM	ZENITH	
12	MICRO	KODAK	
13	MICRO	TI	
14	MICRO	ZENITH	
15	PRINTER	HP	
16	PRINTER	KODAK	
17	PRINTER	TI	
18	PRINTER	ZENITH	
19	RECORDER	HP	
20	RECORDER	IBM	
21	RECORDER	KODAK	
22	RECORDER	TI	
23	TERMINAL	HP	
24	TERMINAL	KODAK	
25	TERMINAL	TI	
26	TV	HP	
27	TV	IBM	
28	TV	KODAK	
29	TV	TI	
30	CALCULATOR	HP	In Supply
31	CALCULATOR	TI	
32	CAMERA	KODAK	
33	FILM	KODAK	
34	MICRO	HP	
35	MICRO	IBM	
36	PRINTER	IBM	
37	RECORDER	ZENITH	
38	TERMINAL	IBM	
39	TERMINAL	ZENITH	
40	TV	ZENITH	

where the two occurrences of the atom true are associated with the logical operator · and can be deleted. Hence, we have the simpler formula

$$F_{10}(x \leftarrow \mu_x, z \leftarrow COMPUTER) := \forall y(ITEM\ SUPPLIER)$$
$$(SUPPLY(y)$$
$$+ \ y(SUPPLIER) \neq ``IBM"$$
$$+ \ \mu_x(ITEM) = y(ITEM)), \tag{3.12c}$$

where $\mu_x(DEPT) = $ "COMPUTER" was previously chosen. Since the free tuple variable y in the three subformulas of (3.12c) is universally quantified and these subformulas are disjuncted, i.e.,

$$F_9(x \leftarrow \mu_x, \; y, \; z \leftarrow COMPUTER) := \overline{SUPPLY(y)}$$
$$+ \; y(SUPPLIER) \neq \text{"IBM"} \qquad (3.11b)$$
$$+ \; \mu_x(ITEM) = y(ITEM),$$

we interpret separately these subformulas involving $\mu_x(DEPT) = $ "COMPUTER".

The first subformula $\overline{SUPPLY(y)}$ is interpreted to true if SUPPLY(y) is interpreted to false by substituting μ_{y_j} (that is any one of the first twenty-nine rows with tuple numbers 1 through 29 in table 3-2) to y. Since the three subformulas in (3.11b) are disjuncted,

$$i(\overline{SUPPLY(y \leftarrow \mu_{y_j})}) = \text{true} \Longrightarrow i(F_9(x \leftarrow \mu_x, \; y \leftarrow \mu_{y_j}, \; z \leftarrow COMPUTER)) = \text{true}$$

for each μ_{y_j}, $1 \leq j \leq 29$, in table 3-2.

The second subformula $y(SUPPLIER) \neq$ "IBM", i.e.,

$$\overline{F_5(y)} := y(SUPPLIER) \neq \text{"IBM"} \qquad (3.7)$$

is interpreted to true by substituting μ_{y_j} (that is any one of the eight rows with tuple numbers 30 through 34, 37, 39, and 40 in table 3-2) to y in (3.7). Hence, we have

$$i(\mu_{y_j}(SUPPLIER) \neq \text{"IBM"}) = \text{true}$$
$$\Longrightarrow i(F_9(x \leftarrow \mu_x, \; y \leftarrow \mu_{y_j}, \; z \leftarrow COMPUTER)) = \text{true}$$

for each μ_{y_j}, $j = 30, 31, 32, 33, 34, 37, 39, 40$, in table 3-2.

The remaining three rows with tuple numbers 35, 36, and 38 in table 3-2 cannot satisfy any one of the three subformulas in (3.11b) if $\mu_x = \mu_{x_1} = $ COMPUTER CALCULATOR (tuple number 22 in table 3-1). Thus, we have

$$i(F_9(x \leftarrow \mu_{x_1}, \; y \leftarrow \mu_{y_k}, \; z \leftarrow COMPUTER)) = \text{false}$$

for $k = 35, 36, 38$ in table 3-2 and $\mu_{x_1} = $ COMPUTER CALCULATOR. Consequently, we have

$$i(F_{10}(x \leftarrow \mu_{x_1}, \; z \leftarrow COMPUTER)) = i(F_{11}(z \leftarrow COMPUTER)) = \text{false}$$

for $\mu_{x_1} = $ COMPUTER CALCULATOR. However, if we try $\mu_x = \mu_{x_2} = $ COMPUTER MICRO with tuple number 23 in table 3-1, then we obtain

$$i(\mu_{x_2}(ITEM) = \mu_{y_{35}}(ITEM)) = \text{true}$$
$$\Longrightarrow i(F_9(x \leftarrow \mu_{x_2}, \; y \leftarrow \mu_{y_{35}}, \; z \leftarrow COMPUTER)) = \text{true}$$

for $\mu_{y_{35}} = $ MICRO IBM in table 3-2, since $\mu_{x_2}(ITEM) = \mu_{y_{35}}(ITEM) = $ MICRO. Similarly, if we try $\mu_x = \mu_{x_3} = $ COMPUTER PRINTER with tuple number 24 in table 3-1, then we obtain

$$i(\mu_{x_3}(ITEM) = \mu_{y_{36}}(ITEM)) = \text{true}$$
$$\Longrightarrow i(F_9(x \leftarrow \mu_{x_3}, \; y \leftarrow \mu_{y_{36}}, \; z \leftarrow COMPUTER)) = \text{true}$$

for $\mu_{y_{36}} = $ PRINTER IBM in table 3-2, since $\mu_{x_3}(ITEM) = \mu_{y_{36}}(ITEM) = $ PRINTER. Finally, if we try $\mu_x = \mu_{x_4} = $ COMPUTER TERMINAL with tuple number 25 in table 3-1, then we have

$$i(\mu_{x_4}(\text{ITEM}) = \mu_{y_{38}}(\text{ITEM})) = \text{true}$$
$$=> i(F_9(x \leftarrow \mu_{x_4}, y \leftarrow \mu_{y_{38}}, z \leftarrow \text{COMPUTER})) = \text{true}$$

for $\mu_{y_{38}}$ = TERMINAL IBM in table 3-2, since $\mu_{x_4}(\text{ITEM}) = \mu_{y_{38}}(\text{ITEM})$ = TERMINAL. Hence, there exist three tuples μ_{x_2}, μ_{x_3}, and μ_{x_4} in SALES to satisfy

$$i(F_9(x \leftarrow \mu_x, y \leftarrow \mu_y, z \leftarrow \text{COMPUTER})) = \text{true}$$

for all forty tuples μ_{y_1} through $\mu_{y_{40}}$ in table 3-2, and we have

$$i(F_{10}(x \leftarrow \mu_x, z \leftarrow \text{COMPUTER})) = i(F_{11}(z \leftarrow \text{COMPUTER})) = \text{true},$$

which implies that COMPUTER ϵ $\mathbf{Et}_1(\text{db})$.

Following the same method as demonstrated above, we can show that DP ϵ $\mathbf{Et}_1(\text{db})$; PHOTO and VIDEO are not in $\mathbf{Et}_1(\text{db})$.

Definition 3:10: A tuple calculus expression $\mathbf{Et} := \{x(R) \mid F(x)\}$ is *safe* if the following conditions are satisfied:

(1) Either one of the following equivalent implications is true, i.e.,

$$i(F(x \leftarrow \mu)) = \text{true} => \mu \,\epsilon\, \text{ETUP}(R, F), \qquad (3.17a)$$

$$i(F(x \leftarrow \mu)) = \text{false} + \mu \,\epsilon\, \text{ETUP}(R, F). \qquad (3.17b)$$

(2) For each subformula of $F(x)$ of the form $\exists y(S)G(y, z_1, \cdots, z_k \leftarrow \mu_k)$,

$$i(G(y \leftarrow \mu, z_1 \leftarrow \mu_1, \cdots, z_k)) = \text{true} => \mu \,\epsilon\, \text{ETUP}(S, G) \qquad (3.18a)$$

is true where $y, z_1, \ldots, z_{k-1}$, and z_k are the free tuple variables in G or, equivalently,

$$i(G(y \leftarrow \mu, z_1 \leftarrow \mu_1, \cdots, z_k \leftarrow \mu_k)) = \text{false} + \mu \,\epsilon\, \text{ETUP}(S, G) \quad (3.18b)$$

is true.

(3) For each subformula of $F(x)$ of the form $\forall y(S)G(y, z_1, \ldots, z_k)$,

$$\mu \notin \text{ETUP}(S, G) => i(G(y \leftarrow \mu, z_1 \leftarrow \mu_1, \ldots, z_k \leftarrow \mu_k)) = \text{true} \,(3.19a)$$

is true where $y, z_1, \ldots, z_{k-1}$, and z_k are the free tuple variables in G or, equivalently,

$$\mu \,\epsilon\, \text{ETUP}(S, G) + i(G(y \leftarrow \mu, z_1 \leftarrow \mu_1, \ldots, z_k \leftarrow \mu_k)) = \text{true} \quad (3.19b)$$

is true.

Among the three rules in definition 3.10, the rules (3.17a), (3.17b), (3.18a), and (3.18b) are intuitively easier to understand. However, by means of the following equivalence similar to (0.13), we have

$$\exists y(S)\overline{G} \equiv \overline{\forall y(S)G}$$

and

$$\forall y(S)G \equiv \overline{\exists y(S)\overline{G}} \,.$$

Consider the unsafe conditions corresponding to (2) and (3) of definition 3.10. The formula $\exists y(S)\bar{G}$ is *unsafe* if

$$i(\overline{G(y \leftarrow \mu, z_1 \leftarrow \mu_1, \ldots, z_k \leftarrow \mu_k)}) = \text{true} \cdot \mu \notin \text{ETUP}(S, \bar{G}) \quad (3.20a)$$

is true or, equivalently,

$$i(G(y \leftarrow \mu, z_1 \leftarrow \mu_1, \ldots, z_k \leftarrow \mu_k)) = \text{false} \cdot \mu \notin \text{ETUP}(S, G) \quad (3.20b)$$

is true where ETUP(S, G) is identical to ETUP(S, $\bar{G}$). The subformulas $\exists y(S)(\bar{G})$ and $\overline{\forall y(S)G}$ are both unsafe if (3.20b) is true; or equivalently, $\forall y(S)G$ is safe if (3.20b) is false or the negation of (3.20b) is true, i.e.,

$$i(G(y \leftarrow \mu, z_1 \leftarrow \mu_1, \ldots, z_k \leftarrow \mu_k)) = \text{true} + \mu \in \text{ETUP}(S, G) \quad (3.19b)$$

is true, which is condition (3) of definition 3.10.

In summary, we can state that **Et** is *unsafe* if some one of the of the following conditions is satisfied:

(1) The implication

$$i(F(x \leftarrow \mu)) = \text{true} \cdot \mu \notin \text{ETUP}(R, F)$$

is true, which is the negation of condition (1) in definition 3.10.

(2) For some subformula of F(x) of the form $\exists y(S)G(y, z_1, \cdots, z_k)$,

$$i(G(y \leftarrow \mu, z_1 \leftarrow \mu_1, \cdots, z_k \leftarrow \mu_k)) = \text{true} \cdot \mu \notin \text{ETUP}(S, G)$$

is true, which is the negation of condition (2) in definition 3.10.

(3) For some subformula of F(x) of the form $\exists y(S)G(y, z_1, \ldots, z_k)$, the negation of condition (3) of definition 3.10 represented by (3.19b) is true.

Example 3.10:

We examine the tuple calculus expression

$$\textbf{Et}_1 := \{z(\text{DEPT}) \mid F_{11}(z)\}$$

to determine the safeness of $\textbf{Et}_1$ where

$$
\begin{aligned}
F_{11}(z) := \ & \exists x(\text{DEPT ITEM}) \ \forall y(\text{ITEM SUPPLIER}) \\
& (z(\text{DEPT}) = x(\text{DEPT}) \\
& \cdot (\overline{\text{SUPPLY}(y)} \\
& + y(\text{SUPPLIER}) \neq \text{``IBM''} \\
& (\text{SALES}(x) \cdot x(\text{ITEM}) = y(\text{ITEM})))).
\end{aligned}
\quad (3.13a)
$$

Consider the subformula $F_9(x, y, z)$ that is universally quantified in $F_{10}(x, z)$ of (3.12a), i.e.,

$$F_{10}(x, z) := \forall y(\text{ITEM SUPPLIER})F_9(x, y, z).$$

As shown in example 3.9, we have

$$
\begin{aligned}
F_9(x \leftarrow \mu_x, y, z \leftarrow \text{COMPUTER}) := \ & \overline{\text{SUPPLY}(y)} \\
& + y(\text{SUPPLIER}) \neq \text{``IBM''} \\
& + \mu_x(\text{ITEM}) = y(\text{ITEM}),
\end{aligned}
\quad (3.11b)
$$

where $\mu_x(\text{DEPT}) = \text{"COMPUTER"}$ and y is the only free tuple variable.
Consider the extended active complex product

$$\text{ETUP(ITEM SUPPLIER, } F_9) = \text{EDOM(ITEM, } F_9) * \text{EDOM(SUPPLIER, } F_9)$$

that is identical to ATUP(ITEM SUPPLIER) as shown in table 3-2. Any tuple μ_y whose
ITEM-value $\mu_y(\text{ITEM})$ is not in EDOM(ITEM, F_9) = ADOM(ITEM) = {CALCULATOR,
CAMERA, FILM, MICRO, PRINTER, RECORDER, TERMINAL, TV} and/or whose
SUPPLIER-value $\mu_y(\text{SUPPLIER})$ is not in EDOM(SUPPLIER, F_9) = ADOM(SUPPLIER)
= {HP, IBM, KODAK, TI, ZENITH} is also not in the extended active complex product
ETUP(ITEM SUPPLIER, F_9). For example, μ_y being equal to WATCH ZENITH, MICRO
FORD, or WATCH FORD is such a tuple. Since WATCH ZENITH is not in SUPPLY, we
have

$$i(\text{SUPPLY(y} \leftarrow \text{WATCH ZENITH)}) = \underline{\text{false}}$$
$$\Longrightarrow i(\overline{\text{SUPPLY(y)} \leftarrow \text{WATCH ZENITH)}} = \text{true.}$$

Therefore, we have

$$i(F_9(x \leftarrow \mu_x, y \leftarrow \text{WATCH ZENITH}, z \leftarrow \text{COMPUTER})) = \text{true.}$$

Thus, (3.19a) in condition (3) of definition 3.10 is satisfied. Note that there are an infinite, or
at least a very large, number of such tuples μ_y like WATCH ZENITH such that $i(F_9(x \leftarrow \mu_x,$
$y \leftarrow \mu_y, z \leftarrow \text{COMPUTER})) = \text{true}$. These tuples may be included in the complex product
TUP(ITEM SUPPLIER) but are not contained in the extended active complex product
ETUP(ITEM SUPPLIER, F_9) so that we need not involve any of them during limited interpretation. This is why extended active domains and extended active complex products are so
practical and useful.

Secondly, consider the subformula $F_{10}(x, z)$ as shown in (3.12a) that is existentially
quantified in $F_{11}(z)$ of (3.13a), i.e.,

$$F_{11}(z) := \exists x(\text{DEPT ITEM})F_{10}(x, z).$$

As shown in example 3.9, we have

$$\begin{aligned}
F_{10}(x, z \leftarrow \text{COMPUTER}) := \ &\forall y(\text{ITEM SUPPLIER}) \\
&(\text{"}\underline{\text{COMPUTER}}\text{ "} = x(\text{DEPT}) \\
&\cdot \overline{\text{(SUPPLY) (y)}} \\
&+ y(\text{SUPPLIER}) \neq \text{"IBM"} \\
&+ (\text{SALES}(x) \cdot x(\text{ITEM}) = y(\text{ITEM})))).
\end{aligned} \qquad (3.12b)$$

As found in example 3.9, the implication.

$$i(F_{10}(x \leftarrow \mu_x, z \leftarrow \text{COMPUTER})) = \text{true} \Longrightarrow \mu_x \in \{\mu_{x_2}, \mu_{x_3}, \mu_{x_4}\}$$

is true for each μ_y in ATUP(ITEM SUPPLIER) of table 3-2 where

$$\mu_{x_2} = \text{COMPUTER MICRO,}$$

$$\mu_{x_3} = \text{COMPUTER PRINTER,}$$

and

$$\mu_{x_4} = \text{COMPUTER TERMINAL}$$

are contained in ATUP(DEPT ITEM) that properly contains SALES. Thus, (3.18a) in condition (2) of definition 3.10 is satisfied.

Finally, the implication

$$iF_{11}((z \leftarrow COMPUTER)) = true \Longrightarrow COMPUTER \in EDOM(DEPT, F_{11})$$

is true. Thus, (3.17a) in condition (1) of definition 3.10 is satisfied. Since all three conditions of definition 3.10 are satisfied, **Et$_1$** is safe.

Since the limited interpretation based on extended active domains of attributes as defined in definitions 3.8 and 3.9 and the unlimited interpretation based on the domains of attributes produce the same value for any safe tuple calculus expression, we omit the latter aspect for simplification.

*3.3 REDUCTION OF RELATIONAL ALGEBRA TO TUPLE CALCULUS

We shall prove that for any algebraic expression over the relational algebra, there is an equivalent tuple calculus expression over the tuple calculus.

Theorem 3.1:   If **Ea** is an algebraic expression over the relational algebra, then there is an expression, **Et,** in the tuple calculus equivalent to **Ea.** That is, for a database db, **Ea**(db) = **Et**(db).

Proof: The proof proceeds by induction on the number of occurrences of operators in **Ea.**

Basis: No Operators. Then **Ea** is either a constant relation over R, i.e., $\{\mu_j \mid sch(\mu_j) = R, 1 \leq j \leq p\}$, or a single relation $r_j(U_j)$ in db. In the former case, **Ea** is equivalent to

$$\textbf{Et} := \{x(R) \mid (x(R) = \mu_1(R)) + (x(R) = \mu_2(R)) + \cdots + (x(R) = \mu_p(R))\}$$

where the tuple variable x(R) (tuple variable x with scheme R) or each constant tuple $\mu_j(R)$ (tuple μ_j, with scheme R) is a shorthand to denote $x(A_{i_1}) x(A_{i_2}) \cdots x(A_{i_q})$ or $\mu_j(A_{i_1}) \mu_j(A_{i_2}) \cdots \mu_j(A_{i_q})$ for $R = A_{i_1} A_{i_2} \ldots A_{i_q}$. The equality $x(R) = \mu_j(R)$ means that $(x(A_{i_1}) = \mu_j(A_{i_1})) \cdot (x(A_{i_2}) = \mu_j(A_{i_2})) \cdot \ldots \cdot (x(A_{i_q}) = \mu_j(A_{i_q}))$ for each j, $1 \leq j \leq p$. In the latter case, **Ea** is equivalent to **Et** := $\{x(U_j) \mid r_j(x)\}$ where x is the tuple variable with scheme U_j.

Induction: Assume that the theorem holds for any algebraic expression with fewer than k operators. Let **Ea** have k operators. There are six cases to consider (since there are six basic algebraic operators).

(1) Renaming: **Ea** := $\delta_{A_{i_1} \cdots A_{i_l} \leftarrow B_1 \cdots B_l}(\textbf{Ea}_1)$.
Let $\{x(R) \mid G(x)\}$ be a tuple calculus expression equivalent to **Ea$_1$** that has fewer than k operators. Then **Ea** is equivalent to

$$\textbf{Et} := \{y(S) \mid \exists x(R)(G(x) \cdot H(x, y))\}$$

where $S = (R - A_{i_1} \cdots A_{i_j}) \cup B_1 \cdots B_j$ is the resulting set of attributes after each A_{i_v} is renamed, respectively, to its corresponding B_v for each v, $1 \leq v \leq j$; and $H(x, y)$ is the formula that is the conjunction of the atoms $y(C) = x(C)$ for each C in $R - A_{i_1} \cdots A_{i_j}$ and $y(B_v) = x(A_{i_v})$ for each v, $1 \leq v \leq j$.

(2) Union: $\mathbf{Ea} = \mathbf{Ea}_1 \cup \mathbf{Ea}_2$.

By the inductive hypothesis, we can find tuple calculus expressons $\{x(R) \mid G(x)\}$ and $\{y(R) \mid H(y)\}$ equivalent to $\mathbf{Ea}_1$ and $\mathbf{Ea}_2$, respectively, where $\mathbf{Ea}_1$ and $\mathbf{Ea}_2$ have fewer than k operators. Then $\mathbf{Ea}$ is equivalent to

$$\mathbf{Et} := \{z(R) \mid G(z) + H(z)\}.$$

(3) Difference: $\mathbf{Ea} = \mathbf{Ea}_1 - \mathbf{Ea}_2$.

Suppose that $\mathbf{Ea}_1$ and $\mathbf{Ea}_2$ have fewer than k operators. Then $\mathbf{Ea}$ is equivalent to

$$\mathbf{Et} := \{z(R) \mid G(z) \cdot \overline{H(z)}\}$$

where $G(z)$ and $H(z)$ are shown in case (2) and $\overline{H(z)}$ is the negation of $H(z)$.

(4) Complex Product: $\mathbf{Ea} = \mathbf{Ea}_1 * \mathbf{Ea}_2$.

Suppose that $\mathbf{Ea}_1$ and $\mathbf{Ea}_2$ have fewer than k operators. By the inductive hypothesis, we can find tuple calculus expressions $\{x(R) \mid G(x)\}$ and $\{y(S) \mid H(y)\}$ equivalent to $\mathbf{Ea}_1$ and $\mathbf{Ea}_2$, respectively. Then $\mathbf{Ea}$ is equivalent to

$$\mathbf{Et} := \{z(R\ S) \mid \exists x(R) \exists y(S)(G(x) \cdot H(y) \cdot (z(R) = x(R)) \cdot (z(S) = y(S)))\}$$

where $z(R) = x(R)$ and $z(S) = y(S)$ are shorthands, as defined in the basis.

(5) Projection: $\mathbf{Ea} = \pi_{A_{i_1}\ A_{i_2} \cdots A_{i_j}}(r)$.

If r is a relation with scheme R and $A_{i_1}, \ldots, A_{i_{j-1}}$, and A_{i_j} are attributes contained in R, then $\mathbf{Ea}$ is equivalent to

$$\mathbf{Et} := \{z(A_{i_1} \cdots A_{i_j}) \mid \exists x(R)(r(x) \cdot (z(A_{i_1}) = x(A_{i_1})) \cdots \cdot (z(A_{i_j}) = x(A_{i_j})))\}.$$

(6) Selection: $\mathbf{Ea} = \sigma_F(r)$.

If r is a relation with scheme R, and F is a formula applicable to r, then $\mathbf{Ea}$ is equivalent to

$$\mathbf{Et} := \{z(R) \mid r(z) \cdot G\}$$

where G is the formula obtained from F by replacing each attribute A_i occurring in F by $z(A_i)$ that is the A_i-component of the tuple variable z.

Other operations can be expressed in terms of the six basic ones, as above.

3.4 DOMAIN RELATIONAL CALCULUS

As mentioned in the introduction of section 3.1, both versions of the relational calculus are very similar except that a domain variable with scheme A defines A-values in the domain $DOM(A)$, whereas a tuple variable with scheme U_j defines tuple-values in $TUP(U_j)$. The domain relational calculus (or simply domain calculus) is also a sextuple $\mathbf{C}_d$

$= (U, Dom, dom Db, db, \Omega)$ where all symbols in the sextuple are defined in definition 3.1 of section 3.2.

Definition 3.11:   *Atoms*, the basic building blocks of the domain calculus, are defined recursively as follows:

(1) If $r_j(U_j)$ is a relation in a database, db, with scheme $U_j = A_{i_1} A_{i_2} \cdots A_{i_k}$, then $r_j(a_1 a_2 \cdots a_k)$ is an atom where each a_i, for $1 \leq i \leq k$, is either a domain variable with scheme A_{i_j} or a constant in $DOM(A_{i_j})$.

(2) If a and b are domain variables with the same scheme, ϑ is an arithmetic comparison operator, and c is a constant in $DOM(U)$ whose scheme is identical to that of a, then $a \vartheta b$, $a \vartheta c$, and $c \vartheta a$ are all atoms.

(3) The truth values, true and false, are atoms.

(4) Nothing else is an atom.

Formulas in the domain calculus are defined analogously as in definition 3.3 for the tuple calculus by changing tuple variables with domain variables along with their schemes.

Example 3.11:

The domain calculus formula for $F_{11}(z)$ of (3.13a) is

$$F_{11}(d) := \exists a_1(DEPT) \exists a_2(ITEM) \; \forall b_1(ITEM) \; \forall b_2(SUPPLIER)(d = a_1$$
$$\cdot(SUPPLY(b_1 \; b_2) + b_2 \neq \text{``IBM''} + (SALES(a_1 \; a_2) \cdot a_2 = b_1)))), \qquad (3.13c)$$

where d is the free domain variable with scheme DEPT; a_1, a_2, b_1, and b_2 are bound domain variables; and IBM is a constant.

Example 3.12:

Given the query
Q_2: Find the departments selling both items PRINTER and MICRO.
The domain calculus expression is $\textbf{Ed}_2 := \{d(DEPT) \mid F_{14}(d)\}$ in which the domain calculus formula is

$$F_{14}(d) := \exists a(DEPT) \exists b(DEPT)$$
$$(SALES(a \; \text{``PRINTER''}) \qquad (3.21a)$$
$$\cdot d = a \cdot SALES(b \; \text{``MICRO''}) \cdot d = b).$$

Example 3.13:

Given the query
Q_3: Find the departments selling item PRINTER or MICRO.
The domain calculus expression is $\textbf{Ed}_3 := \{d(DEPT) \mid F_{15}(d)\}$ in which the domain calculus formula is

$$F_{15}(d) := \exists a(DEPT) \exists b(DEPT)$$
$$((SALES(a \; \text{``PRINTER''}) \cdot d = a) \qquad (3.22a)$$
$$+ (SALES(b \; \text{``MICRO''}) \cdot d = b)).$$

The determination of freedom and boundedness of a domain variable is analogous to that of a tuple variable in a tuple calculus formula. For example, the domain variable d is free in (3.21a) and (3.22a) of examples 3.12 and 3.13.

In addition to the requirement that a quantified domain variable must occur free in the scope of its quantified formula, the domain variable must have a scheme. The scheme of a domain variable d relative to a formula F, denoted by sch(d, F), is equal to sch(d) if d occurs either free or bound in F and is undefined if d does not occur in F. Then legal domain calculus formulas are analogous to legal tuple calculus formulas.

The substitution of a constant c for a domain variable d occurring free in a formula F, denoted by $F(d \leftarrow c)$, is analogous to substitution of a constant tuple for a tuple variable. In the substitution, we assume that $c \in EDOM(sch(d), F)$. Every free occurrence of a domain variable d in a formula F is replaced by c, and then each atom composed entirely of constants is replaced by true or false when the atom is interpreted to true or false. A domain calculus formula is called *closed* if it consists of no free domain variables, and is open otherwise. The limited interpretation of a closed domain calculus formula is denoted by i(F). When F is $\exists d(A_j)G(d)$, i(F) = true if there is a constant c in $EDOM(A_j, F)$ such that $i(G(d \leftarrow c))$ = true. Similarly, when F is $\forall d(A_j)G(d)$, i(F) = true if, for every constant c in $EDOM(A_j, F)$, $i(G(d \leftarrow c))$ = true.

Definition 3.12: A *domain calculus expression* **Ed** over C_d has the form

$$Ed := \{a_1(A_1) \cdots a_k(A_k) \mid F(a_1, \ldots, a_k)\},$$

where

(1) F is a legal domain calculus formula with the free domain variables $a_1, a_2, \ldots, a_{k-1}$, and a_k.

(2) $A_1, A_2, \ldots, A_{k-1}$, and A_k are attributes in U, and

(3) $sch(a_j) = A_j$ for each j, $1 \leq j \leq k$.

The *value* of this expression under limited interpretation is the relation over scheme $A_1 \cdots A_k$ consisting of those tuples of the form $c_1 \cdots c_k$ such that $c_j \in EDOM(A_j, F)$ for each j, $1 \leq j \leq k$ and

$$i(F(a_1 \leftarrow c_1, a_2 \leftarrow c_2, \ldots, a_k \leftarrow c_k)) = true.$$

The value of a domain calculus expression **Ed** for a database db is denoted by **Ed**(db).

A domain calculus expression

$$Ed := \{a_1(A_1) \, a_2(A_2) \cdots a_k(A_k) \mid F(a_1, a_2, \ldots, a_k)\}$$

is *safe* if the following three conditions are satisfied.

(1) For constants $c_1, c_2, \ldots, c_{k-1}$, and c_k, the implication

$$i(F(a_1 \leftarrow c_1, \ldots, a_k \leftarrow c_k)) = true \Rightarrow c_j \in EDOM(A_j, F) \text{ for each } j, 1 \leq j \leq k$$
    is true.

(2) For each subformula of F of the form $\exists a(A_j)G(a)$, the implication

$$i(G(a \leftarrow c)) = \text{true} => c \in \text{EDOM}(A_j, G)$$

is true.

(3) For each subformula of the form $\forall a(A_j)G(a)$, the implication

$$c \notin \text{EDOM}(A_j, G) => i(G(a \leftarrow c)) = \text{true}$$

is true.

Similar to the tuple calculus, we can show that for any safe domain calculus expression **Ed,** the unlimited and limited interpretations of **Ed** are the same.

*3.5 REDUCTION OF TUPLE CALCULUS TO DOMAIN CALCULUS

Similar to the prenex normal form, as defined in section 0.5.5 of chapter 0, any tuple calculus formula can be transformed into an equivalent prenex normal form. Let **Et** := $\{x(R) \mid F(x)\}$ be a tuple calculus expression in which $F(x)$ is in a prenex normal form, and x is the free tuple variable.

A tuple calculus expression **Et** can be trivially transformed into an equivalent domain calculus expression **Ed** as follows: let x be a tuple variable with scheme $S = A_{i_1} A_{i_2} \cdots A_{i_k}$ occurring in F. Then

(1) any atom $r(x)$ in F is replaced by $r(a_1 a_2 \cdots a_k)$ where a_j is the domain variable with scheme A_{i_j} for each j, $1 \le j \le k$;

(2) any atom $x(A_{i_j}) \vartheta c$ or $c \vartheta x(A_{i_j})$ for c being a component of another tuple variable or a constant is replaced, respectively, by $a_j \vartheta c$ or $c \vartheta a_j$ where a_j is the domain variable denoting the A_j-component of the tuple variable x;

(3) any atom $x(A_{i_j}) \vartheta y(B_j)$ is replaced by $a_j \vartheta b_j$ where b_j is the domain variable denoting the B_j-component of the tuple variable y, and $x(A_{i_j})$ and a_j are defined in (2);

(4) a quantified subformula $\exists x(S)G$ is replaced by $\exists a_1(A_{i_1}) \exists a_2(A_{i_2}) \cdots \exists a_k(A_{i_k})G$;

(5) a quantified subformula $\forall x(S)G$ is replaced by $\forall a_1(A_{i_1}) \forall a_2(A_{i_2}) \cdots \forall a_k(A_{i_k})G$; and

(6) if $y = x$ and $R = S$ are in **Et,** then $y(R)$ is replaced by $a_1(A_{i_1}) a_2(A_{i_2}) \cdots a_k(A_{i_k})$.

*3.6 REDUCTION OF DOMAIN CALCULUS TO RELATIONAL ALGEBRA

We show that the relational algebra is as expressive as the domain calculus.

Theorem 3.2:   Let **Ed** be a domain calculus expression. There is an algebraic expression **Ea** that is equivalent to **Ed.** That is, **Ed**(db) = **Ea**(db) for a database db.

Proof: Let a domain calculus expression be

$$\mathbf{Ed} := \{a_1(A_1)\ a_2(A_2)\ \cdots\ a_n(A_n) \mid F(a_1, a_2, \ldots, a_n)\}. \qquad (3.23a)$$

The domain calculus expression for a subformula $G(b_1, b_2, \ldots, b_m)$ of F is

$$\mathbf{Ed}_g := \{b_1(B_1)\ b_2(B_2)\ \cdots\ b_m(B_m) \mid G(b_1, b_2, \ldots, b_m)\}. \qquad (3.24a)$$

Note that although all domain variables $a_1, \ldots, a_{n-1}$, and a_n in (3.23a) are distinct, some of their schemes $A_1, \ldots, A_{n-1}$, and A_n are not necessarily different. Similarly, although all domain variables $b_1, \ldots, b_{m-1}$, and b_m are distinct in (3.24a), some of their schemes $B_1, \ldots, B_{m-1}$, and B_m are not necessarily distinct. In addition, some scheme B_k may be identical to some scheme A_j [for example, the subformula $G_{14}(a, b, d)$:= SALES(a "PRINTER") $\cdot$ d = a $\cdot$ SALES(b "MICRO") $\cdot$ d = b) of the formula $F_{14}(d)$ as shown in (3.21a) has the domain calculus expression {a(DEPT) b(DEPT) d(DEPT) $\mid$ $G_{14}(a, b, d)$} in which the schemes of the domain variables a, b, and d are all equal to DEPT]. For appropriately referencing a domain variable a_j and its corresponding scheme A_j in an expression, we will use the variable symbol sch(a_j) to rename the constant symbol A_j. Thus, we replace (3.23a) and (3.24a) by (3.23b) and (3.24b) respectively as follows:

$$\mathbf{Ed} := \{a_1(\text{sch}(a_1))\ \cdots\ a_n(\text{sch}(a_n)) \mid F(a_1, \ldots, a_n)\} \qquad (3.23b)$$

$$\mathbf{Ed}_g := \{b_1(\text{sch}(b_1))\ \cdots\ b_m(\text{sch}(b_m)) \mid G(b_1, \ldots, b_m)\}. \qquad (3.24b)$$

Then we can find an algebraic expression $\mathbf{Ea}_g$ being equivalent to $\mathbf{Ed}_g$.

Firstly, we represent F in a prenex normal form so that no domain variable occurs bound in two places or occurs both free and bound in F. Secondly, note that every domain variable is associated with an attribute as its scheme either bounded by a quantifier or appearing to the left side of $\mid$ in $\mathbf{Ed}_g$.

For a constant symbol A denoting an attribute, or a variable symbol sch(a) denoting the scheme of a domain variable a, there is an algebraic expression for DOM(A) or DOM(sch(a)), denoted by [A] or [sch(a)] (where the pair of square brackets does not mean a multiset).

We now define recursively an algebraic expression $\mathbf{Ea}_g$ for each domain calculus subformula G of F such that $\mathbf{Ea}_g$ will be equivalent to the domain calculus expression $\mathbf{Ed}_g$ of (3.24b).

(1) Subformula G is an atom of the form a ϑ b, a ϑ c, or c ϑ a where a and b are not necessarily distinct domain variables, and c is a constant. There are two cases to consider.

    (i) If $\mathbf{Ed}_g$:= {a(sch(a)) b(sch(b)) $\mid$ a ϑ b}, then its equivalent algebraic expression $\mathbf{Ea}_g$ is

$$\sigma_{\text{sch(a)}\ \vartheta\ \text{sch(b)}}([\text{sch(a)}]\ |x|\ [\text{sch(b)}])\ \text{if}\ a \neq b \qquad (3.25a)$$

where the join [sch(a)] $|x|$ [sch(b)] is equal to the complex product [sch(a)] * [sch(b)] by (2.14b), and,

$$\sigma_{sch(a)\ \vartheta\ sch(a)}([sch(a)])\ \text{if}\ a = b \qquad (3.25b)$$

where [sch(a)] = [sch(a) $|x|$ [sch(a)] is a special case of a join as described in the remark following (2.14c).

(ii) If $\mathbf{Ed_g} := \{a(sch(a))\ |\ a\ \vartheta\ c\}$, then its equivalent algebraic expression $\mathbf{Ea_g}$ is

$$\sigma_{sch(a)\ \vartheta\ c}([sch(a)]), \qquad (3.25c)$$

and if $\mathbf{Ed_g} := \{a(sch(a))\ |\ c\ \vartheta\ a\}$, then its equivalent algebraic expression $\mathbf{Ea_g}$ is

$$\sigma_{c\ \vartheta\ sch(a)}[sch(a)]). \qquad (3.25d)$$

(2) Subformula G is an atom of the form $r(a_1\ a_2\ \cdots\ a_m)$ where a_j for each j, $1 \leqslant j \leqslant m$, is either a constant or a domain variable. When a_j is a constant in the atom r, we denote its scheme by A_j. On the other hand, when a_j is a domain variable in r, we denote its scheme by the renamed symbol $sch(a_j)$. Let X be the following string

$$X := sch(a_{j_1})\ sch(a_{j_2})\ \cdots\ sch(a_{j_k})$$

in which each a_{j_i}, for $1 \leqslant i \leqslant k$, is a domain variable in the atom r. Let F be the formula which is formed by the conjunction of atoms $A_j = a_j$ for each constant a_j occurring in r. An equivalent algebraic expression is

$$\mathbf{Ea_g} := \pi_X(\delta_{A_{i_1}}\ \cdots\ {}_{A_{i_k}\ \leftarrow\ sch(a_{i_1})}\ \cdots\ {}_{sch(a_{i_k})}(\sigma_F(\ r))).$$

(3) Subformula G is $\bar{H}$. Let $\mathbf{Ea_h}$ be an algebraic expression equivalent to $\mathbf{Ed_h}$. Then $\mathbf{Ea_g} = {\sim}_a\mathbf{Ea_h}$ where ${\sim}_a\mathbf{Ea_h}$ is the active complement of $\mathbf{Ea_h}$ relative to ATUP(sch($\mathbf{Ea_h}$)) where ATUP stands for active complex product.

(4) Subformula G is $H_1 \cdot H_2$. Let H_1 and H_2 have the free domain variables u_1, $u_2, \ldots, u_k, v_1, v_2, \ldots, v_p$, and $u_1, u_2, \ldots, u_k, w_1, w_2, \ldots, w_q$, respectively, where v_i's for $1 \leqslant i \leqslant p$ and w_j's for $1 \leqslant j \leqslant q$ are mutually distinct. Let $\mathbf{Ea_{h_1}}$ and $\mathbf{Ea_{h_2}}$ be the algebraic expressions equivalent to $\mathbf{Ed_{h_1}}$ and $\mathbf{Ed_{h_2}}$, respectively, such that

$$\mathbf{Ea_1} := *(\mathbf{Ea_{h_1}}, [sch(w_1)], \ldots, [sch(w_q)])$$

and

$$\mathbf{Ea_{2*}} : = *(\mathbf{Ea_{h_2}}, [sch(v_1)], \ldots, [sch(v_p)]).$$

Then

$$\mathbf{Ea_2} := \pi_{sch(u_1)\ \cdots\ sch(u_k)\ sch(v_1)\ \cdots\ sch(v_p)\ sch(w_1)\ \cdots\ sch(w_g)}(\mathbf{Ea_{2*}}).$$

Note that $\mathbf{Ea_1}$ is $\mathbf{Ea_{h_1}}$ with columns added for all attributes in $sch(\mathbf{Ea_{h_2}})$ − $sch(\mathbf{Ea_{h_2}})$, and $\mathbf{Ea_2}$ is $\mathbf{Ea_{h_2}}$ with columns added for all attributes in $sch(\mathbf{Ea_{h_1}})$ − $sch(\mathbf{Ea_{h_2}})$. Note also that

$$sch(\mathbf{Ea_1}) = sch(\mathbf{Ea_2}) = \{sch(d) \mid d \text{ is a free domain variable in } G\}$$

and $\mathbf{Ea_{2*}}$ and $\mathbf{Ea_2}$ are equivalent except that their columns may have different orderings. The algebraic expression $\mathbf{Ea_g}$ is $\mathbf{Ea_1} \cap \mathbf{Ea_2}$.

(5) Subformula G is $H_1 + H_2$. The algebraic expression $\mathbf{Ea_g}$ is $\mathbf{Ea_1} \cup \mathbf{Ea_2}$ as defined similarly in case (4).

(6) Subformula G has the form $\exists a(A)H$. $\mathbf{Ea_h}$ is an algebraic expression equivalent to $\mathbf{Ed_h}$. The algebraic expression $\mathbf{Ea_g}$ is $\pi_{X - sch(a)}(\mathbf{Ea_h})$ where $X = sch(\mathbf{Ea_h})$.

(7) Subformula G is $\forall a(A)H$. $\mathbf{Ea_h}$ is an algebraic expression equivalent to $\mathbf{Ed_h}$. By using the scheme of the domain variable a by $sch(a)$ rather than A, the algebraic expression $\mathbf{Ea_g}$ equivalent to $\mathbf{Ed_g}$ is $\mathbf{Ea_h} / [sch(a)]$.

Recursively, using these seven cases, we can construct an algebraic expression $\mathbf{Ea}$ that is equivalent to $\mathbf{Ed}$ of (3.23b).

We are not assured that $sch(a_j)$ is necessarily A_j, so we need one final renaming operation to obtain the algebraic expression $\mathbf{Ea}$ equivalent to $\mathbf{Ed}$ of (3.23a).

Example 3.14:

Given the domain calculus expression $\mathbf{Ed_2} := \{d(DEPT) \mid F_{14}(d)\}$ where $F_{14}(d)$ is shown in (3.21a), i.e.,

$$F_{14}(d) := \exists a(DEPT)\exists b(DEPT)$$
$$(SALES(a \text{ ``PRINTER''}) \cdot d = a \qquad (3.21a)$$
$$\cdot SALES(b \text{ ``MICRO''}) \cdot d = b),$$

we transform it into an equivalent algebraic expression $\mathbf{Ea_2}$ as follows.
For the domain calculus subformula

$$G_1(a) := SALES(a \text{ ``PRINTER''})$$

with $r = SALES$, $a_1 = a$ being a domain variable, and $a_2 = $ ``PRINTER'' being a constant, case (2) of theorem 3.2 defines its equivalent algebraic expression as

$$\mathbf{Ea_{g_1}} := \pi_{sch(a)}(\delta_{DEPT \leftarrow sch(a)}(\sigma_{ITEM = \text{``PRINTER''}}(SALES)))$$

based on $A_1 = DEPT$, $A_2 = ITEM$, $X = sch(a_1)$, and $F := DEPT = $ ``PRINTER''. Similarly, the domain calculus subformula

$$G_2 := SALES(b \text{ ``MICRO''})$$

has its equivalent algebraic expression

$$\mathbf{Ea}_{g_2} := \pi_{\text{sch}(b)}(\delta_{\text{DEPT} \leftarrow \text{sch}(b)}(\sigma_{\text{ITEM} = \text{``MICRO''}}(\text{SALES}))).$$

For the subformulas

$$G_3(a, d) := d = a$$

and

$$G_4(b, d) := d := b,$$

(3.25a) in case (1) of theorem 3.2 defines

$$\mathbf{Ea}_{g_3} := \sigma_{\text{sch}(d) = \text{sch}(a)}([\text{sch}(d)] \,|\!\times\!| \, [\text{sch}(a)])$$

and

$$\mathbf{Ea}_{g_4} := \sigma_{\text{sch}(d) = \text{sch}(b)}([\text{sch}(d)] \,|\!\times\!| \, [\text{sch}(b)]).$$

For the domain calculus subformula

$$G_5(a, d) := G_1(a) \cdot G_3(a, d)$$

where $G_1(a)$ has the free domain variable a, and $G_2(a, d)$ has the free domain variables a and d, case (4) of theorem 3.2 defines $u_1 = a$, $w_1 = d$, and the equivalent algebraic expression

$$\mathbf{Ea}_{g_5} := (\mathbf{Ea}_{g_1} * [\text{sch}(d)]) \cap \pi_{\text{sch}(a)\ \text{sch}(d)}(\mathbf{Ea}_{g_3}).$$

Similarly, the domain calculus subformula

$$G_6(b, d) := G_2(b) \cdot G_4(b, d)$$

has the equivalent algebraic expression

$$\mathbf{Ea}_{g_5} := (\mathbf{Ea}_{g_2} * [\text{sch}(d)]) \cap \pi_{\text{sch}(b)\ \text{sch}(d)}(\mathbf{Ea}_{g_4}).$$

For the domain calculus subformula

$$G_7(d) := \exists a(\text{DEPT})G_5(a, d),$$

condition (6) of theorem 3.2 defines $X = \text{sch}(\mathbf{Ea}_{g_5}) = \text{sch}(a)\ \text{sch}(d)$, $X - \text{sch}(a) = \text{sch}(d)$, and the equivalent algebraic expression

$$\mathbf{Ea}_{g_7} := \pi_{\text{sch}(d)}(\mathbf{Ea}_{g_5}).$$

Similarly, the domain calculus subformula

$$G_8(d) := \exists b(\text{DEPT})G_6(b, d)$$

has the equivalent algebraic expression

$$\mathbf{Ea}_{g_8} := \pi_{\text{sch}(d)}(\mathbf{Ea}_{g_6}).$$

TABLE 3-3 INTERPRETATIONS OF ALGEBRAIC
EXPRESSIONS IN EXAMPLE 3.14

ONE	sch(a)
	COMPUTER DP

TWO	sch(b)
	COMPUTER DP

THREE	sch(d)	sch(e)
	COMPUTER DP PHOTO VIDEO	COMPUTER DP PHOTO VIDEO

FOUR	sch(d)	sch(b)
	COMPUTER DP PHOTO VIDEO	COMPUTER DP PHOTO VIDEO

FIVE	sch(a)	sch(d)
	COMPUTER DP	COMPUTER DP

SIX	sch(b)	sch(d)
	COMPUTER DP	COMPUTER DP

SEVEN, EIGHT, NINE, OR TEN	sch(d)
	COMPUTER DP

For the subformula

$$G_9(d) := G_7(d) \cdot G_8(d),$$

condition (4) again defines $\mu_1 = d$ and the equivalent algebraic expression

$$\mathbf{Ea}_{g_9} := \mathbf{Ea}_{g_7} \cap \mathbf{Ea}_{g_8}.$$

By renaming sch(d) to DEPT, we have

$$\mathbf{Ea}_2 := \delta_{sch(d) \leftarrow DEPT}(\mathbf{Ea}_{g_9}).$$

For the department store database, the values of the algebraic expressions $\mathbf{Ea}_{g_1}$ through $\mathbf{Ea}_{g_9}$ and $\mathbf{Ea}_2$ interpreted based on active domains are shown by the relations named *ONE* through *TEN*, respectively in table 3-3. In these tables, the active domains are [sch(a)] = [sch(b)] = [sch(d)] = ADOM(DEPT) = {COMPUTER, DP, PHOTO, VIDEO}. The answer is $\mathbf{Ea}_2(db) = \mathbf{Ed}_2(db) = TEN(DEPT)$ in which each department sells both items PRINTER and MICRO.

Example 3.15:

Similar to example 3.14, the domain calculus expression

$$\mathbf{Ed}_3 = \{d(DEPT) \mid F_{15}(d)\}$$

where F_{15} is shown in (3.22a) is equivalent to

$$\mathbf{Ea}_3 := \delta_{sch(d) \leftarrow DEPT}(\mathbf{Ea}_{g_7} \cup \mathbf{Ea}_{g_8})$$

where $\mathbf{Ea}_{g_7}$ and $\mathbf{Ea}_{g_8}$ are found in example 3.14. The answer is $\mathbf{Ea}_3(db) = \mathbf{Ed}_3(db) = $ {COMPUTER, DP} in which each department sells item PRINTER or MICRO.

EXERCISES

3.1 Show that the formula

$$\begin{aligned}
F_{16}(z) := \ &\exists x(DEPT\ ITEM)\forall y(ITEM\ SUPPLIER) \\
&(z(\underline{DEPT}) = x(DEPT) \\
&\cdot (SALES(x) + x(ITEM) \neq y(ITEM) \\
&+ (SUPPLY(y) \cdot y(SUPPLIER) = \text{``IBM''})))
\end{aligned}$$

is a legal formula. Find the mention sets and the schemes of the free tuple variable z relative to F_{16} and those of the free tuple variables x and y in the scopes of the quantifiers. What is the corresponding query?

3.2 Given the query

Q_5: Find the suppliers supplying both items "CALCULATOR" and "MICRO" in the SUP-PLY relation as shown in table 3-2. The corresponding tuple calculus expression for this query is

Et$_5$:= {x(SUPPLIER) | ∃y(ITEM SUPPLIER)∃z(ITEM SUPPLIER)
      (SUPPLY(y) · x(SUPPLIER) = y(SUPPLIER) · y(ITEM) = "CALCULATOR"
      · SUPPLY(z) · x(SUPPLIER) = z(SUPPLIER) · z(ITEM) = "MICRO")}.

Find **Et**$_5$(db).

3.3 Given the query

Q_6: Find the suppliers supplying item "PRINTER" or "CAMERA" in the SUPPLY relation. The corresponding tuple calculus expression for this query is

    Et$_6$:= {x(SUPPLIER) | ∃y(ITEM SUPPLIER)∃z(ITEM SUPPLIER)
      ((SUPPLY(y) · x(SUPPLIER) = y(SUPPLIER) · y(ITEM) = "PRINTER")
      + (SUPPLY(z) · x(SUPPLIER) = z(SUPPLIER) · z(ITEM) = "CAMERA"))}.

Find **Et**$_6$(db).

3.4 Given the query

Q_7: Find the departments selling only all those items supplied by "IBM" from the relations SALES and SUPPLY as shown in tables 3-1 and 3-2. The corresponding tuple calculus expression for this query is

    Et$_4$:= {z(DEPT) | ∃x(DEPT ITEM) ∀y(ITEM SUPPLIER)
      (z(DEPT) = x(DEPT)

      · $\overline{\text{(SUPPLY(y)}}$ + y(SUPPLIER) ≠ "IBM" + (SALES(x) · x(ITEM) = y(ITEM))

      · $\overline{\text{(SALES(x)}}$ + x(ITEM) ≠ y(ITEM) + (SUPPLY(y) · y(SUPPLIER) = "IBM"))))}.

Find **Et**$_7$(db).

3.5 Find the tuple calculus expressions equivalent to

    (a) (2.1a) of subset renaming,

    (b) (2.2a) of union,

    (c) (2.3a) of difference,

    (d) (2.6) of complex product,

    (e) (2.7a) of projection,

    (f) (2.10a) of selection,

    (g) (2.13c) of intersection,

    (h) (2.14b) of ϑ-join, and

    (i) (2.15b) of quotient.

3.6 Find the domain calculus expressions equivalent to the tuple calculus expressions in exercise 3.5.

3.7 Given the query Q_7 as shown in exercise 3.4, the corresponding domain calculus expression is
    Ed$_7$:= {d(DEPT) | F_{17}(d)} where

$F_{17}(d) := \exists a_1(DEPT) \; \exists a_2(ITEM) \forall b_1(ITEM) \; \forall b_2(SUPPLIER)$

$(d = a_1 \cdot \overline{(SUPPLY(b_1 \; b_2)} + b_2 \neq \text{``IBM''} + (SALES(a_1 \; a_2) \cdot a_2 = b_1)$

$\overline{\cdot(SALES(a_1 \; a_2)} + a_2 \neq b_1 + SUPPLY(b_1 \; \text{``IBM''}))))\},$

find the equivalent algebraic expression **Ea$_7$**.

chapter 4

FUNCTIONAL DEPENDENCIES

4.1 INTRODUCTION

Data dependencies are constraints imposed on data in a database. In addition to a set of attributes, a set of data dependencies is also an essential part of a relation or database scheme. The class of functional dependencies was the first type of data dependencies to be taken into consideration and has been thoroughly investigated by many researchers such as Codd [Cod70], who proposed the concept, Delobel and Casey [Del73], who developed a set of inference rules, and Armstrong [Arm74], who showed that some inference rules are independent, sound, and complete. The relevance of functional dependencies in the design of a relational database scheme has been conjectured by the observation that, in most cases, a set of functional dependencies plus one join dependency (chapter 6) are enough to express the dependency structure of a relational database scheme and are essential to assume the universal relation scheme [Fag82, Mai83a].

This chapter covers inference rules (including their independence, soundness, and completeness), logical equivalences of functional dependencies, derivations, logical implications, closures, keys, superkeys, coverings, and graphical representations. By means of the propositional logic, simpler proofs of most theorems can be achieved, and many notions involving functional dependencies are easier to understand.

4.2 FUNCTIONAL DEPENDENCIES

We introduce the concept of the basic class of data dependencies known as *functional dependencies*.

Definition 4.1:   Let U be the universal set of attributes and U_j be a subset of U. A *functional dependency* (abbreviated as FD) is a constraint on U_j and is of the form $X \rightarrow Y$ where X and Y are subsets of U_j. Relation $r(U_j)$ *satisfies* FD $X \rightarrow Y$, or $X \rightarrow Y$ *holds* in $r(U_j)$, if for every two tuples in $r(U_j)$, say μ_1 and μ_2, whenever their X-values are identical, their Y-values are also the same, i.e.,

$$\mu_1[X] = \mu_2[X] => \mu_1[Y] = \mu_2[Y].$$

When $X \rightarrow Y$ holds in $r(U_j)$, we say that X *functionally determines* Y in $r(U_j)$ or that Y is *functionally dependent on* X in $r(U_j)$.

In this definition the symbol $=>$ stands for "implies" as shown in (0.5) of chapter 0, and $\mu_1[X]$ is the X-value of tuple μ_1. Let TUP(X) and TUP(Y) be the complex products consisting of all possible tuples over X and Y respectively. An FD $X \rightarrow Y$ defines a (many-to-one including one-to-one) function from TUP(X) to TUP(Y) such that all tuples of an identical X-value in $r(U_j)$ must have the same Y-value in $r(U_j)$. For example, the FD NAME $\rightarrow$ DEPT means that each employee belongs to a unique department and a department may have many employees, i.e., more than one NAME-value may share the same DEPT-value but not vice versa. Thus, it corresponds to a function from DOM(NAME) to DOM(DEPT).

Two FDs $X \rightarrow Y$ and $Y \rightarrow X$ define a one-to-one function between TUP(X) and TUP(Y), denoted by $X \longleftrightarrow Y$, if there exists no proper subset X' of X or Y' of Y such that $X' \rightarrow Y$ or $Y' \rightarrow X$ coexists with $X \rightarrow Y$ and $Y \rightarrow X$. For example, DEPT $\longleftrightarrow$ MGR means that each department has only one manager and each manager controls only one department.

4.3 LOGICAL EQUIVALENCE

Using the propositional logic to prove theorems involving FDs, we can view each attribute A_j in $U = A_1 A_2 \cdots A_n$, as an *atom*. Each atom can assume only two possible truth values as defined in the following:

$$A_j = \left[\begin{array}{l} \text{true if } \mu_1(A_j) = \mu_2(A_j), \\ \text{false if } \mu_1(A_j) \neq \mu_2(A_j) \end{array} \right.$$

for any two tuples μ_1 and μ_2 in a relation $r(U)$.

Let $X = A_{i_1} A_{i_2} \cdots A_{i_k}$ be a subset of U. We can view X as a *formula*, which is the conjunction of the atoms $A_{i_1}, A_{i_2}, \ldots, A_{i_{k-1}}$, and A_{i_k}, i.e.,

$$X = A_{i_1} \cdot A_{i_2} \cdots \cdots A_{i_k} \qquad (4.1)$$

where the symbol $\cdot$ stands for the "logical and" or "conjunction" operator. A conjunction operator $\cdot$ can be also omitted. Hence, the conjunction of two atoms A_j and A_k and the concatenation of two attributes A_j and A_k are both represented by the same string $A_j A_k$ separated by at least one blank. The truth value of formula X is true if all of its atoms A_{i_1} through A_{i_k} are true, and is false otherwise. When X is equal to U and a relation over U consists of at least two tuples, the truth value of U is always false because any two distinct tuples in this relation must have at least one atom with the truth value false (otherwise these two tuples cannot be different). Thus, the scheme U of a relation consisting of at least two tuples corresponds to a *contradiction,* denoted by **F.** Note that since $1 \leq k$ in (4.1), X is a nonempty subset of U and is also viewed a a non-null formula. Note also that the scheme U of a relation consisting of at most one tuple corresponds to a *tautology* but cannot be viewed as a contradiction since each attribute in U has at most one value (exactly one value if null is not allowed), and the corresponding atom in U is always true. From now on, we exclude a relation consisting of, at most, one tuple since it satisfies any FD.

We define the *negation* of A_j, denoted by $\overline{A_j}$, as follows:

$$\overline{A_j} = \left[\begin{array}{l} \text{true if } A_j \text{ is false.} \\ \text{false if } A_j \text{ is true.} \end{array} \right.$$

An atom or a negated atom (i.e., the negation of an atom) is known as a *literal.* The negation of X, denoted by $\overline{X}$, is the formula that is the disjunction of the negations of all atoms A_{i_1} through A_{i_k} in X, i.e.,

$$\overline{X} = \overline{A_{i_1}} + \overline{A_{i_2}} + \cdots + \overline{A_{i_k}}$$

where the symbol $+$ stands for the "logical or" or "disjunction" operator. The truth value of $\overline{X}$ is true if some atom in X is false, or equivalently, some negated atom in $\overline{X}$ is true; and is false otherwise. When X coincides with U (i.e., X = U) and U is the scheme of a relation (consisting of at least two tuples), the negated formula $\overline{U}$ is always true since the formula U is always false as mentioned above. Consequently, the negated formula $\overline{U}$ of the formula U that corresponds to the scheme of a relation (consisting of at least two tuples) is a *tautology,* denoted by **T.** When a relation over U consists of at most one tuple, $\overline{U}$ is not a tautology (why).

Let X be a formula as defined by (4.1) corresponding to a nonempty set of attributes. Let Y be a formula corresponding to a set of attributes. As a special case, Y is the null formula ø consisting of no literals if Y corresponds to the empty set ø. The (formula) *difference* between X and Y, denoted by X − Y, is the formula that is the conjunction of those atoms appearing in X but not in Y. This difference also corresponds to the set of attributes where the set is the difference between the two sets of attributes corresponding to the formulas X and Y. We consider two special cases.

(1) When U is the universe of attributes and X = Y = U, the (formula) difference between U and U is U − U = ø where ø is the null formula corresponding to the empty set ø of attributes. We can view the null formula ø as the negated formula $\overline{U}$, i.e., $\overline{U}$ = U − U = ø.

(2) When X = U and Y = ø, the (formula) difference between U and ø is U − ø = U. We can view the formula U as the negated formula $\overline{ø}$, i.e., $\overline{ø}$ = U − ø = U.

In both cases (1) and (2), the formulas U and ø both correspond to sets of attributes. U − U is the complement of U relative to U, and U − ø is the complement of ø relative to U.

Hence, we have $\overline{U} = \emptyset$ corresponding to $\sim U = U - U$ and $\overline{\emptyset} = U$ corresponding to $\sim\emptyset = U - \emptyset$. Thus, after we exclude any relation consisting of at most one tuple and redefine the $\emptyset$-value of any tuple as the null value, we can view the formulas U and $\emptyset$ corresponding to the sets U and $\emptyset$ as a contradiction and a tautology, respectively. However, when $X = U$, and Y is a formula corresponding to a nonempty proper subset of U, we cannot view the negation $\overline{Y}$ of formula Y as the set difference $U - Y$, which is the complement $\sim Y$ of set Y relative to the universe U, i.e.,

$$\overline{Y} \neq U - Y \tag{4.2a}$$

or equivalently

$$\overline{Y} \neq \sim Y. \tag{4.2b}$$

We will provide a counterexample for the opposite case of (4.2a), i.e., $\overline{Y} = U - Y$. In other words, we cannot substitute the negated formula $\overline{Y}$ by the set difference $U - Y$ when the formula Y corresponds to a nonempty proper subset of U.

Based on the logical approach, the FD $X \to Y$ is equivalent to the formula that is the disjunction of $\overline{X}$ and Y [Sag81], i.e.,

$$X \to Y \equiv \overline{X} + Y \tag{4.3}$$

such that $X \to Y$ holds in $r(U)$ if $\overline{X} + Y$ is valid (true for every two tuples in $r(U)$). In (4.3), if X is true, then $\overline{X}$ is false. Consequently, the truth value of $\overline{X} + Y$ depends completely on Y. On the other hand, if X is false in (4.3), then $\overline{X}$ is true. Consequently, the truth value of Y is immaterial. When a relation $r(U)$ consists of at most one tuple, and X and Y are subsets of U, both X and Y are valid, and Y being valid implies that (4.3) is valid. Thus, this type of relation satisfies $X \to Y$, and U does not correspond to a contradiction under this circumstance. This is the reason that we need to exclude this type of relation for viewing U as a contradiction and $\emptyset$ as a tautology.

4.4. INDEPENDENT INFERENCE RULES FOR FUNCTIONAL DEPENDENCIES

We introduce the independent inference rules for FDs. The proofs of soundness and completeness are postponed until relevant definitions are proposed. Let W, X, Y, and Z be subsets of U or formulas denoted by their string representations. The inference rules, denoted by FD0 through FD2, form an independent set, i.e., these rules are individually independent from one another.

FD0 (Reflexivity): If $Y \subseteq X$, then $X \to Y$.

Definition 4.2: An FD $X \to Y$ is *trivial* if $Y \subseteq X$.
    If $X \to Y$ is a trivial FD on U, then any relation with scheme U satisfies $X \to Y$. This characteristic can be easily shown by the logical equivalence (4.3). Since Y is a

subset of X, we can let X = Y Z where Y and Z are disjoint and Y Z is a shorthand of the union of Y and Z or the conjunction of two formulas Y and Z. Then we have $X \rightarrow Y \equiv \bar{Y} + \bar{Z} + Y$ where $\bar{X} = \bar{Y} + \bar{Z}$ by (0.12b) and $\bar{Y} + Y$ is a tautology **T** by (0.9a) in chapter 0. Thus, the FD Y Z → Y is valid.

The inference rule FD0 derives a trivial FD. Since $\emptyset \subseteq X \subseteq U$, X → ∅ and U → X are trival FDs. Since $X \subseteq X$, X → X is trivial FD. Among the trivial FDs, the first type of the form X → ∅ is useless in application. The second type of the form X → Y for $\emptyset \neq Y \subseteq X$ can be used as an aid in a proof (such as used in the derivation sequences to verify the inference rule FD5), to reflect the reflexive property to some equivalence relation (such as the subset or node equivalence as will be defined in definition 4.20a or 4.20b) when Y = X, or to define dotted arcs (X, A) for each A in X as will be defined in definition 4.14.

FD1 (Augmentation):   If $Z \subseteq W$ and X → Y, then X W → Y Z.

Note that FD1 has several special cases. When Z = ∅, if X → Y, then X W → Y for any subset W of U. When W = Z, if X → Y, then X W → Y W. If X → Y, then X → X Y since X X = X ∪ X reduces to X.

FD2 (Transitivity):   If X → Y and Y → Z, then X → Z.

Relation r(U) satisfies the FD ∅ → Y where Y is a subset of U and ∅ is the empty set if for every two tuples μ_1 and μ_2 in r(U), we have $\mu_1[Y] = \mu_2[Y]$ ($\mu_1[\emptyset]$ and $\mu_2[\emptyset]$ are defined as the null value). Thus, r(U) must have the same Y-value for all its tuples. By the logical equivalence (4.3), $\emptyset \rightarrow Y \equiv Y$ since the negation of ∅ is U, which is a contradiction **F** and $(\mathbf{F} + Y) \equiv Y$ by (0.7a) in chapter 0. Thus, the truth values of Y for all pairs of tuples determine the truth value of the FD ∅ → Y. Consequently, ∅ → Y holds in r(U) whenever Y is valid (true for every pair of tuples) in r(U). When Y = U in ∅ → Y, the logical equivalence yields $\emptyset \rightarrow U \equiv U$, where U, a contradiction **F**, implies that $\mu_1(U) \neq \mu_2(U)$ for every pair of distinct tuples μ_1 and μ_2 in r(U) (consisting of at least two tuples). This result is consistent with the fact that all tuples in r(U) must be mutually distinct (when r(U) consists of at least two tuples).

The notation X ↛ Y means that X does not functionally determine Y and is called an *afunctional dependency* (abbreviated as AFD). For instance, ∅ ↛ U holds in relation r(U) (consisting of at least two tuples) since ∅ → U does not hold in such a relation.

4.5 OTHER INFERENCE RULES FOR FUNCTIONAL DEPENDENCIES

In addition to the inference rules FD0-FD2, there are other inference rules for FDs that are not independent of FD0-FD2 and are useful in subsequent sections.

FD3 (Pseudo-transitivity):   If X → Y and Y W → Z, then X W → Z.

In FD3, if W = ∅, then FD3 coincides with FD2. Thus, FD2 is a special case of FD3, or FD3 is a generalization of FD2. We can show that FD3 is valid by various methods.

Logical equivalence: The implication

$$X \rightarrow Y \text{ and } Y \ W \rightarrow Z => X \ W \rightarrow Z$$

is equivalent to

$$\overline{(\overline{X} + Y) \ (\overline{Y} \ \overline{W} + Z)} + \overline{(X \ W} + Z),$$

which can be simplified as

$$\overline{Y} + Y + \overline{X} + \overline{W} + Z.$$

Since $\overline{Y} + Y$ is a tautology **T,** FD3 is valid. Note that the simplified result may not be unique or is not necessarily in a minimized form.

Truth table: Let $F1 := X \rightarrow Y$, $F2 := Y \ W \rightarrow Z$, and $F3 := X \ W \rightarrow Z$. Table 4-1 is the truth table for verifying FD3. In table 4-1, F and T stand for, respectively, the truth values false and true. This method involves exponential time $0(2^n)$ for n formulas since there are 2^n interpretations (truth assignments). In this example, there are sixteen interpretations for four formulas: W, X, Y, and Z. Since all sixteen interpretations for FD3 are true, FD3 is valid.

Key Table 4-1.

Proof or derivation sequence: By this method, we need a formal definition to define a proof or derivation sequence.

Definition 4.3: Let Σ be a set of FDs on U and σ be a single FD on U. A *proof* or

TABLE 4-1 THE TRUTH TABLE FOR FD3

W X Y Z	F1	F2	F1 and F2	F3	FD3
F F F F	T	T	T	T	T
F F F T	T	T	T	T	T
F F T F	T	T	T	T	T
F F T T	T	T	T	T	T
F T F F	F	T	F	T	T
F T F T	F	T	F	T	T
F T T F	T	T	T	T	T
F T T T	T	T	T	T	T
T F F F	T	T	T	T	T
T F F T	T	T	T	T	T
T F T F	T	F	F	T	T
T F T T	T	T	T	T	T
T T F F	F	T	F	F	T
T T F T	F	T	F	T	T
T T T F	T	F	F	F	T
T T T T	T	T	T	T	T

derivation sequence of σ from Σ, written as $\Sigma \mid\!- \sigma$, is a finite sequence of FDs σ_1, $\sigma_2, \ldots, \sigma_k$ where

(1) each FD σ_j in the sequence can be derived from (a subset of) $\Sigma \cup \{\sigma_1, \ldots, \sigma_{j-1}\}$, or equivalently, σ_j is a member of Σ or can be derived from (a subset of) $\{\sigma_1, \ldots, \sigma_{j-1}\}$ by an application of some inference rule for FDs; and

(2) σ is the last element σ_k in the sequence.

If $\Sigma \mid\!- \sigma$, then we say that Σ *proves* or *derives* σ, and we also say that σ is *provable* or *derivable* from Σ. If Σ' is a set of FDs, then $\Sigma \mid\!- \Sigma'$ means that each FD in Σ' is provable from Σ. By this extension, $\Sigma \mid\!- \{\sigma\}$ and $\Sigma \mid\!- \sigma$ can be used interchangeably.

In condition (1) of definition 4.3, if the subset is the empty set $\emptyset$ and $\emptyset \mid\!-\sigma$, then σ is trivial since the corresponding inference rule applied to derive σ is FD0 of reflexivity.

Based on this definition, we can establish a proof for FD3 (i.e., $\{X \rightarrow Y, Y W \rightarrow Z\} \mid\!- X W \rightarrow Z$ where the left and right sides are, respectively, Σ and σ).

(a) $\sigma_1 := X \rightarrow Y$ (a given FD),

(b) $\sigma_2 := X W \rightarrow Y W$ ($\{\mu_1\} \mid\!- \sigma_2$ by applying FD1),

(c) $\sigma_3 := Y W \rightarrow Z$ (a given FD),

(d) $\sigma_4 := X W \rightarrow Z$ ($\{\sigma_2, \sigma_3\} \mid\!- \sigma_4$ by applying FD2).

Since σ is the last member σ_4 in the proof and is the FD to be derived, FD3 is valid.

FD4 (Union or Additivity):   If $X \rightarrow Y$ and $X \rightarrow Z$, then $X \rightarrow Y Z$. We show that $\{X \rightarrow Y, X \rightarrow Z\} \mid\!- X \rightarrow Y Z$ by the following proof.

(a) $X \rightarrow Y$ (a given FD),

(b) $X \rightarrow X Y$ (by applying FD1 on (a)),

(c) $X \rightarrow Z$ (a given FD),

(d) $X Y \rightarrow Y Z$ (by applying FD1 on (c)),

(e) $X \rightarrow Y Z$ (by applying FD2 on (b) and (d)).

FD5 (Decomposition or Projectivity):   If $X \rightarrow Y Z$, then $X \rightarrow Y$ and $X \rightarrow Z$. We show that $\{X \rightarrow Y Z\} \mid\!- \{X \rightarrow Y, X \rightarrow Z\}$ by providing two proofs.

(a) $X \rightarrow Y Z$ (a given FD),

(b) $Y Z \rightarrow Y$ (a trivial FD),

(c) $X \rightarrow Y$ (by applying FD2 on (a) and (b)).

This shows $\{X \rightarrow Y Z\} \mid\!- X \rightarrow Y$. Similarly, we establish the following proof showing $\{X \rightarrow Y Z\} \mid\!- X \rightarrow Z$.

(a) $X \rightarrow Y Z$ (a given FD),

(b) $Y Z \rightarrow Z$ (a trivial FD),

(c) $X \rightarrow Z$ (by applying FD2 on (a) and (b)).

The inference rule FD5 of projectivity is the converse of FD4 of union. FD4 is used to merge two FDs with the same left subset X into a single FD with the same left subset X to decrease the number of FDs by one, whereas FD5 is used to decompose a single FD into two FDs where all three left subsets are identical.

Given U, and Σ on U, the problem of checking whether a relation r(U) satisfies each FD X $\to$ Y in Σ, known as the *FD satisfaction problem,* can be solved by a polynomial time algorithm. One algorithm based on definition 4.1 requires the examination of $|r| \times (|r| - 1) / 2$ pairs of distinct tuples for a single FD in Σ where $|r|$ is the number of tuples in r(U). Thus, its overall time complexity is $O(|\Sigma| \times |r|^2)$ where $|\Sigma|$ is the number of FDs in Σ.

Another algorithm is required to sort all tuples in r(U) based on their X-values to partition r(U) into blocks such that each block consists of those tuples having the same X-value. If r(U) satisfies X $\to$ Y in Σ, then $\pi_Y \sigma_{X\,=\,x}(r)$ consists of exactly one Y-value if nulls are not allowed, and at most one Y-value otherwise, where x is an X-value, σ stands for a "selection," and π indicates a "projection." This needs $O(|r| \times \log|r|)$ time for sorting $|r|$ tuples for each FD in Σ and also needs additional time $O(|r|)$ to check the Y-values in each block. Thus, the overall time complexity is $O(|\Sigma| \times |r|^2 \times \log |r|)$.

4.6 CLOSURE OF A SET OF FUNCTIONAL DEPENDENCIES

We now look at the process of deriving new, potentially useful, FDs from a given set Σ of FDs by means of inference rules.

Definition 4.4:   Given a set Σ of FDs on U, the *closure* of Σ, written as Σ^+, is defined in the following:

(1) Σ is a subset of its closure (i.e., $\Sigma \subseteq \Sigma^+$).
(2) If $\Sigma' \vdash X \to Y$ for some subset Σ' of Σ, then X $\to$ Y is in Σ^+ where X and Y are subsets of U.
(3) Nothing else is in Σ^+

Mathematically, we can express Σ^+ as

$$\Sigma^+ = \Sigma \cup \{X \to Y \mid \Sigma' \vdash X \to Y \text{ for some } \Sigma' \subseteq \Sigma, \text{ and X Y} \subseteq U\}, \quad (4.4)$$

which consists of all FDs on U, each of which is derivable from Σ.

The closure of a set of FDs is referred to as an *FD-closure*. In (4.4), if the subset Σ' of Σ is empty, then the empty set $\emptyset$ derives each trivial FD X $\to$ Y, Y $\subseteq$ X. Since each relation r(U) satisfies any trivial FD on U, a trivial FD is indeed not a constraint on a relation. In addition, the trivial FDs derived by $\emptyset$ can be classified into two forms: X $\to$ X (including X $\to$ A for each A in X) for each nonempty subset X of U, and X $\to \emptyset$ for each subset X of U. The numbers of the trivial FDs of the first and second form are both in the order $O(2^{|U|})$. These numbers are exponential functions of $|U|$ (referred to as *exponential numbers*) since U has $2^{|U|}$ subsets. Is it required or worthwhile to follow an exhaustive process for enumerating an exponential number of trivial FDs? Since each FD of the form

$X \rightarrow \emptyset$ is useless in applications, we might ignore them by excluding them in any FD-closure. We still have an exponential number of useful FDs of the form $X \rightarrow X$ where X is nonempty. If we want to exclude all trivial FDs from an FD-closure, we can simply replace (1) $\Sigma \subseteq \Sigma^+$ of definition 4.4 by (1) $\Sigma - \{X \rightarrow Y \mid Y \subseteq X \text{ and } X \subseteq U\}$ and also replace "subset" by "nonempty subset" in (2) of definition 4.4 to obtain a modified version. In later applications, whenever excluding trivial FDs is not harmful to the developing results, we can adopt the modified version. Otherwise, we still need to use the original definition to assure mathematical rigor.

To compute Σ^+ based on (the modified version of) definition 4.4, Σ^+ is initialized to Σ ($\Sigma - \{X \rightarrow Y \mid Y \subseteq X \subseteq U\}$) by (1), and then it is augmented by each new FD that is derived from a (nonempty) subset Σ' of Σ by (2). An important problem remaining to be solved is how we can find a subset Σ' of a given set Σ of FDs such that Σ' derives $X \rightarrow Y$. As will be defined in section 4.10, construction of an *implication graph* [Yan85] from node X to node Y in the graphical representation of Σ systematically solves this important problem. In applications, do we require generation of all possible nontrivial FDs in an FD-closure? In some applications, we may involve only the membership problem to determine whether a specific FD is in an FD-closure or not. In this case, we need not to generate all of them. In other applications such as the determination of two FD-closures being equal or not, we may not need to try all possibilities, as will be illustrated by an example.

Example 4.1:

Given $U_a = A\ B\ C$, and $\Sigma_{a1} = \{A \rightarrow B, B \rightarrow C\}$, the closure Σ_{a1}^+ based on the original definition consists of the FDs $A \rightarrow A\ B\ C$, $A\ B \rightarrow A\ B\ C$, $A\ C \rightarrow A\ B\ C$, $A\ B\ C \rightarrow A\ B\ C$, $B \rightarrow B\ C$, $B\ C \rightarrow B\ C$, $C \rightarrow C$, and $X \rightarrow \emptyset$ for each subset X of A B C.
In this closure Σ_{a1}^+, fifteen trivial FDs of the form $X \rightarrow Y$ for each $Y \subseteq X \subseteq A\ B\ C$ can be derived from $\emptyset$ by applying FD0 of reflexivity, i.e.,

$$\emptyset \mid - \{X \rightarrow Y \mid Y \subseteq X \subseteq A\ B\ C\}.$$

In this example, there are seven trivial FDs $X \rightarrow X$ for each nonempty subset X of A B C and eight useless trivial FDs $X \rightarrow \emptyset$ for each subset X of A B C.
Many nontrivial FDs of the form $X \rightarrow Y$ can be easily derived from $Z \rightarrow Y$ for some $Z \subset X$ by applying FD1 of augmentation, i.e.,

$$\{Z \rightarrow Y\} \mid - \{X \rightarrow Y \mid Z \subset X \subseteq U \text{ and } X \not\supseteq Y \subseteq U\}$$

In this example, we have

$$\{B \rightarrow C\} \mid - A\ B \rightarrow C$$

and

$$\{A \rightarrow B\} \mid - A\ C \rightarrow B.$$

Other nontrivial FDs of the form $X \rightarrow Y$ can be derived from $X \rightarrow Z$ and $Z \rightarrow Y$ by applying FD2 of transitivity, i.e.,

$$\{X \rightarrow Z, Z \rightarrow Y\} \mid - X \rightarrow Y$$

where X, Y, and Z are subsets of U. In this example, we have

$$\{A \rightarrow B, \ B \rightarrow C\} \ |- \ A \rightarrow C.$$

Each trivial FD will be defined as redundant. The nontrivial FDs A B $\rightarrow$ C, A C $\rightarrow$ B, and A $\rightarrow$ C, just derived, will also be defined as redundant.

The FD-closure Σ_{a1}^{+}, based on the modified version of definition 4.4, consists only of the nontrivial FDs A $\rightarrow$ B C, A B $\rightarrow$ C, A C $\rightarrow$ B, and B $\rightarrow$ C. This FD-closure is much simpler. Note that excluding trivial FDs from an FD-closure does not affect the existence of trivial FDs.

Definition 4.5:   An FD σ in Σ is *redundant* if it can be derived from $\Sigma - \{\sigma\}$ and is *nonredundant* otherwise. A set Σ of FDs is *nonredundant* if it consists of no redundant FDs and is *redundant* otherwise.

An FD-closure is redundant since some nontrivial FDs can be derived by means of the inference rule FD1 and FD2. Note that a trivial FD is also redundant, but a redundant FD is not necessarily trivial.

Example 4.2:

$\Sigma_{a1} = \{A \rightarrow B, \ B \rightarrow C\}$ is nonredundant, whereas $\Sigma_{a2} = \{A \rightarrow B \ C, \ B \rightarrow C\}$ is redundant. Since both sets are defined on A B C, we use the same symbol U_a, rather than U_{a1} and U_{a2}. We will follow this approach in subsequent examples.

An FD X $\rightarrow$ Y with X $\cap$ Y $\neq$ ø (where ø is the empty set) does not have the cancellation property (i.e, the common attributes in X and Y of X $\rightarrow$ Y cannot be canceled from X and Y). By the logical equivalence (4.3), we show that the above statement is correct. Let X = W S and Y = W T such that X $\cap$ Y = W $\neq$ ø and S $\cap$ T = ø. We prove it by contradiction. Suppose that X $\rightarrow$ Y => X $-$ (X $\cap$ Y) $\rightarrow$ Y $-$ (X $\cap$ Y), i.e.,

$$W \ S \rightarrow W \ T => S \rightarrow T.$$

This implication is equivalent to

$$\overline{W \ S} + W \ T + \overline{S} + T,$$

which can be minimized to W $+ \overline{S} +$ T. This minimized form does not contain any tautology since $\overline{W} \ S \ \overline{T}$ is missing. Thus, the above implication is invalid, i.e.,

$$W \ S \rightarrow W \ T \neq> S \rightarrow T.$$

Two FDs X $\rightarrow$ Y and X $\rightarrow$ Y $-$ X are equivalent, i.e., X $\rightarrow$ Y iff (if and only if) X $\rightarrow$ Y $-$ X. We show that, by the inference rule FD5 of projectivity or by the logical equivalence (4.3), the implication X $\rightarrow$ Y => X $\rightarrow$ Y $-$ X is valid. Let X = W S and Y = W T such that X $\cap$ Y = W $\neq$ ø and S $\cap$ T = ø. Then we have X $\rightarrow$ T as decomposed from X $\rightarrow$ W T by FD5 or

$$\overline{X + W \ T} + \overline{X} + T \equiv \overline{W} + \overline{T} + \overline{X} + T,$$

which includes the tautology $\overline{T} +$ T. Similarly, we can show that the other implication X $\rightarrow$ Y $-$ X => X $\rightarrow$ Y is valid. We will refer to the FD X $\rightarrow$ Y $-$ X as a *right-reduced* version of the FD X $\rightarrow$ Y.

As a counterexample to $\bar{X} = U - X$ and $\bar{Y} = U - Y$ where $X\,Y = U$, if we take $\bar{X}$ $= \sim X = U - X$ and $\bar{Y} = \sim Y = U - Y$, then we would have $\bar{X} = T$ and $\bar{Y} = S$ from X $= W\,S$, $Y = W\,T$, and $U = W\,S\,T$. Consequently, $X \rightarrow Y => X \rightarrow Y - X$ is equivalent to $\bar{Y} + \bar{X} + (Y - X)$, which is simplified to $S + T$ by substituting $\bar{X} = T$, $\bar{Y} = S$, and Y $- X = T$. Since $S + T$ does not contain any tautology, the implication $X \rightarrow Y => X \rightarrow$ $Y - X$ is not shown to be valid by assuming that $\bar{X} = U - X$ and $\bar{Y} = U - Y$. Hence, we must have $\bar{X} \neq U - X$ and $\bar{Y} \neq U - Y$ and cannot substitute a negated formula (such as $\bar{X}$) by its corresponding (set) complement (such as $U - X$), where X and Y are nonempty proper subsets of U.

Definition 4.6:   Given a set Σ of FDs on U and a subset X of U, the *closure* of X, written as X^+, is defined as follows:

(1) X is a subset of its closure (i.e., $X \subseteq X^+$).
(2) If $Z \subseteq X^+$ (as previously defined) and the FD $Z \rightarrow Y$ is in Σ, then $Y \subseteq X^+$.
(3) Nothing else is in X^+.

Mathematically, we can express X^+ as

$$X^+ = X \cup \{Y \mid Z \subseteq X^+ \text{ and } Z \rightarrow Y \in \Sigma\},$$

which contains all attributes, each of which is functionally dependent on X under Σ.

The closure of a subset is referred to as a *subset closure*. To compute X^+ based on this definition, X^+ is initialized to X by (1) of definition 4.6 since $X \rightarrow X$ is derived by FD0 of reflexivity. From (2) of definition 4.6, there are two possibilities. If $Z = X$ and (2) is satisfied (i.e., $X \subseteq X^+$ and $X \rightarrow Y \in \Sigma$), then Y is a subset of X^+ for each $X \rightarrow Y$ in Σ because of FD4 of union. If $Z \neq X$ and (2) is satisfied (i.e., $Z \subseteq X^+$ and $Z \rightarrow Y \in \Sigma$), then $X \rightarrow Z$ (that previously established $Z \subseteq X^+$) and $Z \rightarrow Y \in \Sigma$ imply that $X \rightarrow Y$ is in Σ^+ by the inference rule FD2 of transitivity. The FD $X \rightarrow Y$ in turn implies $Y \subseteq X^+$. Thus, X^+ is constructed by applying the inference rules of reflexivity, union, and transitivity, and it is the largest subset of U such that the FD $X \rightarrow X^+$ is in Σ^+. After a subset closure X^+ is found, the closure must contain the closure A^+ for each attribute A in X^+, and the closure Y^+ for each nonsingleton subset of X^+ such that Y is the left subset of some FD in Σ.

Example 4.3:

Given $U_a = A\,B\,C$ and $\Sigma_{a1} = \{A \rightarrow B, B \rightarrow C\}$, we show that $A^+ = A\,B\,C$ as follows: By (1) of definition 4.6,

$$A \subseteq A^+. \tag{4.5a}$$

By (2) of definition 4.6, $A \subseteq A^+$ of (4.5a) and $A \rightarrow B \in \Sigma_{a1}$ imply that

$$B \subseteq A^+. \tag{4.5b}$$

By (2) again, $B \subseteq A^+$ of (4.5b) and $B \rightarrow C \in \Sigma_{a1}$ imply that

$$C \subseteq A^+. \tag{4.5c}$$

Since A, B, and C are all in A^+, we have $A^+ = A\,B\,C$. Similarly, we obtain $B^+ = B\,C$, C^+ $= C$, $(A\,B)^+ = (A\,C)^+ = (A\,B\,C)^+ = A\,B\,C$, and $(B\,C)^+ = B\,C$.

When $|U| = n$, U has 2^n subsets. Must we find an exponential number of subset closures? In many applications, we may need only to find the closures of those subsets each of which is the left subset of some FD in Σ or in some other relevant Σ'. Based on the closures of the subsets of U, it is easy to find $\Sigma^+ - \{X \rightarrow \emptyset \mid X \subseteq U\}$, but it still involves an exponential number of enumerations. More specifically, based on the subset closure X^+ of each nonempty subset X of U, the FD $X \rightarrow X^+$ (including the trivial FD $X \rightarrow X$ but not including the trivial FD $X \rightarrow \emptyset$) is in Σ^+. Similarly, the nontrivial FD $X \rightarrow X^+ - X$ for each subset X of U is in Σ^+. If X is further constrained to be the left subset of some FD in Σ, then the result consists only of those FDs each of which is in Σ or is derived from some nonempty subset of Σ by FD2 of transitivity.

Example 4.4:

The closure Σ^+_{a1} of $\Sigma_{a1} = \{A \rightarrow B, B \rightarrow C\}$ on $U_a = A\,B\,C$, based on the subset closures as already found in example 4.3, can be trivially determined by means of $X \rightarrow X^+$ as follows: $A^+ = A\,B\,C => A \rightarrow A\,B\,C \in \Sigma^+_{a1}$. Similarly, we find that $B \rightarrow B\,C$, $C \rightarrow C$, $A\,B \rightarrow A\,B$ C, $A\,C \rightarrow A\,B\,C$, $A\,B\,C \rightarrow A\,B\,C$, and $B\,C \rightarrow B\,C$ are all in Σ^+_{a1}. This result shows that trivial FDs of the form $X \rightarrow X$ are included but trivial FDs of the other form $X \rightarrow \emptyset$ are excluded. When all trivial FDs are ignored, Σ^+_{a1} consists only of nontrivial FDs $A \rightarrow B\,C$, $B \rightarrow C$, $A\,B \rightarrow C$, and $A\,C \rightarrow B$ as determined by $X \rightarrow X^+ - X$. When X is further limited to the left subset of an FD in Σ_{a1}, the FD-closure consisting only of the FDs $A \rightarrow B\,C$ and $B \rightarrow C$ is the most simplified result.

*4.7 SOUNDNESS AND COMPLETENESS OF INFERENCE RULES

In this section, we show that the set of inference rules FD0-FD2 is sound and complete.

Definition 4.7: Let Σ be a set of FDs on U and σ be a single FD on U. Σ *logically implies* σ, or σ is a *logical consequence* of Σ, written as $\Sigma \models \sigma$, if every relation r(U) that satisfies each FD in Σ also satisfies σ, i.e.,

$$r(U) \in SAT(\Sigma) => r(U) \in SAT(\Sigma \cup \{\sigma\})$$

where $SAT(\Sigma)$ is the set of all possible relations with scheme U and satisfying every FD in Σ.

Let SAT(U) be the set of all possible relations with scheme U. Since a relation r in SAT(U) is constrained only by the scheme U, it is sufficient to denote it by the symbol r(U). Since a relation s in $SAT(\Sigma)$ (where Σ is a set of FDs on U) is constrained not only by U but also by Σ, we use $S = (U, \Sigma)$ to denote its scheme and use s(S) to denote the relation s with scheme S. Note that $SAT(\Sigma)$ is always a subset of SAT(U).

Let Σ be a set of FDs on U and σ be a single FD on U. In definition 4.3, we defined $\Sigma \mid - \sigma$. The notation $\Sigma \models \sigma$ means that "if each FD in Σ holds in a relation r(U), then σ also holds in r(U)."

Definition 4.8: Let IR be a set of inference rules for Σ. The set IR is *sound* if $\Sigma \mid - \sigma$ using the inference rules in IR implies $\Sigma \models \sigma$. The set IR is *complete* if $\Sigma \models \sigma$ implies $\Sigma \mid - \sigma$ using the inference rules in IR.

Lemma 4.1:   The set of inference rules FD0-FD2 is sound.

Proof: FD0 of reflexivity (i.e., if $Y \subseteq X$, then $X \rightarrow Y$) is valid since $X \rightarrow Y$ with $Y \subseteq X$ is derivable from the empty set (i.e., $\emptyset \vert- Y Z \rightarrow Y$ where $X = Y Z$) and every relation r(U) with $X \subseteq U$ satisfies this trivial FD $X \rightarrow Y$. Contrary to this fact, we must have the case in which r(U) has at least two tuples whose X-values are the same yet whose Y-values are different. This is an impossible case since the Y-value of each tuple is embedded in the X-value of the tuple.

FD1 of augmentation (i.e., if $Z \subseteq W$ and $X \rightarrow Y$, then $X W \rightarrow Y Z$) is valid since, if $Z \subseteq W$, there is a relation r(U) with $X Y W \subseteq U$ satisfying $X \rightarrow Y$, and there are two tuples in r, say μ_1 and μ_2, such that $\mu_1[X W] = \mu_2[X W]$; then we must have $\mu_1[Y Z] = \mu_2[Y Z]$. Suppose that $\mu_1[X W] = \mu_2[X W]$, but $\mu_1[Y Z] \neq \mu_2[Y Z]$. By this assumption, if $\mu_1[X] = \mu_2[X]$, then we must have $\mu_1[Y] \neq \mu_2[Y]$, which contradicts the assumption that r satisfies $X \rightarrow Y$.

To prove FD2 of transitivity (i.e., if $X \rightarrow Y$ and $Y \rightarrow Z$, then $X \rightarrow Z$), we again prove it by contradiction. Suppose that r satisfies both $X \rightarrow Y$ and $Y \rightarrow Z$, but does not satisfy $X \rightarrow Z$. Then r has two tuples μ_1 and μ_2 such that $\mu_1[X] = \mu_2[X]$ and $\mu_1[Z] \neq \mu_2[Z]$. If $\mu_1[Y] = \mu_2[Y]$, then $\mu_1[Z] \neq \mu_2[Z]$ contradicts the assumption that $Y \rightarrow Z$ holds in r. If $\mu_1[Y] \neq \mu_2[Y]$, then $\mu_1[X] = \mu_2[X]$ contradicts the assumption that $X \rightarrow Y$ holds in r.

Theorem 4.1:   The set of inference rules FD0-FD2 is complete.

Proof: We need only to show that if $\Sigma \models X \rightarrow Y$, then $\Sigma \vert- X \rightarrow Y$ (or equivalently if $\Sigma \vert+ X \rightarrow Y$, then $\Sigma \not\models X \rightarrow Y$).

Let $U = A_1 \cdots A_n$ be a set of attributes and FD(U) be the set of all possible FDs on U. Consider the set Σ of FDs, which is a subset of FD(U), and the relation scheme $R = (U, \Sigma)$. Let a_j and b_j be two distinct elements of $DOM(A_j)$, $1 \leq j \leq n$. Consider a relation r with scheme R. There will be only two tuples in r, say ν and μ. Tuple ν will be $a_1 a_2 \cdots a_n$. Tuple μ is defined as

$$\mu(A_j) = \left[\begin{array}{l} a_j \text{ if } A_j \notin X^+. \\ b_j \text{ if } A_j \not\subseteq X^+. \end{array} \right.$$

where X is a subset of U.

Let an FD $X \rightarrow Y$ be in $FD(U) - \Sigma^+$. We need to show that r satisfies all FDs in Σ^+ but does not satisfy the FD $X \rightarrow Y$.

Firstly, we show that r does not satisfy $X \rightarrow Y$. Suppose that r satisfies $X \rightarrow Y$. Then $\nu[X] = \mu[X]$ implies $\nu[Y] = \mu[Y]$. By definition of r as defined above, $\mu[Y]$ must be all a's since $\nu[Y]$ is a string of all a's. Hence, $Y \subseteq X^+$ or, equivalently, $X^+ \rightarrow Y$ by FD0 of reflexivity. But since $X \rightarrow X^+$ is in Σ^+, by FD2 of transitivity, $X \rightarrow Y$ is in Σ^+, a contradiction to $X \rightarrow Y \in FD(U) - \Sigma^+$. Thus, r does not satisfy $X \rightarrow Y$.

Secondly, we show that r satisifes all FDs in Σ^+. The only FDs that need be considered are those of the form $W \rightarrow Z$ where $W \subseteq X^+$, because if $W \not\subseteq X^+$, then $\nu[W] \neq \mu[W]$ ($\nu[W]$ is a string of a's and $\mu[W]$ is a string of b's) and the Z-values of ν and μ are immaterial. Since $W \subseteq X^+$, by FD0 of reflexivity, $X^+ \rightarrow W$ is in Σ^+, and by FD4 of union, $X \rightarrow X^+$ is in Σ^+, which in turn imply, by FD2 of transitivity, $X \rightarrow W \in^+ \Sigma^+$. By one more application of FD2, $X \rightarrow W$ and $W \rightarrow Z$ imply $X \rightarrow Z \in \Sigma^+$. Hence, $Z \subseteq X^+$ and $\nu[Z] = \mu[Z]$ (both $\nu[Z]$ and $\mu[Z]$ are strings of a's). So r satisfies $W \rightarrow Z$.

Since the set of inference rules FD0-FD2 is sound and complete, $\Sigma \mid- \sigma$ iff $\Sigma \mid= \sigma$. Thus, we can use $\mid-$ and $\mid=$ interchangeably.

*4.8 KEYS AND SUPERKEYS

In section 1.5 of chapter 1, we defined a key for a relation or for a relation scheme and discussed its related problems. Key dependencies are special cases of FDs. In addition, keys and key dependencies are among the most important concepts in relational databases. Hence, we repeat the definition of a key and define a superkey here. Since keys and superkeys must involve FDs, a relation scheme is not only determined by a set U of attributes but also by a set Σ of FDs on U. Thus, a relation scheme R is represented by an ordered pair of U and Σ, i.e., $R = (U, \Sigma)$ as discussed in the remark preceding definition 4.8.

Definition 4.9:   Let $R = (U, \Sigma)$ be a relation scheme. A subset X of U is a *superkey* for a relation scheme R if $X \rightarrow U$ is in Σ^+. A subset X of U is a *key* for R if X is a superkey for R and $Y \rightarrow U$ is not in Σ^+ for every proper subset Y of X. If X is a key for R, then it is also a key for a relation with scheme R.

Since $\emptyset \rightarrow U$ does not hold in a relation consisting of at least two tuples, as discussed in the remark preceding section 4.5, a superkey or key must be a nonempty subset of U. An FD of the form $X \rightarrow U$ is referred to as a *key dependency* where X is a key or superkey.

Example 4.5

> For the relation scheme $R_{b1} = (U_b, \Sigma_{b1})$ with $U_b = A\,B\,C\,D\,E\,F\,G$ and $\Sigma_{b1} = \{A \rightarrow B\,C\,F, C \rightarrow D, B\,D \rightarrow E, E\,F \rightarrow G\}$, $A^+ = U_b$, $C^+ = C\,D$, $(B\,D)^+ = B\,D\,E$, and $(E\,F)^+ = E\,F\,G$. Thus, we have the key A since the left subset A of the key dependency $A \rightarrow U$ is a singleton set. The union of A and any subset of $U - A$ is a superkey.

By definition 4.9, a key for a relation scheme R and a key for a relation r(R) can be used interchangeably, and a superkey must contain a key. Note that some relation r(R) may have more than one key. Each key is known as a *candidate key*. When a candidate key is chosen as the key for a relation, this key is called the *primary key* for the relation.

When X is a key for a relation r(R) or for a relation scheme $R = (U, \Sigma)$, the key dependency $X \rightarrow U$ is in Σ^+ or, equivalently, $X^+, = U$. If $X \rightarrow U$ holds in a relation r(R), then the logical equivalence $\bar{X} + U \equiv \bar{X}$ being valid implies that X must be false for every pair of distinct tuples in r(R) since U is a contradiction. This guarantees that the X-values of every two distinct tuples in r(R) are different, which in turn insures that X contains enough information to differentiate all tuples in r(R).

If a relation r with scheme $R = (U, \Sigma)$ has a very large set U and has U as its only key known as the *all-key* for r(R), then retrieving a tuple in r(R) is not efficient since the retrieval must need the maximum possible extent of information that can be provided only by an all-key value. In this case, it would be beneficial to add an additional attribute to U and to use this single attribute as the key for a relation with the modified scheme. For example, a personnel relation may use the single attribute "social security number" as the key, no matter how many attributes are included in the relation scheme.

The problem of finding a minimal sized key for a relation scheme is NP-complete [Luc78]. Thus, finding such a key for a relation scheme is generally a very difficult problem.

4.9 COVERINGS OF A SET OF FUNCTIONAL DEPENDENCIES

In this section, we define a covering of a set Σ of FDs, a covering being nonredundant, minimal, LR-minimal, and optimal.

Definition 4.10: Let FD(U) be the set of all possible FDs on U. Let Σ_1 and Σ_2 be nonempty subsets of FD(U). We say that Σ_1 is a *covering* for Σ_2 if $\Sigma_1^+ = \Sigma_2^+$.

A covering for a set of FDs is referred to as an *FD-covering*. This type of covering defines a binary equivalence relation on FD(U) since it has the properties of reflexivity, symmetry, and transitivity. Thus, given a set Σ of FDs, we can say that Σ is an FD-covering for itself because of the reflexive property. An FD-covering Σ_1 for a given set Σ of FDs is equivalent to Σ, written as $\Sigma_1 \equiv \Sigma$. In addition, the power set of the set FD(U), excluding the empty set, can be partitioned into (mutually disjoint) equivalence classes such that each class consists of mutually equivalent FD-coverings.

Example 4.6:

The redundant set $\Sigma_{a2} = \{A \rightarrow B\ C,\ B \rightarrow C\}$ (since $A \rightarrow C$ is redundant) and the nonredundant set $\Sigma_{a1} = \{A \rightarrow B,\ B \rightarrow C\}$ are equivalent. The equivalence is determined by $A^+ = A\ B\ C$, and $B^+ = B\ C$, which imply the same nontrivial FDs $A \rightarrow B\ C$ and $B \rightarrow C$ in both FD-closures. This example illustrates that the examination of both FD-closures for equality needs to consider only the subset closures A^+ and B^+ where A and B are the left subsets of the FDs in both FD-coverings. In this example, Σ_{a1} happens to be a proper subset of Σ_{a2} since $A \rightarrow B\ C$ can be decomposed into $A \rightarrow B$ and $A \rightarrow C$.

Example 4.7:

Let $U_c = A\ B\ C\ D\ E\ F$, $\Sigma_{c1} = \{A\ B \rightarrow E,\ A\ C \rightarrow F,\ A\ D \rightarrow B,\ B \rightarrow C,\ C \rightarrow D\}$, and $\Sigma_{c2} = \{A\ D \rightarrow B\ E\ F,\ B \rightarrow C,\ C \rightarrow D\}$. Then $\Sigma_{c1} \equiv \Sigma_{c2}$. However, there is no inclusion relationship between Σ_{c1} and Σ_{c2}. By comparing the FDs in Σ_{c1} and Σ_{c2}, two FDs, $A\ B \rightarrow E$ and $A\ C \rightarrow F$ in Σ_{c1} are not in Σ_{c2}, but both of these FDs are adjusted as the FD $A\ D \rightarrow E\ F$ included in the FD $A\ D \rightarrow B\ E\ F$ in Σ_{c2}. Since Σ_{c2} has fewer FDs as well as fewer attributes, it is superior in the design of a database scheme. Given a set Σ of FDs, how can we find an FD-covering that is not only equivalent to, but also better than Σ? As will be seen in section 4.10, when Σ_{c1} is graphically represented, the nodes A B, A C, and A D can be determined to be equivalent, and in addition, A B and A C can be determined to be superfluous so that a systematic method is provided to find a better FD-covering, such as Σ_{c2}. In addition to Σ_{c1} and Σ_{c2} as shown above, let $\Sigma_{c3} = \{A\ B \rightarrow E,\ A\ D \rightarrow B\ F,\ B \rightarrow C,\ C \rightarrow D\}$ and $\Sigma_{c4} = \{A\ C \rightarrow F,\ A\ D \rightarrow B\ E,\ B \rightarrow C,\ C \rightarrow D\}$ be nonredundant sets of FDs. Since Σ_{c1}, Σ_{c2}, Σ_{c3}, and Σ_{c4} are mutually equivalent, each one of them has three other nonredundant FD-coverings. In this example, the determination of two given FD-closures to be equal must consider the subset closures of the left subsets of all FDs in the union of the two given sets of FDs. For example, when Σ_{c1}^+ and Σ_{c2}^+ are examined, we must consider all subset closures of the left subsets A B, A C, A D, B, and C for both FD-closures, although A B and A C are not left subsets in Σ_{c2}. By this method, we can avoid examining an exponential number of subset closures, since U has $2^{|U|}$ subsets. FD-covering is a very important notion is designing a better database scheme, since we can find a better FD-covering equivalent to a given set of FDs. In this example, Σ_{c2} is better than all others mentioned above because it has fewer attributes, and needs fewer columns for implementation.

Example 4.8:

The redundant set of FDs, Σ_{d1} = { A B → C, B C → D, B E → C, C D → B, C E → A F, C F → B D, C → A, D → E F}, has two nonredundant FD-coverings. When we first delete the redundant FD C D → A (since {C → A} $|-$ C E → A by FD1 of augmentation) and then delete the redundant FD C F → B (since {C F → D, C D → B} $|-$ C F → B by FD3 of pseudo-transitivity), the first nonredundant FD-covering is Σ_{d2} = {A B → C, B C → D, B E → C, C D → B, C E → F, C F → D, C → A, D → E F}. The other nonredundant FD-covering is Σ_{d3} = {A B → C, B C → D, B E → C, C D → B, C E → F, C F → B, C → A, D → E F} by firstly, deleting the redundant FD C D → B (since {D → F} $|-$ C D → C F and {C D → C F, C F → B} $|-$ C D → B), secondly, eliminating the redundant FD C E → A (since {C → A} $|-$ C E → A), and finally, erasing the redundant FD C F → D (since {C F → B} $|-$ C F → B C and {C F → B C, B C → D} $|-$ C F → D). The second FD-covering Σ_{d3} has fewer FDs and fewer attributes and is superior in the design of a database scheme. This example demonstrates that when a redundant set of FDs has more than one redundant FD, the order of examining the FDs for redundancy is not immaterial since the result is not unique and is order dependent or sensitive. Before an examination proceeds, how do we know in advance which order should be taken to yield a better result? There is no systematic method available to solve this order-sensitive problem until the graphical approach in section 4.10 is developed.

Definition 4.11:   An attribute A in X, or B in Y of an FD X → Y is *extraneous* if $(X - A) \rightarrow Y$ is in Σ^+, or X → B is redundant. An FD X → Y is called *left- or right-reduced* if X or Y does not contain any extraneous attributes. An FD X → Y is called *reduced* if both X and Y do not contain any extraneous attributes.

Although a nonredundant set of FDs consists of no redundant FDs, some FD may contain extraneous attributes. If the left subset of an FD contains an extraneous attribute, then this attribute can be deleted. This deletion is called a *left-reduction*. Similarly, we can define a deletion on the right subset of an FD called a *right-reduction*. However, to avoid completely any right-reduction, if X → Y and Y = $A_{i_1} A_{i_2} \cdots A_{i_k}$ for $1 \leq k \leq n$, then we can decompose X → Y into $X \rightarrow A_{i_1}, \cdots, X \rightarrow A_{i_{k-1}}$, and $X \rightarrow A_{i_k}$ by means of FD5 of projectivity. Consequently, we need only to decide whether to delete $X \rightarrow A_{i_j}$ if it is redundant or to delete any extraneous attributes in X otherwise. By this consideration, we can avoid obtaining a trivial FD of the form X → ∅ if each attribute in Y of an FD X → Y under examination is extraneous. This approach will be adopted to decide whether or not an arc (X, A) corresponding to an FD of the form X → A in Σ is redundant where X and A are nodes in an FD-graph (definition 4.14).

Definition 4.12:   Let Σ be a subset of FD(U). The set Σ is *minimal* if the number of FDs in Σ is the minimum as compared to any of its FD-coverings. The set Σ is *LR-minimal* if it is minimal and each FD in it is reduced.

Since this definition requires that the number of FDs in Σ be the minimum, all FDs with the same left subset must be merged into a single FD by FD4 of additivity to reduce the number of FDs. A set of reduced FDs containing FDs of the only form $X \rightarrow A$ may not be minimal since its FDs of the same left subset are not merged into one FD by FD4 of union. A minimal set of FDs may not be LR-minimal since it may contain some FD that is not reduced, and an LR-minimal set of FDs may not contain the minimum number of attributes occurring in it.

Example 4.9:

Let $\Sigma_{e1} = \{A\,B \rightarrow D\,E\,F, A\,C \rightarrow G, A \rightarrow C\}$. The attribute C in A C $\rightarrow$ G is extraneous since $(A\,C)^+ = A^+ = A\,C\,G$ implies that $A \rightarrow G$ is in Σ_{e1}^+. Thus, we can replace A C $\rightarrow$ G in Σ_{e1} by $A \rightarrow G$ to yield the FD-covering $\Sigma_{e2} = \{A\,B \rightarrow D\,E\,F, A \rightarrow C\,G\}$. In this example, Σ_{e1} is not minimal, and Σ_{e2} is not only minimal but also LR-minimal.

Example 4.10:

The sets $\Sigma_{f1} = \{A\,B\,C \rightarrow E, B\,C \rightarrow D, D \rightarrow B\,C\}$ and $\Sigma_{f2} = \{A\,D \rightarrow E, B\,C \rightarrow D, D \rightarrow B\,C\}$ are equivalent since $(A\,B\,C)^+ = (A\,D)^+ = A\,B\,C\,D\,E$, $(B\,C)^+ = D^+ = B\,C\,D$, and both are LR-minimal. However, Σ_{f2} has nine attributes occurring in it, whereas Σ_{f1} has ten attributes. This demonstrates that an LR-minimal FD-covering is not necessarily optimal in the sense of having the minimum number of attributes. If Σ_{f1} is given and Σ_{f2} is unknown, how do we know that there exists a better FD-covering Σ_{f2} (that is equivalent to Σ_{f1})?

Definition 4.13:   Let Σ be a subset of FD(U). Σ is *optimal* if the number of attributes occurring in Σ is the minimum as compared to any of its FD-coverings.

Example 4.11:

The set of FDs $\Sigma_{a1} = \{A \rightarrow B, B \rightarrow C\}$ of example 4.6 is optimal. The other sets of FDs, such as $\Sigma_{c2} = \{A\,D \rightarrow B\,E\,F, B \rightarrow C, C \rightarrow D\}$ of example 4.7, $\Sigma_{d3} = \{A\,B \rightarrow C, B\,C \rightarrow D, B\,E \rightarrow C, C\,E \rightarrow F, C\,F \rightarrow B, C \rightarrow A, D \rightarrow E\,F\}$ of example 4.8, $\Sigma_{e2} = \{A\,B \rightarrow D\,E\,F, A \rightarrow C\,G\}$ of example 4.9, and $\Sigma_{f2} = \{A\,D \rightarrow E, B\,C \rightarrow D, D \rightarrow B\,C\}$ example 4.10 are all at least LR-minimal and are the best FD-coverings obtained from their corresponding FD-coverings mentioned in these examples. It is difficult to determine an FD-covering to be optimal since the problem is NP-complete [Theorem 4, Mai80].

There exist polynomial time algorithms to

(1) solve the FD membership problem (i.e., $\Sigma \mathrel{|\!-} \sigma$ or equivalently $\sigma \in \Sigma^+$?) with $O(|\Sigma|)$ time [Bee79a] or $O(|ATTR(\Sigma)|)$ time [Gal82], and to find

(2) a nonredundant FD-covering by deleting redundant FDs [Bee79a],

(3) an extraneous attribute B in X by testing if $(X - B) \rightarrow A$ is in Σ^+,

(4) a minimal FD-covering [Aus83], and

(5) an LR-minimal FD-covering [Aus83].

Note that the optimal FD-covering problem is NP-complete. This is a hard problem to solve since we may need to try an exponential number of possible cases in order to search for an optimal covering.

4.10 GRAPHICAL REPRESENTATIONS OF FUNCTIONAL DEPENDENCIES

Given a set Σ of FDs, we can represent Σ by a graph known as the FD-graph for Σ. In this section, we introduce an FD-graph; the closure and a covering of an FD-graph; and the nonredundancy, minimality, LR-minimality, and optimality of FD-coverings. This section is based on a generalization [Yan85] from the FD-path proposed in [Aus83].

To achieve better algorithm complexities, a set Σ of FDs is assumed to have the following properties:

(1) There exist no FDs having the same left subset (i.e., $X \rightarrow Y$ and $X' \rightarrow Z$ in Σ imply $X \neq X'$).

(2) For each FD of the form $X \rightarrow Y$, X and Y are disjoint, i.e., $X \rightarrow Y$ is right-reduced.

If there are two FDs, $X \rightarrow Y$ and $X \rightarrow Z$, then we can derive $X \rightarrow Y Z$ by FD4 of additivity to decrease $|\Sigma|$, the number of FDs in Σ. If X and Y of any FD $X \rightarrow Y$ is not disjoint, then we can replace the FD by the right-reduced version $X \rightarrow Y - X$ to decrease $|MATTR(\Sigma)|$, the number of attributes appearing in Σ (where $MATTR(\Sigma)$ is the multiset of attributes appearing in Σ). An FD $X \rightarrow Y$ possessing both properties (1) and (2) may contain some extraneous attributes.

Definition 4.14:   Given a set Σ of FDs on U, the *FD-graph* for Σ, denoted by G_Σ = (V, E), is the graph where V is a nonempty finite set of nodes partitioned into subsets V^s and V^c such that

(1) for every attribute A in U, there is a *simple node* labeled by A in V^s, and

(2) for every FD $X \rightarrow Y$ in Σ with $|X| > 1$, there is a *compound node* labeled by X in V^c; and E is a nonempty finite set of arcs partitioned into subsets E^f and E^d such that

(3) for every FD $X \rightarrow B_1 \cdots B_p$ in Σ (where X is in V^s or V^c), there are p *full arcs* (X, B_k) in E^f for each k, $1 \leq k \leq p$ and

(4) for every compound node $X = C_1 \cdots C_q$, there are q *dotted arcs* (X, C_k) in E^d for each k, $1 \leq k \leq q$. The simple nodes C_1 through C_q, adjacent from the compound node X, are referred to as the *component nodes* of X.

By rule (1) for constructing an FD-graph, each simple node is labeled by a single attribute of U or a singleton set that is a subset of U. By rule (2), each compound node is labeled by a subset X of at least two attributes in U (since $|X| > 1$). All node-labels are distinct so that we can use the set of node-labels to denote the set V of nodes. By the assumed property (2) of Σ, G does not contain any trivial FD so that each node does not have a self-loop, and therefore, an FD-graph is not reflexive. A compound node X should have at least one outgoing full arc to a simple node so that the corresponding FD is nontrivial and should also have at least two outgoing dotted arcs to its component nodes (since $|X| > 1$). Each dotted arc (X, C_k) in G_Σ as constructed by rule (4) defines a trivial FD $X \to C_k$ in Σ^+, since $C_k \in X$, and is useful in definition of an implication graph (definition 4.15). Each full arc (X, B_k) as constructed by rule (3) defines a nontrivial FD $X \to B_k$ in Σ. The number of nodes is implied by rules (1) and (2) and satisfies $|V| \leq |U| + |\Sigma|$ where the inequality holds if some FD involves only a singleton set as its left subset. The number of full arcs is implied by rule (3) and is $|E^f| = |MATTR(\Sigma_r)|$ where $MATTR(\Sigma_r)$ is the multiset of attributes appearing in the right subset Y of an FD $X \to Y$ in Σ. The number of dotted arcs is implied by rule (4) and satisfies $|E^d| \leq |MATTR(\Sigma_1)|$ where $MATTR(\Sigma_1)$ is the multiset of attributes appearing in the left subset X of an FD $X \to Y$ in Σ, and the inequality holds if some FD involves only a singleton set as its left subset. The total number of arcs is $|E| = |E^f| + |E^d| \leq |MATTR(\Sigma)|$.

Example 4.12:

Given the set $\Sigma_{b1} = \{A \to B\ C\ F, C \to D, B\ D \to E, E\ F \to G\}$ with $|\Sigma_{b1}| = 4$ and $|MATTR(\Sigma_{b1})| = 12$, the corresponding FD-graph $G_{\Sigma_{b1}} = (V_{b1}, E_{b1})$ is given in Fig. 4-1 where $|V_{b1}| = 9 (<|U| + |\Sigma_{b1}| = 7 + 4 = 11$ since there are two FDs $A \to B\ C\ F$ and $C \to D$ involving only singleton sets A and C as their left subsets). Also $|E^f_{b1}| = |MATTR((\Sigma_{b1})_r)| = |[B, C, D, E, F, G]| = 6$ and $|E^d_{b1}| = 4 (<|MATTR((\Sigma_{b1})_1)| = |[A, B, C, D, E, F]| = 6$ since there are two FDs $A \to B\ C\ F$ and $C \to D$ involving only singleton sets as their left subsets).

In an FD-graph, we define implication graphs [Yan85] as subgraphs of the FD-graph. Then we can define the closure of an FD-graph, redundant nodes, superfluous nodes, and redundant arcs.

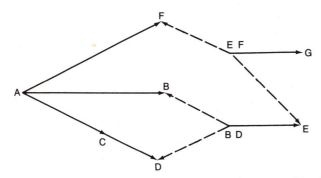

Figure 4-1   The FD-graph $G_{\Sigma_{b1}}$

Definition 4.15:   Given an FD-graph $G_\Sigma = (V, E)$ and two distinct nodes i and j in V, an *implication graph from the initial node i to the final node j* is a subgraph $G^*_\Sigma(i.j) = (V^*_{ij}, E^*_{ij})$ of the FD-graph G_Σ such that the following rules are initialized by x := j and are recursively applied to construct the subgraph depending on the characteristics of the final node x.

(1) Case 1: The final node x of $G^*_\Sigma(i,x)$ is simple. If there exists a node k such that the full arc (k, x) is in E^*_{ix} (implied by $(k, x \in E^f)$, then

   (i) the arc (i, k) is in E^*_{ix} (implied by $(i, k) \in E$), or else

(ii) an implication graph from i to k exists and is in $G_\Sigma^*(i, x)$ (if $(i, k) \notin E$).

(2) Case 2: The final node x of $G_\Sigma^*(i, x)$ is compound and has component nodes $m_1, \ldots, m_{r-1}$, and m_r. The r dotted arcs $(x, m_1), (x, m_2), \ldots, (x, m_{r-1})$, and (x, m_r) are in E_{ix}^*, at most one of the r component nodes is equal to i, and for each component node $m_s \neq i$, $s \in \{1, 2, \ldots, r\}$,

(i) the arc (i, m_s) is in E_{ix}^* (implied by $(i, m_s) \in E$), or else

(ii) an implication graph from i to m_s exists and is in $G_\Sigma^*(i, x)$ (if $(i, m_s) \notin E$).

An implication graph from i to j is *dotted* if there are only dotted arcs incident from i, and is *full* otherwise.

An implication graph constructed by rule (1i) alone has two possible minimal types. One of them, shown in Fig. 4-2(a), is a full implication graph that is the (directed) path (i, k), (k, j), and generates, by transitivity, the full arc (i, j), in the closure of its corresponding FD-graph, which will be defined later. The other one, shown in Figure 4-2(b), is a dotted implication graph that is the (hybrid) path (i, k), (k, j), and generates, by transitivity, the dotted arc (i, j) in the closure of its corresponding FD-graph. Note that the nodes i, j, and k are distinct since (k, j) and (i, k) are both in E, and E does not contain any self-loop.

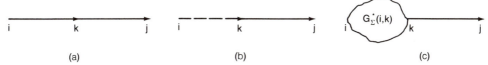

(a)   (b)   (c)

Figure 4-2   Basic types of implication graphs with simple final nodes

An implication graph constructed by rule (1ii) properly contains an implication graph from i to k as a subgraph and is shown in Fig. 4-2(c). Although the nodes i, j, and k are distinct, an implication graph from i to j of this type may contain the full arc (i, j) of E if the implication graph from i to j is not dotted. As an example, an implication graph from A B to C of the FD-graph $G_{\Sigma_{d1}}$ (do exercise 4.17) for $\Sigma_{d1} = \{A\,B \rightarrow C, B\,C \rightarrow D, B\,E \rightarrow C, C\,D \rightarrow B, C\,E \rightarrow A\,F, C\,F \rightarrow B\,D, C \rightarrow A, D \rightarrow E\,F\}$ contains the full arc (A B, C), as shown in Fig. 4-3.

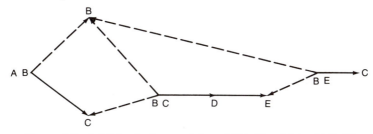

Figure 4-3   A full implication graph from A B to C containing (A B, C)

An implication graph constructed by rule (2i) alone has one possible minimal type, as shown in Fig. 4-4(a), if the final node j has two component nodes and one of them is equal to the initial node i. In addition, when both component nodes of j are not equal to i, there exist three possible minimal types of implication graphs as shown in Fig. 4-4 (ci), (cii), and (ciii). If each compound node except the initial node consists of two component nodes, then all other possible types of implication graphs from i to j are shown in Figs. 4-4(b) and 4-4 (di), (dii), and (diii). When these compound nodes consist of more than two component nodes, the generalization is straightforward and is omitted in this section.

Let a node in an implication graph be called *intermediate* if it is not the initial or final node of the implication graph. From Figs. 4-2 and 4-4, it is easy to see that if an implication graph from i to j exists, it must have at least one intermediate node k such that (k, j) is in E^f, or at least two intermediate nodes m_1 and m_2 such that (j, m_1) and (j, m_2) are in E^d. The initial node, i, must have at least one arc incident from it. More specifically, an implication graph constructed by rule (1) must have $|V_{ij}^*| \geq 3$ and $|E_{ij}^*| \geq 2$ where at least one element in E_{ij}^* is a full arc. Similarly, an implication graph constructed by rule (2) must have $|V_{ij}^*| \geq 3$ and $|E_{ij}^*| \geq 3$ where at least two elements in E_{ij}^* are dotted arcs. Hence, the arc (i, j) in E is excluded as an implication graph from i to j since an implication graph of this type is of no practical significance.

An implication graph from i to i is useless and is excluded from the definition. A dotted implication graph from i to any other node requires that all arcs incident from i in

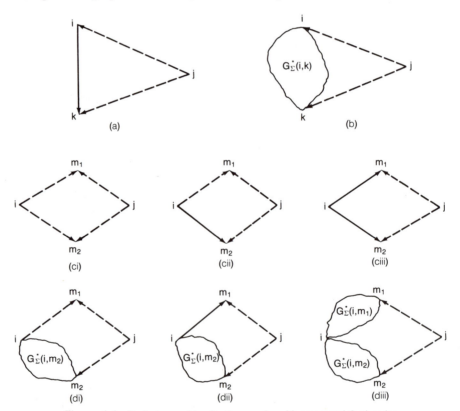

Figure 4-4   Basic types of implication graphs with compound final nodes

the graph are dotted. Thus, a dotted implication graph from a simple node to any other node does not exist. An implication graph from i to j that includes the arc (i, j) in E is also useless. However, it is still defined, for otherwise, the rules for constructing an implication graph must be modified and might become very complicated; and particularly, an algorithm for finding an implication graph from i to j without containing the arc (i, j) might be less efficient.

Theorem 4.2:   If arc (i, j) is in E or an implication graph from i to j exists in the FD-graph for a set Σ of FDs, then the FD $i \rightarrow j$ is in Σ^+ or, equivalently, j is in i^+.

Proof: If arc (i, j) is in E^f, then the FD $i \rightarrow j$ must be in Σ and is nontrivial by rule (3) of definition 4.14. On the other hand, if arc (i, j) is in E^d, then the FD $i \rightarrow j$ is in $\Sigma^+ - \Sigma$ and is trivial by rule (4) of definition 4.14. We need only to show that if an implication graph from i to j exists in the FD-graph for Σ, then there is a subset Σ_{ij} of Σ such that $\Sigma_{ij} \mid\!- i \rightarrow j$ where Σ_{ij} consists of each nontrivial FD of the form $X \rightarrow A$ corresponding to the full arc (X, A) in E_{ij}^*. We prove this theorem by a mathematical induction on the number of intermediate nodes in the implication graph.

Basis: If an implication graph from i to j has only one intermediate node k, then this graph must be one of the three possible types as shown in Figs. 4-2(a), 4-2(b), and 4-4(a). By Fig. 4.2(a), we have the minimal set

$$\Sigma_{ij} = \{i \rightarrow k, k \rightarrow j\} \mid\!- i \rightarrow j \tag{4.6a}$$

by the inference rule FD2 of transitivity. By Fig. 4-2(b), we have the minimal set

$$\Sigma_{ij} = \{k \rightarrow j\} \mid\!- i \rightarrow j \tag{4.6b}$$

by the inference rule FD1 of augmentation since $i = i'\ k$ and $i \rightarrow k$ is trivial. By Fig. 4-4(a), we have the minimal set

$$\Sigma_{ij} = \{i \rightarrow k\} \mid\!- i \rightarrow j \tag{4.6c}$$

by FD1 of augmentation since $j = i\ k$, and $j \rightarrow i$ and $j \rightarrow k$ are both trivial.

When j is a compound node, we can assume without loss of generality that j has two component nodes. If an implication graph from i to j has two intermediate nodes, then this graph must be one of the three possible types as shown in Fig. 4-4(ci), (cii), and (ciii). By Fig. 4.4(ci), we have the minimal set

$$\Sigma_{ij} = \varnothing \mid\!- i \rightarrow j \tag{4.6d}$$

by the inference rule FD0 of reflexivity since $j = m_1\ m_2 \subseteq i$ and the FDs $i \rightarrow m_1\ m_2$ and $j \rightarrow m_1\ m_2$ are trivial. By Fig. 4-4(cii), we have the minimal set

$$\Sigma_{ij} = \{i'\ m_1 \rightarrow m_2\} \mid\!- i'\ m_1 \rightarrow m_1\ m_2 \tag{4.6e}$$

by the inference rule FD1 of augmentation where $i = i'\ m_1$, $j = m_1\ m_2$, and the FDs $i \rightarrow m_1$ and $j \rightarrow m_1\ m_2$ are trivial. By Fig. 4-4(ciii), we have the minimal set

$$\Sigma_{ij} = \{i \rightarrow m_1, i \rightarrow m_2\} \mid\!- i \rightarrow j \tag{4.6f}$$

by the inference rule FD4 of union since $j = m_1\ m_2$ and the FD $j \rightarrow m_1\ m_2$ is trivial.

Hypothesis: Suppose that an implication graph from i to j properly contains at least one implication graph from i to some intermediate node x. Since x is an intermediate node in $G_\Sigma^*(i, j)$ but is the final node in $G_\Sigma^*(i, x)$, $G_\Sigma^*(i, x)$ must have fewer intermediate nodes than $G_\Sigma^*(i, j)$, so that we can assume that the set Σ_{ix} of FDs corresponding to the full arcs in $G_\Sigma^*(i, x)$ derives the FD $i \rightarrow x$. When x is compound, we assume without loss of generality that x has two component nodes. We want to show that when $G_\Sigma^*(i, j)$ is structured as any one of the five possible types as shown in Figs. 4-2, 4-4 (b), (di), (dii), and (diii), the FD $i \rightarrow j$ is derived. By Fig. 4-2(c), we have

$$\Sigma_{ij} = \Sigma_{ik} \cup \{k \rightarrow j\} \mid - \{i \rightarrow k, k \rightarrow j\} \mid - i \rightarrow j \qquad (4.6g)$$

by FD2 of transitivity since $\Sigma_{ik} \mid - i \rightarrow k$ in Σ^+ is assumed in the hypothesis. Similarly, by Fig. 4-4(b), we have

$$\Sigma_{ij} = \Sigma_{ik} \mid - \{i \rightarrow k\} \mid - i \rightarrow j \qquad (4.6h)$$

by FD1 of augmentation since $j = i\,k$, and $i \rightarrow k$ in Σ^+ is assumed in the hypothesis. By Fig. 4-4(di), we have

$$\Sigma_{ij} = \Sigma_{im_2} \mid - \{i \rightarrow m_2\} \mid - i \rightarrow j \qquad (4.6i)$$

by FD1 of augmentation since $j = m_1\,m_2$, $m_1 \in i$, and $i \rightarrow m_2$ in Σ^+ is assumed in the hypothesis. By Fig. 4-4(dii), we have

$$\Sigma_{ij} = \{i \rightarrow m_1\} \cup \Sigma_{im_2} \mid - \{i \rightarrow m_1, i \rightarrow m_2\} \mid - i \rightarrow j \qquad (4.6j)$$

by FD4 of union since $j = m_1,\, m_2$, and $i \rightarrow m_2$ in Σ^+ is assumed in the hypothesis. By Fig. 4-4(diii), we we have

$$\Sigma_{ij} = \Sigma_{im_1} \cup \Sigma_{im_2} \mid - \{i \rightarrow m_1, i \rightarrow m_2\} \mid - i \rightarrow j \qquad (4.6k)$$

by FD4 of union since $j = m_1\,m_2$, and both $i \rightarrow m_1$ and $i \rightarrow m_2$ are assumed in the hypothesis. Since all possible types of implication graphs have been examined, the proof is complete.

Note that each set Σ_{ij} in (4.6g) through (4.6k) is not necessarily nonredundant unless Σ_{ix} for x in $\{k, m_1, m_2\}$ is nonredundant. For example, if Σ_{ix} consists of the FD $i \rightarrow x$ corresponding to the full arc (i, x) in E, then every other FD in Σ_{ix} is redundant, since $\{i \rightarrow x\}$ alone derives the FD $i \rightarrow x$. Note also that each FD corresponding to a dotted arc in an implication graph is trivial and is not included in (4.6b) through (4.6f). Thus, no trivial FD is involved in theorem 4.2. Since the implication graph from i to j will be used to define an arc (i, j) in the closure of an FD-graph or the corresponding subset Σ_{ij} will be used to derive the FD $i \rightarrow j$ in Σ^+, we do not require that such a graph or subset be minimal and unique.

Corollary 4.1:   An implication graph from i to j does not exist if j is not in the subset closure i^+.

The converse of corollary 4.1 is not true, since the arc (i, j) of E is excluded as an implication graph from i to j although the FD $i \rightarrow j$ is in Σ and implies $j \in i^+$.

Example 4.13:

The FD-graph $G_{\Sigma_{g_1}}$ for $\Sigma_{g_1} = \{A\ B \to E, C\ D \to F, A \to C, B \to D, C \to A, D \to B, F \to A\ D\}$ is shown in Fig. 4-5(a). There are two implication graphs from C D to A B, as shown in Figs. 4-5(b) and 4-5(c), both containing six nodes and six arcs.

Figure 4-5(b) shows a dotted implication graph from C D to A B. The full arcs (C, A) and (D, B) derive the FD C D $\to$ A B, i.e.,

$$\{C \to A, D \to B\} \mid - C\ D \to A\ B.$$

Figure 4-5(c) shows a full implication graph with the same initial and final nodes C D and A B. The full arcs (C D, F), (F, A), (F, D), and (D, B) derive C D $\to$ A B, i.e.,

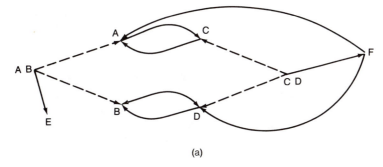

(a)

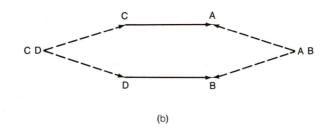

(b)

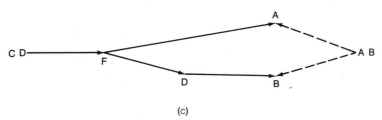

(c)

Figure 4-5   Nonunique implication graphs in (a)

$$\{C\ D \to F, F \to A, F \to D, D \to B\} \mid - C\ D \to A\ B.$$

Since a dotted implication graph from i to j derives a redundant FD i $\to$ j, it provides more useful information than a full implication graph from i to j. We say that the former graph supersedes the latter graph when both of them exist.

Note that a sequence of arcs connecting i to j in an implication graph from i to j is not necessarily a path from i to j consisting of full and dotted arcs oriented in the same direction. For example, each of the four sequences of arcs connecting the initial node C D to the final node A B in Figs 4-5(b) and 4-5(c) are not paths as defined in chapter 0.

Lemma 4.2: If an arc (i, j) is in E^f and a dotted implication graph from i to j exists, then the FD $i \rightarrow j$ corresponding to the full arc (i, j) is redundant or, equivalently, the arc (i, j) is redundant.

Proof: We can prove this lemma by a mathematical induction similar to the proof of theorem 4.2. The reader is encouraged to complete this proof as an exercise (do exercise 4.11).

Definition 4.16: The *closure* of an FD-graph $G_\Sigma = (V, E)$ is the graph $G_\Sigma^+ = (V, E^+)$ where the multiset E^+ composed of the set E^{d+} of dotted arcs and the multiset E^{f+} of full arcs is defined in the following:

Firstly, we define additional dotted arcs in $E^{d+} - E^d$ such that

$$E^{d+} = E^d \cup \{(i, j) \mid i, j \in V, (i, j) \notin E^d, \text{ and a dotted } G_\Sigma^*(i, j) \text{ exists}\}. \quad (4.7a)$$

Then we define additional full arcs in $E^{f+} - E^{d+}$ such that

$$E^{f+} = [(i, j) \mid (i, j) \in E^f; \text{ or } (i, j \in V, (i, j) \notin E^{d+},$$
$$\text{and a full } G_\Sigma^*(i, j) \text{ exists})] \quad (4.7b)$$

where the right side is a multiset as denoted by square brackets.

In (4.7a) if the dotted arc (i, j) is in E^d, we do not define a duplicated dotted arc even if a dotted implication graph from i to j exists, since a duplicate of a dotted arc is useless. However, the dotted arc (i, j) is defined by a dotted implication graph from i to j even if the arc (i, j) is in E^f, since the FD $i \rightarrow j$ derived by any dotted implication graph is redundant and can supersede the FD $i \rightarrow j$ defined by the full arc (i, j). In (4.7b), the duplicated full arc (i, j) is defined by a full implication graph from i to j if the arc (i, j) is not in E^{d+} (since the dotted arc (i, j) that defines the redundant FD $i \rightarrow j$ can supersede the full arc (i, j)). Since E^+ may have a full arc (i, j) in E^f, a duplicated full arc (i, j) in $E^{f+} - E^f$, and a dotted arc (i, j) in $E^{d+} - E^d$, E^+ and E^{f+} are multisets, and E^{f+} and E^{d+} are not disjoint in general. Thus, $\{E^{f+}, E^{d+}\}$ is not a partition on E^+. The closure of an FD-graph will be referred to as a *graph closure*.

Example 4:14:

Let $\Sigma_h = \{ B \rightarrow C, C \rightarrow D, A D \rightarrow B\}$. The full implication graph from A D to D is the path (A D, B), (B, C), (C, D) and does not define the full arc (A D, D), since the arc (A D, D) is in E^d. The reason behind this exclusion is that the dotted arc (A D, D) has already defined the trivial FD A D $\rightarrow$ D and the full arc (A D, D) defined by the full implication graph from A D to D is useless in application.

Corollary 4.2:   If arc (i, j) is in E^+, then the FD $i \to j$ is in Σ^+.

Proof: If arc (i, j) is in E^f, then the FD $i \to j$ must be in Σ, which defines the full arc (i, j) by rule (3) of definition 4.14. On the other hand, if (i, j) is in E^d, then $i \to j$ is in $\Sigma^+ - \Sigma$, which defines the dotted arc (i, j) by rule (4) of definition 4.14.

If arc (i, j) is in $E^+ - E$, then an implication graph from i to j exists by (4.7a) or (4.7b) which derives the FD $i \to j$ by theorem 4.2.

Given a set Σ of FDs on U, the set Σ_G of FDs defined by the arcs in the closure G_{Σ}^+ is only a proper subset of the FD-closure Σ^+, since Σ_G contains only those FDs whose left subsets are the left subsets of the FDs in Σ, whereas Σ^+ contains additional FDs whose left subsets are supersets of the left subsets of the FDs in Σ. For example, given $\Sigma_{a1} = \{A \to B, B \to C\}$, $\Sigma_G = \{A \to B \; C, B \to C\}$ is properly contained in Σ_{a1}^+ as shown in example 4.1. This means that the converse of corollary 4.2 is not true. This is one of the reasons why the graphical approach is very valuable in the design of a better database scheme.

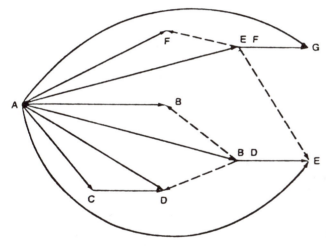

Figure 4-6   The closure $G_{\Sigma_{b1}}^+$

Example 4.15:

The closure of the FD-graph of Fig. 4-1 is shown in Fig. 4-6. There are five additional full arcs (A, E F), (A, G), (A, D), (A, B D), and (A, E) in E_{b1}^{f+} (what are their corresponding implication graphs). There exist no implication graphs from E F to any node. An implication graph from E F to A, B, C, D, or B D does not exist since $(E F)^+ = E F G$. An implication graph from E F to E, F, or G does not exist since a single arc cannot be an implication graph, although $(E F)^+$ coantains E, F, and G.

Based on definition 4.16 and the inference rules of reflexivity, union, and transitivity, an efficient algorithm to find the closure of an FD-graph can be designed without constructing each individual implication graph. Such an algorithm is available in

[Aus83] and its corrected version is in [Yan85]. The algorithm has time complexity $O(|\text{MATTR}(\Sigma)| \times |\Sigma|)$. If an FD-graph has no compound nodes, then this algorithm is an algorithm for finding the transitive closure of a directed graph.

So far we have used implication graphs to define arcs in a graph closure. By means of impliation graphs, we can detect redundant or superfluous nodes. We first define a redundant node and develop a method to detect it.

Definition 4.17:   A compound node i in an FD-graph is *redundant* if each full arc (i, j) in E is redundant (in the sense of definition 4.5).

Theorem 4.3:   A compound node i in an FD-graph is redundant if, for each full arc (i, j) in E, a dotted implication graph from i to j exists.

Proof: If a dotted implication graph from i to j exists, then the implication graph does not include the full arc (i, j) and derives the redundant FD i → j as proved in lemma 4.2. When all full arcs incident from node i are redundant as determined by their corresponding dotted implication graphs, deletion of node i does not alter the corresponding FD-closure. Thus, node i is redundant.

Example 4.16:

Let Σ_{i1} = {A B C → F G, A B → D G, D E → F, C → E}. The compound node A B C is redundant since for both full arcs (A B C, F) and (A B C, G) in $G_{\Sigma_{i1}}$ (do exercise 4.16) there are corresponding dotted implication graphs from A B C to F and from A B C to G. These dotted implication graphs imply that {A B → D, C → E, D E → F} |− A B C → F and {A B → G} |− A B C → G. When the given FDs A B → D, C → E, D E → F, and A B → G are all retained, the redundant FDs A B C → F and A B C → G derived by these retained FDs can be deleted without altering the corresponding FD-closure. In other words, all attributes appearing in A B C → F G are extraneous so that their associated node A B C and full arcs (A B C, F) and (A B C, G) can be deleted. Note that a simple node is not defined to be redundant so that F and G cannot be deleted.

Note that since a dotted implication graph defines a dotted arc, we can check arcs in E^+ incident from a compound node i to determine whether i is redundant or not. If there is a one-to-one function between the set of full arcs incident from i in E^f and the set of dotted arcs incident from i in E^{d+}, then i is redundant. In example 4.16, for the given full arcs (A B C, F) and (A B C, G) in E^f, there are dotted arcs (A B C, F) and (A B C, G) in E^{d+} so that A B C is redundant. Note also that some FD-graphs may have more than one node satisfying theorem 4.3, but these nodes cannot all be considered as redundant since after the deletion of some of them, the remaining ones may no longer satisfy theorem 4.3. For example, in the FD-graph (do exercise 4.18) for Σ = {A → B C, B C → A, A D → E F, B C D → E F}, both A D and B C D satisfy theorem 4.3. When one of them is considered to be redundant and is deleted, the other one no longer satisfies theorem 4.3 and is not redundant. We should delete B C D rather than A D for otherwise the number of attributes is not minimized.

Definition 4.18:   An FD-graph G_{Σ} is *nonredundant* if it consists of no redundant nodes and is *redundant* otherwise.

A nonredundant FD-graph has no redundant nodes, but it may contain superfluous nodes (definition 4.22) and/or redundant arcs (definition 4.25). Thus, its corresponding Σ may contain redundant FDs and is not nonredundant in the sense of definition 4.5. In other words, definitions 4.5 and 4.18 define different redundancies.

Example 4.17:

The FD-graph $G_{\Sigma_{i1}}$ (do exercise 4.16) is redundant since the node A B C is redundant, whereas the FD-graph $G_{\Sigma_{i2}}$ (a subgraph of $G_{\Sigma_{i1}}$) is nonredundant where $\Sigma_{i_2} = \{A\,B \rightarrow D\,G,$ $D\,E \rightarrow F, C \rightarrow E\}$, which is a proper subset of $\Sigma_{i1} = \{A\,B\,C \rightarrow F\,G, A\,B \rightarrow D\,G, D\,E \rightarrow F,$ $C \rightarrow E\}$.

Similar to definition 4.10, which defines an FD-covering, we refer to an FD-graph being a covering for an FD-graph as a *graph covering*. To define a compound node as being superfluous, we need the concepts of graph coverings and node equivalence in addition to implication graphs. Furthermore, for definition of two nodes being equivalent such that the corresponding relation on a set of nodes is an equivalence relation, we need to add all self-loops to an FD-graph and a graph closure. We call these graphs, *reflexive*.

Definition 4.19:   Given two FD-graphs G_{Σ_1} and G_{Σ_2}, we say that G_{Σ_1} is a *covering* for G_{Σ_2} if $\Sigma_1 \equiv \Sigma_2$.

Similar to FD-covering, graph covering is also a binary equivalence relation since it has the properties of reflexivity, symmetry, and transitivity. Thus, when an FD-graph is a covering for another FD-graph, both of these FD-graphs are equivalent.

Example 4.18:

Let two nonredundant sets of FDs be $\Sigma_{g1} = \{A\,B \rightarrow E, A \rightarrow C, C \rightarrow A, B \rightarrow D, D \rightarrow B, C\,D$ $\rightarrow F, F \rightarrow A\,D\}$ and $\Sigma_{g2} = \{A\,B \rightarrow E\,F, A \rightarrow C, C \rightarrow A, B \rightarrow D, D \rightarrow B, F \rightarrow A\,D\}$. Their corresponding FD-graphs, $G_{\Sigma_{g1}}$ (Fig. 4-5(a)) and $G_{\Sigma_{g2}}$ (similar to Fig. 4-5(a)), are equivalent, since $\Sigma_{g1} \equiv \Sigma_{g2}$. This example shows that two equivalent FD-graphs do not have the same set of nodes. Although both graph coverings $G_{\Sigma_{g1}}$ and $G_{\Sigma_{g2}}$ do not have any redundant node, $G_{\Sigma_{g1}}$ has a superfluous node (which will be defined).

Definition 4.20a: Two subsets, i and j, of U are said to be *equivalent*, written as i $\equiv$ j, if the FDs i $\rightarrow$ j and j $\rightarrow$ i are both in Σ^+. When i $\equiv$ j, i $\rightarrow$ k and j $\rightarrow$ k in Σ^+ are *equivalent*.

Theorem 4.4:   Let X and Y be two subsets of U. If $X^+ = Y^+$ then $X \equiv Y$.

Proof: If $X^+ = Y^+$, then $X \rightarrow X^+$ and $Y \rightarrow Y^+$ in Σ^+ become, respectively, $X \rightarrow Y^+$ and $Y \rightarrow X^+$ by substitution. Since $X \subseteq X^+$ and $Y \subseteq Y^+$, $X \rightarrow Y$ and $Y \rightarrow X$ derived, respectively, from $X \rightarrow Y^+$ and $Y \rightarrow X^+$ by FD5 of projectivity are both in Σ^+. Thus, $X \equiv Y$ is established by definition 4.20a.

Example 4.19:

In $G_{\Sigma_{g1}}$ and $G_{\Sigma_{g2}}$ for $\Sigma_{g1} = \{A\,B \rightarrow E, C\,D \rightarrow F, A \rightarrow C, B \rightarrow D, C \rightarrow A, D \rightarrow B, F \rightarrow A\,D\}$ and $\Sigma_{g2} = \{A\,B \rightarrow E\,F, A \rightarrow C, B \rightarrow D, C \rightarrow A, D \rightarrow B, F \rightarrow A\,D\}$, $A \rightarrow C$ and $C \rightarrow A$ corresponding to (A, C) and (C, A) imply $A \equiv C$. Similarly, $B \rightarrow D$ and $D \rightarrow B$ corresponding to (B, D) and (D, B) imply $B \equiv D$. $G_{\Sigma_{g1}}$ (Fig. 4-5(a)) has A B $\equiv$ C D $\equiv$ F and $G_{\Sigma_{g2}}$ (similar to Fig. 4-5(a)) has A B $\equiv$ F, which can be seen from their subset closures $((A\ B)^+ = (C\ D)^+ = F^+ = A\ B\ C\ D\ E\ F)$ satisfying theorem 4.4.

When X and Y are left subsets of some FDs in Σ and after all self-loops are augmented to G_Σ, we can define node equivalence.

Definition 4.20b: Two nodes, i and j, in a reflexive graph covering or closure are said to be *equivalent,* written as $i \equiv j$, if both arcs (i, j) and (j, i) are in E^+.

Corollary 4.3:   The subset equivalence and the node equivalence in a reflexive graph covering or closure are equivalent.

Proof: We need only to show that

$$\{j \mid X \rightarrow j \in \Sigma^+\} \text{ iff } \{j \mid (X, j) \in E^+\}$$

for each X where X is a subset of U as well as a node in V, and the closure X^+ is alternatively represented by a set of some subsets of U rather than the union of these subsets. By the reflexive property $(X \equiv X)$, $X \rightarrow X$ is in Σ^+ and (X, X) is in E^{d+}. By the symmetric property $(X \equiv Y => Y \equiv X)$, $X \rightarrow Y$ and $Y \rightarrow X$ are both in Σ^+ and (X, Y) and (Y, X) are both in E^+. By the transitive property $(X \equiv Y$ and $Y \equiv Z => X \equiv Z)$, $X \rightarrow Y$, $Y \rightarrow Z$, and $X \rightarrow Z$ are all in Σ^+, and (X, Y), (Y, Z), and (X, Z) are all in E^+.

The subset equivalence having the properties of reflexivity, symmetry, and transitivity is a binary equivalence relation on a set of some subsets of U. By corollary 4.3, the node equivalence is also a binary equivalence relation on the set V of nodes in a reflexive graph covering or closure. Note that if all self-loops are not added to a graph covering or closure, then this graph is not reflexive, and the relation defined on V of a nonreflexive graph covering or closure has only the properties of symmetry and transitivity and is mathematically not an equivalence relation on V. Thus, to achieve a mathematical rigor, we should use a reflexive graph covering or closure to define the node equivalence relation. Besides this purpose, an FD-graph or its closure being reflexive is not an important issue since a self-loop defines only a trivial FD and can be ignored. From now on, when the existence of self-loops is understood and kept in mind, we do not need actually to add any self-loop to such a graph to complicate the graphical representation.

Example 4.20:

When $\Sigma_{c1} = \{A\ B \rightarrow E, A\ C \rightarrow F, A\ D \rightarrow B, B \rightarrow C, C \rightarrow D\}$, the nodes A B, A C, and A D are equivalent by theorem 4.4 since $(A\ B)^+ = (A\ C)^+ = (A\ D)^+ = A\ B\ C\ D\ E\ F$. The subsets A B, A C, and A D are the keys and form an equivalence class. Obviously, $\{A\ B \rightarrow U_c, A\ C \rightarrow U_c, A\ D \rightarrow U_c\} \mid- \{A\ B \rightarrow A\ C, A\ B \rightarrow A\ D, A\ C \rightarrow A\ B, A\ C \rightarrow A\ D, A\ D \rightarrow A\ B, A\ D \rightarrow A\ C\}$ by FD5 of projectivity where $U_c = A\ B\ C\ D\ E\ F$. Let the sets on both sides of $\mid-$ be Σ_1 and Σ_2, respectively. The set Σ_1 of all key dependencies derives the set Σ_2 of FDs. However, a single key dependency in Σ_1 does not derive Σ_2. On the other hand, Σ_2 does not define Σ_1 or even a single key dependency in Σ_1. This example also demonstrates that a Hamiltonian cycle exists in Σ_2 corresponding to a node equivalence class. In this example, $\{A\ B \rightarrow A\ C, AC \rightarrow A\ D, A\ D \rightarrow A\ B\}$ is one of the Hamiltonian cycles (what are others).

Definition 4.21:   Given an FD-graph G_Σ, an *equivalence class of nodes* in G_Σ is a maximal set of mutually equivalent nodes as determined by the node equivalence relation on V of nodes.

Example 4.21:

In $G_{\Sigma_{g1}}$ (Fig. 4-5(a)) for $\Sigma_{g1} = \{A\,B \to E, C\,D \to F, A \to C, B \to D, C \to A, D \to B, F \to A\,D\}$, there are five equivalence classes of nodes: $\{A\,B, C\,D, F \mid A\,B \equiv C\,D \equiv F\}$, $\{A, C \mid A \equiv C\}$, $\{B, D \mid B \equiv D\}$, $\{E \mid E \equiv E\}$.

Theorem 4.5:   If $X \equiv Y$, then $X\,Z \equiv Y\,Z$.

Proof: We show that

$$X \to Y \text{ and } Y \to X \Rightarrow X \equiv Y \Rightarrow X\,Z \equiv Y\,Z$$

is equivalent to

$$X \to Y \text{ and } Y \to X \Rightarrow X\,Z \to Y\,Z \text{ and } Y\,Z \to X\,Z \Rightarrow X\,Z \equiv Y\,Z.$$

Since "$X \to Y$ and $Y \to X \Rightarrow X \equiv Y$" and "$X\,Z \to Y\,Z$ and $Y\,Z \to X\,Z \Rightarrow X\,Z \equiv Y\,Z$" are true by definition 4.20a, we want only to prove that

$$\{X \to Y, Y \to X\} \vdash \{X\,Z \to Y\,Z, Y\,Z \to X\,Z\},$$

which is valid by individually applying FD1 of augmentation to $\{X \to Y\} \vdash \{X\,Z \to Y\,Z\}$ and $\{Y \to X\} \vdash \{Y\,Z \to X\,Z\}$.

Corollary 4.4:   When $X \equiv Y$ with $|X| \geq |Y|$, and $X\,Z$ and $Y\,Z$ are also nodes in an FD-graph, the replacement of the FD $X\,Z \to V$ in Σ^+ by the FD $Y\,Z \to V$ does not alter the FD-closure Σ^+.

Proof: By theorem 4.5, $X \equiv Y$ implies $X\,Z \equiv Y\,Z$. This is equivalent to saying that $X^+ = Y^+$ implies $(X\,Z)^+ = (Y\,Z)^+$. Hence, $V \subseteq (X\,Z)^+$ iff $V \subseteq (Y\,Z)^+$ and the replacement of $X\,Z \to V$ by $Y\,Z \to V$ does not alter the FD-closure.

By this Corollary, when $|X| > |Y|$, the replacement of $X\,Z \to V$ by $Y\,Z \to V$ can reduce the number of attributes. This is a necessary step to achieve an optimal FD-covering.

Example 4.22:

Let $\Sigma_{j1} = \{A \to B\,C, B\,C \to A, A\,D \to E, B\,C\,D \to F\}$ with $|\Sigma_{j1}| = 4$ and $\{MATTR(\Sigma_{j1})| = 13$. Based on the node equivalence $A \equiv B\,C$ and $A\,D \equiv B\,C\,D$, two coverings for Σ_{j1} are

$$\Sigma_{j2} = \{A \to B\,C, B\,C \to A, B\,C\,D \to E\,F\}$$

as obtained by replacing $A\,D \to E$ by $B\,C\,D \to E$ and

$$\Sigma_{j3} = \{A \to B\,C, B\,C \to A, A\,D \to E\,F\}$$

as obtained by replacing $B\,C\,D \to F$ by $A\,D \to F$. Since $|MATTR(\Sigma_{j2})| = 11$ and $|MATTR(\Sigma_{j3})| = 10$, Σ_{j3} is superior in the design of a database scheme.

Definition 4.22:   A compound node i of an FD-graph $G_\Sigma = (V, E)$ is *superfluous* if $i \equiv j$ for some j in V and the replacement of each existing full arc (i, k) in E by the full arc (j, k) does not alter the graph closure.

Theorem 4.6:   A compound node i of an FD-graph $G_\Sigma = (V, E)$ is superfluous if i $\equiv$ j for some j in V, and either the arc (i, j) is in E^d or a dotted implication graph from i to j exists.

Proof: If i is equivalent to j, then the arcs (i, j) and (j, i) must be in E^+ or equivalently the FD $j \to i$ and $i \to j$ must be in Σ^+.

We first consider the FD $i \to j$. This FD corresponds to either the arc (i, j) in E or is derived by an implication graph from i to j. There are two possible cases to be examined.

(1) If (i, j) is in E^d, then deletion of this dotted arc does not alter the FD-closure Σ^+ whenever i is deleted, since the FD $i \to j$ is trivial.

(2) If (i, j) is in E^f and there exists a dotted implication graph from i to j, then (i, j) is redundant by lemma 4.2 and deletion of this full arc does not alter Σ^+ whenever i is deleted. In addition, this dotted implication graph does not contain any full arc incident from i. Whenever i is deleted, all full arcs contained in this implication graph are still in the FD-graph since the component nodes of i are not deleted.

We consider the FD $j \to i$. There is only one possible case in which node i is compound. Since i is compound, it is impossible to have any full arc incident to i (including (j, i)). Because FD $j \to i$ exists in Σ^+ and any full arc incident to i is not in E, an implication graph from j to i exists, and this implication graph does not contain any full arc incident to i. When i is deleted, its component nodes are still in the FD-graph so that the full arcs contained in this implication graph are not affected.

It remains to show the necessary arc adjustment. By means of the logical implication $\{j \to i, i \to x\} \mid - j \to x$ where $j \to i$ is derived by an implication graph from j to i, whenever i is deleted, (i, x) is also deleted, and consequently, $j \to x$ is no longer derived if $i \to x$ is not trivial. Hence, if (i, x) is full, then $i \to x$ is not trivial, and we need arc adjustment to maintain Σ^+ unchanged.

To perform a necessary arc adjustment, we consider the following cases.

(1) When the full arc (j, x) is in E, no arc adjustment is required.

(2) When the full arc (j, x) is not in E and after node i is deleted, if there exists an implication graph from j to x, then no arc adjustment is required.

(3) When the full arc (j, x) is not in E and after node i is deleted, if there exists no implication graph from j to x, then the new full arc (j, x) must be added.

When node i is superfluous, it can be shown by contradiction that the dotted arc (j, x) cannot be in E.

Example 4.23:

In $G_{\Sigma_{g1}}$ of Fig. 4-5(a) for $\Sigma_{g1} = \{A\,B \to E, C\,D \to F, A \to C, B \to D, C \to A, D \to B, F \to$

A D}, either A B or C D is superfluous. Node A B is superfluous, since A B ≡ C D ≡ F and the dotted implication graphs from A B to C D and from A B to F exist. We can delete A B and replace (A B, E) by (C D, E) or by (F, E). Similarly, C D is superfluous, since C D ≡ A B and the dotted implication graph from C D to A B exists. We can delete C D and replace (C D, F) by (A B, F). After one superfluous node is removed, the other one is no longer superfluous. Although F is also equivalent to A B and C D, F is not superfluous, since F is simple so that a dotted implication graph from F to any node does not exist.

Example 4.24:

In Σ_{c1} = {A B → E, A C → F, A D → B, B → C, C → D} of example 4.20, A B and A C are superfluous, but A D is not superfluous. Node A B is superfluous, since A B ≡ A D and there exists a dotted implication graph from A B to A D. When A B is deleted, the full arcs (B, C) and (C. D) in the implication graph from A B to A D are not affected, and only the full arc (A B, E) is deleted. Thus, the new full arc (A D, E) must be added. Similarly, A C is superfluous, since A C ≡ A D and a dotted implication graph from A C to A D exists. However, A D is not superfluous, since the implication graph from A D to A B or from A D to A C is full and includes the full arc (A D, B). When A D is deleted, the full arc (A D, B) is also deleted. Then the full arc (A D, A B) or (A D, A C) that can be defined by the full implication graph from A D to A B or from A D to A C is no longer defined because the node A D is deleted. In addition, even if we use the new arc (A B, B) or (A C, B) to replace (A D, B), Σ^+ is still changed because of the deletion of (A D, B) that is included in both implication graphs from A D to A B and from A D to A C.

Example 4.25:

The compound node A C in the FD-graph $G_{\Sigma_{e1}}$ (do exercise 4.16) for Σ_{e1} = {A B → D E F, A C → G, A → C} is superfluous by theorem 4.6, since A C ≡ A and the arc (A C, A) is dotted. Thus, we have an LR-minimal covering Σ_{e2} = {A B → D E F, A → C G}. Note that the implication graph from A to A C is full and is of the type as shown in Fig. 4-4(a).

Example 4.26:

For Σ_{j1} = {A → B C, B C → A, A D → E, B C D → F}, either A D or B C D is superfluous. As discussed in the remark following corollary 4.4 and as illustrated in example 4.22, we should delete B C D to obtain a better FD-covering. If we delete A D, then the resulting FD-covering is worse because of having more attributes.

Definition 4.23:   An FD-graph G_Σ is *minimal* if there exist no coverings for G_Σ having fewer nodes. An FD-graph G_Σ is *LR-minimal* if it is minimal and has the minimum number of full arcs.

A graph covering has the minimum number of nodes iff its corresponding FD-closure has the minimum number of FDs.

Lemma 4.3 [Aus83]:   An FD-graph G_Σ = (V, E) is minimal iff Σ consists of the minimum number of FDs.

Proof: Given an FD-graph G_Σ = (V, E), the number of nodes is equal to $|V_{sk}| + |\Sigma|$ where V_{sk} is the set of sink nodes (i.e., simple nodes without outgoing arcs). Since all coverings for G_Σ have the same set V_{sk}, the number of nodes depends only on $|\Sigma|$; hence, G_Σ is minimal iff $|\Sigma|$ is minimal.

Example 4.27:

The FD-graphs $G_{\Sigma_{b2}}$ (do exercise 4.16) for $\Sigma_{b2} = \{A \rightarrow B\ C\ F, C \rightarrow D, B\ D \rightarrow E, B\ D\ F \rightarrow G\}$ and the FD-graph $G_{\Sigma_{b1}}$ of Fig. 4-7 for $\Sigma_{b1} = \{A \rightarrow B\ C\ F, C \rightarrow D, B\ D \rightarrow E, E\ F \rightarrow G\}$ that is not equivalent to Σ_{b2} (since $(E\ F)^+$ is E F G or E F with respect to Σ_{b1} or Σ_{b2} respectively) are both minimal as well as LR-minimal.

Theorem 4.7[Aus83]: An FD-graph $G_\Sigma = (V, E)$ is minimal iff it has no superfluous nodes.

The reader is encouraged to provide a proof as an exercise. Although a minimal FD-graph does not have any redundant or superfluous node, it may have redundant full arcs. It remains to define an arc being redundant.

Definition 4.24: Given a set Σ of FDs, the FD-graph G_Σ is *optimal* if Σ is optimal (in the sense of definition 4.13).

An LR-minimal graph covering may not have the minimum number of attributes. In order to determine an optimal covering for an FD-graph G_Σ, we have to eliminate all redundant arcs from a minimal covering for G_Σ. However, eliminating all redundant arcs from a minimal covering is not sufficient to obtain an optimal covering. For example, the FD-graphs (do exercise 4.16) for Σ_{j2} and Σ_{j3}, as shown in example 4.22, are both LR-minimal, but they have different numbers of attributes.

Definition 4.25: A full arc (i, j) is *redundant* if either a dotted implication graph from i to j exists or a full implication graph from i to j that does not include the arc (i, j) exists.

We do not define a dotted arc being redundant, since dotted arcs are useful in constructing implication graphs and in finding graph closures and cannot, therefore, be deleted from an FD-graph. However, an FD corresponding to a dotted arc in E is trivial, and an FD derived by a dotted implication graph is redundant by lemma 4.2 so that they are not included in any minimal FD-covering.

Example 4.28:

Given the FD-graph (do exercise 4.16) for the set Σ_{d4} of FDs, i.e.,

$\Sigma_{d4} = \{A\ B \rightarrow C, B\ C \rightarrow D, B\ E \rightarrow C, C\ E \rightarrow A\ F, C\ F \rightarrow B, C \rightarrow A, D \rightarrow E\ F\}$,

the arc (C E, A) is redundant since definition 4.25 is satisfied, i.e., a dotted implication graph from C E to A that is the path (C E, C), (C, A) exists. Since $\{C \rightarrow A\} \mid - C\ E \rightarrow A$, when the FD $C \rightarrow A$ is retained, the FD $C\ E \rightarrow A$ is redundant so that the corresponding arc (C E, A) is also redundant and can be deleted. Since Σ_{d4} has the redundant FD $C\ E \rightarrow A$ $G_{\Sigma_{d4}}$ is not LR-minimal.

Example 4.29:

The FD-graph for $\Sigma_{j3} = \{A \rightarrow B\ C, B\ C \rightarrow A, A\ D \rightarrow E\ F\}$ is at least LR-minimal. However, the FD-graph for $\Sigma_{j2} = \{A \rightarrow B\ C, B\ C \rightarrow A, B\ C\ D \rightarrow E\ F\}$ is worse since it contains more attributes, although it is also LR-minimal. Recall that the optimal FD-covering problem is NP-complete and is extremely difficult.

EXERCISES

4.1 Let X, G, and H be formulas as defined in (4.1).

    (a) Show that $X + \bar{X} = \mathbf{T}$ and $X \cdot \bar{X} = \mathbf{F}$.

    (b) Show that all equivalences (0.5) through (0.13) are applicable to a formula involving FD logical equivalences.

4.2 Show that FD4 (i.e., $\{X \rightarrow Y, X \rightarrow Z\} \mid\!- X \rightarrow Y Z$) is valid by using its logical equivalence.

4.3 Show that FD5 (i.e., $\{X \rightarrow Y Z\} \mid\!- \{X \rightarrow Y, X \rightarrow Z\}$) is valid by using its logical equivalence.

4.4 Show that $\{X \rightarrow Y Z, Z \rightarrow C W\} \mid\!- X \rightarrow C W Y Z$.

4.5 Let X^+ be the closure of subset X of attributes. Show that the FD $X \rightarrow X^+$ is in Σ^+.

4.6 Show that

    (a) $\{X \rightarrow Y\} \mid\!- W X \rightarrow Y$ and

    (b) $\{W X \rightarrow Y\} \mid\!\not- X \rightarrow Y$.

4.7 Prove that

    (a) a key K_1 and a superkey $X K_2$ where K_2 is a key for a relation r(U) are equivalent, and

    (b) two candidate keys for a relation r(U) are equivalent.

4.8 Show that

    (a) $\{\emptyset \rightarrow W, W X' \rightarrow W Y'\} \mid\!- X' \rightarrow Y'$, and

    (b) $\{\emptyset \rightarrow Y', W X' \rightarrow W Y'\} \mid\!- X' \rightarrow Y'$.

4.9 Let R = (A B C D, {A $\rightarrow$ B, B $\rightarrow$ C}). Find the key and all superkeys for a relation r(R).

4.10 Show that the FDs A C $\rightarrow$ F in $\Sigma_{c5} = \{A B \rightarrow E, A C \rightarrow F, A D \rightarrow B F, B \rightarrow C, C \rightarrow D\}$ is redundant and $\Sigma_{c5} \equiv \Sigma_{c3}$ where $\Sigma_{c3} = \Sigma_{c5} - \{A C \rightarrow F\}$.

4.11 Complete the proof of lemma 4.2.

4.12 Prove theorem 4.5 and disprove its converse.

    (a) Prove theorem 4.5 by the logical equivalence of $\{X \rightarrow Y, Y \rightarrow X\} \mid\!- \{X Z \rightarrow Y Z, Y Z \rightarrow X Z\}$.

    (b) Disprove the converse of theorem 4.5, i.e., $\{X Z \rightarrow Y Z, Y Z \rightarrow X Z\} \mid\!- \{X \rightarrow Y, Y \rightarrow X\}$.

4.13 Referring to Fig. 4-1,

    (a) find all implication graphs, and

    (b) show that there does not exist an implication graph from a sink node (such as B, D, E, F, or G) to any other node.

4.14 For $\Sigma_{g1} = \{A B \rightarrow E, C D \rightarrow F, A \rightarrow C, B \rightarrow D, C \rightarrow A, D \rightarrow B, F \rightarrow A D\}$,

    (a) find the closure $G^+_{\Sigma_{g1}}$;

    (b) prove the following logical implications:

(i) $\{C \rightarrow A, D \rightarrow B\} \models C\,D \rightarrow A\,B$,

(ii) $\{C\,D \rightarrow F, F \rightarrow A\,D, D \rightarrow B\} \models C\,D \rightarrow A\,B$; and

(c) show that $\Sigma_{g3} = \{A \rightarrow C, B \rightarrow D, C \rightarrow A, D \rightarrow B, F \rightarrow A\,D, C\,D \rightarrow E\,F\}$ is equivalent to Σ_{g1}.

4.15 Find the equivalence classes of nodes in $G_{\Sigma_{g2}}$ for $\Sigma_{g2} = \{A\,B \rightarrow E\,F, A \rightarrow C, B \rightarrow D, C \rightarrow A, D \rightarrow B, F \rightarrow A\,D\}$.

4.16 Find the FD-graphs for

(a) $\Sigma_{b2} = \{A \rightarrow B\,C\,F, C \rightarrow D, B\,D \rightarrow E, B\,D\,F \rightarrow G\}$,

(b) $\Sigma_{d4} = \{A\,B \rightarrow C, B\,C \rightarrow D, B\,E \rightarrow C, C\,E \rightarrow A\,F, C\,F \rightarrow B, C \rightarrow A, D \rightarrow E\,F\}$,

(c) $\Sigma_{e1} = \{A\,B \rightarrow D\,E\,F, A\,C \rightarrow G, A \rightarrow C\}$,

(d) $\Sigma_{i1} = \{A\,B\,C \rightarrow F\,G, A\,B \rightarrow D\,G, D\,E \rightarrow F, C \rightarrow E\}$,

(e) $\Sigma_{j2} = \{A \rightarrow B\,C, B\,C \rightarrow A, B\,C\,D \rightarrow E\,F\}$, and

(f) $\Sigma_{j3} = \{A \rightarrow B\,C, B\,C \rightarrow A, A\,D \rightarrow E\,F\}$.

4.17 Let $\Sigma_{d1} = \{A\,B \rightarrow C, B\,C \rightarrow D, B\,E \rightarrow C, C\,D \rightarrow B, C\,E \rightarrow A\,F, C\,F \rightarrow B\,D, C \rightarrow A, D \rightarrow E\,F\}$. Find the FD-graph, and determine

(a) the equivalence classes of nodes,

(b) the compound node C D being redundant (definition 4.17),

(c) the compound node C F not being superfluous (definition 4.22),

(f) the full arc (C E, A) being redundant (definition 4.25), and

(e) the implication graph from A B to C including the arc (A B, C).

4.18 Let $\Sigma = \{A \rightarrow B\,C, B\,C \rightarrow A, A\,D \rightarrow E\,F, B\,C\,D \rightarrow E\,F\}$. Find the FD-graph, and show that

(a) A D and B C D are the candidates for redundant nodes,

(b) either A D or B C D (but not both) can be deleted, and

(c) B C D should be deleted.

4.19 Let V, W, and Z be subsets of U and A and B be attributes in U. Let $X = V\,Z$ and $Y = W\,Z$.

(a) Prove that $\{V \rightarrow W, W \rightarrow V, X \rightarrow A\} \models Y \rightarrow A$.

(b) Disprove that $\{V \rightarrow W, W \rightarrow V, X \rightarrow A\} \models Y \rightarrow B$.

4.20 Given a set Σ of FDs on U and a subset X of U, design an algorithm for finding the subset closure of X based on definition 4.6. By means of this algorithm, solve the FD membership problem, i.e., the problem of deciding whether $\Sigma \models Y \rightarrow Z$. Design an algorithm for solving this membership problem based on the fact that $\Sigma \models Y \rightarrow Z$ iff Z is in Y^+. What are the complexities of these algorithms?

chapter 5

MULTIVALUED DEPENDENCIES

5.1 INTRODUCTION

Multivalued dependencies were independently introduced by Fagin [Fag77c], Zaniolo [Zan76], and Delobel [Del78]. This class of data dependencies is a generalization of the class of functional dependencies, since multivalued dependencies provide (many-to-many) relations, whereas functional dependencies provide only (many-to-one) functions.

This chapter covers multivalued dependencies, logical equivalence, inference rules, dependency basis, embedded multivalued dependencies, and conflict-free virtual keys. By means of the propositional logic and the Venn diagram, simpler proofs of most theorems can be achieved; and many notions involving multivalued and functional dependencies are easier to understand.

5.2 MULTIVALUED DEPENDENCIES

We define a multivalued dependency on a set U of attributes as follows.

Definition 5.1: A *multivalued dependency* (abbreviated as MVD) is a constraint on the set U of attributes and is of the form $X \rightarrow \rightarrow Y$ where X and Y are subsets of U. Relation r(U) *satisfies* MVD $X \rightarrow \rightarrow Y$, or $X \rightarrow \rightarrow Y$ *holds* in r(U) if for every pair of tuples in r(U), say μ_1 and μ_2, $\mu_1(X\ Y\ Z) = x\ y_1\ z_1$ and $\mu_2(X\ Y\ Z) = x\ y_2\ z_2$, there is a tuple μ_3 in r(U) such that $\mu_3(X\ Y\ Z) = x\ y_1\ z_2$ where $Z = U - X\ Y$, $x = \mu_1[X] = \mu_2[X] = \mu_3[X]$, $y_1 = \mu_1[Y] = \mu_3[Y]$, $y_2 = \mu_2[Y]$, $z_1 = \mu_1[Z]$, and $z_2 = \mu_2[Z] = \mu_3[Z]$. When

X → → Y holds in r(U), we say that X *multivalued determines* Y or Y is *multivalued dependent* on X in r(U).

In this definition, $\mu_1[X]$ is the X-value of the tuple μ_1, and X Y is the shorthand of the union of X and Y. By the symmetric property of this definition, if two tuples $\mu_1(X\ Y\ Z) = x\ y_1\ z_1$ and $\mu_2(X\ Y\ Z) = x\ y_2\ z_2$ exist, then not only the tuple $\mu_3(X\ Y\ Z) = x\ y_1\ z_2$ exists, but also the tuple $\mu_4(X\ Y\ Z) = x\ y_2\ z_1$ exists. As a direct consequence of this definition, we have the following theorem.

Theorem 5.1: An MVD X → → Y holds in a relation r(U) iff X → → U − X Y holds in r(U).

Proof: Let Z = U − X Y. As already stated in the remark following definition 5.1, if relation r(U) satisfies MVD X → → Y, then whenever $\mu_1(X\ Y\ Z) = x\ y_1\ z_1$ and $\mu_2(X\ Y\ Z) = x\ y_2\ z_2$ are in r(U), r(U) consists of not only the tuple $\mu_3(X\ Y\ Z) = x\ y_1\ z_2$, but also the tuple $\mu_4(X\ Y\ Z) = x\ y_2\ z_1$. Consequently, distinct tuples of the same X-value with identical Y-value (or Z-value) must have different Z-values (or Y-values) so as to maintain all tuples distinct. By this symmetric property, relation r(U) satisfies MVD X → → Y iff it satisfies MVD X → → Z.

This theorem will be used as one of the inference rules for MVDs to yield completeness. We will alternatively prove this theorem by the logical equivalence of an MVD.

Example 5.1:

Given a relation scheme R = (A B C D, {B C → → A}), the following relation r(R) satisfies the MVD B C → → A.

TABLE 5-1. A RELATION
SATISFYING B C → → A

r	A	B	C	D
	b	a	c	a
	b	a	c	f
	b	a	e	a
	b	a	e	f
	d	a	c	a
	d	a	c	f
	d	a	e	a
	d	a	e	f

This relation also satisfies the MVD B C → → D.

5.3 LOGICAL EQUIVALENCE

The logical equivalence described in section 4.3 for FDs (Functional Dependencies) can be extended to MVDs. In addition, we will use a Venn diagram as an aid in evaluation of a (formula) difference to achieve much simplification.

The MVD $X \to \to Y$ is equivalent to the formula $\bar{X} + Y + (U - X\,Y)$ [Sag81], i.e.,

$$X \to \to Y \equiv \bar{X} + Y + (U - X\,Y) \tag{5.1}$$

where X, Y, and $U - X\,Y$ on the right side are formulas corresponding to the subsets X, Y, and $U - X\,Y$, respectively; and $\bar{X}$ is the negation of X and does not correspond to the set difference $U - X$.

When MVD $X \to \to Y$ holds in relation r(U), its logical equivalence $\bar{X} + Y + (U - X\,Y)$ must be true in the following cases.

(1) When any two tuples are of different X-values, X is false, $\bar{X}$ is true, and $\bar{X} + Y + (U - X\,Y)$ is also true so that the corresponding Y-values and $(U - X\,Y)$-values are immaterial.

(2) On the other hand, when any two tuples, say μ_1 and μ_2, are of the same X-value, X is true, and $\bar{X}$ is false so that the truth value of $\bar{X} + Y + (U - X\,Y)$ is determined by the subformula $Y + (U - X\,Y)$. There are four possible cases to consider.

  (i) If Y and $U - X\,Y$ are both true, then μ_1 and μ_2 are not distinct.

  (ii) If Y is true and $U - X\,Y$ is false, then the subformula is true.

  (iii) If $U - X\,Y$ is true and Y is false, then the subformula is true.

  (iv) If both Y and $U - X\,Y$ are false, then the subformula is false. In this case, r(U) must have two additional tuples, say μ_3 and μ_4, such that they have the same X-value, μ_1 and μ_3 must satisfy (ii), and μ_2 and μ_4 must satisfy (iii).

Now, we can provide a formal proof of theorem 5.1 by means of the logical equivalence and a Venn diagram. Let A, B, C, and D be subsets of the set $U = X\,Y\,D$ of attributes. Without loss of generality, we can also view these symbols as attributes each denoting an atom in a formula. Let $X = A\,C$, $Y = B\,C$, and $U = X\,Y\,D$ such that $X \cap Y = C$ as shown in the Venn diagram of Fig. 5-1. By means of (5.1), we have

$$X \to \to Y \equiv \bar{X} + Y + (U - X\,Y)$$

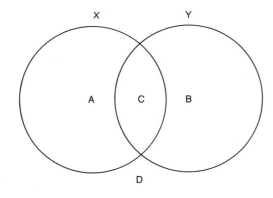

Figure 5-1 The Venn diagram for proving Theorem 5.1

and

$$X \to \to U - X \ Y \equiv \overline{X} + (U - X \ Y) + [U - X \ (U - X \ Y)].$$

We show that both formulas on the right sides of $\equiv$ are in fact identical after they are simplified to

$$\overline{X} + Y + (U - X \ Y) \equiv \overline{A} + \overline{C} + B + D$$

where $\overline{X} = \overline{A} + \overline{C}$ and $U - X \ Y = D$, and

$$\overline{X} + (U - X \ Y) + [U - X \ (U - X \ Y)] = \overline{A} + \overline{C} + D + B$$

where $U - X \ (U - X \ Y) = B$. Thus, we can conclude that $X \to \to Y$ iff $X \to \to U - X$ Y.

This proof is general enough, since it is not required that $\{X, Y, Z\}$ be a partition on U, i.e., X, Y, and Z need not be mutually disjoint.

In MVD $X \to \to Y$, X and Y are not necessarily disjoint. Hence, the right subset Y may not be reduced. We prove that the right-reduced version $X \to \to Y - X$ of $X \to \to Y$ is equivalent to $X \to \to Y$.

Theorem 5.2:   An MVD $X \to \to Y$ holds in a relation r(U) iff its right-reduced version $X \to \to Y - X$ holds in r(U).

The reader is encouraged to provide a proof of this theorem (do exercise 5.1).

Theorem 5.3:   Let X, Y, and Z be subsets of the set U of attributes such that X Y Z = U. An MVD $X \to \to Y$ holds in a relation r(U) iff r(U) is the join of the projections r[X Y] and r[X Z] where Z = U − X Y.

Proof: Let $r_1 = r[X \ Y]$ and $r_2 = r[X \ Z]$. To prove the necessity, we need to show that every tuple μ in the join $r_1 \ |x| \ r_2$ is also in r(U) (i.e., $r_1 \ |x| \ r_2 \subseteq r(U)$), since we always have the converse (i.e., $r(U) \subseteq r_1 \ |x| \ r_2$). Suppose that $X \to \to Y$ holds in r(U). Let μ be a tuple in the join $r_1 \ |x| \ r_2$. Then there must be a tuple μ_1 in r_1 and a tuple μ_2 in r_2 such that $\mu[X] = \mu_1[X] = \mu_2[X] = x$, $\mu[Y] = \mu_1[Y] = y$, and $\mu[Z] = \mu_2[Z] = z$. Since r_1 and r_2 are projections of r, there must be tuples ν_1 and ν_2 in r with $\mu_1[X \ Y] = \nu_1[X \ Y] = x \ y$ and $\mu_2[X \ Z] = \nu_2[X \ Z] = x \ z$. Let $\nu_1(X \ Y \ Z) = x \ y \ z'$ and $\nu_2(X \ Y \ Z) = x \ y' \ z$. By definition 5.1, r(U) satisfying $X \to \to Y$ implies that there exists a tuple ν_3 in r(U) such that $\nu_3(X \ Y \ Z) = x \ y \ z$. Thus, $\nu_3 = \mu$.

To prove the sufficiency, we need to show that for any two tuples $\nu_1(X \ Y \ Z) = x \ y \ z'$ and $\nu_2(X \ Y \ Z) = x \ y' \ z$ in r(U), there is a tuple μ in r(U) such that $\mu(X \ Y \ Z) = x \ y \ z$, i.e., $X \to \to Y$ holds in r(U). Let r_1 and r_2 be defined as before, and let ν_1 and ν_2 be tuples in r(U). Since r(U) decomposes losslessly onto X Y and X Z (i.e., $r(U) = r[X \ Y] \ |x| \ r[X \ Z]$), r_1 and r_2 consist of, respectively, tuples μ_1 and μ_2 with $\mu_1 = \nu_1[X \ Y] = x \ y$ and $\mu_2 = \nu_2[X \ Z] = x \ z$. The result of joining μ_1 and μ_2 yields a tuple μ with $\mu(X \ Y \ Z) = x \ y \ z$. Since $r(U) = r_1 \ |x| \ r_2$, μ must be in r(U). Since ν_1, ν_2, and μ satisfy definition 5.1, $X \to \to Y$ must hold in r(U).

This theorem provides a method to solve the MVD $X \to \to Y$ satisfaction problem by examining the equality $r(X \ Y \ Z) = (r[X \ Y] \ |x| \ r[X \ Z])$. However, the test requires two projections and one join so that it may be time consuming. Another method for solving this problem requires that the tuples of r(U) be sorted based on their X-values and then, for each X-value x, the following equality be tested.

$$|\sigma_{X=x}(r)| = |\pi_{X\ Y}(\sigma_{X=x}(r))| \times |\pi_{X\ Z}(\sigma_{X=x}(r))| \qquad (5.2a)$$

where $|r|$ means the cardinality of relation r, and σ and π stand for "selection" (definition 2.7) and "projection" (definition 2.6), respectively. Since

$$|\pi_{X\ W}(\sigma_{X=x}(r))| = |\pi_W(\sigma_{X=x}(r))|, \qquad (5.2b)$$

(5.2a) can be simplified as

$$|\sigma_{X=x}(r)| = |\pi_Y(\sigma_{X=x}(r))| \times |\pi_Z(\sigma_{X=x}(r))|. \cdot \qquad (5.2c)$$

Note that the empty relation and each relation consisting of a single tuple with scheme U satisfy an MVD $X \rightarrow \rightarrow Y$ on U. When U is viewed as a contradiction, we still need to exclude a relation consisting of at most one tuple. Note also that (5.2c) is not applicable to either $Y = \emptyset$ or $Z = \emptyset$, since projecting a relation onto $\emptyset$ is undefined.

Example 5.2:

The relation r(A B C D) of table 5-1 satisfies theorem 5.3. The projections r[B C A] and r[B C D] are shown in table 5-2.

The join of r[B C A] and r[B C D] is equal to r(A B C D). The equality (5.2c) is satisfied since

(1) $|\pi_A(\sigma_{B\ C=a\ c}(r))| = |\pi_D(\sigma_{B\ C=a\ c}(r))| = 2$, and $|\pi_{B\ C=a\ c}(r)|$ 4; and

(2) $|\pi_A(\sigma_{B\ C=a\ e}(r))| = |\pi_D(\sigma_{B\ C=a\ e}(r))| = 2$, and $|\sigma_{B\ C=a\ e}(r)| = 4$.

On the other hand, if any tuple in r(A B C D) is missing, then the MVDs B C $\rightarrow \rightarrow$ A and B C $\rightarrow \rightarrow$ D do not hold.

TABLE 5-2. TWO
PROJECTIONS OF r(A B C D)

r[B C A]	B	C	A
	a	c	b
	a	e	b
	a	c	d
	a	e	d

r[B C D]	B	C	D
	a	c	a
	a	c	f
	a	e	a
	a	e	f

5.4 INDEPENDENT INFERENCE RULES FOR MULTIVALUED DEPENDENCIES

Similar to the set of FD0-FD2 for FDs, there is a sound and complete set of inference rules for MVDs.

MVD0 (Complementation or Symmetry):   Let X Y Z = U, X → → Y iff X → → Z where Z = U − X Y.
The validity of this rule was proved in theorem 5.1.

MFD1 (Reflexivity):   If Y ⊆ X, then X → → Y.

Proof: Since Y ⊆ X, we can let X = (X − Y) Y. By the logical equivalence (5.1), we have

$$X \rightarrow \rightarrow Y \equiv \overline{X} + Y + (U - X) \equiv \overline{X - Y} + \overline{Y} + Y + (U - X),$$

which includes the tautology $\overline{Y} + Y$.

Since ø ⊆ X ⊆ U, X → → ø and U → → X are special cases of MVD1. These MVDs are trivial and hold in every relation r(U).

MVD2 (Augmentation):   If Z ⊆ W and X → → Y, then X W → → Y Z.

Proof: By theorem 5.2, we can merely assume that X ∩ Y = ø. Let X = A D F, Y = B E G, Z = F G H, and W = C D E Z as shown in the Venn diagram of Fig. 5-2 such that Z ⊆ W, and U = X Y W I. By the logical equivalence (5.1), we have

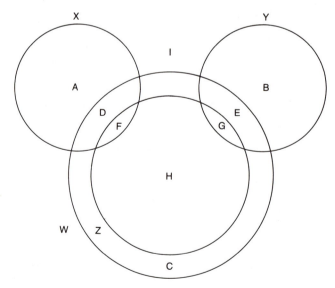

Figure 5-2 The Venn diagram for proving MVD2

$$\overline{X} + Y + (U - X \, Y) + \overline{X \, W} + Y \, Z + (U - X \, W \, Y),$$

which can be simplified to

$$\overline{C} + \overline{H} + \overline{I} + \overline{X} + \overline{Z} + Y + I$$

including the tautology $\overline{I} + I$.

Note that in the proof of MVD2, once a simplified form contains a tautology, the simplification terminates so that no further simplification is needed. Thus, the logical approach may not involve a minimization process, i.e., a simplified form is not necessarily a minimized form. Note also that a simplified form containing a tautology is not necessarily unique.

MVD3 (Transitivity):   If $X \to \to Y$ and $Y \to \to Z$, then $X \to \to Z - Y$.

Proof: By theorem 5.2, we can merely assume that $X \cap Y = X \cap Z = \emptyset$. However, we canot assume $Y \cap Z = \emptyset$, otherwise $Z - Y = Z$, and the generality is lost. Let $Y = B \, D$, $Z = C \, D$, and $U = X \, Y \, Z \, A$ such that $X \cap Y = X \cap Z = \emptyset$, and $Y \cap Z = D$, as shown in the Venn diagram of Fig. 5-3. By logical equivalence, we have

$$\overline{[\overline{X} + Y + (U - X \, Y)][\overline{Y} + Z + (U - Y \, Z)]} + \overline{X} + (Z - Y) + [U - X \, (Z - Y)],$$

which can be simplified to

$$\overline{Y} + \overline{C} + \overline{D} + \overline{X} + C + A$$

including the tautology $\overline{C} + C$.

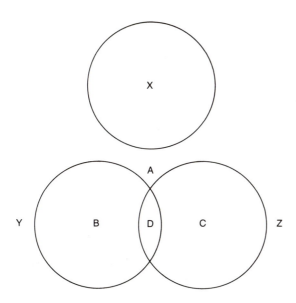

Figure 5-3 The Venn diagram for proving MVD3

5.5 *OTHER INFERENCE RULES FOR MULTIVALUED DEPENDENCIES*

In addition to the inference rules MVD0-MDV3, there are other inference rules for MVDs that are useful in later applications.

MVD4 (Pseudo-transitivity):   If $X \rightarrow \rightarrow Y$ and $Y\ W \rightarrow \rightarrow Z$, then $X\ W \rightarrow \rightarrow Z - Y\ W$.

Proof: We can define a derivation sequence by extending definition 4.3 and show that

$$\{X \rightarrow \rightarrow Y,\ Y\ W \rightarrow \rightarrow Z\} \ |- \ X\ W \rightarrow \rightarrow Z - Y\ W$$

by providing such a sequence based on MVD2 and MVD3.

(a) $X \rightarrow \rightarrow Y$ (given MVD),
(b) $X\ W \rightarrow \rightarrow Y\ W$ (by applying MDV2 on (a)),
(c) $Y\ W \rightarrow \rightarrow Z$ (given MVD),
(d) $X\ W \rightarrow \rightarrow Z - Y\ W$ (by applying MVD3 on (b) and (c)).

The above derivation sequence (a), (b), (c), (d) proves the validity of MVD4 and also shows that MVD4 is dependent on MVD2 and MVD3.

MVD5 (Union or Additivity):   If $X \rightarrow \rightarrow Y$ and $X \rightarrow \rightarrow Z$, then $X \rightarrow \rightarrow Y\ Z$.

Proof: We prove MVD5 by establishing a derivation sequence based on MVD0, MVD2, and MVD3 as follows.

(a) $X \rightarrow \rightarrow Z$ (given MVD),
(b) $X \rightarrow \rightarrow X\ Z$ (by applying MVD2 on (a)),
(c) $X \rightarrow \rightarrow Y$ (given MVD),
(d) $X\ Z \rightarrow \rightarrow Y\ Z$ (by applying MVD2 on (c)),
(e) $X\ Z \rightarrow \rightarrow U - X\ Y\ Z$ (by applying MVD0 on (d)),
(f) $X \rightarrow \rightarrow U - X\ Y\ Z$ (by applying MVD3 on (b) and (e) since $(U - X\ Y\ Z) - X\ Z \equiv U - X\ Y\ Z$),
(g) $X \rightarrow \rightarrow U - X\ (U - X\ Y\ Z)$ (by applying MVD0 on (f)).

It can be shown that $(U - X\ (U - X\ Y\ Z)) \equiv Y\ Z$ by using the Venn diagram as shown in Fig. 5-3.

MVD6 (Decomposition or Projectivity):   If $X \rightarrow \rightarrow Y$ and $X \rightarrow \rightarrow Z$, then $X \rightarrow \rightarrow Y \cap Z$, $X \rightarrow \rightarrow Y - Z$, and $X \rightarrow \rightarrow Z - Y$.

Proof: By means of MVD0, MVD5, and the Venn diagram of Fig. 5-3, we show that

$$\{X \to \to Y, X \to \to Z\} \mid- \{X \to \to Y \cap Z, X \to \to Y - Z, X \to \to Z - Y\}$$

by the following derivation sequence.

(a) $X \to \to B\ D$ (given MVD $X \to \to Y$),

(b) $X \to \to C\ D$ (given MVD $X \to \to Z$),

(c) $X \to \to A\ C$ (by applying MVD0 on (a)),

(d) $X \to \to A\ C\ D$ (by applying MVD5 on (b) and (c)),

(e) $X \to \to B$ (by applying MVD0 on (d)),

(f) $X \to \to A\ B$ (by applying MVD0 on (b)),

(g) $X \to \to A\ B\ D$ (by applying MVD5 on (a) and (f)),

(h) $X \to \to C$ (by applying MVD0 on (g)),

(i) $X \to \to A\ B\ C$ (by applying MVD5 on (c) and (f)),

(j) $X \to \to D$ (by applying MVD0 on (i)).

The MVDs derived in (e), (h), and (j) are, respectively, the MVDs $X \to \to Y - Z$, $X \to \to Z - Y$, and $X \to \to Y \cap Z$.

By using the Venn diagram shown in Fig. 5-3 and the logical equivalence, we can alternatively prove

$$\{X \to \to Y, X \to \to Z\} \mid- X \to \to Y \cap Z,$$

which is equivalent to

$$\overline{Y} \cdot \overline{A\ C} + \overline{Z} \cdot \overline{A\ B} + \overline{X} + D + A\ B\ C.$$

Further simplification yields the formula

$$\overline{A} + \overline{B} + \overline{C} + \overline{X} + D + C,$$

which includes the tautology $\overline{C} + C$. The other two MVDs can be similarly verified (do exercise 5.8).

The inference rule MVD5 of union (i.e., $\{X \to \to Y, X \to \to Z\} \mid- X \to \to Y\ Z$) is the counterpart of the inference rule FD4 of union (i.e., $\{X \to Y, X \to Z\} \mid- X \to Y\ Z$). However, the inference rule MVD6 of projectivity (i.e., $\{X \to \to Y, X \to \to Z\} \mid- \{X \to \to Y \cap Z, X \to \to Y - Z, X \to \to Z - Y\}$) does not parallel the inference rule FD5 of projectivity (i.e., $\{X \to Y\ Z\} \mid- \{X \to Y, X \to Z\}$). By FD5, if $X \to Y$ and $Y = A_{i_1} A_{i_2} \cdots A_{i_k}$, then we have k FDs $X \to A_{i_j}$ for each j, $1 \le j \le k$. By MVD6, if $X \to \to Y$ and $Y = A_{i_1} A_{i_2} \cdots A_{i_k}$, then we do not have any MVD $X \to \to A_{i_j}$ for any j, $1 \le j \le k$, unless there exists some subset Z such that $X \to \to Z$ and either $Y \cap Z = A_{i_j}$ or $Y - Z = A_{i_j}$ for some j, $1 \le j \le k$. Similarly, if $X \to \to Z$ and $Z = B_{i_1} B_{i_2} \cdots B_{i_k}$, then we do not have any MVD $X \to \to B_{i_j}$ for any j, $1 \le j \le k$, unless there exists some subset Y such that $X \to \to Y$ and either $Y \cap Z = B_{i_j}$ or $Z - Y = B_{i_j}$ for some j, $1 \le j \le k$.

The inference rules MVD5 of union and MVD6 of projectivity indicate that the family of subsets S of U, such that $X \to \to S$ exists for each subset S in the family, is closed under union, intersection, and (set) difference.

The set of inference rules MVD0-MVD3 is sound and complete for a set of MVDs on U. The soundness was shown and the proof of the completeness can be found in [Bee77] or [Sag81].

5.6 INFERENCE RULES FOR FUNCTIONAL AND MULTIVALUED DEPENDENCIES

Let Σ be a set of FDs and MVDs on U, and σ be a single FD or MVD. There are mixed inference rules that can be used to decide whether $\Sigma \mid= \sigma$ or not. Let W, X, Y, and Z be formulas or subsets of U.

FM1 (Replication):   If $X \rightarrow Y$, then $X \rightarrow \rightarrow Y$.

Proof: By the logical equivalences (4.3) and (5.1), we have

$$\overline{X + Y} + \overline{X} + Y + (U - X\,Y),$$

which contains the tautology $\overline{(\overline{X + Y})} + (\overline{X} + Y)$.

By FM1, the MVD $X \rightarrow \rightarrow Y$ is called the *MVD counterpart* of the FD $X \rightarrow Y$. By FM1 and exercise 5.9, an FD $X \rightarrow Y$ is a special case of its MVD counterpart $X \rightarrow \rightarrow Y$, since if a relation r(U) satisfies the FD $X \rightarrow Y$, then it also satisfies $X \rightarrow \rightarrow Y$. An FD $X \rightarrow Y$ defines a (many-to-one) function from TUP(X) to TUP(Y), whereas an MVD $X \rightarrow \rightarrow Y$ defines a (many-to-many) relation between TUP(X) and TUP(Y).

Example 5.3:

Let $r_1 = r[B\ C\ A] = \{a\,c\,b, a\,e\,b, a\,c\,d, a\,e\,d\}$ and $r_2 = r[B\ C\ D] = \{a\,c\,a, a\,c\,f, a\,e\,a, a\,e\,f\}$ as shown in table 5-2 of example 5.2. Both MVDs $B\ C \rightarrow \rightarrow A$ and $B\ C \rightarrow \rightarrow D$ define two-to-two relations between TUP(B C) and DOM (A) and between TUP(B C) and DOM(D). These relations imply that the keys for r_1 and r_2 must be the all-keys (i.e., A B C for r_1 and B C D for r_2). However, if $r_1'(A\ B\ C)$ and $r_2'(B\ C\ D)$ satisfy, respectively, the FDs $B\ C \rightarrow A$ and $B\ C \rightarrow D$, then r_1' and r_2' must be proper subsets of r_1 and r_2 respectively such that only functions are defined and the key for both relations r_1' and r_2' is B C.

FM2 (Coalescence):   If $X \rightarrow \rightarrow Y$ and $Z \rightarrow W$ where $W \subseteq Y$, and $Y \cap Z = \emptyset$, then $X \rightarrow W$.

Proof: Since $W \subseteq Y$, $Y \cap Z = \emptyset$, and $U = X\ Y\ Z\ E$, the subsets W, X, Y, and Z can be assumed, as shown in Fig. 5-4, the Venn diagram for proving FM2. From this Venn diagram, we have $X = A\ B$, $Z = B\ D$, and $Y = C\ W$. By the logical equivalences (4.3) and (5.1), we have the following equivalence:

$$\overline{[X + Y + (U - X\,Y)]\ (\overline{Z} + W)} + \overline{X} + W \equiv \overline{D} + \overline{E} + B + \overline{A} + \overline{B} + W,$$

which contains the tautology $B + \overline{B}$.

The next mixed inference rule is not independent but may be useful.

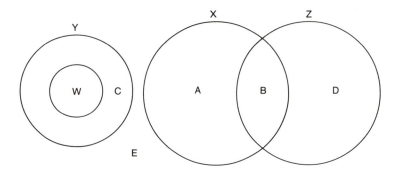

Figure 5-4   The Venn diagram for proving FM2

FM3:   If $X \rightarrow \rightarrow Y$ and $X\,Y \rightarrow Z$, then $X \rightarrow Z - Y$.
For a proof of FM3, do exercise 5.10.

Definition 5.2:   An MVD $X \rightarrow \rightarrow Y$ is *trivial* if either $Y \subseteq X$ or $X\,Y = U$, and is *nontrivial* otherwise.

By this definition, the inference rule MVD1 of reflexivity derives only trivial MVDs. Each relation r(U) satisfies a trivial MVD on U.

Theorem 5.4:   Let $V \rightarrow \rightarrow W$ be a nontrivial MVD on U. If $\{K \rightarrow U\} \models V \rightarrow \rightarrow W$, then K is a nonempty subset of V.

Proof: Since $V \rightarrow \rightarrow W$ is nontrivial (i.e., $W \not\subseteq V$ and $V\,W \subset U$), we can let $V \cap W = \emptyset$ and $(U - V\,W) = A$. By the logical equivalences (4.3) and (5.1), we have

$$\overline{K + U} + \overline{V} + W + (U - V\,W) \equiv K + \overline{V} + W + A$$

Since the subformula $\overline{V} + W + A$ does not contain any tautology and only V is negated, the formula $K + \overline{V} + W + A$ is valid iff $K + \overline{V}$ contains a tautology. This condition results iff K is a nonempty subset of V ($K \neq \emptyset$ since $K \rightarrow U$ is a key dependency and $\emptyset$ cannot be a key).

By this theorem, if a key dependency logically implies a nontrivial MVD, then the left subset of the MVD is a superkey.

The set of inference rules FD0-FD2, MVD0-MVD3, and FM1-FM2 is sound and complete. A proof of the completeness can be found in [Bee77].

5.7 DEPENDENCY BASIS

Let X be a subset of U. Let Σ be a set of FDs and MVDs on U, and Σ^+ be the closure of Σ whose elements are derivable from Σ by applying inference rules.

Definition 5.3:   The *dependency basis* of X, written as DEPBS(X), relative to Σ is the finest partition on U, i.e.,

$$\text{DEPBS(X)} = \{W_1, \ldots, W_k \mid 1 \leq k \leq n\}$$

where $n = |U|$ such that

(1) $X \to\to W_j$ is in Σ^+ for some j, $1 \leq j \leq k$, and

(2) $X \to\to Y$ is in Σ^+ iff Y is a union of some W_js in DEPBS(X).

Note that the dependency basis DEPBS(X) may be defined as the finest partition on $U - X$ that eliminates all trivial elements of the partition on U. These trivial elements can be derived by applying the inference rule MVD1 of reflexivity.

Example 5.4:

Let $U = A B C D E F G H I J$ and $\Sigma = \{A B \to\to D E F G, C G J \to\to A D H I\}$. We find the dependency bases DEPBS(A B) and DEPBS(C G J) as follows.

(a) $A B \to\to A$ (by applying MVD1),

(b) $A B \to\to B$ (by applying MVD1),

(c) $A B \to\to D E F G$ (given MVD),

(d) $A B \to\to C H I J$ (by applying MVD0 on (c)).

Thus, we have

$$\text{DEPBS(A B)} = \{A, B, C H I J, D E F G\}.$$

We may alternatively denote the dependency basis DEPBS(A B) by the notation

$$A B \to\to C H I J \mid D E F G,$$

which does not include the trivial MVDs in (a) and (b) of the above sequence. This notation is only a shorthand of "$A B \to\to C H I J$ and $A B \to\to D E F G$," and the symbol $\mid$ does not mean "such that." Similarly, we have the following sequence.

(a) $C G J \to\to C$ (by applying MVD1),

(b) $C G J \to\to G$ (by applying MVD1),

(c) $C G J \to\to J$ (by applying MVD1),

(d) $C G J \to\to A D H I$ (given MVD),

(e) $C G J \to\to B E F$ (by applying MVD0 on (d)).

Thus, we have

$$\text{DEPBS(C G J)} = \{C, G, J, B E F, A D H I\}$$

or alternatively,

$$C G J \to\to B E F \mid A D H I.$$

There exists a polynomial time algorithm [GAL82] to find the dependency basis DEPBS(X) with complexity $O((1 + \min(|\Sigma_m|, \log|DEPBS(X)|)) \times |ATTR(\Sigma)|)$ where min stands for "minimum," $|\Sigma_m|$ means the number of MVDs in Σ, and $|ATTR(\Sigma)|$ means the number of distinct attributes each appearing in Σ (Σ may consist of FDs).

*5.8 EMBEDDED MULTIVALUED DEPENDENCIES

We consider a generalization of an MVD and call it an embedded MVD.

Definition 5.4:   An *embedded MVD* (abbreviated as EMVD) is a constraint on U and is written as $X \rightarrow \rightarrow Y \mid Z$ (U) where X Y Z is a proper subset of U. Relation r(U) *satisfies* EMVD $X \rightarrow \rightarrow Y \mid Z$ (U), or $X \rightarrow \rightarrow Y \mid Z$ (U) *holds* in r(U), if MVD $X \rightarrow \rightarrow Y$ holds in the projection r[X Y Z].

Note that the notation $X \rightarrow \rightarrow Y \mid Z$ (U) is a shorthand of "$X \rightarrow \rightarrow Y$ and $X \rightarrow \rightarrow Z$ for X Y Z $\subset$ U," and the symbol $\mid$ does not mean "such that."

Example 5.5:

Let a relation r(A B C D) be shown in table 5-3. The projections r[A B C] = {a b c, a b′ c′, a b c ′, a b′ c} and r[A B D] = {a b d, a b′ d′, a b d′, a b′ d} satisfy $A \rightarrow \rightarrow C$ and $A \rightarrow \rightarrow D$, respectively. By the inference rule MVD0 of complementation, both projections satisfy $A \rightarrow \rightarrow B$. However, the relation r(A B C D) does not satisfy the MVDs $A \rightarrow \rightarrow B$ and $A \rightarrow \rightarrow C$ D, since the tuples a b c′ d′ and a b′ c d are missing from table 5-3, and definition 5.1 is not satisfied. Thus, $A \rightarrow \rightarrow B \mid C$ (A B C D) and $A \rightarrow \rightarrow B \mid D$ (A B C D) are EMVDs.

TABLE 5-3. A RELATION
SATISFYING AN EMVD

r	A	B	C	D
a	b	c	d
ap	b′	c′	d′
a	b	c′	d
a	b′	c	d′
a	b	c	d′
a	b′	c′	d

We show that the logical equivalence for an MVD cannot be extended to any EMVD by the following counterexample.

Example 5.6:

Consider the EMVDs $A \rightarrow \rightarrow B \mid C$ (A B C D) and $A \rightarrow \rightarrow B \mid D$ (A B C D), and the MVD $A \rightarrow \rightarrow B$. For MVD $A \rightarrow \rightarrow B$, we have $\overline{A} + B + C D$. Suppose that we were able to apply the same logical equivalence to any EMVD. Then for EMVDs $A \rightarrow \rightarrow B \mid C$ (A B C D) and $A \rightarrow \rightarrow B \mid D$ (A B C D), we must have

$$(\overline{A} + B + C) (\overline{A} + B + D) \equiv \overline{A} + B + C D$$

where the "logical and" operator is omitted. Hence, we obtain

$$\{A \rightarrow \rightarrow B \mid C \ (A \ B \ C \ D), \ A \rightarrow \rightarrow B \mid D \ (A \ B \ C \ D)\} \mid - A \rightarrow \rightarrow B,$$

which is equivalent to the tautology

$$\overline{\overline{A} + B + C \ D} + (\overline{A} + B + C \ D).$$

However, as already demonstrated in example 5.5, $A \rightarrow \rightarrow B$ does not hold in the relation $r(A \ B \ C \ D)$, although the MVDs $A \rightarrow \rightarrow B$ and $A \rightarrow \rightarrow C$ hold in the projection $r[A \ B \ C]$, and the MVDs $A \rightarrow \rightarrow B$ and $A \rightarrow \rightarrow D$ hold in the projection $r[A \ B \ D]$. Thus, the logical approach that is applicable for FDs and MVDs cannot be extended to EMVDs. Since MVDs $X \rightarrow \rightarrow Y$ and $X \rightarrow \rightarrow Z$ are an EMVD $X \rightarrow \rightarrow Y \mid Z \ (U)$ for $X \ Y \ Z = U$, the former is a special case of the latter, or the latter is a generalization of the former.

Although there are finite sets of inference rules for EMVDs, for mixed FDs and EMVDs, and for mixed MVDs and EMVDs, each of these sets is sound but is not complete. In addition, there exists no finite complete set of inference rules for EMVDs.

*5.9 CONFLICT-FREE VIRTUAL KEYS

As already discussed in example 5.3, the left subset X of a nontrivial MVD $X \rightarrow \rightarrow Y$ does not form a key for the projection $r[X \ Y]$ of any relation $r(U)$ satisfying this MVD. We refer to X as a *virtual key* instead of a key for proper differentiation. Then we define an important property of two virtual keys.

Definition 5.5: Two virtual keys X and Y are called *conflict-free* if their dependency bases DEPBS(X) and DEPBS(Y) satisfy the following condition. For some $i \geq 0$, $j \geq 0$, and $k \geq 0$; and for possibly empty subsets Z_x and Z_y,

$$\text{DEPBS}(X) - \{A \mid A \in X\}$$
$$= \{V_1, \cdots, V_k, X_1, \cdots, X_i, Z_x \ Y_1 \cdots Y_j\} \qquad (5.3a)$$

and

$$\text{DEPBS}(Y) - \{B \mid B \in Y\}$$
$$= \{V_1, \ldots, V_k, Y_1, \cdots, Y_j, Z_y \ X_1 \cdots X_i\} \qquad (5.3b)$$

where

$$\{V_1, \cdots, V_k\} \subseteq \text{DEPBS}(X \cap Y) \qquad (5.3c)$$

and

$$Z_x \cup X = Z_y \cup Y. \qquad (5.3d)$$

We assume that $\text{DEPBS}(\emptyset) = \emptyset$. If X and Y are not conflict-free, then the pair (X, Y) is said to be a *conflict*. Let Σ be a set of MVDs on U. If all virtual keys in Σ are mutually conflict-free, then Σ is *conflict-free*.

Example 5.7 [Lie 82]:

> Let U = DEPT NAME DEP PROJ PART SUPPLIER where the attributes DEPT, NAME, DEP, PROJ, PART, and SUPPLIER denote, respectively, department, employee name, dependent, project, part, and supplier; and Σ = {NAME $\rightarrow\rightarrow$ DEPT | DEP | PROJ PART SUPPPLIER, PROJ $\rightarrow\rightarrow$ NAME DEPT DEP | PART SUPPLIER, PART $\rightarrow\rightarrow$ DEPT NAME DEP PROJ | SUPPLIER} where the three elements denote the dependent bases of the three virtual keys NAME, PROJ, and PART.
>
> We show that NAME and PROJ are conflict-free. By (5.3a), we have
>
> $$\text{DEPBS(NAME)} - \{\text{NAME}\} = \{\text{DEPT, DEP, PROJ PART SUPPLIER}\}$$
>
> where X = NAME, X_1 = DEPT, X_2 = DEP, Z_x = PROJ, Y_1 = PART, and Y_2 = SUPPLIER. By (5.3b), we have
>
> $$\text{DEPBS(PROJ)} - \{\text{PROJ}\} = \{\text{PART SUPPLIER, NAME DEPT DEP}\}$$
>
> where Y = PROJ, Y_1 = PART, Y_2 = SUPPLIER, Z_y = NAME, X_1 = DEPT, and X_2 = DEP. Since X $\cap$ Y = NAME $\cap$ PROJ = ø and DEPBS(ø) = ø, we have k = 0 in (5.3c). Condition (5.3d) is also satisfied since $Z_x \cup$ X = {PROJ, NAME} and $Z_y \cup$ Y = {NAME, PROJ}. Hence, NAME and PROJ are conflict-free. Similarly, we find that NAME and PART are conflict-free, and so are PROJ and PART. Thus, Σ is conflict-free.

Example 5.8 [Lie 82]:

> Let U = A B C D and Σ = {A B $\rightarrow\rightarrow$ C | D, C D $\rightarrow\rightarrow$ A | B}. The left subsets A B and C D are virtual keys, and their dependency bases are DEPBS(A B) = DEPBS(C D) = {A, B, C, D}. Thus, DEPBS(A B) $-$ {A, B} = {C, D} and DEPBS(C D) $-$ {C, D} = {A, B} do not satisfy (5.3a), (5.3b), and (5.3d). The pair (A B, C D) is a conflict.

Definition 5.6:   An MVD V $\rightarrow\rightarrow$ W *splits* two attributes A and B if one of A and B is in W and the other one is in U $-$ V W.

By theorem 5.3, if V $\rightarrow\rightarrow$ W holds in relation r(U), then r(U) is decomposed as r[V W] and r[U $-$ W]. If A is in W and B is in U $-$ V W or vice versa, then A and B must belong to two different projections. In this sense, V $\rightarrow\rightarrow$ W splits A and B.

Example 5.9:

> Given U = A B C D, the MVD A B $\rightarrow\rightarrow$ C splits C and D. Similarly, the MVD C D $\rightarrow\rightarrow$ A splits A and B.

In example 5.9, if the relation scheme R = (A B C D, {A B $\rightarrow\rightarrow$ C, C D $\rightarrow\rightarrow$ A}) is projected based on the MVD A B $\rightarrow\rightarrow$ C onto A B C and A B D, then only the constraint A B $\rightarrow\rightarrow$ C | D is enforced, whereas the constraint C D $\rightarrow\rightarrow$ A | B is left out and cannot be applied to the two projections for further splitting A and B (since C D $\rightarrow\rightarrow$ A | B does not imply either C $\rightarrow\rightarrow$ A | B or D $\rightarrow\rightarrow$ A | B). This is known as the *split virtual key problem*. This problem presents a difficulty for explicitly enforcing the constraint during updates. Consequently, only a conflict-free set of MVDs can possibly yield a good decomposition based on some MVDs in the set.

5.10 FINAL REMARKS ON LOGICAL EQUIVALENCE

In chapters 4 and 5, we have extensively used the logical approach to solve various problems involving FDs and/or MVDs. We have also provided a counterexample to demonstrate that this logical approach cannot be extended to EMVDs.

By using the logical equivalences and the inclusion and exclusion relationships among some subsets of attributes depicted by means of Venn diagrams, we can provide straightforward verifications of most theorems involving FDs and/or MVDs. These techniques are much easier to understand than conventional proofs of those theorems.

As shown in [Fag77b] and [Sag81], the inference rules for FDs and MVDs interpreted as logical formulas are also sound and complete. Most importantly, the equivalence theorem between data dependencies including FDs and MVDs and a fragment of the propositional logic is formally developed. This equivalence theorem entails the following. Let Σ be a set of FDs and MVDs on a set U of attributes, and let σ be a single FD or MVD. Then the following statements are equivalent.

(1) Σ implies σ.

(2) Σ implies σ in the world of two tuple relations (i.e., each such relation has only two tuples rather than each tuple has only two components).

(3) Σ logically implies σ when FDs and MVDs are interpreted as formulas.

Because of this important theorem, the determination of whether an FD $X \rightarrow Y$ or an MVD $X \rightarrow \rightarrow Y$ holds in a relation r(U) may be made solely by evaluating the truth value of its equivalent logical formula, $\overline{X} + Y$ or $\overline{X} + Y + (U - X\ Y)$, for the two tuples of a two tuple relation over U. This implies that use of the logical approach to solving problems involving FDs and/or MVDs is more than adequate.

EXERCISES

5.1 Prove theorem 5.2 by using the Venn diagram of figure 5-1 and the logical equivalence (5.1).

5.2 Let $r(A\ B\ C) = \{a\ b_1\ c_1,\ a\ b_2\ c_2,\ a\ b_1\ c_2,\ a\ b_2\ c_1\}$.

    (a) Show that the MVD $A \rightarrow \rightarrow B$ holds in $r(A\ B\ C)$.

    (b) Find four subsets of $r(A\ B\ C)$ each consisting of three tuples. Show that the MVD $A \rightarrow \rightarrow B$ does not hold in each such subset.

    (c) Find six subsets of $r(A\ B\ C)$ each consisting of two tuples. Show that two of these subsets do not satisfy the MVD $A \rightarrow \rightarrow B$ and four of these subsets satisfy the MVD $A \rightarrow \rightarrow B$.

5.3 Show that

    (a) any relation r(U) satisfies the MVDs $X \rightarrow \rightarrow \emptyset$, $X \rightarrow \rightarrow X$, and $X \rightarrow \rightarrow U - X$ where X is a subset of U, and

    (b) the MVD $\emptyset \rightarrow \rightarrow Y$ holds in a relation r(U) iff r(U) is the complex product of the projections r[Y] and r[U - Y] where Y is a subset of U.

5.4 Disprove that if $Z \subseteq W$ and $X \rightarrow \rightarrow Y$, then $X\ W \rightarrow Y\ Z$.

5.5 Show that

    (a) $\{X \rightarrow \rightarrow Y, Y \rightarrow \rightarrow Z\} \not\vdash X \rightarrow \rightarrow Z$ when $Y \cap Z \neq \emptyset$, and

    (b) $\{X \rightarrow \rightarrow Y, Y \rightarrow \rightarrow Z\} \vdash X \rightarrow \rightarrow Z$ when $Y \cap Z = \emptyset$.

5.6 Prove the inference rule MVD4 (i.e., $\{X \rightarrow \rightarrow Y, Y\,W \rightarrow \rightarrow Z\} \vdash X\,W \rightarrow \rightarrow Z - Y\,W$) by assuming that $X \cap Y = \emptyset$ and $Y\,W \cap Z = \emptyset$.

5.7 Prove MVD5 (i.e., $\{X \rightarrow \rightarrow Y, X \rightarrow \rightarrow Z\} \vdash X \rightarrow \rightarrow Y\,Z$) by using the Venn diagram as shown in Fig. 5-3.

5.8 Prove MVD6 (i.e., $\{X \rightarrow \rightarrow Y, X \rightarrow \rightarrow Z\} \vdash \{X \rightarrow \rightarrow Y \cap Z, X \rightarrow \rightarrow Y - Z, X \rightarrow \rightarrow Z - Y\}$) by using the Venn diagram as shown in Fig. 5-3.

5.9 Disprove that if $X \rightarrow \rightarrow Y$, then $X \rightarrow Y$.

5.10 Prove FM3 (i.e., $\{X \rightarrow \rightarrow Y, X\,Y \rightarrow Z\} \vdash X \rightarrow Z - Y$) by letting $X = A\,B$, $Y = C\,D$, and $Z = D\,E$ such that $X\,Y\,Z = U$.

5.11 Let $V \rightarrow \rightarrow W$ be a trivial MVD on U. Show that $\emptyset \models V \rightarrow \rightarrow W$.

5.12 Let $V \rightarrow \rightarrow W$ be an MVD on U. If $\{V \rightarrow \rightarrow W\} \models K \rightarrow U$, then $K = U$ where K is a key.

5.13 Given $\Sigma = \{A\,B \rightarrow \rightarrow D\,E\,F\,G, C\,G\,J \rightarrow \rightarrow A\,D\,H\,I\}$, find DEPBS(A C G J).

5.14 Let $U = A\,B\,C\,D\,E$ and $\Sigma = \{E \rightarrow \rightarrow B, A\,E \rightarrow \rightarrow C\}$. Show that the virtual keys E and A E are conflict-free.

5.15 An MVD $X \rightarrow \rightarrow Y$ in Σ is called *elementary* if it is nontrivial and there exists no MVD $X' \rightarrow \rightarrow Y'$ where X' is a proper subset of X and Y' is a subset of Y. An elementary MVD is called *multiple* if Σ contains other elementary MVDs with the same left subset (i.e., virtual key), and is called *single* otherwise. A relation scheme involving only trivial MVDs is called *atomic*. Show that a relation scheme is atomic iff it does not involve any multiple elementary MVDs.

5.16 Let H be the hypergraph of a database scheme and H_1 be any component of the subhypergraph of H after the removal of an articulation set X of U from H. If Y denotes the vertex set of H_1, then $X \rightarrow \rightarrow Y$ is in Σ of the database scheme. Provide a proof.

chapter 6

JOIN DEPENDENCIES

6.1 INTRODUCTION

In definition 2.10 of chapter 2, we defined the join of two relations and introduced some of its properties. In section 4.1, we stated that a set of functional dependencies plus one join dependency are conjectured to be sufficient in most cases for expressing the dependency structure of a relational database scheme. This means that the join dependency is one of the most important data dependencies in the theory of relational databases.

In chapter 5, theorem 5.3 establishes a connection between the MVD $X \rightarrow \rightarrow Y$ and the join of two projections r[X Y] and r[X Z] where r is a relation with scheme X Y Z. If r satisfies this MVD, then r equals the join of the projections r[X Y] and r[X Z]. This provides a means to perform a viable decomposition of a relation into two projections. However, a relation can have only a viable decomposition into more than two projections. This chapter covers a generalization of an MVD as well as an EMVD in which a join dependency involves more than two projected relation schemes.

6.2 JOIN DEPENDENCIES

The join of two relations was formally defined in chapter 2. We consider the m-ary version of a join in more detail, and define a full join dependency and an embedded join dependency.

Definition 6.1: Let U_j be a subset of the universal set U of attributes and r_j be a relation with scheme U_j for each j, $1 \leq j \leq m$. The *natural join* (or simply *join*) of relations $r_1, \ldots, r_{m-1}$, and r_m, written as $|x|(r_1, \ldots, r_m)$, is the relation with scheme $U' = U_1 \ldots U_m \subseteq U$ such that

$$|x|(r_1, \ldots, r_m) = \{\mu \mid \mu[U_j] = \mu_j \text{ and } \mu_j \in r_j(U_j) \text{ for each } j, 1 \leq j \leq m\}. \quad (6.1)$$

The join $|x|(r_1, \ldots, r_m)$ of relations $r_1, \ldots, r_{m-1}$, and r_m has a corresponding *join dependency* (abbreviated as JD) on U', which is a constraint on U' and is of the form $|x|(U_1, U_2, \ldots, U_m)$. The join dependency is *full* (abbreviated as FJD) if $U' = U$, and is *embedded* (abbreviated as EJD) if U' is a proper subset of U (where U' is the union of U_1 through U_m).

In this definition, we use the notation $|x|(r_1, \ldots, r_m)$ to denote the join of m named relations r_1 through r_m and the notation $|x|(U_1, \ldots, U_m)$ to denote the JD of m relation schemes U_1 through U_m. Wherever the underlying relations are unnamed, we will use the schemes of the unnamed relations to represent the relations and use the JD notation to denote a join, i.e., we do not differentiate a JD and a join. The differentiation can be resolved in the context. We extend definition 1.3 to define a full database scheme. In (6.1), a special case $|x|(r_1) = r_1$ arises, and r_1 satisfies the JD $|x|(U_1)$. Note that the m-ary join is naturally extended from its binary version and has the associative property. For example, $|x|(|x|(r_1, r_2), r_3) = |x|(r_1, |x|(r_2, r_3)) = |x|(r_1, r_2, r_3)$.

Definition 6.2: A database scheme Db of relation schemes $R_1, \ldots, R_{m-1}$, and R_m with $R_j = (U_j, \Sigma_j)$ where U_j is a subset of U and Σ_j is a set of data dependencies on U_j, simply represented by the set $\{R_1, \ldots, R_m\}$, is called a *full database scheme* if $ATTR(Db) = U_1 \ldots U_m = U$.

If Db is a full database scheme, then $|x|(U_1, \ldots, U_m)$ is an FJD, and is an EJD otherwise. In subsequent sections, we will use R_j and U_j interchangeably when Σ_j is understood.

TABLE 6-1. RELATION
r(A B C)

r	A	B	C
	a	b	c
	a	b'	c'
	a'	b	c''

Example 6.1:

Let r be a relation over A B C, as shown in table 6-1. The JDs $|x|(A B, A C, B C)$, $|x|(A B, A C)$, $|x|(A B, B C)$, and $|x|(A C, B C)$ are FJDs. For the first join dependency, $U = A B C$, $U_1 = A B$, $U_2 = A C$, and $U_3 = B C$ imply that $U' = U_1 U_2 U_3 = U$ and the JD is full.

Example 6.2:

The EMVDs

$$A \rightarrow \rightarrow B \mid C \ (A B C D)$$

and

$$A \rightarrow \rightarrow B \mid D \, (A \, B \, C \, D),$$

as shown in table 6-2 have, respectively, their corresponding EJDs

$$|x|(A \, B, \, A \, C)$$

in which D does not occur and

$$|x|(A \, B, \, A \, D)$$

in which C does not occur.

Definition 6.3: Relation $r(U)$ *satisfies* the FJD $|x|(U_1, \ldots, U_m)$, or the FJD *holds* in $r(U)$, if $r(U)$ decomposes onto $U_1, \ldots, U_{m-1}$, and U_m such that

$$r(U) = |x|(r[U_1], \ldots, r[U_m]). \qquad (6.2a)$$

Relation $r(U)$ *satisfies* the EJD $|x|(U_1, \ldots, U_m)$ or the EJD *holds* in $r(U)$, if the projection $r[U']$ of $r(U)$ satisfies the EJD with respect to U as an FJD with respect to U', i.e.,

$$r[U'] = |x|(r[U_1], \ldots, r[U_m]) \qquad (6.2b)$$

TABLE 6-2. A RELATION
SATISFYING EJDs

r'	A	B	C	D
	a	b	c	d
	a	b′	c′	d′
	a	b	c′	d
	a	b′	c	d′
	a	b	c	d′
	a	b′	c′	d

where $U' = U_1 \ldots U_m$ is a proper subset of U. If (6.2a) holds (for $r(U)$), then the full join on the right side of = is *lossless*, and is *lossy* otherwise. Similarly, if (6.2b) holds (for $r[U']$), then the embedded join on the right side of = is *lossless*, and is *lossy* otherwise.

If $U' = U$, then (6.2a) and (6.2b) coincide. Thus, (6.2a) is a special case of (6.2b), i.e., every FJD is also an EJD. Consequently, EJDs are generalizations of FJDs. From now on, we will refer to an FJD as a JD whenever there is no need to differentiate JDs and FJDs. By definition 6.3, ''a relation r satisfying a JD j'' is equivalent to ''the join of the projections decomposed from r based on the JD j being lossless.'' We may also say that a JD is lossless in the sense that the join of the projections of a relation decomposed based on the JD is lossless.

Example 6.3:

The relation $r(A \, B \, C) = \{1 \, 2 \, 3, \, 1 \, 4 \, 5, \, 6 \, 2 \, 7\}$ of table 6-1 satisfies the JDs $|x|(A \, B, \, A \, C, \, B \, C)$ and $|x|(A \, C, \, B \, C)$, since (6.2a) is satisfied. The relations ra and rb corresponding to the

TABLE 6-3.
RELATIONS rc AND rd

rc	A	B	C
	a	b	c
	a	b	c″
	a	b′	c′
	a′	b	c
	a′	b	c″

rd	A	B	C
	a	b	c
	a	b	c′
	a	b′	c
	a	b′	c′
	a′	b	c″

lossless joins $|x|(r[A\ B],\ r[A\ C],\ r[B\ C])$ and $|x|(r[A\ C],\ r[B\ C])$ respectively, are identical to r. However, the relation r does not satisfy the JDs $|x|(A\ B,\ B\ C)$ and $|x|(A\ B,\ A\ C)$ since (6.2a) is not satisfied. The relations rc and rd corresponding to the lossy joins $|x|(r[A\ B],\ r[B\ C])$ and $|x|(r[A\ B],\ r[A\ C])$ are shown in table 6-3. Relation rc(A B C) or rd(A B C) properly contains relation r(A B C) in table 6-1.

Definition 6.4:   A tuple in the join of some projections of a given relation r is called *spurious* if it is in the join but is not in r.

Example 6.4:

In the joins rc and rd, as shown in table 6-3, there are spurious tuples a b c′ and a′ b c in rc; and a b c′ and a b′ c in rd.

Examples 6.3 and 6.4 demonstrate that a lossy join contains at least one spurious tuple rather than losing any tuples. A relation r is, in general, a subset of the join of its projections r_1 through r_m, i.e., $r \subseteq |x|(r_1, \ldots, r_m)$.

Example 6.5:

The relation r(A B C D) as shown in table 6-2 satisfies the EMVDs

$$A \to\to B\ |\ C\ (A\ B\ C\ D)$$

and

$$A \to\to B\ |\ D\ (A\ B\ C\ D)$$

and also satisfies the EJDs $|x|(A\ B,\ A\ C)$ and $|x|(A\ B,\ A\ D)$ but does not satisfy the JD $|x|(A\ B,\ A\ C\ D)$, since relation r does not satisfy the MVD $A \to\to B$ (and $A \to\to C\ D$ by theorem 5.1 or the inference rule MVD0 of complementation). This example demonstrates that an EJD is a generalization of an EMVD.

6.3 TESTING OF LOSSLESSNESS

An algorithm for testing the losslessness of a join or JD by the tableau method [Aho79] is introduced. Let a_i be a *distinguished variable* and b_{jk} be a *nondistinguished variable*.

Input: $|x|(U_1, \ldots, U_m)$ and Σ.

Output: Return "lossless" if the tableau for the JD has a row with all distinguished variables, and return "lossy" otherwise.

Method:

(1) Define the tableau T_{JD} for the JD that has $|ATTR(JD)|$ columns labeled by the attributes appearing in the JD and m rows labeled by $w_1, \ldots, w_{m-1}$, and w_m corresponding to the subsets $U_1, \ldots, U_{m-1}$, and U_m, respectively. Row w_i has the distinguished variable a_j in A_j-column iff A_j of the JD is in U_i. The remaining entries of w_i are unique nondistinguished variables b_{ik} for each A_k-column, $k \neq j$.

(2) For each FD $X \rightarrow A$ in Σ, if $w_i[X] = w_j[X]$, $w_i[A] = v_1$ and $w_j[A] = v_2$ for every two rows w_i and w_j, then rename one of v_1 and v_2 to be the other by the following rule known as the *F-rule*.

   (a) If only one of v_1 and v_2 is a distinguished variable, then every occurrence of the nondistinguished variable is replaced by the distinguished variable or,

   (b) If both v_1 and v_2 are nondistinguished, then every occurrence of the one with the larger subscript is replaced by the one with the smaller subscript.

(3) After the replacements are performed for all FDs in Σ, check if there is a row with all distinguished variables known as a *target row*. If there is a target row, then return "lossless" and return "lossy" otherwise.

Example 6.6:

Let U = A B C D E F, $\Sigma = \{A \rightarrow B, F \rightarrow E\}$, and JD = $|x|$(A B D E, A C D F, B C E F). Following the algorithm, step (1) yields the initial tableau as shown in table 6-4(a). This table has three rows since $|JD| = 3$ and six columns since $|ATTR(JD)| = 6$. The first row, w_1, corresponds to the subset U_1 = A B D E in the JD. Thus, the (1,1), (1,2), (1.4), and (1,5) entries are filled by distinguished variables a_1, a_2, a_4, and a_5, respectively; and the remaining (1,3) and (1,6) entries are filled by nondistinguished variables b_{13} and b_{16}, respectively. The entries of the other two rows are similarly defined. Applying the FD A $\rightarrow$ B in step (2), we obtain the tableau modified by A $\rightarrow$ B as shown in table 6-4(b) where $w_2(B) = a_2$, since b_{22} in table 6-4(a) is replaced by a_2. Applying F $\rightarrow$ E in step (2), we get the tableau modified by F $\rightarrow$ E, as shown in table 6-4(c). In table 6-4(c), $w_2(E) = a_5$, since b_{25} in table 6-4(b) is replaced by a_5. Since $w_2 = a_1 a_2 a_3 a_4 a_5$ is a target row, a relation r(A B C D E F) satisfies the JD $|x|$(A B D E, A C D F, B C E F), or the join $|x|$(r[A B D E], r[A C D F], r[B C E F]) is lossless.

This algorithm takes $O(s^4)$ time where s is the space needed to write down the relation schemes in Db, the attributes in U, and the FDs in Σ.

Theorem 6.1:   Relation r(X Y) satisfies the JD $|x|$(X, Y) iff $X \cap Y \rightarrow \rightarrow X - Y$

TABLE 6-4(a). THE INITIAL TABLEAU T_{JD}

	A	B	C	D	E	F
w_1	a_1	a_2	b_{13}	a_4	a_5	b_{16}
w_2	a_1	b_{22}	a_3	a_4	b_{25}	a_6
w_3	b_{31}	a_2	a_3	b_{34}	a_5	a_6

TABLE 6-4(b). TABLEAU MODIFIED BY $A \rightarrow B$

	A	B	C	D	E	F
w_1	a_1	a_2	b_{13}	a_4	a_5	b_{16}
w_2	a_1	a_2	a_3	a_4	b_{25}	a_6
w_3	b_{31}	a_2	a_3	b_{34}	a_5	a_6

TABLE 6-4(c). TABLEAU MODIFIED BY $F \rightarrow E$

	A	B	C	D	E	F
w_1	a_1	a_2	b_{13}	a_4	a_5	b_{16}
w_2	a_1	a_2	a_3	a_4	a_5	a_6
w_3	b_{31}	a_2	a_3	b_{34}	a_5	a_6

or $X \cap Y \rightarrow \rightarrow Y - X$ is in Σ^+ where Σ^+ is the closure of Σ, which contains MVDs.

Proof: By theorem 5.1 or the inference rule MVD0 of complementation, $X \cap Y \rightarrow \rightarrow X - Y$ iff $X \cap Y \rightarrow \rightarrow U - (X \cap Y) (X - Y)$. By theorem 5.3, $X \cap Y \rightarrow \rightarrow X - Y$ holds in $r(X \ Y)$ iff

$$r(X \ Y) = |x|(r[(X \cap Y) (X - Y)], r[(X \cap Y) (U - (X \cap Y) (X - Y))]). \qquad (6.3a)$$

That is, by (6.2a), the join on the right side of (6.3a) is lossless iff $X \cap Y \rightarrow \rightarrow X - Y$ holds in $r(X \ Y)$. We want to show that the JD corresponding to the join in (6.3a) is equivalent to the JD $|x|(X, Y)$, i.e.,

$$|x|((X \cap Y) (X - Y), (X \cap Y) (U - (X \cap Y) (X - Y))) = |x|(X, Y). \qquad (6.3b)$$

Let $X = V \ Z$, $Y = W \ Z$, and $U = V \ W \ Z$ such that $X \cap Y = Z$, $X - Y = V$, and $U - (X \cap Y) (X - Y) = W$. It is trivial to establish (6.3b) by substitution. The other alternative follows from the property of symmetry.

In theorem 6.1, the left side $X \cap Y$ and the right side $X - Y$ of the first MVD are disjoint and so are $X \cap Y$ and $Y - X$ of the second MVD. This restriction can be relaxed by theorem 5.2. Thus, we have the following corollary in which the left subset $X \cap Y$ and the right subset X or Y of the FD $X \cap Y \rightarrow X$ or $X \cap Y \rightarrow Y$ are not disjoint.

Corollary 6.1:   Relation $r(X \; Y)$ satisfies the JD $|x|(X, Y)$ iff $X \cap Y \to \to X$ or $X \cap Y \to \to Y$ is in Σ^+.

By theorem 6.1 and the inference rule FM1, we have another corollary.

Corollary 6.2:   If $X \cap Y \to X - Y$ or $X \cap Y \to Y - X$ is in Σ^+, then the JD $|x|(X, Y)$ holds in a relation $r(X \; Y)$.

By definition 6.1 and theorem 6.1, MVDs are special cases of FJDs where each MVD involves only two projections.

Example 6.7:

> The join $rb = |x|(r[A \; C], r[B \; C])$ is lossless since $C \to \to A$ holds in $r(A \; B \; C)$ as shown in table 6-1 where the left subset C of the MVD $C \to \to A$ is the intersection of A C and B C, and the right subset $A = A \; C - B \; C$. However, the joins $rc = |x|(r[A \; B], r[B \; C])$ and $rd = |x|(r[A \; B], r[A \; C])$ are both lossy, since $B \to \to A$ and $A \to \to B$ do not hold in $r(A \; B \; C)$ as shown in table 6-1.

The previous algorithm for testing the losslessness of a join or JD involves only FDs in Σ. When Σ contains also MVDs, we need an additional rule to add rows in the tableau following definition 5.1, i.e., the rule known as the *J-rule* [Mai79]. For every MVD $X \to \to Y$ with $X \cap Y = \emptyset$, the set U of attributes can derive two subsets, X Y and U − Y, each defining the scheme of a projection where $U - Y = X \; (U - X \; Y)$. We initially add two rows in the tableau such that one row has distinguished variables for all attributes in X Y and nondistinguished variables for all attributes in U − X Y, and the other row has distinguished variables for all attributes in U − Y and nondistinguished variables for all attributes in Y. For every pair of distinct rows (say w_i, w_j) in the tableau, if $W_i[X] = w_j[X]$, then we add a new row w_k (not in the tableau) such that $w_k[X] = w_i[X]$, $w_k[Y] = w_i[Y]$ and $w_k[U - X \; Y] = w_j[U - X \; Y]$. The algorithm terminates if a target row is yielded or no additional new rows can be added to the tableau. The join is lossless if a target row appears in the tableau. This algorithm may require exponential time and space because of adding new rows.

Example 6.8:

> Let $U = A \; B \; C$ and $\Sigma = \{A \to \to B\}$. Then U can derive two subsets A B and A C by the MVD $A \to \to B$. We initially have the following tableau.

TABLE 6-5.   THE INITIAL TABLEAU DEFINED BY $A \to \to B$

	A	B	C
w_1	a_1	a_2	b_{13}
w_2	a_1	b_{22}	a_3

Since $A \to \to B$, we add a new row $w_3 = a_1 \; a_2 \; a_3$, which is a target row. Thus, the join $|x|(r[A \; B], r[A \; C])$ is lossless, and the algorithm terminates (i.e., we need not to add $w_4 = a_1 \; b_{22} \; b_{13}$).

6.4 AN EXISTENCE THEOREM

This existence theorem is based on [Aho79]. The proof is modified to reflect practical considerations.

Theorem 6.2:   For each $n \geq 3$, there is a set of n relation schemes such that the JD of these schemes is lossless, but the JD of fewer than n such schemes is lossy.

Proof: Let U consist of the attributes A_1, A_2, . . . , A_{n-1}, B_1, B_2, . . . , B_{n-2}, and B_{n-1}. Let $\Sigma = \{A_i \rightarrow B_i \mid 1 \leq i \leq n - 1\}$. Let the relation schemes be

$$U_0 = A_1 \, A_2 \, . \, . \, . \, A_{n-1},$$

and

$$U_i = A_i \, B_i, \, 1 \leq i \leq n - 1.$$

The initial tableau is shown below in table 6-6.

TABLE 6-6.   THE INITIAL TABLEAU DEFINED BY RELATION
SCHEMES

A_1	A_2	. . .	A_{n-1}	B_1	B_2	. . .	B_{n-1}
a_1	a_2	. . .	a_{n-1}	b_{1n}	$b_{1(n+1)}$	. . .	$b_{1(2n-2)}$
a_1	b_{22}	. . .	$b_{2(n-1)}$	a_n	$b_{2(n+1)}$	. . .	$b_{2(2n-2)}$
b_{31}	a_2	. . .	$b_{3(n-1)}$	b_{3n}	a_{n+1}	. . .	$b_{3(2n-2)}$
. . .							
b_{n1}	b_{n2}	. . .	a_{n-1}	b_{nn}	$b_{n(n+1)}$	. . .	a_{2n-2}

By applying $A_i \rightarrow B_i$, $1 \leq i \leq n - 1$, we obtain

$$b_{1(n+i-1)} = a_{n+i-1}, \, 1 \leq i \leq n - 1.$$

Thus, the first row is a target row, and the JD $|x|(U_0, U_1, \ldots, U_{n-1})$ is lossless.

However, the JD involving any proper subset S of $\{U_0, U_1, \ldots, U_{n-1}\}$ with $2 \leq |S| \leq n - 1$ is lossy. Suppose U_0 is in S, but U_i for some i, $1 \leq i \leq n - 1$ is not in S. Since A_i for each i, $1 \leq i \leq n - 1$, appears in exactly two relation schemes U_0 and U_i in table 6-6, all entries in the A_i-column are distinct after the row corresponding to U_i is deleted from table 6-6. Since A_i does not appear on the right side of any FD in Σ, no two variables in the A_i-column can be made equal. Although $A_i \rightarrow B_i$ is in Σ, the $(1, n+i-1)$-entry originally filled by the nondistinguished variable $b_{1(n+i-1)}$ under the B_i-column is never changed to the distinguished variable a_{n+i-1}, and the first row contains at least one nondistinguished variable $b_{1(n+i-1)}$. If U_j for any $j \geq 1$ and $j \neq i$ is in S, then the (j, i)-entry originally filled by the nondistinguished variable b_{ji}, is never changed to the distinguished variable a_i, and the j-th row cannot be a target row. Therefore the JD over S is lossy.

Suppose $|S| \geq 2$, and U_0 is not in S (i.e., the first row is deleted from table 6-6). Then no entries have the same variable in any of the columns for the $n - 1$ A attributes, so no FDs in Σ can be applied to change any nondistingushed variable. It follows that no row can be made as a target row, and the JD is lossy.

6.5 THE MEMBERSHIP PROBLEM FOR FULL JOIN DEPENDENCIES

Let Σ be a set of FJDs and j be a single FJD. The problem of deciding whether $\Sigma \models j$ is known as the membership problem. Without providing a formal proof, we state that $\Sigma \models$ j iff the corresponding tableau contains a target row. This logical implication is demonstrated by an example.

Example 6.9:

Let U = A B C D E, $\Sigma = \{|x|(A\ C, A\ B\ D, B\ D\ E), |x|(A\ B\ D, C\ D\ E)\}$, and j $= |x|(A\ C, A\ B\ D, D\ E)$. Define the initial tableau T_j based on j as shown in the following. In table 6-7(a), the three rows w_1, w_2, and w_3 are, respectively, determined by the three relation schemes A C, A B D, and D E in the FJD j. We make the projections $\pi_{A\ B\ D}(T_j)$ and $\pi_{C\ D\ E}(T_j)$ as shown in tables 6-7(b) and 6-7(c), respectively, based on the FJD $|x|(A\ B\ D, C\ D\ E)$ in Σ.

Now, we need to define a subsumption relation on a set of tuples or rows in a (projected) tableau.

Definition 6.5: Let w_i and w_j be two rows in a (projected) tableau involving U', a subset of U, as its set of column labels. Whenever a distinguished variable $w_j[A]$ implies that $w_i[A]$ is also a distinguished variable for attribute A in U', w_i *subsumes* w_j, or w_j is *subsumed by* w_i. A row having only nondistinguished variables is subsumed by any row in the tableau.

In this definition, if w_i subsumes w_j, then w_j being distinguished requires that $w_i[A]$ also be distinguished; but conversely, $w_i[A]$ being distinguished does not require that $w_j[A]$ also be distinguished. Hence, the subsumption relation on a set of rows in a tableau has the properties of reflexivity, transitivity, and antisymmetry.

We continue to solve the membership problem of example 6.9 by the tableau approach. In the projection $\pi_{A\ B\ D}(T_j)$ as shown in table 6-7(b), the second row $a_1\ a_2\ a_4$ subsumes the other two rows $a_1\ b_{12}\ b_{14}$ and $b_{31}\ b_{32}\ a_4$ since a_1 and a_4 in the first and third row imply, respectively, a_1 and a_4 in the second row. Similarly, in the projection $\pi_{C\ D\ E}(T_j)$ as shown in table 6-7(c), the third row $b_{33}\ a_4\ a_5$ subsumes the second row $b_{23}\ a_4\ b_{25}$, since a_4 in the second row implies a_4 in the third row. The first row of table 6-7(c) is not subsumed by any other row since neither the second nor the third row has a_3.

We delete the subsumed rows in both projections and then join the resulting projections to yield the new row $a_1\ a_2\ b_{33}\ a_4\ a_5$, denoted by w_4, and add w_4 to T_j, as shown in table 6-7(a), to yield the tableau T_j, as shown in table 6-7(d).

By repeating the previous process, we make the projections $\pi_{A\ C}(T'_j)$, $\pi_{A\ B\ D}(T'_j)$, and $\pi_{B\ D\ E}(T'_j)$ based on the FJD $|x|(A\ C, A\ B\ D, B\ D\ E)$ in Σ; determine and then delete all subsumed

TABLE 6-7(a). THE INITIAL
TABLEAU T_j

	A	B	C	D	E
w_1	a_1	b_{12}	a_3	b_{14}	b_{15}
w_2	a_1	a_2	b_{23}	a_4	b_{25}
w_3	b_{31}	b_{32}	b_{33}	a_4	a_5

TABLE 6-7(b). $\pi_{A\ B\ D}(T_j)$

A	B	D
a_1	b_{12}	b_{14}
a_1	a_2	a_4
b_{31}	b_{32}	a_4

TABLE 6-7(c). $\pi_{C\ D\ E}(T_j)$

C	D	E
a_3	b_{14}	b_{15}
b_{23}	a_4	b_{25}
b_{33}	a_4	a_5

TABLE 6-7(d).   TABLEAU
$T'_j = T_j \cup \{w_4\}$

	A	B	C	D	E
w_1	a_1	b_{12}	a_3	b_{14}	b_{15}
w_2	a_1	a_2	b_{23}	a_4	b_{25}
w_3	b_{31}	b_{32}	b_{33}	a_4	a_5
w_4	a_1	a_2	b_{33}	a_4	a_5

rows in these projections; and finally, join the resulting projections to yield new rows. In this example, the only new row generated is $a_1\ a_2\ a_3\ a_4\ a_5$, which is a target row so that the process no longer repeats and $\Sigma \models j$ is true.

This tableau method is applicable only to FJDs. The problem of testing whether a single JD j is logically implied by a JD and a set of FDs [Mai81b] or by a JD and a set of MVDs [Bee80] is NP-complete.

*6.6 INFERENCE RULES FOR JOIN DEPENDENCIES

Sciore [Sci82] proposed a set of inference rules for JDs. The set is sound, but it seems unlikely that the set is complete.

JD0: $\emptyset \models |x|(X)$ for a subset X of U.
This inference rule means that any relation r(X) satisfies the JD $|x|(X)$, since r(X) = $|x|(r[X])$, i.e., (6.2b) holds.

JD1:   Let $|x|(S) = |x|(U_1, \ldots, U_k)$ and $ATTR(S) = U_1 U_2 \ldots U_k$. $\{|x|(S)\} |=$ $|x|(S, Y)$ if $Y \subseteq ATTR(S)$ where $U_1, \ldots, U_k$, and Y are relation schemes.

Recall that $U_1 \ldots U_k$ is the union of U_1 through U_k and $|x|(|x|(S), Y) = |x|(S, Y) =$ $|x|(U_1, \ldots, U_k, Y)$.

Example 6.10:

Let $|x|(S) = |x|(A\,C, B\,C)$ and $Y = A\,B$. Then $\{|x|(A\,C, B\,C)\} |= |x|(A\,C, B\,C, A\,B)$. This means that a relation r(A B C) satisfying the left JD $|x|(A\,C, B\,C)$ also satisfies the right JD $|x|(A\,C, B\,C, A\,B)$, or equivalently, r(A B C) is in $SAT(\{|x|(A\,C, B\,C)\})$ implies that r(A B C) is in $SAT(\{|x|(A\,C, B\,C, A\,B)\})$. This example involves FJDs on both sides of $|=$ so that it can be checked by the tableau method in section 6.5. In example 6.3, r(A B C) = {a b c, a b′ c′, a′ b c″} satisfying the JD $|x|(A\,C, B\,C)$ also satisfies the JD $|x|(A\,C, B\,C, A\,B)$.

JD2: $\{|x|(S, Y, Z)\} |= |x|(S, Y\,Z)$ where Y and Z are relation schemes and $|x|(S) = |x|(U_1, \ldots, U_k)$.

Example 6.11:

Let $|x|(S) = |x|(A\,C, D\,E)$, $Y = A\,B\,D$, and $Z = B\,D$. Then $\{|x|(A\,C, D\,E, A\,B\,D, B\,D)\} |= |x|(A\,C, D\,E, A\,B\,D)$. Since both JDs are full, the tableau method can be used to verify the logical consequence.

JD3: $\{|x|(S, Y), |x|(R)\} |= |x|(S, R)$ if $ATTR(R) = Y$ where Y is a relation scheme and $|x|(S)$ and $|x|(R)$ are JDs.

Example 6.12:

Let $|x|(S) = |x|(A\,C, A\,B\,D)$, $Y = B\,D\,E$, and $|x|(R) = |x|(B\,D, D\,E)$. Then $\{|x|(A\,C, A\,B\,D, B\,D\,E), |x|(B\,D, D\,E)\} |= |x|(A\,C, A\,B\,D, B\,D, D\,E)$. Since $ATTR(R) = B\,D\,E \subset ATTR(S\,Y) = A\,B\,C\,D\,E$, R is not a FJD so that the tableau method cannot be used to verify the logical implication.

JD4: $\{|x|(S, Y\,A)\} |= |x|(S, Y)$ if $A \notin ATTR(S)$ where Y A is a relation scheme and $|x|(S)$ is a JD.

Example 6.13:

View $|x|(S) = |x|(B\,C\,D)$ and $Y\,A = D\,E\,A$ where $A \notin ATTR(S) (= B\,C\,D)$. Then $\{|x|(B\,C\,D, D\,E\,A\} |= |x|(B\,C\,D, D\,E)$. Similarly, we have $\{|x|(B\,C\,D, C\,D\,E)\} |= |x|(B\,C\,D, C\,D)$ where $E \notin ATTR(S) (= B\,C\,D)$ by viewing E as A in JD4. Since the right JDs $|x|(B\,C\,D, D\,E)$ and $|x|(B\,C\,D, C\,D)$ in both cases are not full, the tableau method cannot be used.

Definition 6.6:   A JD $|x|(U_1, U_2, \ldots, U_m)$ over $U = U_1 \ldots U_m$ is *trivial* if it is satisfied by every relation r(U).

Theorem 6.3:   A JD $|x|(U_1, \ldots, U_m)$ over $U = U_1 \ldots U_m$ is trivial iff $U_i = U$ for some i, $1 \leq i \leq m$.

The proof of this theorem is left as an exercise (exercise 6.4).

Theorem 6.4:   The set of inference rules JD0 through JD4 is sound. For a proof, the interested reader should refer to [Sci82].

The inference rules JD3 and JD4 involve EJDs. We can combine them to obtain an equivalent JD5 involving only FJDs.

JD5:   Let $|x|(S, Y)$ and $|x|(R)$ be FJDs such that $\{A \mid A$ appears in more than one relation scheme of $R\} \subseteq Y$. If $|x|(R) = |x|(Y_1, \ldots, Y_m)$, then $\{|x|(S, Y), |x|(R)\} |= |x|(S, Y_1 \cap Y, \ldots, Y_m \cap Y)$.

Example 6.14:

$\{|x|(A\,C, A\,B\,D, B\,D\,E), |x|(A\,B\,D, C\,D\,E)\} |= |x|(A\,C, A\,B\,D, B\,D, D\,E)$ by viewing $|x|(S) = |x|(A\,C, A\,B\,D)$, $Y = B\,D\,E$, $|x|(R) = |x|(A\,B\,D, C\,D\,E)$, $Y_1 = A\,B\,D$, and $Y_2 = C\,D\,E$.

EXERCISES

6.1 Given r(A B C), as shown in table 6-1, find the joins $|x|(r[A\ B], r[B\ C])$ and $|x|(r[A\ B], r[A\ C])$.

6.2 Let a relation scheme R = (A B C, $\{A\ B \rightarrow C, C \rightarrow A\}$). A relation r(R) and its projections r[A B] and r[A C] are shown in table 6-8(a), (b), and (c).

TABLE 6-8(a).   A RELATION
r(R)

r(R)	A	B	C
	a	b1	c1
	a	b2	c2

TABLE 6-8(b).   PROJECTION
r[A B]

r[A B]	A	B
	a	b1
	a	b2

TABLE 6-8(c).   PROJECTION
r[A C]

r[A C]	A	C
	a	c1
	a	c2

Show that the join corresponding to the JD $|x|(A\ B, A\ C)$ is lossy.

6.3 Let U = A B C D E F G H, Σ = {B → E, C → E, E F → G, G → A B H}, and Db = {A B F G, B C, C D F H, A E H}. Determine the losslessness of the join corresponding to the JD ⋈(A B F G, B C, C D F H, A E H).

6.4 Prove theorem 6.3 by the tableau method.

6.5 Check the logical implication of {⋈(A C, A B D, B D E), ⋈(A B D, C D E)} ⊨ ⋈(A C, A B D, B D, D E) by the tableau method.

chapter 7

NORMALIZATION

7.1 INTRODUCTION

To decompose a relation into a number of subrelations is known as a *normalization*. There are two approaches to normalization: vertical and horizontal normalization. Vertical normalization requires the use of operations called "projection" and "join"; horizontal normalization is based on the operations known as "selection" and "union."

There are two methods for vertical normalization: normalization through vertical decomposition from first normal form up to project-join normal form, and normalization through synthesis from first normal form up to elementary key normal form. There are synthesis algorithms available in the literature [Ber76, Aus83]. The recently proposed algorithm [Aus83, Yan85] based on finding an LR-minimal FD-covering is very valuable in the design of a better database scheme, since systematic methods for finding superfluous nodes, redundant nodes, and redundant arcs in an FD-graph are all provided.

This chapter covers in detail various normal forms including the first, second, third, elementary key, Boyce-Codd, fourth, and project-join normal forms by vertical normalization. The synthesis algorithm using FD-graphs and a case study for horizontal normalization are included.

7.2 FIRST NORMAL FORM

As mentioned in section 1.2, the domains of attributes are assumed to be simple, i.e., their values are atomic (nondecomposable by the underlying database management system).

Definition 7.1:   A relation scheme $R = A_{i_1} \ldots A_{i_k}$ is in *first normal form* (abbreviated as 1NF) if the domain of each attribute A_{i_j} for $1 \leqslant j \leqslant k$ is simple. A database scheme is in *1NF* if each relation scheme in it is in 1NF.

Example 7.1:

> Let DEPT, STOCK, MGR, and QTY, denoting, respectively, the department, stock, manager, and stock quantity, be the attributes of U_k whose domains are all simple. The relation scheme U_k = DEPT STOCK MGR QTY is in 1NF. Let DTSK = DEPT STOCK. Then the relation scheme DTSK MGR QTY is not in 1NF, since DTSK is composite and can be decomposed into DEPT and STOCK.

7.3 SECOND NORMAL FORM

Let $U = A_1 \ldots A_n$ be the universal set of attributes and Σ be a set of FDs on U. To obtain a second normal form database scheme, we need a set Σ of FDs as the basis for normalization. For defining a relation scheme in second normal form, we must identify an attribute as either prime or nonprime, and an FD as either a partial or full dependency as defined in the following.

Definition 7.2:   An attribute A in U is *prime* if A belongs to some key (definition 1.4 or 4.9), and is *nonprime* otherwise.

Definition 7.3:   Let $X \rightarrow A$ be a nontrivial FD (i.e., A is not in X). Attribute A is *partially dependent on* X if $Y \rightarrow A$ exists for some proper subset Y of X. When both FDs $X \rightarrow A$ and $Y \rightarrow A$ exist with $Y \subset X$, we say that $X \rightarrow A$ is a *partial dependency*. An FD $X \rightarrow A$ is a *full dependency* if $Y \nrightarrow A$ for all proper subsets Y of X.

In this definition, the FD $X \rightarrow A$ is required to be nontrivial. By this requirement, a trivial FD $X \rightarrow A$ (i.e., $A \in X$) is not defined as a partial dependency, although the trivial FD $A \rightarrow A$ exists by the inference rule FD0 of reflexivity.

Definition 7.4:   A 1NF relation scheme $R = (U, \Sigma)$ is in *second normal form* (abbreviated as 2NF) if each nonprime attribute in U is not partially dependent on every key for R. A database scheme is in *2NF* if each relation scheme in it is in 2NF.

A relation scheme R being in 2NF is determined by all partial dependencies involving keys and nonprime attributes. On the other hand, R not being in 2NF is determined by some nonprime attribute A_i and some key K_j for R such that $K_j \rightarrow A_i$ is a partial dependency. A prime attribute being partially dependent on a key can be ignored. In addition, since a partial dependency $X \rightarrow A$ where X is not a superkey is redundant (since $\{Y \rightarrow A\} \vdash X \rightarrow A$ for some $Y \subset X$), it can be ignored. Recall that a key is also a superkey.

The problems of testing the primeness of each attribute and of deciding whether a relation scheme has a minimal-sized key are both NP-complete [Bee79a, Luc78]. Thus, the determination of a database scheme being in 2NF is a difficult problem.

Example 7.2:

If the relation scheme U_k = DEPT STOCK MGR QTY in example 7.1 is constrained by the two FDs in Σ_k:

$$\text{DEPT} \rightarrow \text{MGR}, \tag{7.1a}$$

meaning that each department has a unique manager—and

$$\text{DEPT STOCK} \rightarrow \text{QTY}, \tag{7.1b}$$

meaning that each pair of department and stock has a unique stock quantity—then the only key is DEPT STOCK, since (DEPT STOCK)$^+$ = U_k, DEPT$^+$ = DEPT MGR, and STOCK$^+$ = STOCK. The attributes MGR and QTY are nonprime. Since (7.1a) involves the nonprime attribute MGR and the partial dependency

$$\text{DEPT STOCK} \rightarrow \text{MGR} \tag{7.1c}$$

is in Σ_k^+, the relation scheme RK = (U_k, Σ_k) is not in 2NF.

   Insertion anomaly arises when the insertion of the first inventory item (i.e., the first STOCK-value) for a particular department (i.e., DEPT-value) into a relation over RK creates a new connection between that specific department and its manager (i.e., MGR-value).

   Deletion anomaly arises when the deletion of the last inventory item for a particular department from a relation over RK removes the connection between that specific department and its manager.

   Update anomaly arises when the repetition of the connection between a department and its manager for each stock in that department can lead to an inconsistency if arbitrary updates on individual tuples are permitted.

   To avoid the anomalies, we should separate the nonprime attribute MGR from the key DEPT STOCK (since MGR is partially dependent on DEPT STOCK) by decomposing RK into two subrelation schemes:

$$RK_1 = \underline{\text{DEPT}} \text{ MGR}, \tag{7.2a}$$

where the nonprime attribute MGR can coexist with the proper subset DEPT of the key DEPT STOCK, and

$$RK_2 = \underline{\text{DEPT STOCK}} \text{ QTY}, \tag{7.2b}$$

which does not include the nonprime attribute MGR. In (7.2a) and (7.2b), each underscored set of attributes denotes the key and induces a key dependency for the underlying relation scheme. For example, DEPT is the key, and DEPT $\rightarrow$ DEPT MGR is a key dependency for RK_1. Similarly, DEPT STOCK is the key, and DEPT STOCK $\rightarrow$ DEPT STOCK QTY is a key dependency for RK_2. By this decomposition, RK_1 and RK_2 are both in 2NF, and the two given FDs in Σ_k are, respectively, preserved or enforced by the relation schemes of (7.2a) and (7.2b).

   Note that (7.2a) and (7.2b) are alternative representations for the relation schemes (DEPT MGR, {(7.1a)}) and (DEPT STOCK QTY, {(7.1b)}). This alternative representation is limited to the case in which the key is unique. Otherwise it is not convenient to underscore more than one key in a relation scheme.

Example 7.3:

Let U_m = A B C D E F and Σ_m consists of the following FDs:

$$A B \rightarrow C D, \tag{7.3a}$$
$$A \rightarrow E, \tag{7.3b}$$
$$B \rightarrow F, \tag{7.3c}$$

and

$$E F \rightarrow C. \tag{7.3d}$$

This scheme has a practical significance, since its FD-graph is isomorphic [Yan79] to that of the stock inventory universal relation scheme in [Lin81]. In (7.3a), A B $\rightarrow$ C is redundant, since there exists a dotted implication graph from A B to C (what is it). In (7.3a), we can also view C as extraneous, so that the FD of (7.3a) is not right-reduced.

Let two relation schemes be

$$RM_1 = (U_m, \{(7.3a), (7.3b), (7.3c)\}) \tag{7.4a}$$

and

$$RM_2 = (E F C, \{(7.3d)\}). \tag{7.4b}$$

The keys for relation schemes RM_1 and RM_2 are, respectively, the sets A B and E F. Each relation scheme is individually examined. The relation scheme RM_2 is obviously in 2NF. The relation scheme RM_1 is not in 2NF because of the existence of the following partial dependencies in Σ_m^+:

$$A B \rightarrow E \tag{7.3e}$$

(since its left subset is the key for RM_1) relative to (7.3b) for nonprime attribute E in RM_1 and

$$A B \rightarrow F \tag{7.3f}$$

(since its left subset is the key for RM_1) relative to (7.3c) for nonprime attribute F in RM_1 (E and F are both prime in RM_2).

Example 7.4:

Let the relation scheme RNONE = (U_n, Σ_{n1}), where U_n = A B C D E F and

$$\Sigma_{n1} = \{C \rightarrow A, A E \rightarrow B, B F \rightarrow C, C D \rightarrow E F, E F \rightarrow A D\}. \tag{7.5a}$$

The subset closures C^+ = A C, $(A E)^+$ = A B E, $(B F)^+$ = A B C F, $(C D)^+$ = $(E F)^+$ = U_n, D^+ = D, E^+ = E, and F^+ = F imply that C D and E F are the keys for the relation scheme RNONE. Hence, A and B are nonprime attributes. The FD C D $\rightarrow$ A (implied by C D $\rightarrow$ E F and E F $\rightarrow$ A) in Σ_{n1}^+ is a partial dependency, since C $\rightarrow$ A is in Σ_{n1}. In obtaining a 2NF database scheme, the nonprime attribute A cannot coexist with C D and E F where E F $\equiv$ C D. Thus, we must use the FD-covering

$$\Sigma_{n2} = \{C \rightarrow A, A E \rightarrow B, B F \rightarrow C, C D \rightarrow E F, E F \rightarrow C D\} \tag{7.5b}$$

to decompose the relation scheme RNTWO = (A B C D E F, Σ_{n2}) into two subrelation schemes based on C D $\rightarrow$ A and E F $\rightarrow$ A by separating A from C D and from E F:

$$RNTWO_1 = (A\ B\ C\ E, \{C \rightarrow A,\ A\ E \rightarrow B\}), \tag{7.5c}$$

in which only the first two FDs in (7.5a) are selected and

$$RNTWO_2 = (B\ C\ D\ E\ F, \{B\ F \rightarrow C,\ C\ D \rightarrow E\ F,\ E\ F \rightarrow C\ D\}), \tag{7.5d}$$

in which the set of attributes B C D E F is obtained by deleting A from U_n = A B C D E F. In (7.5d), the selected FDs are B F → C, C D → E F, and E F → D, and the additional E F → C in Σ_{n1}^+ is used to replace E F → A in Σ_{n1}. The reason behind this replacement is to maintain C D ≡ E F; otherwise we will have {B F → C, CD → E F, E F → D} from which $(C\ D)^+$ = C D E F and $(E\ F)^+$ = D E F, which imply that C D and E F are no longer equivalent. As will be seen in example 7.25, there is a systematic method, based on the graphical representation of FDs, to solve this FD adjustment problem.

In the first subrelation scheme $RNTWO_1$, the key becomes A C E (since $(A\ E)^+$ = A B E). Consequently, B is the only nonprime attribute that is partially dependent on the key A C E. Thus, we must further decompose this scheme based on the partial dependency A C E → B, by separating B from A C E, into the following 2NF subrelation schemes:

$$RNTWO_{1a} = (A\ C, \{C \rightarrow A\}) \tag{7.5e}$$

and

$$RNTWO_{1b} = (A\ B\ E, \{A\ E \rightarrow B\}). \tag{7.5f}$$

Example 7.5:

Let a relation scheme be

$$ROONE = (A\ B\ C\ D\ E, \\ \{A\ B \rightarrow C\ E,\ A\ C \rightarrow B\ D,\ B \rightarrow C\ E,\ C \rightarrow B\ D\}). \tag{7.6a}$$

This relation scheme has two keys, A B and A C, so that D and E are nonprime. There exist the partial dependencies A B → D E and A C → D E (since {B → D E} |− A B → D E and {C → D E} |−A C → D E for A B → D, B → D, A C → E, and C → E in Σ_{o1}^+) for nonprime attributes D and E. This means that D cannot coexist with A B and A C in a single relation scheme, and similarly, E cannot coexist with A B and A C in a single relation scheme. Hence, based on the partial dependencies A B → D and A C → D, we need to decompose ROONE into

$$ROONE_1 = (A\ B\ C\ E, \{A\ B \rightarrow C\ E,\ A\ C \rightarrow B,\ B \rightarrow C\ E,\ C \rightarrow B\}), \tag{7.6b}$$

where A B and A C are the keys and E is non-prime, and

$$ROONE_2 = (C\ D, \{C \rightarrow D\}), \tag{7.6c}$$

where C is the key. In $ROONE_1$ of (7.6b), since E is still partially dependent on the keys A B and A C, we must further decompose $ROONE_1$ into

$$ROONE_{1a} = (A\ B\ C, \{A\ B \rightarrow C,\ A\ C \rightarrow B,\ B \rightarrow C,\ C \rightarrow B\}), \tag{7.6d}$$

where A B and A C are the keys and no attribute is nonprime, and

$$ROONE_{1b} = (B\ E, \{B \rightarrow E\}), \tag{7.6e}$$

where B is the key. The 2NF database scheme becomes

$$Db_{o1} = \{ROONE_{1a}, ROONE_{1b}, ROONE_2\}. \tag{7.6f}$$

Example 7.6:

Let a relation scheme be $U_e = A\ B\ C\ D\ E\ F\ G$ and

$$\Sigma_{e1} = \{A\ B \rightarrow D\ E\ F, A\ C \rightarrow G, A \rightarrow C\}$$

as used in examples 4.9 and 4.25. The key is A B, and the nonprime attributes are C, D, E, F, and G. The FDs $A\ B \rightarrow C$ and $A\ B \rightarrow G$ in Σ_{e1}^+ (implied, respectively, by $A \rightarrow C$ and $A \rightarrow G$ where $A \rightarrow G$ is derived by $\{A \rightarrow C, A\ C \rightarrow G\}$) and the FD $A\ C \rightarrow G$ in Σ_{e1} (implied by $A \rightarrow G$) are partial dependencies. We need to separate C from A B and also to separate G from A B and A C to yield a database scheme as

$$Db_{e1} = \{(A\ B\ D\ E\ F, \{A\ B \rightarrow D\ E\ F\}),$$
$$(A\ C, \{A \rightarrow C\}), (A\ G, \{A \rightarrow G\})\}.$$

As shown in example 4.9, the attribute C in $A\ C \rightarrow G$ is extraneous. As shown in example 4.25, the node A C in the FD-graph $G_{\Sigma_{e1}}$ is superfluous by definition 4.22 or theorem 4.6. Hence, we have the following LR-minimal FD-covering

$$\Sigma_{e2} = \{A\ B \rightarrow D\ E\ F, A \rightarrow C\ G\},$$

where the key is still A B; the nonprime attributes are still C, D, E, F, and G; and the partial dependencies are $A\ B \rightarrow C$ and $A\ B \rightarrow G$ ($A\ C \rightarrow G$ is deleted with the addition of $A \rightarrow G$ and is no longer a partial dependency). We need only to separate C G from A B to obtain a better database scheme

$$Db_{e2} = \{(A\ B\ D\ E\ F, \{A\ B \rightarrow D\ E\ F\}), (A\ C\ G, \{A \rightarrow C\ G\})\}.$$

This example demonstrates that whenever a given set of FDs is not minimized, the normalized database scheme through decomposition may not have the minimal number of relation schemes. This is one of the disadvantages of normalization through decomposition.

7.4 THIRD NORMAL FORM

To obtain a third normal form database scheme, we still need a set Σ of FDs on U and to use transitive dependencies involving keys and nonprime attributes. Third normal form was first proposed by Codd in [Cod72a].

Definition 7.5:   Let X and Y be nonempty subsets of U, and A be an attribute in U. Attribute A is *transitively dependent* on X via Y if the following conditions are all satisfied:

(1) $X \rightarrow Y$,

(2) $Y \nrightarrow X$ (i.e., Y is not functionally dependent on X),

(3) $Y \rightarrow A$, and

(4) A is not in X Y (where X Y is the union of X and Y).

In this definition, conditions (1) and (3) imply $X \rightarrow A$ by the inference rule FD2 of transitivity. Condition (2) is essential, otherwise $X \equiv Y$ and, consequently, $X \rightarrow A$ and $Y \rightarrow A$ are equivalent (definition 4.20a). Condition (4) is also essential, otherwise $X \rightarrow A$ can be derived by the inference rule FD0 of reflexivity if A is in X, or by the inference rule FD5 of projectivity if A is in Y. When $X \rightarrow A$ satisfies definition 7.5, it is a *transitive dependency*.

Example 7.7:

The nonprime attribute MGR in example 7.2 is transitively dependent on the key DEPT STOCK via DEPT since

(1) DEPT STOCK $\rightarrow$ DEPT (by FD0),

(2) DEPT $\nrightarrow$ DEPT STOCK (DEPT is a proper subset of the key DEPT STOCK),

(3) DEPT $\rightarrow$ MGR (given FD (7.1a)), and

(4) MGR is not in DEPT STOCK.

Theorem 7.1:   A nonprime attribute that is partially dependent on a key K is also transitively dependent on K.

Proof: Let $R = (U, \Sigma)$ be a relation scheme. Suppose that a nonprime attribute A in U is partially dependent on a key K for R (i.e., $K \rightarrow A$ is in Σ^+ and $K' \rightarrow A$ is also in Σ^+, where K' is a proper subset of K by definition 7.3). Since K' is a subset of K, by the inference rule FD0 of reflexivity, $K \rightarrow K'$ is in Σ^+, and condition (1) of definition 7.5 is satisfied. Since K is a key and K' is a proper subset of K, it is impossible to have $K' \rightarrow K$ in Σ^+, and condition (2) of definition 7.5 is satisfied. Condition (3) of definition 7.5 was defined to be true (i.e., $K' \rightarrow A$). Since A is nonprime and K is a key, A is not in K by definition 7.2. Since K' is a subset of K, A is also not in K'. Hence, condition (4) of definition 7.5 is satisfied. Therefore, A is transitively dependent on K via K'.

Example 7.8:

In example 7.2, the FDs DEPT $\rightarrow$ MGR of (7.1a) in Σ_k and DEPT STOCK $\rightarrow$ MGR of (7.1c) in Σ_k^+ imply that (7.1c) is a partial dependency. In example 7.7, it was shown that (7.1c) is also a transitive dependency via DEPT.

Definition 7.6a: A 1NF relation scheme $R = (U, \Sigma)$ is in *third normal form* (abbreviated as 3NF) if each nonprime attribute is not transitively dependent on any key for R. A database scheme is in *3NF* if each relation scheme in it is in 3NF.

To determine a relation scheme R being in 3NF all nonprime attributes must not be transitively dependent on any key to satisfy definition 7.6a. On the other hand, R is not in 3NF if, for some nonprime attribute A_i and some key K_j for R, $K_j \rightarrow A_i$ is a transitive dependency. An attribute being transitively dependent on X where X is not a superkey can be ignored, since the corresponding FD, implied by the inference rule of transitivity, is redundant.

A relation scheme that is in 3NF is also in 2NF (or equivalently, a relation scheme that is not in 2NF is also not in 3NF), since a nonprime attribute that is partially dependent on a key is also transitively dependent on the key. Equivalently, a nonprime attribute that is not transitively dependent on a key is also not partially dependent on the key. However, a nonprime attribute not being partially dependent on a key K does not preclude its being transitively dependent on K.

Theorem 7.2: If a nonprime attribute is transitively dependent on a key K, then it may be or may not be partially dependent on K.

Proof: Let K be a key for $R = (U, \Sigma)$ and A in U be a nonprime attribute. By this assumption, A is not in K, and a part of condition (4) is satisfied. Suppose that $K \rightarrow A$ is a transitive dependency via X. Then by conditions (1), (2), (3), and (4) of definition 7.5, $K \rightarrow X$, $X \nrightarrow K$, $X \rightarrow A$, and $A \notin X$. There are two possible relationships between X and K:

(1) X is a proper subset of K: In this case, $K \rightarrow A$ and $X \rightarrow A$ imply that $K \rightarrow A$ is a partial dependency on K.

(2) X is not a proper subset of K: In this case, $K \rightarrow A$ and $X \rightarrow A$ do not imply that $K \rightarrow A$ is a partial dependency on K.

Example 7.9:

The relation schemes $RK_1 = \underline{DEPT}$ MGR and $RK_2 = \underline{DEPT \ STOCK}$ QTY of example 7.2 are both in 3NF, since there are no transitive dependencies in each individual relation scheme.

Example 7.10:

Let the relation scheme EMPNO-DEPT be equal to

(EMPNO NAME DEPT MGR, {EMPNO $\rightarrow$ NAME DEPT, DEPT $\rightarrow$ MGR})

where EMPNO stands for the number of an employee. This relation scheme has the key EMPNO. It is not in 3NF, since the nonprime attribute MGR is transitively dependent on the key EMPNO via DEPT. However, it is in 2NF, since MGR is not partially dependent on the key EMPNO. This demonstrates case (2) in the proof of theorem 7.2.

Inserting the first or deleting the last EMPNO-value for a particular DEPT-value creates an anomaly, since a DEPT-MGR connection is created or destroyed in the process. The repetition of the DEPT-MGR connection for each EMPNO in that department creates the inconsistency problem.

EMPNO-DEPT should be decomposed into the subrelation schemes by separating MGR from EMPNO (since MGR is nonprime and is transitively dependent on the key EMPNO):

$$\text{EMPLOYEE} = (\text{EMPNO NAME DEPT}, \{\text{EMPNO} \rightarrow \text{NAME DEPT}\}) \qquad (7.7a)$$

and

$$\text{DEPARTMENT} = (\text{DEPT MGR}, \{\text{DEPT} \rightarrow \text{MGR}\}), \qquad (7.7b)$$

which are both in 3NF and preserve the two given FDs.

Example 7.11:

Let a relation scheme be RPONE = (A B C D, $\{A \rightarrow B, B \rightarrow C\}$). Since $A^+ = A B C$ and $B^+ = B C$, A D is the key for RPONE; and B and C are nonprime. Since $A D \rightarrow B$ is in Σ_{p1}^+ and $A \rightarrow B$ is in Σ_{p1}, the nonprime attribute B is partially dependent on A D. This partial dependency $A D \rightarrow B$ is also a transitive dependency via A. Hence, we need to decompose RPONE into

$$\text{RPONE}_1 = (A C D, \{A D \rightarrow C\}),$$

where the FD $A D \rightarrow C$ is derived by projecting the key dependency $A D \rightarrow A B C D$ onto A C D to yield $A D \rightarrow A C D$ and then by eliminating the trivial FD $A D \rightarrow A D$; and

$$\text{RPONE}_2 = (A B, \{A \rightarrow B\}).$$

In this 3NF database scheme, the given FD $B \rightarrow C$ in Σ_{p1} is not enforced. Although this database scheme is in 3NF, $A \rightarrow C$ in Σ_{p1}^+ ($\{A \rightarrow B, B \rightarrow C\} \mid - A \rightarrow C$) derives the partial dependency $A D \rightarrow C$; and $A D \rightarrow A$ and $A \rightarrow C$ imply the transitive dependency $A D \rightarrow C$ via A. This FD $A D \rightarrow C$ is known as a *hidden partial dependency* and a *hidden transitive dependency* through decomposition. The existence of a hidden partial or transitive dependency involving a nonprime attribute is also one of the disadvantages of normalization through decomposition.

Definition 7.6b: A 1NF relation scheme R = (U, Σ) is in 3NF if every attribute being transitively dependent on a key is prime.

Example 7.12:

The database scheme Db_{n2} consisting of RNTWO_{1a} of (7.5e), RNTWO_{1b} of (7.5f), and RNTWO_2 of (7.5d), as developed in example 7.4, i.e.,

$$\{(A C, \{C \rightarrow A\}), (A B E, \{A E \rightarrow B\}),$$
$$(B C D E F, \{B F \rightarrow C, C D \rightarrow E F, E F \rightarrow C D\})\}$$

is in 3NF. It is in 3NF since the first two relation schemes RNTWO_{1a} and RNTWO_{1b} do not have any transitive dependency, the attributes in the third relation scheme RNTWO_2 are all prime (since the keys are B C D, B D F, and B E F), and the transitive dependencies B C D $\rightarrow$ E F, B D F $\rightarrow$ C, and B E F $\rightarrow$ C D involve only prime attributes.

Lemma 7.1:   Let R = (U, Σ) be a 1NF relation scheme and A be an attribute in U.

If K is a key for R, A is nonprime, and A is partially dependent on K, then A is transitively dependent on every key for R.

Proof: By theorem 7.1, A is also transitively dependent on the key K. We need to show that A is transitively dependent on every other key K' for R.

Since A is nonprime, A does not belong to any key and any subset of a key. Since A is partially dependent on K, there must exist a proper subset X of K such that $X \rightarrow A$ is in Σ^+. Now, for any other key K' for R, $K' \rightarrow X$ is in Σ^+, $X \nrightarrow K'$, $X \rightarrow A$ is in Σ^+, and A is not in K' X. Thus, $K' \rightarrow A$ is a transitive dependency via X in Σ^+.

Lemma 7.2: Let $R = (U, \Sigma)$ be a 1NF relation scheme and A be an attribute in U. If K is a key for R, A is nonprime, and A is transitively dependent on K, then A is transitively dependent on every key for R.

The proof of this lemma is similar to those of lemma 7.1 and theorem 7.2 and is left to the reader as an exercise (do exercise 7.5).

Lemmas 7.1 and 7.2 imply the following result.

Theorem 7.3: A 1NF relation scheme $R = (U, \Sigma)$ is in 3NF if each nonprime attribute is not transitively dependent on an arbitrarily chosen key for R.

By this theorem, determining that a 1NF relation scheme is in 3NF requires only to check each nonprime attribute with a single key for R (but not with all keys for R). Since the problem of testing the primeness of each attribute is NP-complete [Bee79a, Luc78], the determination of a 3NF database scheme by the normalization through decomposition based on non-prime attributes, keys, and transitive dependencies is a hard problem. This difficulty is one of the disadvantages of the normalization through decomposition to obtain a 3NF database scheme.

Example 7.13:

Let the relation scheme RQ be

$$RQ = (A\ B\ C, \{A\ B \rightarrow C, C \rightarrow A\}). \qquad (7.8a)$$

RQ has two keys A B and B C. All attributes are prime. Hence, RQ is in 3NF by definition 7.6b. However, the prime attribute A, being transitively dependent on the key A B via C, causes the following drawbacks:

(1) We cannot arbitrarily change the C-value for a particular A-B-value because by doing so, the FD $C \rightarrow A$ can be violated.

(2) The insertion of the first A-B-value for a particular C-value creates a new A-C connection.

(3) Although RQ enforces the given FD A B $\rightarrow$ C, it does not enforce the other given FD C $\rightarrow$ A.

Although A is partially dependent on the key B C (since B C $\rightarrow$ A and C $\rightarrow$ A are both in Σ_q^+) and A is transitively dependent on this key via C (since B C $\rightarrow$ C, C $\nrightarrow$ B C,

C → A, and A is not in B C), A is not partially and transitively dependent on the other key A B. In the first case, A B → A and C → A have disjoint left subsets; and for the second case, although A B → C, C $\not\to$ A B, and C → A, A is not in C, but A is in A B.

Example 7.14:

The following relation scheme

$$RCONE = (A\ B\ C\ D\ E\ F, \{A\ B \to E,\ A\ C \to F,$$
$$A\ D \to B,\ B \to C,\ C \to D\}), \tag{7.9a}$$

as used in examples 4.7, 4.20 and 4.24 has three keys A B, A C, and A D. Attributes E and F are nonprime but are not transitively dependent on any key. Thus, RCONE is in 3NF.

3NF relation schemes are used to avoid certain kinds of update anomalies and consistency difficulties among nonprime attributes. They do not eliminate similar problems caused by a prime attribute being transitively dependent on a key.

7.5 ELEMENTARY KEY NORMAL FORM

We introduce a normal form known as *elementary key normal form* [Lin81, Zan82c], which is an improved form and implies 3NF.

Definition 7.7:   A nontrivial FD X → A (i.e., A is not in X) is *elementary* if it is not a partial dependency. A key K for a relation scheme R = (U, Σ) is *elementary* if K → A is an elementary FD in Σ^+ for some attribute A in U. An attribute in an elementary key is called *elementary prime*.

A trivial FD and a partial dependency are not elementary. We refer them to as *nonelementary FDs*.

Example 7.15:

In the relation scheme of example 7.5, i.e.,

$$ROONE = (A\ B\ C\ D\ E, \{A\ B \to C\ E,\ A\ C \to B\ D,\ B \to C\ E,\ C \to B\ D\}), \tag{7.6a}$$

$(A\ B)^+ = (A\ C)^+ = A\ B\ C\ D\ E$, $B^+ = C^+ = B\ C\ D\ E$, and $A^+ = A$ imply that A B and A C are the keys for ROONE. The trivial FDs A B → A, A B → B, A C → A, A C → C, A → A, B → B, and C → C are nonelementary. The partial dependencies A B → C (since B →C), A B → D (since B → C and C → D), A B → E (since B → E), A C → B (since C → B), A C → D (since C → D), and A C → E (since C → B and B → E) are nonelementary. Hence, the keys A B and A C are not elementary; and the attributes A, B, and C are prime but are not elementary prime. The other FDs, B → C, B → E, C → B, and C → D in Σ_{o1} and B → D and C → E in Σ_{o1}^+ are elementary.
     Similarly, in ROONE$_{1a}$, i.e.,

$$ROONE_{1a} = (A\ B\ C, \{A\ B \to C,\ A\ C \to B,\ B \to C,\ C \to B\}), \tag{7.6d}$$

B ≡ C, A B ≡ A C, A B and A C are keys for ROONE$_{1a}$ but are not elementary keys, since B → C and C → B are the only elementary FDs. Hence, A, B, and C are prime but are not elementary prime.

Definition 7.8:   A 1NF relation scheme is in *elementary key normal form* (abbreviated as EKNF) if, for every elementary FD of the form $X \rightarrow A$, one of the following conditions is satisfied:

(1) X is a key, or

(2) A is an elementary prime attribute.

A database scheme is in *EKNF* if each relation scheme in it is in EKNF.

A relation scheme being in EKNF is determined by each elementary FD satisfying condition (1) or (2) of definition 7.8, whereas each nonelementary FD does not play a role in the determination and can be ignored. A relation scheme not being in EKNF is determined by existence of some elementary FD that does not satisfy both conditions (1) and (2) of definition 7.8.

Example 7.16:

The 3NF database scheme Db_{o1} of (7.6f) is not in EKNF, since the relation scheme $ROONE_{1a}$, i.e.,

$$ROONE_{1a} = (A\ B\ C,\ \{A\ B \rightarrow C,\ A\ C \rightarrow B,\ B \rightarrow C,\ C \rightarrow B\}), \quad (7.6d)$$

is not in EKNF, because the left subset B of the elementary FD $B \rightarrow C$ is not a key for $ROONE_{1a}$, and the right attribute C is not elementary prime.

To obtain an EKNF database scheme, we can delete the redundant nodes A B and A C to obtain the LR-minimal FD-covering

$$\Sigma_{o2} = \{B \rightarrow C\ E,\ C \rightarrow B\ D\},$$

where the keys are B and C, and the nonprime attributes are D and E. Based on this LR-minimal FD-covering, we have the EKNF database scheme

$$Db_{o2} = \{(B\ C\ D\ E,\ \{B \rightarrow C\ E,\ C \rightarrow B\ D\})\}.$$

This EKNF database scheme has only one relation scheme, whereas the 3NF database scheme Db_{o1} of (7.6f) has three relation schemes and is not in EKNF.

Example 7.17:

The 3NF database scheme $\{RPONE_1,\ RPONE_2\}$ where $RPONE_1 = \underline{A\ D}\ C$ and $RPONE_2 = \underline{A}$ B in example 7.11 is in EKNF, since the keys for $RPONE_1$ and $RPONE_2$ are A D and A respectively; the left subset of the elementary FD $A\ D \rightarrow C$ is the key A D, and the left subset of the elementary FD $A \rightarrow B$ is the key A.

Example 7.18:

The relation scheme RQ in example 7.13, i.e.,

$$RQ = (A\ B\ C,\ \{A\ B \rightarrow C,\ C \rightarrow A\}), \quad (7.8a)$$

is in EKNF, since the left subset of the elementary FD A B $\rightarrow$ C is a key and the right attribute of the elementary FD C $\rightarrow$ A is elementary prime.

Example 7.19:

The relation scheme in example 7.14, i.e.,

$$RCONE = (A \ B \ C \ D \ E \ F, \{A \ B \rightarrow E, \ A \ C \rightarrow F,$$
$$A \ D \rightarrow B, \ B \rightarrow C, \ C \rightarrow D\}, \quad\quad (7.9a)$$

is in EKNF, since the left subsets A B, A C, and A D of the elementary FDs A B $\rightarrow$ E, A C $\rightarrow$ F, and A D $\rightarrow$ B in Σ_{c1} and of other elementary FDs A B $\rightarrow$ F, A C $\rightarrow$ B, A C $\rightarrow$ E, A D $\rightarrow$ C, A D $\rightarrow$ E, and A D $\rightarrow$ F in Σ_{c1}^+ are all keys. The right attributes C and D of the remaining elementary FDs, B $\rightarrow$ C and C $\rightarrow$ D in Σ_{c1} and B $\rightarrow$ D in E_{c1}^+, are both elementary prime.

Example 7.20:

The 3NF database scheme $Db_{n2} = \{RNTWO_{1a}, RNTWO_{1b}, RNTWO_2\}$ in example 7.4, i.e.,

$$\{(A \ C, \{C \rightarrow A\}), (A \ B \ E, \{A \ E \rightarrow B\}),$$
$$(B \ C \ D \ E \ F, \{B \ F \rightarrow C, \ C \ D \rightarrow E \ F, \ E \ F \rightarrow C \ D\})\},$$

is not in EKNF, since the third relation scheme $RNTWO_2 = (B \ C \ D \ E \ F, \{B \ F \rightarrow C, \ C \ D \rightarrow E \ F, \ E \ F \rightarrow C \ D\})$ does not satisfy definition 7.8 for all elementary FDs B F $\rightarrow$ C, C D $\rightarrow$ E F, and E F $\rightarrow$ C D. In this relation scheme the subsets B C D, B D F, and B E F are keys but are not elementary keys; and consequently, the right attributes C, D, E, and F of the elementary FDs are prime but are not elementary prime, and the left subsets B F, C D, and E F of the elementary FDs are not keys.

To obtain an EKNF database scheme, we must further decompose the third relation scheme $RNTWO_2$ into

$$RNTWO_{2a} = (B \ C \ F, \{B \ F \rightarrow C\})$$

with the elementary key B F and

$$RNTWO_{2b} = (C \ D \ E \ F, \{C \ D \rightarrow E \ F, \ E \ F \rightarrow C \ D\})$$

with the elementary keys C D and E F.

7.6 A SYNTHESIS ALGORITHM BASED ON FD-GRAPHS

In section 4.10 we introduced FD-graphs and their closures and coverings. This section presents the synthesis algorithm based on the above concepts to find a better database scheme in EKNF by a systematic method. We assume that each compound node does not contain any extraneous attribute. If A in X is extraneous, then it can be detected by the fact that $(X - A)^+ = X^+$.

7.6.1. An Algorithm for Finding a Nonredundant Graph Covering

Given an FD-graph $G_\Sigma = (V, E)$, we find a graph covering $G'_\Sigma = (V', E')$, which is nonredundant in the sense of having no redundant nodes as defined in definition 4.18.

Input: An FD-graph $G_\Sigma = (V, E)$.

Output: A nonredundant graph covering $G'_\Sigma = (V', E')$.

Method:

(1) If V consists of no compound node, then the algorithm terminates, and the output graph covering is equal to the input FD-graph.

(2) Examine a compound node with the largest cardinality and delete it, along with all arcs incident from it if it is a redundant node.

(3) Repeat step (2) until there is no remaining compound node to be examined for redundancy.

(4) The graph $G'_\Sigma = (V', E')$, generated from $G_\Sigma = (V, E)$ by eliminating all redundant nodes, is the output graph covering. Then the algorithm terminates.

Example 7.21:

Let an FD-covering for Σ_{j1} through Σ_{j3} in example 4.22 be

$$\Sigma_{j4} = \{A \rightarrow B\ C,\ B\ C \rightarrow A,\ A\ D \rightarrow E\ F,\ B\ C\ D \rightarrow E\ F\}.$$

The FD-graph $G_{\Sigma_{j4}}$ is shown in Fig. 7-1(a). The compound nodes A D, B C, and B C D do not contain any extraneous attributes.

In Fig. 7-1(a), the compound node B C D has the largest cardinality, and so it is the first one to be examined for redundancy. The dotted implication graphs from B C D to E and from B C D to F are shown in Fig. 7-1(b) and imply that B C D is redundant. After B C D is deleted, the compound nodes A D and B C are successively examined and are not redundant. Thus, the nonredundant graph covering is updated from Fig. 7-1(a) by deleting B C D and the five arcs incident from it. The resulting LR-minimal FD-covering becomes

$$\Sigma_{j3} = \{A \rightarrow B\ C,\ B\ C \rightarrow A,\ A\ D \rightarrow E\ F\}.$$

Note that if we delete the redundant node A D, then the resulting FD-covering is

$$\Sigma_{j2} = \{A \rightarrow B\ C,\ B\ C \rightarrow A,\ B\ C\ D \rightarrow E\ F\},$$

which is LR-minimal but is worse than Σ_{j3}, because of containing one more attribute.

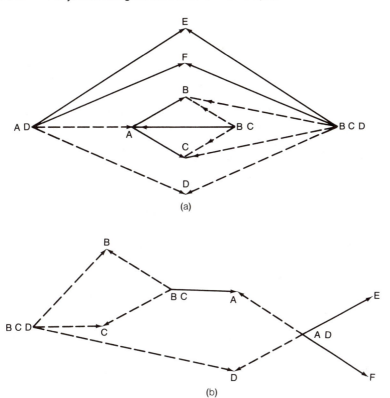

Figure 7-1   (a) The FD-graph $G_{\Sigma_{j4}}$; (b) dotted implication graphs from B C D to E and to F

7.6.2 An Algorithm for Finding a Minimal Graph Covering

Given a nonredundant graph covering $G_\Sigma = (V, E)$, a minimal graph covering $G'_\Sigma = (V', E')$ can be found by deleting any superfluous node and by making necessary arc adjustments based on theorem 4.6. An algorithm for finding a minimal graph covering for a nonredundant graph covering entails the following:

Input: A nonredundant graph covering $G_\Sigma = (V, E)$.

Output: A minimal graph covering $G'_\Sigma = (V', E')$.

Method:

(1) Find the graph closure $G^+_\Sigma = (V, E^+)$, which is defined by definition 4.16 in section 4.10.

(2) Find the equivalence classes of nodes in V, which is defined by definition 4.21 in section 4.10.

(3) If each equivalence class is a singleton set or consists of only simple nodes, then the algorithm terminates, and the output graph covering is equal to the input graph covering.

(4) Examine a nonsingleton equivalence class consisting of at least one compound node to find the candidates of possible superfluous nodes in the class. If there exists such a candidate, then choose a node j that is not a candidate (if the class has a simple node and/or a nonsuperfluous compound node) or a candidate j (if all nodes in the class are candidates) with the minimum cardinality as the representative of the class. For each candidate i that is not the representative (i.e., $i \neq j$), delete i from G_Σ^+, and make necessary arc adjustments as follows.

  (a) If there exists a node k such that (i, k) is a full arc in E, (j, k) is not in E^+, and there exists no implication graph from j to k after i is deleted, then add the new full arc (j, k) to E^+.

  (b) If both (i, k) and (j, k) are full arcs, then no arc adjustment is needed.

  (c) If (i, k) is full and there exists an implication graph from j to k after i is deleted, then no arc adjustment is required.

  Store each pair of nodes (i, j) in a list L for subsequent execution of step (6) where i is a superfluous node deleted from G_Σ^+, and j is the representative of an equivalence class of nodes. Note that when i is superfluous, (j, k) cannot be dotted.

(5) Repeat step (4) until all nonsingleton equivalence classes have been examined for superfluity. The final graph closure $G_\Sigma'^+$, updated from G_Σ^+, is the graph closure of the minimal covering.

(6) The FD-graph G_Σ is updated in accordance with the contents of the list L by eliminating each superfluous node i and by moving its full outgoing arcs to its equivalent node j, which is the representative of its equivalence class, to yield the minimal graph covering G'_Σ. Then the algorithm terminates.

This algorithm has time complexity $O(\max(|\Sigma|^2 + |\Sigma| \times |U|, p))$ [Aus83], where max means the maximum and p is the total length of the strings of symbols needed to represent Σ, the set of functional dependencies.

Example 7.22:

Reconsider the set of FDs in examples 4.7, 4.20, and 4.21, i.e.,

$$\Sigma_{c1} = \{A B \rightarrow E, A C \rightarrow F, A D \rightarrow B, B \rightarrow C, C \rightarrow D\}. \qquad (7.9a)$$

The FD-graph $G_{\Sigma_{c1}} = (V_{c1}, E_{c1})$ with

$$V_{c1} = \{A, B, C, D, E, F, A B, A C, A D\},$$

$$E_{c1}^d = \{(A B, A), (A B, B), (A C, A), (A C, C), (A D, A), (A D, D)\},$$

and

$$E_{c1}^f = \{(B, C), (C, D), (A\ B, E), (A\ C, F), (A\ D, B)\}$$

is shown in Fig. 7-2(a).

The graph closure $G_{\Sigma_{c1}}^+ = (V_{c1}, E_{c1}^+)$ has

$$E_{c\ 1}^{d+} = E_{c1}^d \cup \{(A\ B, C), (A\ B, D), (A\ B, F), (A\ B, A\ C), (A\ B, A\ D),$$
$$(A\ C, B), (A\ C, D), (A\ C, E), (A\ C, A\ B), (A\ C, A\ D)\}$$

and

$$E_{c1}^{f+} = \{(B, C), (B, D), (C, D), (A\ B, E), (A\ C, F), (A, D, B),$$
$$(A\ D, C), (A\ D, E), (A\ D, F), (A\ D, A\ B), (A\ D, A\ C)].$$

Note that (A D, D) is not in E_{c1}^{f+} (although the full implication graph (A D, C), (C, D) derives A D → D), since it is in E_{c1}^d and its corresponding FD A D → D is trivial.

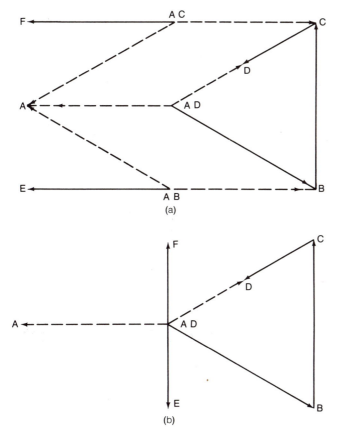

(a)

(b)

Figure 7-2   (a) The FD-graph $G_{\Sigma_{c1}}$; (b) a minimal graph covering $G_{\Sigma_{c2}}$.

Since $(A\ B)^+ = (A\ C)^+ = (A\ D)^+ = U_c$, $A\ B \equiv A\ C \equiv A\ D$. In step (2) of the algorithm the only one nonsingleton equivalence class is $\{A\ B, A\ C, A\ D\}$. In step (4) nodes A B and A C are candidates, since the arcs (A B, A D) and (A C, A D) are dotted. Since A D is the only nonsuperfluous node in the equivalence class, it is the representative of the class. We delete A B and A C and retain only the representative A D. By step (4a), $G^+_{\Sigma_{c1}}$ is further updated by adding the new full arcs (A D, E) and (A D, F). In step (4), $G_{\Sigma_{c1}}$ is updated by eliminating nodes A B and A C and by moving the full arcs (A B, E) and (A C, F) to node A D. A minimal graph covering for $G_{\Sigma_{c1}}$ is $G_{\Sigma_{c2}}$, as shown in Fig. 7-2(b) and the corresponding minimal FD-covering is

$$\Sigma_{c2} = \{A\ D \to B\ E\ F,\ B \to C,\ C \to D\}. \tag{7.9b}$$

Example 7.23:

Let $U_r = A\ B\ C\ D\ E\ F\ G$ and

$$\Sigma_{r1} = \{A \to B\ C,\ B \to A\ D,\ A\ E \to F,\ B\ E \to G\}$$

be a relation scheme. The FD-graph $G_{\Sigma_{r1}}$ is shown in Fig. 7-3(a).
In Fig. 7-3(a) we have

$$V_{r1} = \{A, B, C, D, E, F, G, A\ E, B\ E\},$$

$$E^d_{r1} = \{(A\ E, A), (A\ E, E), (B\ E, B), (B\ E, E)\},$$

and

$$E^f_{r1} = \{(A, B), (A, C), (B, A), (B, D), (A\ E, F), (B\ E, G)\}.$$

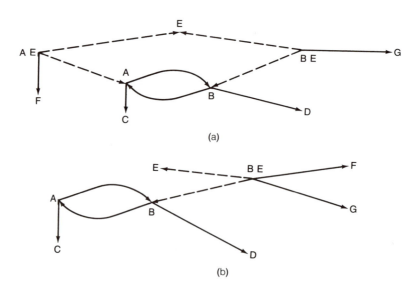

(a)

(b)

Figure 7-3 (a) The FD-graph $G_{\Sigma_{r1}}$; (b) a minimal graph covering $G_{\Sigma_{r2}}$.

The graph closure $G^+_{\Sigma_{rl}} = (V_{rl}, E^+_{rl})$ has

$$E^{d+}_{rl} = E^d_{rl} \cup \{(A\ E,\ B),\ (A\ E,\ C),\ (A\ E,\ D),$$
$$(A\ E,\ G),\ (A\ E,\ B\ E),\ (B\ E,\ A),\ (B\ E,\ C),$$
$$(B\ E,\ D),\ (B\ E,\ F),\ (B\ E,\ A\ E)\}$$

and

$$E^{f+}_{rl} = \{(A,\ B),\ (A,\ C),\ (A,\ D),\ (B,\ A),\ (B,\ C),\ (B,\ D),\ (A\ E,\ F),\ (B\ E,\ G)\}.$$

Since $|V_{rl}| = 9$ and the out-degrees of nodes A E and B E are both eight, $A\ E \equiv B\ E$. $A^+ = B^+ = A\ B\ C\ D$ implies $A \equiv B$. There are two equivalence classes, namely, $\{A, B\}$ and $\{A\ E, B\ E\}$. The dotted arcs (A E, B E) and (B E, A E) in E^{d+}_{rl} and $A\ E \equiv B\ E$ imply that A E and B E are candidates for superfluous nodes, and one of them can be deleted. After eliminating A E and adding the new full arc (B E, F), a minimal graph covering is shown in Fig. 7-3(b), and the minimal FD-covering is

$$\Sigma_{r2} = \{A \rightarrow B\ C,\ B \rightarrow A\ D,\ B\ E \rightarrow F\ G\}.$$

7.6.3 An Algorithm for Finding an LR-Minimal Graph Covering

An algorithm for finding an LR-minimal graph covering is based on definitions 4.23 and 4.25 and on theorem 7.4 (which will be proved) to delete any redundant arcs from a minimal graph covering. An algorithm for finding an LR-minimal graph covering from a minimal graph covering entails the following:

Input: A minimal graph covering $G_\Sigma = (V, E)$.

Output: An LR-minimal graph covering $G'_\Sigma = (V, E')$.

Method:

(1) Find the set of all dotted arcs where each such arc (i, j) is not in E^d and is defined by a dotted implication graph from i to j (based on (4.7a) of chapter 4). Also, for each arc (i, j) not in E^{d+}, find the set of all full arcs (i, j) where each such arc is defined by a full implication graph from i to j (based on (4.7b) of chapter 4) that does not include (i, j) (since it is useless). These arcs will be used in step (3) for arc adjustments.

(2) Find the equivalence classes of nodes in V, and choose a node from each equivalence class as the representative for the equivalence class.

(3) Modify the graph covering G_Σ by replacing each full arc (i, j) connecting nodes i and j of different equivalence classes by the full arc $(\hat{i}, \hat{j})$ connecting the representatives $\hat{i}$ and $\hat{j}$ of such equivalence classes if $(\hat{i}, \hat{j})$ is available as found in step (1). Then provide a Hamiltonian cycle among all nodes in every equivalence class by using arcs in the above modified graph and/or in the sets of available arcs as found in step (1). Each arc that appears in the modified graph but is not included in its corresponding Hamiltonian cycle is deleted.

(4) Find and then eliminate any redundant arc using theorem 7.4. The algorithm terminates.

Theorem 7.4:   Let H_Σ be the graph obtained from a minimal graph covering after steps (1) through (3) of the preceding algorithm. The full arc (î, ĵ) connecting representatives î and ĵ of different equivalence classes is redundant if there exits an implication graph from i to j. If (î, ĵ) is dotted and redundant, then the corresponding implication graph must be dotted.

Proof: If there exists a dotted implication graph from representative î to representative ĵ, then definition 4.25 is satisfied, and the arc (î, ĵ) is redundant. If there exists a full implication graph from î to ĵ, then the nodes included in the implication graph are distinct representatives, since the arc connecting any two representatives is unique. By this uniqueness property, the implication graph can never include the arc (î, ĵ). Thus, if the arc (î, ĵ) is full and the full implication graph from î to ĵ exists, then definition 4.25 is satisfied, and the full arc (î, ĵ is redundant.

Example 7.24:

Let Fig. 7-4(a) be a minimal graph covering corresponding to the redundant set Σ_{s1} of FDs

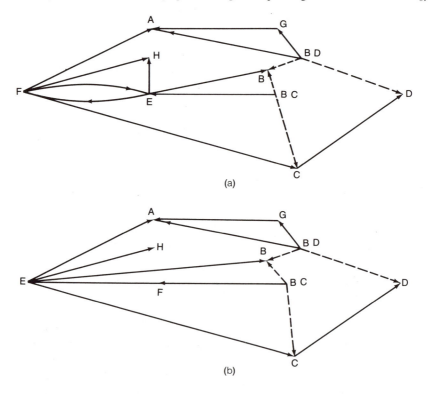

(a)

(b)

Figure 7-4   (a) The FD-graph $G_{\Sigma_{s1}}$; (b) a redundant graph covering for $G_{\Sigma_{s1}}$; (c) a graph covering $G_{\Sigma_{s2}}$; (d) a graph covering $G_{\Sigma_{s3}}$; (e) a graph covering $G_{\Sigma_{s4}}$

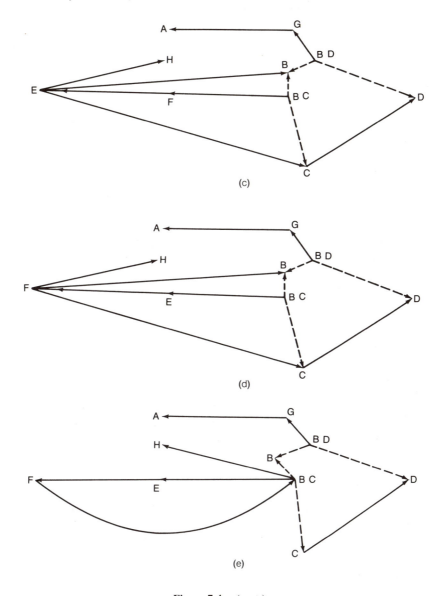

Figure 7-4   (cont.)

$^{+}\Sigma_{s1} = \{C \rightarrow D,\ E \rightarrow B\ F\ H,\ G \rightarrow A,\ F \rightarrow A\ C\ E\ H,\ B\ C \rightarrow E,\ B\ D \rightarrow A\ G\}$

in which there are six FDs and $|\text{MATTR}(\Sigma_{s1})| = 20$.

In step (1), the implication graphs yield the full arcs: (E, A), (E, C), (E, D), (E, G), (E, H), (E, B C), (E, B D), (F, A), (F, B), (F, D), (F, E), (F, G), (F, H), (F, B C), (F, B D), (B C, A), (B C, F), (B C, H), and (B D, A); and the dotted arcs (B C, D), (B C, G), and (B

C, B D). The full arc (B C, E), defined by the full implication graph (B C, E), (E, F), (F, E) including (B C, E), itself is useless and is excluded. The duplicated full arc (E, H), defined by the full implication graph (E, F), (F, H), is included. Other duplicated full arcs (F, A), (F, E), (F, H), and (B D, A) are also included.

In step (2), nodes E, F, and B C are equivalent (where B C is not redundant or superfluous). We choose E as the representative for the equivalence class {E, F, B C}.

In step (3), since node E is chosen as the representative, the full arcs (F, A), (F, C), and (F, H) in Fig. 7-4(a) are, respectively, replaced by the available full arcs (E, A), (E, C), and (E, H) in $E_{s1}^{f^+}$. The Hamiltonian cycle for the equivalence class {E, F, B C} is formed by the set of available arcs {(E, B), (E, C), (B C, B), (B C, C), (B C, F), (F, E)}. The arc (E, F) that appears in Fig. 7-4(a), but is not included in the Hamiltonian cycle, is deleted. The modified graph covering is shown in Fig. 7-4(b).

In step (4), (E, A) and (B D, A) are redundant arcs, since, by definition 4.25, the full implication graph from E to A satisfying theorem 7.4 exists in Fig. 7-4(b), and the full implication graph from B D to A satisfying theorem 7.4 can be trivially determined by the path (B D, G), (G, A). Note that an implication graph considered in step (4) must be a subgraph of Fig. 7-4(b) but may not be a subgraph of Fig. 7-4(a), since some arcs are adjusted in step (3). After the redundant arcs are deleted, a graph covering is shown in Fig. 7-4(c) which defines

$$\Sigma_{s2} = \{C \rightarrow D, E \rightarrow B C H, G \rightarrow A, F \rightarrow E, B C \rightarrow F, B D \rightarrow G\},$$

in which there are six FDs and $|MATTR(\Sigma_{s2})| = 16$. Σ_{s2} is LR-minimal.

If we choose node F as the representative, then an alternative graph covering having 12 arcs is shown in Fig. 7-4(d). In this case, (F, A) and (B D, A) are redundant so that they are not included in Fig. 7-4(d). Fig. 7-4(d) defines

$$\Sigma_{s3} = \{C \rightarrow D, E \rightarrow F, G \rightarrow A, F \rightarrow B C H, B C \rightarrow E, B D \rightarrow G\},$$

in which there are six FDs and $|MATTR(\Sigma_{s3})| = 16$. Σ_{s3} is also LR-minimal.

When we choose node B C as the representative, the resulting graph covering is shown in Fig. 7-4(e) after deleting the redundant arcs (B C, A) and (B D, A). Fig. 7-4(e) defines

$$\Sigma_{s4} = \{C \rightarrow D, E \rightarrow F, G \rightarrow A, F \rightarrow B C, B C \rightarrow E H, B D \rightarrow G\},$$

in which there are six FDs and $|MATTR(\Sigma_{s4})| = 16$. This is once again LR-minimal.

This algorithm requires that a Hamiltonian cycle be found for each equivalent class in finding an LR-minimal graph covering. For each equivalence class of nodes, a Hamiltonian cycle always exists. We need only to find one such cycle in a nonsingleton equivalence class.

Example 7.25:

Reconsider the set of FDs in example 7.4, i.e.,

$$\Sigma_{n1} = \{C \rightarrow A, A E \rightarrow B, B F \rightarrow C, C D \rightarrow E F, E F \rightarrow A D\}, \qquad (7.5a)$$

which was normalized through vertical decomposition in example 7.4. Fig. 7-5(a) shows the FD-graph $G_{\Sigma_{n1}}$. Since the full arc (E F, C D) is defined by the full implication graph from E F to C D and E F $\equiv$ C D, the Hamiltonian cycle is (C D, E F), (E F, C D), where (C D, E F) is in E_{n1}^f. If we choose C D as the representative for the equivalence class {C D, E F}, then the full

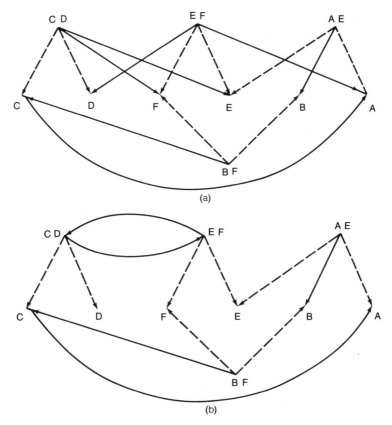

Figure 7-5   (a) The graph $G_{\Sigma_{n_1}}$; (b) a graph covering $G_{\Sigma_{n_2}}$.

arcs (E F, A) and (E F, D) are, respectively, replaced by (C D, A) and (C D, D), since $\{E F \rightarrow C D, C \rightarrow A\} \mid- E F \rightarrow A$ and $\{E F \rightarrow C D\} \mid- E F \rightarrow D$. The replaced full arc (C D, A) is redundant, since the dotted implication graph (C D, C), (C, A) exists and the other replaced dotted arc (C D, D) corresponds to the trivial FD C D $\rightarrow$ D. After (C D, A) is deleted, an LR-minimal graph covering is shown in Fig. 7-5(b) which defines

$$\Sigma_{n2} = \{C \rightarrow A, \ A E \rightarrow B, \ B F \rightarrow C, \ C D \rightarrow E F, \ E F \rightarrow C D\}. \qquad (7.5b)$$

This explains why we must replace the given FD E F $\rightarrow$ A in Σ_{n1} by the FD E F $\rightarrow$ C in Σ_{n2} as discussed in example 7.4. If we choose E F as the representative, the resulting graph covering is identical to Fig. 7-5(b).

7.6.4 Finding a Database Scheme

Once an LR-minimal graph covering is available, a database scheme can easily be defined. In the database scheme, each relation scheme $R_j = (U_j, \{K_{j_i}\})$ is defined as follows:

(1) $\{K_{j_i}\}$ is the set of keys for R_j where each key K_{j_i} corresponds to a node in the underlying node equivalence class α, and

(2) U_j is the set of attributes that is the union of all nodes in α and each representative of a node equivalence class β adjacent from the representative of α.

Theorem 7.5:   A database scheme yielded by the synthesis algorithm is in EKNF.

Proof: We want to examine the FDs corresponding to the three possible types of arcs in an LR-minimal FD-graph covering from which a database scheme is synthesized.

(1) Each dotted arc in the graph covering defines only a trivial FD from a compound node to one of its component nodes, or defines a redundant FD from a compound node to another node by a dotted implication graph. Both types of FDs are not included in the LR-minimal FD-covering corresponding to the graph covering, since they are redundant. Thus, each dotted arc in the graph covering can simply be ignored.

(2) Within each node equivalence class, all nodes contain no extraneous attributes, are not superfluous or redundant, are mutually equivalent, and are synthesized as the keys for the same relation scheme. Each FD defined by a full arc connecting two equivalent nodes is elementary, and its left subset is a key. Suppose that some FD defined by such an arc is not elementary. Then this FD is either trivial or a partial dependency. In the first case, the trivial FD implies that the corresponding arc is dotted, which contradicts the arc being full. In the second case, the FD $i \rightarrow j$ derived by the full arc (i, j) being a partial dependency requires that there exists an arc (k, j) in the graph covering such that k is a proper subset of i. The node k being a proper subset of i implies that there is a dotted arc (i, k) or a dotted implication graph from i to k, which in turn implies the existence of a dotted implication graph from i to j via k. The latter dotted implication graph implies that the full arc (i, j) is redundant, which contradicts the covering being LR-minimal.

(3) Each FD derived by a full arc $(\hat{i}, \hat{j})$ connecting the representatives $\hat{i}$ and $\hat{j}$ of two node equivalence classes is elementary. We can prove it by contradiction similarly to (2) above. In addition, the left subset $\hat{i}$ is a key for a relation scheme synthesized by the node equivalence class with representative $\hat{i}$ and each representative $\hat{j}$ connected from $\hat{i}$.

Since each FD in a synthesized relation scheme is elementary and its left subset is a key for the relation scheme, the relation scheme is in EKNF. Since each relation scheme is in EKNF, the synthesized database scheme is in EKNF.

Example 7.26:

The LR-minimal graph covering of Fig. 7-4(c), 7-4(d), or 7-4(e) defines the following database scheme:

$Db_{sj} = \{(B\ C\ E\ F\ H, \{E, F, B\ C\}), (C\ D, \{C\}), (A\ G, \{G\}), (B\ D\ G, \{B\ D\})\}$

for j = 2, 3, 4, where the second element in each ordered pair is a set of keys. This is the third representation for a relation scheme. All three representations are used interchangeably.

Example 7.27:

The LR-minimal graph covering of Fig. 7-5(b) corresponds to the LR-minimal FD-covering Σ_{n2} of (7.5b) and defines the EKNF database scheme

$$Db_{n2} = \{RNTWO_{1a}, RNTWO_{1b}, RNTWO_{2a}, RNTWO_{2b}\}$$

where

$$RNTWO_{1a} = (A \ C, \{C\}),$$

$$RNTWO_{1b} = (A \ B \ E, \{A \ E\}),$$

$$RNTWO_{2a} = (B \ C \ F, \{B \ F\}),$$

and

$$RNTWO_{2b} = (C \ D \ E \ F, \{C \ D, \ E \ F\}).$$

7.7 BOYCE-CODD NORMAL FORM

The concept of Boyce-Codd normal form is refined from the notion of 3NF [Cod74]. In the determination of a database scheme being in Boyce-Codd normal form, we also need a given set Σ of FDs.

Definition 7.9:   A 1NF relation scheme $R = (U, \Sigma)$ is in *Boyce-Codd normal form* (abbreviated as BCNF) if, for every nontrivial FD of the form $X \rightarrow A$, X is a superkey for R. A database scheme is in *BCNF* if each relation scheme in it is in BCNF.

Example 7.28:

The EKNF relation scheme RQ of (7.8a) in example 7.18, i.e.,

$$RQ = (A \ B \ C, \{A \ B \rightarrow C, \ C \rightarrow A\}), \tag{7.8a}$$

is not in BCNF since C of $C \rightarrow A$ is not a superkey.
  Although the subrelation schemes

$$RQ_1 = \underline{C} \ A \tag{7.8b}$$

and

$$RQ_2 = \underline{A \ B} \tag{7.8c}$$

are both in BCNF where RQ_2 has only the trivial FD $A \ B \rightarrow A \ B$, this database scheme is not acceptable since the JD of RQ_1 and RQ_2 is lossy (why), and the given FD A B $\rightarrow$ C is not enforced or represented. Although the JD of RQ_1 and RQ_3 where

$$RQ_3 = \underline{B\ C} \tag{7.8d}$$

is lossless, the BCNF database scheme $\{RQ_1, RQ_3\}$ is also not acceptable, since the given FD A B $\rightarrow$ C is not enforced.

Example 7.29:

The EKNF RCONE in example 7.19, i.e.,

$$\text{RCONE} = (\text{A B C D E F}, \{\text{A B} \rightarrow \text{E, A C} \rightarrow \text{F, A D} \rightarrow \text{B,}$$
$$\text{B} \rightarrow \text{C, C} \rightarrow \text{D}\}), \tag{7.9a}$$

is not in BCNF, since the left subsets B of B $\rightarrow$ C and C of C $\rightarrow$ D are not superkeys. The synthesis algorithm in section 7.6 produces a good database scheme

$$\text{Db}_{c2} = \{(\text{A B D E F}, \{\text{A D}\}), (\text{B C}, \{\text{B}\}), (\text{C D}, \{\text{C}\})\},$$

which is based on the LR-minimal covering $\Sigma_{c2} = \{\text{A D} \rightarrow \text{B E F, B} \rightarrow \text{C, C} \rightarrow \text{D}\}$ of (7.9b) as obtained in example 7.22, and is in BCNF.

Example 7.30:

Let two equivalent FD-coverings be

$$\Sigma_{ja} = \{\text{A} \rightarrow \text{B C, B C} \rightarrow \text{A, B C D} \rightarrow \text{E F, E} \rightarrow \text{C}\}$$

and

$$\Sigma_{jb} = \{\text{A} \rightarrow \text{B C, B C} \rightarrow \text{A, A D} \rightarrow \text{E F, E} \rightarrow \text{C}\}$$

where A $\equiv$ B C and A D $\equiv$ B C D. Then the relation scheme (A B C D E F, Σ_{jb}) is in EKNF, since it has two elementary keys A D and B C D and four elementary prime attributes: A, B, C and D; the left subsets of the elementary FDs A D $\rightarrow$ E F and B C D $\rightarrow$ E F are keys; and the right attributes of the remaining elementary FDs are elementary prime. However, it is not in BCNF, since A or B C of the nontrivial FD A $\rightarrow$ B C or B C $\rightarrow$ A is not a superkey. After decomposition, the database scheme

$$\text{Db}_{jb} = \{(\text{A B C}, \{\text{A, B C}\}), (\text{A D E F}, \{\text{A D}\}), (\text{C E}, \{\text{E}\})\}$$

is in BCNF. The other relation scheme (A B C D E F, Σ_{ja}) is not in BCNF, although it is in EKNF. After decomposition, the database scheme

$$\text{Db}_{ja} = \{(\text{A B C}, \{\text{A, B C}\}), (\text{B C D E F}, \{\text{B C D}\}), (\text{C E}, \{\text{E}\})\}$$

is still not in BCNF, since the left subset E of the FD E $\rightarrow$ C embodied in the second relation scheme (B C D E F, $\{\text{B C D}\}$) is not a superkey.

The problem of checking the existence of a non-BCNF decomposition is NP-complete [Bee79a]. The problem of determining that there is no BCNF decomposition representing all the given FDs is NP-hard [Bee79a].

*7.8 RELATIONSHIPS AMONG 3NF, EKNF, AND BCNF RELATION SCHEMES

In terms of elementary FDs, the definitions for 3NF and BCNF relation schemes can be reformulated so that a comparative study of 3NF, EKNF, and BCNF relation schemes can be easily accomplished.

Theorem 7.6:   A 1NF relation scheme $R = (U, \Sigma)$ is in 3NF iff for every nontrivial FD of the form $X \rightarrow A$,

(1) X is a superkey for R or

(2) A is a prime attribute.

Proof: Let $X \rightarrow A$ be a nontrivial FD, and K be a key for R. By definition 7.6b, we need not consider the case in which for any prime attribute A, $K \rightarrow A$ is a transitive dependency. We need only to show that for each nonprime attribute A, $K \rightarrow A$ is not a transitive dependency. Hence, we let A be nonprime. Since K is a key for R, $K \rightarrow X$ and $K \rightarrow A$ are both in Σ^+. Then $K \rightarrow A$ is not a transitive dependency via X iff $X \rightarrow K$ is in Σ^+ (i.e., X is a superkey for R). Condition (2) of definition 7.5, is therefore violated.

Theorem 7.7:   A 1NF relation scheme $R = (U, \Sigma)$ is in 3NF iff for every elementary FD of the form $X \rightarrow A$

(1) X is a key for R or

(2) A is a prime attribute.

Proof: Since an elementary FD $X \rightarrow A$ is also nontrivial, X must be a superkey for R in 3NF by theorem 7.6 if A is nonprime. It remains to be shown that X must be a key for R to be in 3NF when $X \rightarrow A$ is not a partial dependency and A is nonprime. Let K be a key for R. Suppose that K is a proper subset of X. Then $K \rightarrow A$ and $X \rightarrow A$ imply that $X \rightarrow A$ is a partial dependency. This contradicts that $X \rightarrow A$ is not elementary and R is not in 3NF (since R is not in 2NF).

Note that in the proof of theorem 7.7, we do not need to consider the case in which X is a proper subset of K, since X as a superkey for R (and given that a key cannot be a proper subset of X) implies that X must be a key. Indeed, if X is a proper subset of a key K, then $K \rightarrow A$ is a transitive dependency via X. The nonprime attribute A, being transitively dependent on a key K, implies that R is not in 3NF. By comparison, the condition ''$X \rightarrow A$ being elementary'' in theorem 7.7 is stronger than the condition ''$X \rightarrow A$ being nontrivial'' in theorem 7.6. Thus, if A is nonprime, then X must be a key in theorem 7.7, whereas X can be a key or a superset of a key in theorem 7.6.

Theorem 7.8:   A 1NF relation scheme $R = (U, \Sigma)$ is in BCNF iff for every elementary FD of the form $X \rightarrow A$, X is a key for R.

Proof: The proof is straightforward, since R is in BCNF iff ''for each nontrivial FD $X \rightarrow A$, X is a superkey'' (definition 7.9); iff ''for each nontrivial FD $X \rightarrow A$ where $X \rightarrow$

A is not a partial dependency, X is a key''; and iff ''for each elementary FD X → A, X is a key.'' We prove it by contradiction. Suppose that for each elementary FD X → A, X is a superkey properly containing a key. We can let X = (X − K) K, where K is a key. K being a key implies that K → A is in Σ^+ for each A not in X, which in turn implies that X → A is a partial dependency and is not elementary.

Theorem 7.9: A 1NF relation scheme R = (U, Σ) is in EKNF iff for every nontrivial FD of the form X → A

(1) X is a superkey for R or
(2) A is an elementary prime attribute.

Proof: The proof of this theorem is similar to that of theorem 7.8. R is in EKNF iff ''for each elementary FD X → A, X is a key or A is elementary prime''; iff ''for each nontrivial FD X → A where X → A is not a partial dependency, X is a key or A is elementary prime''; and iff ''for each nontrivial FD X → A, X is a superkey or A is elementary prime.''

Based on previous theorems and definitions, for each nontrivial FD of the form X → A in Σ, we can determine the following:

(1) R is in 3NF if X is a superkey for R or A is prime (theorem 7.6).
(2) R is in EKNF if X is a superkey for R or A is elementary prime (theorem 7.9).
(3) R is in BCNF if X is a superkey for R (definition 7.9).

Since an elementary prime attribute is also prime but a prime attribute is not necessarily elementary prime, the condition in (1) is weaker than the condition in (2). The condition in (3) is the strongest. Thus, R in BCNF is also in EKNF, and R in EKNF is also in 3NF; but the converses are not necessarily true. Thus, we have the following theorem:

Theorem 7.10: BCNF implies EKNF, and EKNF implies 3NF.

7.9 FOURTH NORMAL FORM

The determination of a relation scheme R = (U, Σ), where U is a set of attributes and Σ is a set of FDs and/or MVDs, being in fourth normal form depends on checking each MVD in Σ and the key dependencies in Σ^+. Fourth normal form was proposed by Fagin [Fag77c].

Definition 7.10: A 1NF relation scheme R = (U, Σ) is in *fourth normal form* (abbreviated as 4NF) if, for every MVD of the form X → → Y,

(1) X → → Y is trivial (i.e., Y ⊆ X or X Y = U) or
(2) X is a superkey for R.

A database scheme is in *4NF* if each relation scheme in it is in 4NF.

Let Σ_{fd} be a set of FDs such that $\Sigma_{fd} \subseteq \Sigma$ and $\Sigma_{fd} \mid- K \rightarrow U$, where K is a key for a relation scheme R = (U, Σ). Let V $\rightarrow\rightarrow$ W be a nontrivial MVD in Σ. In chapter 5, we have proven, in theorem 5.4, that if a relation r(R) satisfying the key dependency K $\rightarrow$ U also satisfies V $\rightarrow\rightarrow$ W (i.e., {K $\rightarrow$ U} $\mid=$ V $\rightarrow\rightarrow$ W), then K is a nonempty subset of V, or equivalently, V is a superkey for R. However, when K is a key for R, as derived by an MVD V $\rightarrow\rightarrow$ W (i.e., {V $\rightarrow\rightarrow$ W} $\mid-$ K $\rightarrow$ U), the key is no longer a nonempty subset of V but is equal to U, as can be seen from the (many-to-many) relations between TUP(V) and TUP(W) and between TUP(V) and TUP(U − V W) or as can be proved from the logical implication {V $\rightarrow\rightarrow$ W} $\mid=$ K $\rightarrow$ U. By definition 7.10, R is not in 4NF, since V $\rightarrow\rightarrow$ W is nontrivial and V is not a superkey for R. When R is decomposed, based on the MVD V $\rightarrow\rightarrow$ W, to yield the subrelation schemes R$_1$ = (V W, {V $\rightarrow\rightarrow$ W}) and R$_2$ = (U − W, {V $\rightarrow\rightarrow$ U − V W}), R$_1$ and R$_2$ are both in 4NF by condition (1) of definition 7.10. If a relation r(R$_1$) satisfying the trivial MVD V $\rightarrow\rightarrow$ W also satisfies the key dependency K' $\rightarrow$ V W, then K' = V W, since the relation between TUP(V) and TUP(W) is still many-to-many. To prove the logical implication {V $\rightarrow\rightarrow$ W} $\mid=$ K' $\rightarrow$ V W, we have

$$\overline{V + W + \emptyset} + \overline{K'} + V W = \overline{K'} + V W,$$

which contains a tautology iff K' = V W. This means that K' cannot be a proper subset of V, since a key for a (many-to-many) relation between TUP(V) and TUP(W) requires more attributes to uniquely identify its tuples. Similarly, for a relation r'(R$_2$), we have

$$\overline{V + (U − V W) + \emptyset} + \overline{K''} + (U − W) = \overline{K''} + U − W,$$

which contains a tautology iff K'' = U − W.

Example 7.31:

Let a relation scheme be RT = (U$_t$, Σ_t) where

$$\Sigma_t = \{A \rightarrow B, B \rightarrow A, A C \rightarrow D, B C \rightarrow D, A D \rightarrow C,$$
$$B D \rightarrow C, A \rightarrow\rightarrow C D, B \rightarrow\rightarrow C D\}. \qquad (7.10)$$

RT is not in 4NF, since the keys determined from a set of FDs are A C, B C, A D, and B D, and the left subsets of both nontrivial MVDs in (7.10) are not superkeys.

Example 7.32:

The relation scheme

$$RU = (A B C, \{A B \rightarrow C, C \rightarrow\rightarrow A\}) \qquad (7.11)$$

has the key A B as defined by the FD A B $\rightarrow$ C, and the left subset C of the nontrivial MVD C $\rightarrow\rightarrow$ A is not a superkey. It is not in 4NF.

In addition to some 4NF decompositions not being unique, such as the 4NF decompositions for the relation scheme RT as shown in (7.10), there exist cases in which a database is in 4NF, but we cannot obtain it by using only the given MVDs.

Example 7.33:

Let U$_v$ = EMPNO PROJ LOC CHILD and Σ_{v1} = {EMPNO $\rightarrow\rightarrow$ PROJ, PROJ $\rightarrow\rightarrow$ LOC}. This relation scheme is not in 4NF, since the given MVDs are nontrivial and EMPNO and

PROJ are not superkeys (the key for (U_v, Σ_{v1}) is U_v, since $\{\text{EMPNO} \rightarrow \rightarrow \text{PROJ}, \text{PROJ} \rightarrow \rightarrow \text{LOC}\} \models U_v \rightarrow U_v$).

We can use the MVD EMPNO $\rightarrow \rightarrow$ PROJ to obtain the 4NF decomposition

$$Db_{v1} = \{(\text{EMPNO PROJ}, \{\text{EMPNO} \rightarrow \rightarrow \text{PROJ}, \text{PROJ} \rightarrow \rightarrow \text{EMPNO}\}),$$
$$(\text{CHILD EMPNO LOC}, \{\text{EMPNO} \rightarrow \rightarrow \text{CHILD LOC}\})\},$$

in which the MVDs are trivial; or we can first use the MVD PROJ $\rightarrow \rightarrow$ LOC for first level decomposition, and then use the MVD EMPNO $\rightarrow \rightarrow$ PROJ for second level decomposition to obtain the 4NF decomposition

$$Db_{v2} = \{(\text{LOC PROJ}, \{\text{PROJ} \rightarrow \rightarrow \text{LOC}\}),$$
$$(\text{CHILD EMPNO PROJ}, \{\text{EMPNO} \rightarrow \rightarrow \text{CHILD LOC},$$
$$\text{PROJ} \rightarrow \rightarrow \text{CHILD EMPNO}\})\}$$
$$= \{(\text{LOC PROJ}, \{\text{PROJ} \rightarrow \rightarrow \text{LOC}\}),$$
$$(\text{EMPNO PROJ}, \{\text{EMPNO} \rightarrow \rightarrow \text{PROJ}, \text{PROJ} \rightarrow \rightarrow \text{EMPNO}\}),$$
$$(\text{CHILD EMPNO}, \{\text{EMPNO} \rightarrow \rightarrow \text{CHILD}\})\}.$$

However, there exist two additional 4NF decompositions as follows:

$$Db_{v3} = \{(\text{EMPNO PROJ}, \{\text{EMPNO} \rightarrow \rightarrow \text{PROJ}, \text{PROJ} \rightarrow \rightarrow \text{EMPNO}\}),$$
$$(\text{EMPNO LOC}, \{\text{EMPNO} \rightarrow \rightarrow \text{LOC}\}),$$
$$(\text{CHILD EMPNO}, \{\text{EMPNO} \rightarrow \rightarrow \text{CHILD}\})\}$$

and

$$Db_{v4} = \{(\text{EMPNO PROJ}, \{\text{EMPNO} \rightarrow \rightarrow \text{PROJ}, \text{PROJ} \rightarrow \rightarrow \text{EMPNO}\}),$$
$$(\text{EMPNO LOC}, \{\text{EMPNO} \rightarrow \rightarrow \text{LOC}\}),$$
$$(\text{CHILD EMPNO}, \{\text{EMPNO} \rightarrow \rightarrow \text{CHILD}\}),$$
$$(\text{LOC PROJ}, \{\text{PROJ} \rightarrow \rightarrow \text{LOC}\})\}.$$

Theorem 7.11:   4NF implies BCNF.

Proof: We prove the equivalent statement: if R is not in BCNF, then R is also not in 4NF. Suppose that R is not in BCNF. Then there must exist at least one FD of the form $X \rightarrow A$ in Σ such that A is not in X and X is not a superkey for R. X not being a superkey, or equivalently, $X \rightarrow U$ not being in Σ^+ implies that U must contain at least one attribute, say B, that is not in A X such that $X \not\rightarrow B$. Hence, B is in $U - A X$ and the MVD counterpart $X \rightarrow \rightarrow A$ of the FD $X \rightarrow A$ is nontrivial. $X \rightarrow \rightarrow A$ being nontrivial and X not being a superkey for R imply that R is not in 4NF.

7.10 PROJECT–JOIN NORMAL FORM

After a database scheme is normalized through decomposition or synthesized by the graphical method, a very important problem is whether the JD (definition 6.1) of all relation schemes in the database scheme is lossless or lossy. If the JD is lossy, then the database scheme is not acceptable.

A database scheme in 4NF is not guaranteed to have a lossless JD unless it consists of two relation schemes decomposed by a nontrivial MVD. It can be shown, by examples, that some 4NF database schemes do not have lossless JDs.

Example 7.34:

Let

$$\Sigma_{w1} = \{A_j \rightarrow B_j \mid 1 \leq j \leq n - 1\}.$$

The corresponding FD-graph consisting of only $2 \times (n - 1)$ simple nodes and $n - 1$ full arcs is LR-minimal. The synthesis algorithm produces the database scheme

$$Db_{w1} = \{\underline{A_1}\ B_1,\ \ldots,\ \underline{A_{n-1}}B_{n-1}\},$$

which is in 4NF, since each MVD counterpart $A_j \rightarrow\rightarrow B_j$ is trivial. However, the JD of the $n - 1$ relation schemes in Db_{w1} is lossy (as proved in theorem 6.2), i.e.,

$$\Sigma_{w1} \mid\neq \mid x \mid (A_1\ B_1,\ \ldots,\ A_{n-1}\ B_{n-1}),$$

where the symbol $\mid\neq$ stands for "not $\mid=$" and $\mid=$ is defined in definition 4.8.

For an improvement, an additional relation scheme,

$$R_0 = \underline{A_1 \ldots A_{n-1}},$$

is required. R_0 is in 4NF, since its corresponding MVD $A_1 \ldots A_{n-1} \rightarrow\rightarrow A_1 \ldots A_{n-1}$ is trivial. Thus, we have the new 4NF database scheme

$$Db_{w2} = \{\underline{A_1 \ldots A_{n-1}},\ \underline{A_1}\ B_1,\ \ldots,\ \underline{A_{n-1}}\ B_{n-1}\}. \tag{7.12}$$

This database scheme has a lossless JD, i.e.,

$$\Sigma_{w1} \mid= \mid x \mid (A_1 \ldots A_{n-1},\ A_1\ B_1,\ \ldots,\ A_{n-1}\ B_{n-1}).$$

This example suggests that if we take a sequence of $n - 1$ decompositions by using the MVDs logically implied by the FDs $A_j \rightarrow B_j$ for $1 \leq j \leq n - 1$ and by MVD0 of complementation, i.e.,

$$A_1 \rightarrow\rightarrow B_1,$$
$$A_1 \rightarrow\rightarrow A_2\ B_2 \ldots A_{n-1}\ B_{n-1},$$
$$A_j \rightarrow\rightarrow B_j,$$

and

$$A_j \rightarrow\rightarrow A_1 \ldots A_{j-1}\ A_{j+1}\ B_{j+1} \ldots A_{n-1}\ B_{n-1}$$

for $2 \leq j \leq n - 1$, then we obtain a 4NF decomposition with a lossless join. The $n - 1$ decompositions are shown in Fig. 7-6, in which each leaf of the binary decomposition tree represents a relation scheme.

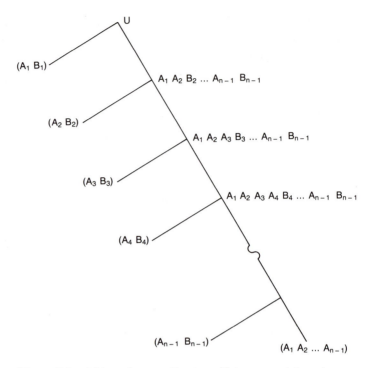

Figure 7-6   A binary decomposition tree with leaves as relation schemes

Definition 7.11:   Let $R = (U, \Sigma)$ be a relation scheme and Db be a database scheme decomposed from R. Let Σ_{Db} be the set of FDs where each FD is represented in Db. A minimum subset K_U of U is a *universal key* for R if $\Sigma_{Db} |- K_U \rightarrow U$, where $|-$ is defined in definition 4.8.

In this definition, Σ_{Db} corresponds to the set of full arcs in an LR-minimal graph covering for an FD-graph G_Σ. Because of possible arc adjustments, Σ_{Db} and Σ are equivalent but may not be equal.

Example 7.35:

Let a relation scheme be

$$RXONE = (A\ B\ C, \{A \rightarrow C, B \rightarrow C\}).$$

The key for RXONE is A B. Thus, RXONE is not in EKNF, since A and B are not keys and C is not prime in the elementary FDs $A \rightarrow C$ and $B \rightarrow C$. The synthesis algorithm yields the database scheme $Db_{x1} = \{\underline{A}\ C, \underline{B}\ C\}$ that is in 4NF (since the MVD counterparts $A \rightarrow \rightarrow C$ and $B \rightarrow \rightarrow C$ are trivial) and has a lossy JD, i.e.,

$$\Sigma_{x1} = \{A \rightarrow C, B \rightarrow C\} |\neq |x|(A\ C, B\ C).$$

From $\Sigma_{Db_{x1}} = \Sigma_{x1} = \{A \rightarrow C, B \rightarrow C\} |- K_{U_{x1}} \rightarrow A\ B\ C$, where K_{U_x} is a universal key for

RXONE, we find $K_{U_x} = A\ B$. This universal key is used to improve the database scheme in such a way that, if an additional relation scheme $\underline{A}\ \underline{B}$ is included in the database scheme, then the new database scheme,

$$Db_{x2} = \{\underline{A}\ C,\ \underline{B}\ C,\ \underline{A}\ \underline{B}\}, \tag{7.13}$$

is in 4NF and has a lossless JD, i.e.,

$$\{A \rightarrow C,\ B \rightarrow C\} \mid= |x|(A\ C,\ B\ C,\ A\ B).$$

By introducing a universal key, a lossy database scheme obtained by the synthesis algorithm can be modified as follows. We add a new attribute $\triangle$ to U and a new FD U $\rightarrow$ $\triangle$ to Σ. The FD U $\rightarrow \triangle$ is not redundant, since no other FD in Σ has $\triangle$ as its right subset. However, the left subset U of U $\rightarrow \triangle$ may contain extraneous attributes that will be detected and then eliminated so that the reduced left subset becomes a universal key K_U for R. Based on the FD $K_U \rightarrow \triangle$, the additional relation scheme consists of $K_U \triangle$. Finally, $\triangle$ is removed from the additional relation scheme in which it appears.

Example 7.36:

For the relation scheme

$$RPONE = (A\ B\ C\ D,\ \{A \rightarrow B,\ B \rightarrow C\}),$$

as normalized through decomposition in example 7.11, the 3NF database scheme

$$Db_{p1} = \{RPONE_1,\ RPONE_2\} = \{\underline{A}\ \underline{D}\ C,\ \underline{A}\ B\}$$

does not enforce the given FD B $\rightarrow$ C in Σ_{p1} and has the hidden partial and transitive dependency A D $\rightarrow$ C. A better database scheme,

$$Db_{p2} = \{\underline{A}\ B,\ \underline{B}\ C\},$$

synthesized by the graphical algorithm is in 4NF (since the MVD counterparts A $\rightarrow \rightarrow$ B and B $\rightarrow \rightarrow$ C are trivial), but involves only an EJD $|x|(A\ B,\ B\ C)$ where an EJD is defined in definition 6.3. From $\Sigma_{Db_{p2}} = \Sigma_{p2} = \{A \rightarrow B,\ B \rightarrow C\} \mid- K_{U_p} \rightarrow A\ B\ C\ D$, A D is the universal key for RPONE. Based on the new FD A D $\rightarrow \triangle$, we have an additional 4NF relation scheme $\underline{A}\ \underline{D}$ and the 4NF new database scheme

$$Db_{p3} = \{\underline{A}\ B,\ \underline{B}\ C,\ \underline{A}\ \underline{D}\},$$

which involves the lossless FJD $|x|(A\ B,\ B\ C,\ A\ D)$, i.e.,

$$\Sigma_{p1} \mid= |x|(A\ B,\ B\ C,\ A\ D).$$

Based on the results from examples 7.34 through 7.36, we define a relation scheme and a database scheme being in project-join normal form.

Definition 7.12:   A 1NF relation scheme R = (U, Σ) where Σ consists of FDs and JDs (MVDs are viewed as JDs) is in *project-join normal form* (abbreviated as PJNF) if, for each FJD $j = |x|(R_1, \ldots, R_t)$ in Σ, the FJD j is trivial or $\Sigma - \{j\} |= j$. A database scheme is in *PJNF* if each relation scheme in it is in PJNF.

In this definition, $\Sigma - \{j\} |= j$ means that a relation over R satisfying each data dependency other than j in Σ also satisfies j.

Example 7.37:

In the database scheme

$$Db_{w2} = \{\underline{A_1 \ldots A_{n-1}}, \underline{A_1} \ B_1, \ldots, \underline{A_{n-1}} \ B_{n-1}\}, \qquad (7.12)$$

the corresponding FJD is $|x|(A_1 \ldots A_{n-1}, A_1 B_1, \ldots, A_{n-1}B_{n-1})$. Since $\{A_j \rightarrow B_j \mid 1 \leq j \leq n - 1\} |=$ the above JD, $\overline{Db_{w2}}$ is in PJNF.

Similarly, the database scheme

$$Db_{x2} = \{\underline{A} \ C, \ \underline{B} \ C, \ \underline{A} \ \underline{B}\} \qquad (7.13)$$

has the corresponding FJD $|x|(A \ C, B \ C, A \ B)$. Since $\{A \rightarrow C, B \rightarrow C\} |= |x|(A \ C, B \ C, A \ B)$, Db_{x2} is in PJNF.

As another example, the database scheme $Db_{p3} = \{\underline{A} \ B, \underline{B} \ C, \underline{A} \ \underline{D}\}$ in example 7.36 is also in PJNF, since $\{A \rightarrow B, B \rightarrow C\} |= |x|(A \ B, B \ C, A \ D)$.

Example 7.38:

Let $U_y = A \ B \ C \ D \ E \ F$ and $\Sigma_y = \{A \rightarrow B \ C \ D \ E, B \ C \rightarrow A \ F, |x|(A \ B \ C, A \ D \ E \ F)\}$. This relation scheme is in PJNF, since $\{A \rightarrow B \ C \ D \ E, B \ C \rightarrow A \ F\} |= |x|(A \ B \ C, A \ D \ E \ F)$. However, if the FJD in Σ_y is replaced by the FJD $|x|(A \ B, A \ D \ E \ F, B \ C \ D \ E \ F)$, then $\{A \rightarrow B \ C \ D \ E, B \ C \rightarrow A \ F\} |\neq |x| (A \ B, A \ D \ E \ F, B \ C \ D \ E \ F)$, although the subsets A D, A D E F, and B C D E F are superkeys for the relation scheme $(U_y, \{A \rightarrow B \ C \ D \ E, B \ C \rightarrow A \ F, |x|(A \ B, A \ D \ E \ F, B \ C \ D \ E \ F)\})$ with the keys A and B C.

Fagin [Fag79] uses the set λ of the key dependencies for R to replace the set $\Sigma - \{j\}$ in definition 7.12 to provide a stronger definition. Since $\Sigma_{fd} |= \lambda$ is always true but the converse may be false, $\Sigma_{fd} |= j$ implies $\lambda |= j$ for each FJD j in Σ where Σ_{fd} contains the FDs in Σ. Thus, Fagin's definition is stronger and is referred to as strong PJNF.

Definition 7.13: A 1NF relation scheme $R = (U, \Sigma)$ where Σ consists of FDs and JDs is in *strong PJNF* if, for each FJD j in Σ, there is a set λ of key dependencies for R such that $\lambda |= j$. A database scheme is in *strong PJNF* if each relation scheme in it is in strong PJNF.

Definition 7.14: In definition 7.13, if the condition "a set λ of key dependencies for R such that $\lambda |= j$" is replaced by the condition "a key dependency $K \rightarrow U$ for R such that $\{K \rightarrow U\} |= j$," then the relation scheme is in *overstrong PJNF*. A database scheme is in *overstrong PJNF* if each relation scheme in it is in overstrong PJNF.

Theorem 7.12: Overstrong PJNF implies strong PJNF, strong PJNF implies PJNF, and PJNF implies 4NF.

Similar to the fact that 3NF implies 2NF (since a partial dependency implies a transitive dependency), PJNF implies 4NF, since an MVD implies a JD; however, in either case the converse may not be true. Strong PJNF implies PJNF, since a set of FDs implies a set of key dependencies, but the converse may not be true (for example, $\{A \to C, B \to C\} \mid - A B \to C$, where A B is the key but $\{A B \to C\} \mid\neq \{A \to C, B \to C\}$). Overstrong PJNF implies strong PJNF, since the former involves only one key dependency, whereas the latter involves all key dependencies.

Let λ be the set of key dependencies in the relation scheme $R = (U, \Sigma)$ and j be a join dependency. A membership algorithm is available in [Fag79] for deciding whether or not $\lambda \mid - j$.

Example 7.39:

The database schemes Db_{w2} of (7.12), Db_{x2} of (7.13), and Db_{p3} in example 7.37 are not in strong PJNF, since only one relation scheme in each such database scheme contains the key and the JD membership algorithm fails.

Example 7.40:

Let $U_z = A B C D$, $j = |x|(A B, A D, B C)$, and $\Sigma_z = \{A \to B D, B \to A C, j\}$. Then $\lambda = \{A \to U, B \to U\}$. The database scheme $Db_z = \{(A B, \{A, B\}), (A D, \{A\}), (B C, \{B\})\}$ is in strong PJNF. It is not in overstrong PJNF, since

$$\{A \to A B C D\} \mid\neq |x|(A B, A D, B C)$$

and

$$\{B \to A B C D\} \mid\neq |x|(A B, A D, B C).$$

7.11 HORIZONTAL NORMALIZATION

In previous sections, we have introduced vertical normalization of relation schemes based on ''projection'' and ''join'' operations. Such a normalization is used to eliminate insertion, deletion, and update anomalies; to avoid inconsistency caused by redundancy; to speed query processing; and to distribute databases. However, less attention has been paid to the normalization based on ''selection'' and ''union'' operations known as horizontal normalization.

The general theory of horizontal normalization has not fully developed. There are only a number of case studies available in the literature [DeB82, Mai83b]. This section introduces only a possible case. The reader may refer to [Mai83b] for a formal definition of ''fragmentation scheme'' and the illustrated example concerning the fires in California.

Let us revisit the following relation scheme,

$$RQ = (A B C, \{A B \to C, C \to A\}). \tag{7.8a}$$

This scheme has practical significance when A, B, and C are mapped to CITY, ADDRESS, and ZIP, respectively. Although the database scheme $\{\underline{C} A, \underline{B} C\}$ is in PJNF, the given FD $A B \to C$ is not enforced. One possible improvement can be accomplished by means of projection, selection, and union to obtain the following subrelation schemes known as *fragments*.

$$RQ_0 = RQ[C\ A] = \underline{C}\ A$$

where C is the key and

$$RQ_j = \pi_{BC}\ (\sigma_{A\ =\ ``C_j"}(RQ)) = (\underline{B}\ C\ |\ A = ``C_j")$$

for each C_j in ADOM(A), $1 \le j$, where B is the key. Since

$$\sigma_{A\ =\ ``C_j"}(RQ) = \{C_j\}\ |x|\ RQ_j,$$

we obtain

$$\overset{t}{\underset{j\ =\ 1}{\cup}}\ \sigma_{A\ =\ ``cj"}\ (RQ) = RQ$$

where t is the number of cities in the database. By this approach, the given FD C $\rightarrow$ A is enforced in RQ_0 and another given FD A B $\rightarrow$ C is enforced in RQ_1 through RQ_t, since the FD B $\rightarrow$ C is enforced in each individual RQ_j.

7.12 FINAL REMARKS ON NORMALIZATION

We have introduced two approaches to normalization, various normal forms, and a synthesis algorithm concerning the design of a database scheme. Many design issues in the area of vertical normalization are NP-hard. Horizontal normalization is still in an infant stage.

In the following sequence of normal forms,

```
overstrong PJNF, strong PJNF, PJNF, 4NF, BCNF, EKNF, 3NF, 2NF, 1NF,
```

a left normal form implies a right one, i.e., overstrong PJNF implies strong PJNF, and so forth. When a database scheme is modeled relationally, it is in 1NF, since every domain is simple. To find a database scheme in 2NF through BCNF, a set of FDs must be specified. We can design a database scheme based on an FD-covering for the given set of FDs. To obtain a 2NF or 3NF database scheme involves nonprime attributes and keys. Since testing the primeness of attributes and finding a minimal sized key for a relation scheme are both NP-complete, these problems are extremely difficult. The polynomial time-bounded synthesis algorithm that is based on FD-graphs and systematically produces a database scheme in EKNF is a very valuable tool in the design of a good database scheme (in EKNF). The graphical method systematically detects redundant nodes, superfluous nodes, and redundant arcs in an FD-graph and the antecedent closure (of the FD-graph) to produce an LR-minimal FD-covering from which an EKNF database scheme is synthesized. However, this graphical technique does not generally yield an optimal FD-covering (the general problem of finding an optimal FD-covering is NP-complete). To check the existence of a non-BCNF decomposition and to determine that there is no BCNF database scheme are both NP-hard. The determination of a database scheme in 4NF and PJNF involves, respectively, additional data dependencies known as MVDs and JDs. There are no systematic methods to find a database scheme in 4NF or PJNF. In particular, the problem of testing a single JD being logically implied by a JD and a set of FDs or MVDs is NP-hard.

EXERCISES

7.1 The relation scheme RM_1 of (7.4a) in example 7.3 is not in 2NF, because of the existence of the partial dependencies as shown in (7.3e) and (7.3f). How should RM_1 be decomposed such that its subrelation schemes are in 2NF and preserve the FDs (7.3a) through (7.3d)? Show that the C in (7.3a) is extraneous and that the FD A B $\rightarrow$ C is redundant.

7.2 The set of FDs for the relation scheme ROONE of (7.6a) in example 7.5 is not LR-minimized. Show that A B and A C are redundant and can be deleted.

7.3 Show that the nonprime attributes E and F in example 7.3 are both transitively dependent on the key A B. How should RM_1 be decomposed into subrelation schemes which are in 3NF?

7.4 Show that definitions 7.6a and 7.6b are equivalent.

7.5 The proof of lemma 7.2 is very similar to those proofs of lemma 7.1 and theorem 7.2. Provide a proof of lemma 7.2.

7.6 In

$$\Sigma_{c1} = \{A\ B \rightarrow E,\ A\ C \rightarrow F,\ A\ D \rightarrow B,\ B \rightarrow C,\ C \rightarrow D\}, \qquad (7.9a)$$

show that the prime attribute C is transitively dependent on the keys A B and A D but is not transitively dependent on the key A C, and show that the prime attribute D is transitively dependent on the keys A B and A C but is not transitively dependent on the key A D.

7.7 For the set

$$\Sigma = \{A\ B \rightarrow C,\ B\ C \rightarrow D,\ B\ E \rightarrow C,\ C\ D \rightarrow B,\ C\ E \rightarrow A\ F,\ C\ F \rightarrow B\ D,$$
$$C \rightarrow A,\ D \rightarrow E\ F\},$$

find an LR-minimal FD-covering, and design a database scheme in EKNF.

7.8 Show that the following database schemes are or are not in BCNF:
   (a) $\{RK_1, RK_2\}$ of (7.2a) and (7.2b) in example 7.2.
   (b) $\{RNTWO_{1a}, RNTWO_{1b}, RNTWO_2\}$ of (7.5e), (7.5f), and (7.5d) in example 7.4.
   (c) $\{ROONE_{1a}, ROONE_{1b}, ROONE_2\}$ of (7.6d), (7.6e), and (7.6c) in example 7.5.
   (d) $\{EMPLOYEE, DEPARTMENT\}$ of (7.7a) and (7.7b) in example 7.10.

7.9 Show that the relation scheme RT of (7.10) in example 7.31 is in EKNF but is not in BCNF. How should RT be decomposed to obtain all possible 4NF database schemes?

7.10 Show that the relation scheme RU of (7.11) in example 7.32 is in BCNF. How should RU be decomposed to obtain a 4NF database scheme?

7.11 Let $U = A\ B\ C$ and $\Sigma = \{A \rightarrow B\ C,\ C \rightarrow A\ B,\ |x|(A\ B,\ B\ C)\}$. Show that $R = (U, \Sigma)$ is not in PJNF, although each element in the JD $|x|(A\ B,\ B\ C)$ is a superkey for R.

7.12 The database schemes $\{RQ_1, RQ_2\}$ and $\{RQ_1, RQ_3\}$ of (7.8b), (7.8c), and (7.8d) in example 7.28 are not acceptable. How would you design an acceptable database scheme?

7.13 Show that if K is a key for a relation scheme $R = (U, \Sigma)$ and X is a superset of K, then $\{K \rightarrow U\}\,|-\,X \rightarrow A$ for each A in U, i.e., $\{K \rightarrow U\}\,|-\,X \rightarrow U$. However, $\{X \rightarrow U\}\,|\nmid\,K \rightarrow U$ unless $K = X$. Thus, R is in BCNF if, for each nontrivial FD $X \rightarrow A$ in Σ, there is a key K for R such that X is a superset of K.

7.14 If $\lambda = \{K_1, \ldots, K_t\}$ is a set of keys for a relation scheme $R = (U, \Sigma)$ and $X \rightarrow A$ is a nontrivial FD in Σ, then $\{K_1 \rightarrow U, \ldots, K_t \rightarrow U\}\,|-\,X \rightarrow A$ iff X is a superkey for R. Prove this by logical approach. Thus, R is in BCNF if $\{K_1 \rightarrow U, \ldots, K_t \rightarrow U\}\,|-\,X \rightarrow A$ for each nontrivial FD $X \rightarrow A$ in Σ.

7.15 Similarly to exercise 7.14, show that if K is a key for a relation scheme $R = (U, \Sigma)$ and X is a superset of K, then $\{K \rightarrow Y\}\,|-\,X \rightarrow \rightarrow Y$ for each nontrivial MVD $X \rightarrow \rightarrow Y$ in Σ or is derived from some FDs in Σ. Thus, R is in 4NF if, for each nontrivial MVD $X \rightarrow \rightarrow Y$ that is in Σ or is an MVD counterpart of some FD in Σ, there is a key K for R such that X is a superset of K.

7.16 Similarly to exercise 7.15, if λ is the set of keys for R and $X \rightarrow \rightarrow Y$ is a nontrivial MVD as defined in exercise 7.15, then $\{K_1 \rightarrow U, \ldots, K_t \rightarrow U\}\,|-\,X \rightarrow \rightarrow Y$ iff X is a superkey for R. Prove this by logical approach. Thus, R is in 4NF if $\{K_1 \rightarrow U, \ldots, k_t \rightarrow U\}$ derives each such MVD.

7.17 An attribute A in U of a relation scheme $R = (U, \Sigma)$ is *abnormal* if for some nontrivial FD $X \rightarrow A$, X is not a superkey for R. Show that A is transitively dependent on a key iff A is nonprime and abnormal.

chapter 8

QUERY LANGUAGES AND DATABASE MANAGEMENT SYSTEMS

8.1. INTRODUCTION

In this chapter, we introduce several query languages and relational database management systems. We examine how the concepts introduced in previous chapters are applied in various implementations. Although the relational algebra introduced in chapter 2 and the tuple and the domain calculus introduced in chapter 3 are complete in expressive power, arithmetic computations cannot be carried out without use of additional operations, such as addition, subtraction, multiplication, division, exponentiation, etc. In addition, a database without additional mechanisms cannot provide data-entry and listing services to satisfy the user requirements. A practical DBMS needs to provide extensions in these aspects in addition to assignment statements, aggregate operations, and built-in functions among others. Thus, a DBMS is more than complete.

An algebraic language ISBL, used in an experimental DBMS PRTV, is introduced in section 8.2. A tuple calculus language QUEL, used in INGRES, is discussed in section 8.3. A domain calculus language Query-by-Example and a logic programming language PROLOG, are also included in this chapter.

8.2. ISBL AND PRTV

8.2.1. Introduction

ISBL (Information System Base Language) is an algebraic-based query language and is used in an experimental interactive DBMS called *PRTV* (Peterlee Relational Test Vehicle). PRTV was developed at IBM's United Kingdom Scientific Center in Peterlee,

TABLE 8-1. CORRESPONDENCE OF
TERMINOLOGY AND NOTATION

Relational algebra	ISBL
not equal $\neq$	$\neg =$
and	&
or $+$	|
not $-$	$\neg$
join $\vert x \vert$	*
union $\cup$	$+$
intersection $\cap$	.
selection $\sigma_F(r)$	r : F
projection $\pi_X(r)$	r % list
domain-element	object
attribute	selector
relation scheme	relation type
relation	named variable
selection criterion	filter
complex product *	full quadratic join

County Durham and was fully operational in 1973. The largest database handled requires 50 megabytes. A database can consist of at most about 50 relations, each containing at most 65,000 rows of at most 128 columns [Tod75, Tod76].

Some terminology and notation used in ISBL are not identical to those defined in the relational algebra of chapter 2. Correspondence between the relational algebra and ISBL is provided in table 8-1. In this table, a "list" specifies the selectors to be projected and possibly their new names for renaming, but X consists only of the columns to be projected. Example 8.3 will illustrate the format of a "list" for projecting and/or renaming.

8.2.2 Objects, Attributes, and Named Variables

The elements in the domain of an attribute are called *objects* in ISBL and are either numeric or character data characterized, respectively, by the keyword **N** or **C** denoting the data type. A new domain can be created at any time by an ISBL statement of the following form:

```
CREATE DOMAIN domain-name, data-type
```

where domain-name is the name of a new domain to be created and the data-type can be assumed to be either **N** or **C**, depending on the characteristics of the objects.

Each column of a tabular relation is identified by a name called a *selector* in ISBL and is an attribute as defined in chapter 1. To represent a relation in an expression, the attributes and their corresponding domain names must be given. A domain name and its corresponding attribute are separated by a colon to form a combination of the form "domain-name : attribute." Such combinations are separated by commas. When a domain name and its corresponding attribute are the same, only one of them is required.

A relation in ISBL is treated as a named variable, but its intermediate values is an expression can be left unnamed. A function that applies to one tuple at a time is treated as a relation. Extensibility is provided by allowing a user to write a PL/I function to be added to the system. Relation schemes are referred to as *relation types*.

Example 8.1:

Let the following relation scheme

$$\text{BOOKORDER (ORDERNO AUTHOR TITLE YEAR PRICE)}$$

be a part of a library database for ordering books. Suppose that there are two domains named as NUMBER (consisting of order numbers, publishing years, and unit prices) with type **N** and NAME (consisting of the names of authors and book titles) with type **C.** Then the relation BOOKORDER can be described as

$$\text{BOOKORDER (NUMBER : ORDERNO, NAME : AUTHOR, NAME : TITLE,}$$
$$\text{NUMBER : YEAR, NUMBER : PRICE)}$$

where the attributes ORDERNO, YEAR, and PRICE share the same domain NUMBER, and the attributes AUTHOR and TITLE share the same domain NAME.

8.2.3 Operations

There are six relational algebraic operations in ISBL: selection, projection, union, intersection, difference, and join (denoted respectively by :, %, +, ·, −, and *).

The notation used for "selection" is of the form

```
                      relation-name : filter
```

where "filter" is the selection criterion defined by a formula in chapter 2. However, the comparison operators allowed are =, ¬=, >, ≥, <, and ≤ for numeric data; and = and ¬= for character data.

Example 8.2:

For the relation SALES(DEPT ITEM) shown in table 8-2, the following selection

$$\text{SALES : (DEPT = COMPUTER | DEPT = DP) \& (ITEM } \neg\text{= CALCULATOR)}$$

yields the following result of the selection

$$\text{\{COMPUTER MICRO, COMPUTER PRINTER, COMPUTER TERMINAL,}$$
$$\text{DP MICRO, DP PRINTER, DP TERMINAL\}.}$$

The notation used for "projection" is of the form

```
                  relation-name % projection-list
```

TABLE 8-2.   RELATION SALES(DEPT ITEM)

SALES	DEPT	ITEM
	COMPUTER	CALCULATOR
	COMPUTER	MICRO
	COMPUTER	PRINTER
	COMPUTER	TERMINAL
	DP	MICRO
	DP	PRINTER
	DP	TERMINAL
	PHOTO	CAMERA
	PHOTO	FILM
	VIDEO	RECORDER
	VIDEO	TV

where the projection-list specifies the selectors to be projected and possibly their new names for renaming. These selectors are separated by commas. To rename some selectors and leave the remaining ones unchanged, a projection-list is given with the new names followed by , . . . (meaning "and so on"). A selector to be renamed is associated with its new name by the symbol $->$ as "old selector $->$ new name." The projection operation in ISBL is a generalization of definition 2.6, where renaming is not allowed.

Example 8.3:

The following projections

$$EMP \ \% \ DEPT, \ MGR$$

and

$$BOOKORDER \ \% \ AUTHOR \ -> \ WRITER, \ . \ . \ .$$

produce, respectively, a relation with attributes DEPT and MGR, and a relation similar to BOOKORDER with AUTHOR renamed to WRITER.

The operations "union" and "intersection" require that both operand relations be of the same scheme. If the relation schemes R and S are not identical but their relations r(R) and s(S) are union-compatible, then one of the relations must be renamed by the renaming option of the projection operation before union or intersection is performed.

The operation "difference" in ISBL was introduced in section 2.2.4 and discussed in section 2.3 of chapter 2. The difference in ISBL is a generalization of definition 2.4. When the schemes of both operand relations are the same, the difference in ISBL becomes the conventional difference as defined by definition 2.4.

In ISBL, the "full quadratic join," which concatenates each tuple in the first operand relation with every tuple in the second operand relation is exactly the complex product as defined in section 2.2.5 of chapter 2. The "natural join" in ISBL is identical to that in section 2.3.3.

*8.2.4. User Extensions

Since the relational operations described in previous sections are incapable of carrying out computations, and a database without additional mechanisms cannot provide listing and data-entry services to satisfy the user requirements, PRTV provides two types of user extensions: tuple-at-a-time extension and general extension. Procedures are provided in PRTV to simplify the linking of new user extensions into the system.

For a tuple-at-a-time extension, the user enters the body of a PL/I procedure and the names and the data types of the parameters of the procedure. This type of extension is used for providing computed fields and user defined selection criteria.

Example 8.4:

The PL/I procedure ISIN shown below is similar to that in [Tod76].

```
ISIN : PROCEDURE(A, B) RETURNS(BIT(1));
       DECLARE (A, B) CHARACTER(*), FLAG BIT(1);
       FLAG = (INDEX(B,A) ¬= 0);
       RETURN(FLAG);
       END ISIN;
```

where A and B are parameters of the procedure ISIN declared as character strings having no specific lengths by an asterisk; FLAG is a Boolean variable declared as a bit string of length one; and **INDEX**(B, A) is a built-in function whose value is zero if (the value of) A is not a substring of (the value of) B and whose value is the position number of the first character of the matched substring otherwise. The procedure ISIN returns '1'B (true) if A occurs in B as a substring, and '0'B (false) otherwise. Then the ISBL statement

```
LIST BOOKORDER * ISIN("RELATIONAL DATABASES", TITLE)
```

selects and then prints the books whose TITLE-values contain ''RELATIONAL DATABASES.'' Note that ISIN is a procedure, whereas ISIN(''RELATIONAL DATABASES'', TITLE) is an operand relation of the join operation *. The operand relation ISIN consists of each tuple whose TITLE-value contains the substring ''RELATIONAL DATABASES'' when the procedure ISIN returns the truth value '1'B. The join yields a subset of BOOKORDER where the title of each book contains ''RELATIONAL DATABASES'' as a substring.

General extensions call the ISBL interpreter recursively, or they use the relational file interface to access and to write data in a database one object at a time. **ENTER** is a system utility, which accepts as parameters the name of a relation to be entered and the attributes of the relation.

Example 8.5:

To enter the BOOKORDER, the ISBL call is

```
CALL ENTER (BOOKORDER | NUMBER : ORDERNO,
                        NAME : AUTHOR,
            NAME : TITLE, NUMBER : YEAR, NUMBER : PRICE)
```

where its input and output parameters are located on the left and right sides of |. In the output part, the domains and their corresponding attributes must be given.

*8.2.5 Other Features of PRTV

The value of a named variable can be changed by an assignment =. In other words, the results of an expression can be evaluated and assigned to a named variable by means of =. For example, S = S + T would insert a set T of tuples into a set S of tuples where the tuples must have the same scheme, since the operand relations S and T of the union + must have identical scheme.

When a variable is used in an expression, ISBL allows binding either by value or by name. The default binding is by value.

(1) A relation name preceded by the delayed evaluation operator **N!** means that the relation is bound by name. If an expression specifies binding by name, the named variable is not evaluated, but its name is held in a procedure that represents the expression. If an expression is used in an assignment statement, any subsequent change of a value in the relation bound by name is reflected as a change of value in the assigned relation. This unary operation that postpones the evaluation of its operand is not new. (In the SNOBOL4 programming language [Gri71], if E is an expression, then *E is an unevaluated or a delayed evaluated expression.)

(2) In the case of binding by value, the current value of a named variable in an expresion is found and inserted into the expression. If an expression is used in an assignment statement, any subsequent change of a value in the original variable is not reflected as a change of value in the assigned variable.

8.2.6 Query Processing

In example 2.12 of chapter 2, we solved the query Q_1 in which we want to find all departments in the department store database such that each such department sells all items supplied by IBM. We can follow the quotient

$$\text{SALES(DEPT ITEM)} / \pi_{\text{ITEM}}(\sigma_{\text{SUPPLIE R = IBM}}(\text{SUPPLY(ITEM SUPPLIER)}))$$

based on (2.8b) to process this query by a procedural approach. We can use the delayed evaluation provision to define relation names by expressions with this capability. By (2.8b), i.e.,

$$r(T\ R) / s(R) = \pi_T(r) - \pi_T((\pi_T(r) * s(R)) - r), \tag{2.8b}$$

we view

$$r(T\ R) = \text{SALES(DEPT ITEM)},$$

$$s(R) = \pi_{\text{ITEM}}(\sigma_{\text{SUPPLIER = IBM}}(\text{SUPPLY(ITEM SUPPLIER)})),$$

and

$$\pi_T(r) = r[T].$$

Then we define

$$RONTOT = N!SALES \% DEPT, \tag{8.1}$$

$$SR = N!SUPPLY: (SUPPLIER = IBM) \% ITEM, \tag{8.2}$$

$$JOINDFONTOT = ((N!RONTOT * N!SR) - N!SALES) \% DEPT, \tag{8.3}$$

and

$$RESULT = N!RONTOT - N!JOINDFONTOT. \tag{8.4}$$

Finally, we use **LIST** RESULT to find the answer as {COMPUTER, DP}. Referring to table 8-2 for SALES and table 8-3 for SUPPLY, when (8.1) is executed by **LIST,** we obtain the relation that is the projection from SALES onto DEPT as shown in table 8-4.

When (8.2) is executed by **LIST,** we obtain the relation SR, which is the projection from the selection of SUPPLY under SUPPLIER = ''IBM'' onto ITEM as shown in table 8-5.

When (8.3) is executed by **LIST,** we obtain the relation JOINDFONTOT which is

TABLE 8-3.   RELATION SUPPLY(ITEM SUPPLIER)

SUPPLY	ITEM	SUPPLIER
	CALCULATOR	HP
	CALCULATOR	TI
	CAMERA	KODAK
	FILM	KODAK
	MICRO	HP
	MICRO	IBM
	PRINTER	IBM
	RECORDER	ZENITH
	TERMINAL	IBM
	TERMINAL	ZENITH
	TV	ZENITH

TABLE 8-4.   RELATION RONTOT(DEPT)

RONTOT	DEPT
	COMPUTER
	DP
	PHOTO
	VIDEO

TABLE 8-5.
RELATION
SR(ITEM)

SR	ITEM
	MICRO PRINTER TERMINAL

TABLE 8-6. RELATION
JOINDFONTOT(DEPT)

JOINDFONTOT	DEPT
	PHOTO VIDEO

the projection from the difference of the complex product RONTOT * SR and SALES onto DEPT as shown in table 8-6.

When (8.4) is executed by **LIST,** we obtain the quotient {COMPUTER, DP}, which is the difference of RONTOT AND JOINDFONTOT.

8.3 QUEL AND INGRES

8.3.1 Introduction

QUEL (QUEry) Language) [Hel75] is a query language that is supported by a relational database management system called INGRES(INteractive Graphics and REtrival System) [Eps77a, Eps77b, Woo81]. QUEL enables the user to be isolated from the implementations of data, storage structures, access methods, and the operations of algorithms on stored data. QUEL also provides a considerable degree of data independence.

INGRES was developed at the University of California, Berkeley in the seventies. A relation can have up to 49 columns and a virtually unlimited number of rows. The tuple width can not exceed 498 bytes, since INGRES never splits a tuple between two pages with 512 bytes per page and there is an overhead of 12 bytes per page plus 2 bytes per tuple. Rows represent entries, and columns are called *domains* in INGRES. The examples in subsequent sections were tested using INGRES version 7.7 (3/7/81).

8.3.2 QUEL

QUEL [Woo81] borrows much from Data Language/Alpha [Sto76]. QUEL provides arithmetic computations and powerful aggregate operations, and is a language based on functions and tuple calculus, but it does not implement the universal quantifier. Each legal name in QUEL is a lowercase string at most 12 characters long, starting with an alphabetic letter, and composed of alphanumeric characters and underscore "___". Because of this limitation, the names of relations and attributes, which will be used in subsequent sections, are changed to lowercase strings. Identifiers, such as **append,** and **from,** among others, are reserved for use as keywords and may not be used as user-defined identifiers. For clarity, boldface names are used to indicate reserved keywords in the context of this chapter (but not in programs).

Three data types characterize the values of attributes, and accordingly, there are three types of constants.

(1) *String constants*—String constants are character strings composed of at most 255 ASCII (American Standard Code for Information Interchange) characters enclosed by a pair of double quotation marks. A double quotation mark or a back-slash "\" embedded in a string must be prefixed by a back-slash. Control characters embedded in a string are converted to blanks, since INGRES does not allow control characters to be stored. The format of string constants is

$$\mathbf{c}j \text{ for } j = 1, 2, \ldots, 255,$$

where **c** indicates the character data type and "j" is the number of bytes indicating the required storage size.

(2) *Integer constants*—There are 1-byte, 2-byte, and 4-byte integers. The format of integer constants is

$$\mathbf{i}j \text{ for } j = 1, 2, 4,$$

where **i** indicates the integer data type and "j" is the number of bytes.

(3) *Floating point constants*—There are 4-byte and 8-byte floating point numbers. The format of floating point constants is

$$\mathbf{f}j \text{ for } j = 4, 8,$$

where **f** indicates the floating point data type and "j" is the number of bytes.

A *variable* in QUEL is associated with a relation by means of a **range** statement of the synopsis "**range of** variable **is** relation-name." This variable is a term defined in the first-order logic indicating a tuple variable belonging to the relation "relation-name." It can be viewed as a marker that moves down the relation to indicate the current location of a tuple when the tuples of the relation are searched during query processing. By means of **range** statement, a variable not only identifies a particular relation but also has the same scheme as that of the relation. This implements an atom "relation-name(tuple-variable)" as defined in (2) of definition 3.2 in chapter 3. For example, the statement "**range of** e **is** emp" implements the atom "emp(e)" standing for e ϵ emp so that sch(e) = sch(emp) = name salary mgr dept. The number of variables appearing in any one query is at most 10.

A term of the form "variable.domain" is called an *attribute* in QUEL and is actually a component of a (tuple) variable and implements the construction of the form "variable(attribute)" as defined in (3) of definition 3.2 in chapter 3. For example, "e.name" is the name-component of the variable e and implements "e(name)."

QUEL supports a number of aggregate operators: **count** and **countu** compute respectively, the numbers of all possible occurrences and all distinct occurrences; **sum** and **sumu** find respectively, the summations of all possible values and all distinct values; **avg** and **avgu** define respectively, the divisions **sum / count** and **sumu / countu; max** and **min** mean the maximum and the minimum; and **any** returns value 1 if the underlying qualification is evaluated to be true and 0 otherwise. A qualification is an expression (which will be defined) prefixed by the key word **where.** A qualification serves as a selection criterion.

There are two types of aggregate operations.

(1) *Simple aggregate operation*—A simple aggregate operation yields a single value. For example, "**avg**(e.salary)" computes the single average salary in the underlying database.

(2) *Aggregate function*—Aggregate functions are extensions of simple aggregates. An aggregate function yields several results based on the specified "**by**-lists." For example, "**avg**(e.salary **by** e.dept)" computes the average salaries of the employees in individual departments. For the department store database, since ADOM(dept) = {COMPUTER, DP, PHOTO, VIDEO}, there are four average salaries, one for each department. Whenever any average value is actually undefined because of no data, INGRES always makes it zero. For example, if ADOM(dept) also contains a new department named ELECTRONICS that has no employee yet, then the average value for this department is undefined and has value 0.

QUEL also supports a number of built-in functions, such as the trigonometric functions. In particular, **abs**(n) finds the absolute value of n, **ascii**(n) converts a numeric number to a character string, **mod**(n, b) means "n modulo b," and **sqrt**(n) computes the square root of n.

An *expression* in QUEL is one of the following:

(1) a constant, such as a string, an integer, or a floating point number;

(2) a component of a variable (i.e., an attribute in QUEL terminology), such as "e.name";

(3) a functional expression, such as a built-in function;

(4) a simple aggregate operation or an aggregate function; or

(5) a combination of numeric expressions and arithmetic operators.

Each expression has a format denoted by a letter in {**c, i, f**} followed by a number of storage bytes. Operators involved in expressions are of three types:

(1) *Comparison operators*—These operators are "=" (equal), "!=" (not equal), "<" (less than), "<=" (less than or equal), ">" (greater than), and ">=" (greater than or equal). All are of the same order of precedence.

(2) *Logical operators*—Operator **not** ("logical not" or "negation") is of the highest order of precedence, and operators **and** ("logical and" or "conjunction") and **or** ("logical or" or "disjunction") are of the same order of precedence.

(3) *Numeric or arithmetic operators*—These operators, arranged in the descending order of precedence, are shown below.

+,−   unary plus, minus
**   exponentiation
*,/   multiplication, division
+,−   binary addition, subtraction

Pattern matching can be done in INGRES. There are three types of pattern matching.

(1) The pattern ''*'' matches any string of zero or more characters. For example, ''**where** e.mgr = ''Y*''''' matches any manager whose name begins with the letter ''Y.''

(2) The pattern ''?'' matches any one nonblank character. For example ''**where** e.name = ''?ANG''''' matches any employee whose name is composed of four characters and ends with the substring ''ANG.''

(3) The pattern ''[ ]'' matches any one character enclosed with the brackets. For example, ''**where** e.name = ''*[AEIOU]*''''' matches any employee whose name begins with at least one vowel and ''**where** e.name = ''[A-M]''''' matches any employee whose name begins with ''A,'' ''B,'' . . . , or ''M.''

Note that INGRES ignores blanks in any string comparison, whether pattern matching is engaged or not. To disable a pattern-matching operation, a back-slash ''\'' is used to prefix a pattern-matching character such as '' *'', ''\?''.

Concatenation of two strings is supported by the built-in function **concat**(a, b) such that all trailing blanks in a are trimmed, b is concatenated, and the remainder is padded by blanks so that the length of the new string is the sum of the lengths of a and b. For example, ''e.salary = **concat**(''$'', e.salary)'' adds the dollar sign ''$'' prefixing a salary value.

Some terminology and notation used in QUEL are different from those defined in chapter 3 for tuple calculus. Correspondence between the tuple calculus and QUEL is listed in table 8-7.

TABLE 8-7. CORRESPONDENCE OF TERMINOLOGY
AND NOTATION

Tuple calculus	QUEL
attribute or column	domain
relation-name(tuple-variable)	**range of** variable **is** relation-name
variable(attribute)	attribute
not equal: ≠	!=
less than or equal: <	<=
greater than or equal: ≥	>=
and: ·	**and**
or: +	**or**
not: −	**not**

When operators, such as the equality "$=$," are not denoted by different symbols, their correspondences are not included in table 8-7.

This and the following sections offer only a brief introduction to QUEL and INGRES so that the reader can start an interactive session to get practical experience when INGRES is available. The interested reader should consult the INGRES reference manual [Woo81] for more detailed information particularly concerning the options of QUEL and UNIX statements.

8.3.3 INGRES

INGRES is implemented on top of the UNIX time-sharing operating system [Sto76, Rit78a, Rit78b, Tho78, Bou78], developed at the Bell Telephone Laboratories. The implementation of INRES is primarily programmed in the C high-level programming language [Rit78c].

There are three major environments involved.

(1) *UNIX environment*—This environment is indicated by "%" appearing on the beginning of each line.

(2) *INGRES environment*—This environment is indicated by "*" rather than "%." In this environment, the statement \g requests processing of the current query. Then INGRES offers the message "Executing . . . " indicating that the query is being processed.

(3) EQUEL (Embedded QUEL) environment—Each EQUEL statement must be prefixed by two number signs "##." EQUEL will be briefly introduced in section 8.3.4.

The primary front end to INGRES is the interactive terminal monitor. The monitor formulates and reviews a query held in the query buffer before issuing the query to INGRES, and offers a variety of messages to inform the user concerning the status of the monitor and the query buffer. This buffer is referred to as the *work space*. The query buffer is empty when the message "go" is printed, and is nonempty when the message "continue" is printed. To manage the query buffer, the user can use a number of commands prefixed by a back-slash "\", such as \r for resetting the query buffer, \p for printing the current contents of the query buffer, and so forth. These commands are executed immediately, without requiring additional requests, using the "go" commands (i.e., \g). The macro facility of the monitor allows some string of text to be removed from the query stream and replaced by another string. For example, a macro is composed of the template and the replacement part. The template part defines when the macro should be invoked in the input stream. When a macro is executed, the template part is removed and replaced by the replacement part. For example, a macro for shortening a **range** statement can be defined as {**define**; rg $r $s; **range of** $r **is** $s}," where **define** is the special macro to define a macro, the template part "rg $r $s" is removed from the input text and replaced by the replacement part "**range of** $r **is** $s." There are also built-in macros for changing the environment upon execution.

*8.3.4 EQUEL

EQUEL (Embedded QUEL) [Sto76, Woo81] is a new language providing the flexibility of the general purpose programming language C, in addition to the database facilities of QUEL. EQUEL consists of a library and a precompiler. The run-time support library contains all the routines necessary for loading an EQUEL program to provide an interface between C and INGRES. The precompiler converts an EQUEL program into a valid C program with QUEL statements converted to appropriate C code and calls to INGRES. The resulting C program is then compiled by the standard C compiler, producing an executable module. When an EQUEL program is run, the executable module is used as the front end process in place of the interactive terminal monitor. Each EQUEL statement is prefixed by two number signs. To exit from INGRES, the EQUEL command is **## exit**.

8.3.5 Creating or Destroying a Database

The tree-structured UNIX file system creates a subtree, whose root is a directory made for the UNIX superuser INGRES when the INGRES system is initially installed. A descendant file contains an authorization list of users who are allowed to create databases and to destroy their own databases. This file can be modified only by the superuser using the UNIX text editor. Creating or destroying a database can be accomplished under the UNIX environment by simply creating a legal database name or destroying an existing database name. The database name must be unique among all INGRES users. After the completion of a login to the UNIX system, the UNIX environment is entered. Then a new database can be created by typing the UNIX command **creatdb** followed by the legal database name to be created. To execute a command or a sequence of commands, the "RETURN" key of the user's terminal must be depressed. From now on, this operation is no longer mentioned. The invoker of a database automatically becomes the database administrator (abbreviated as DBA). A DBA has the following authorities:

(1) destroy his/her database by using the UNX command **destroydb** followed by the existing database name to be destroyed under the UNIX environment;

(2) create relations shared by other user's registered in the users file and specify access control for those users;

(3) run the UNIX statement "**purge** database-name" to report all expired user relations by default, or to destroy them if **-p** flag was specified in the statement; to destroy temporary system relations; and to report extraneous files by default, or to remove them if the **-f** flat was specified;

(4) run the UNIX statement "**restore** database-name" to recover a database from a UNIX crash while INGRES is running, or to recover it whenever INGRES has a system error caused by an inconsistency or a failure returned from UNIX.

Example 8.6:

To create the department store database with name deptstore, the UNIX statement "**creatdb** deptstore" is used. Similarly, to destroy the existing database deptstore, the UNIX statement "**destroydb** deptstore" is the right one to use.

8.3.6 Entering or Leaving INGRES Environment

Before invoking INGRES, the user must be admitted as an INGRES user in the "users file." After the database deptstore is created, the INGRES environment is established by requesting UNIX to invoke INGRES (consult the person responsible for the installation to become familiar with the invocation of INGRES). If the user has been admitted as an INGRES user, then the INGRES login message provided by the interactive terminal monitor is displayed on the screen followed by

```
go /*the work space is empty */
* /* INGRES is ready to accept input */
```

where a message enclosed by ''/*'' and ''*/'' is a comment that is not provided by the monitor. To leave the INGRES environment, the QUEL "quit" command \q can be used. Then the INGRES logout message is displayed followed by

```
% /* UNIX is ready to accept input */
```

8.3.7 Creating a Relation Scheme

So far only a database name has been created. Storing a database requires the creation of relation schemes by creating their (relation) names, declaring their column-names and the data types and the storage sizes of the column-values, and filling tuples into relations. After the INGRES environment has been established, a new relation scheme can be created by the QUEL **create** statement of the form:

```
create relation-name (domain-name = format {, domain-name = format})
```

where ''{, domain-name = format}'' indicates that this optional item may be repeated. Each ''domain-name'' corresponds to a column-name or an attribute, and all domain-names are distinct in a relation scheme. Each ''format'' defines a particular data type and a number of storage bytes for attribute-values. Note that to execute a single INGRES statement or a sequence of INGRES statements, the statement \g or \go, meaning "requesting for processing the current query," must be followed. For simplicity in subsequent examples, this mandatory statement will no longer be explicitly included unless it should be there for clarity. The sequence of objects enclosed by a pair of parentheses in a QUEL statement is called a *target list*.

Example 8.7:

To create the relation named sales, the following statement

```
create sales(dept = c10, item = c12)
```

can be used where each dept-value and item-value are, respectively, character strings of lengths 10 and 12. The ordered pair following SALES is a target list.

8.3.8 Creating or Destroying a Relation

After a relation scheme is defined, a relation with this scheme can be created by filling tuples into the relation. Filling tuples can be accomplished by either a single QUEL **copy** command or a sequence of QUEL **append** commands. By the first method, the QUEL **copy** command copies data in bulk from an existing UNIX file into a relation whose scheme was previously created. In a **copy** statement, the path name of a UNIX file must be used.

Example 8.8:

To fill all tuples into the relation sales, a UNIX file with a specific path name in the DBA's home directory is first created under the UNIX environment.

```
% ed /*invoke UNIX text editor and read editing requests from terminal*/
a /*append */
COMPUTER,CALCULATOR /*first tuple */
COMPUTER,MICRO /*second tuple */
COMPUTER,PRINTER
COMPUTER,TERMINAL
DP,MICRO
DP,PRINTER
DP,TERMINAL
PHOTO,CAMERA
PHOTO,FILM
VIDEO,RECORDER
VIDEO,TV /*last tuple */
  /*end of file */
w unixsale /*write the file unixsale back to the work space */
150 /*number of characters and lines in unixsale displayed by UNIX */
q /*quit the UNIX text editor */
```

where attribute values in the UNIX file unixsale are character strings of variable lengths delimited by commas, new lines, or tabs and the number 150 includes 128 alphabetic letters, 11 commas for separation, and 11 lines. In this example, attribute-values belonging to a tuple are separated by commas, and tuples are entered on different lines. An attribute-value can be null. In this case, a null value defaults to zero or blank when its corresponding data type is numeric or nonnumeric, respectively.

Since the relation scheme for sales was created in example 8.7, data can be copied from the existing UNIX file, unixsale, into the relation sales by executing

```
copy sales(dept = c0, item = c0) from "unixsale" /*use file path name */
```

where the data type **c0** means that a character string ends in a comma, tab, or new line. Other options **c0nl, c0sp, c0z,** and **c0%** denote, respectively, a character string ending in a new line, a space or blank, the character z, and the character %.

Note that the **copy** command is of the general form as follows:

```
copy relation-name(domain-name = format {, domain-name = format})
     direction "file-path-name"
```

where domain-names corresponding to column-names are distinct, and **copy** moves data between an INGRES relation with the name "relation-name" and a UNIX file with the path name "file-path-name." A "domain-name" identifies a column in "relation-name." A "format" indicates the format of a column defined by specific data type and number of storage bytes. The "direction" means either **into** or **from.** The **into** option copies data from an INGRES relation into a UNIX file and is omitted here. The reader should refer to [Eps77a].

The second method to fill tuples into a relation whose scheme was previously defined uses a sequence of **append** commands. The **append** statement is of the general form

```
append[to]relation-name (target-list) [where qualification]
```

To append tuples one at a time, we use

```
append to relation-name (domain-name = "value" {, domain-name = "value"})
```

where domain-names corresponding to column-names are distinct.

Example 8.9:

To fill tuples into the relation with the name supply, the relation scheme supply(item supplier) is created first, and then tuples are filled by a sequence of the QUEL **append** commands.

```
create supply(item = c12, supplier = c10)
append to supply(item = "CALCULATOR", supplier = "HP")
append to supply(item = "CALCULATOR", supplier = "TI")
append to supply(item = "CAMERA", supplier = "KODAK")
append to supply(item = "FILM", supplier = "KODAK")
append to supply(item = "MICRO", supplier = "HP")
append to supply(item = "MICRO", supplier = "IBM")
append to supply(item = "PRINTER", supplier = "IBM")
append to supply(item = "RECORDER", supplier = "ZENITH")
append to supply(item = "TERMINAL", supplier = "IBM")
append to supply(item = "TERMINAL", supplier = "ZENITH")
append to supply(item = "TV", supplier = "ZENITH")
```

followed by \g. Then INGRES produces

```
Executing . . . /*the query is being processed by INGRES */
(1 tuple) /*processed one query */
continue /*the work space is nonempty */
```

where eleven tuples are filled into the relation supply. To enter a large relation using this method involves too much typing, since there are too many duplicated words. However, it is quite convenient to append one or several new tuples to an existing relation. The order of the objects such as "item = value" and "supplier = value" in a given target list is arbitrary, since INGRES follows the order of the columns as defined in the corresponding **create** statement by recognizing and matching column-names.

The invoker of the **create** command becomes the owner of a relation with the scheme created. A user may destroy a relation that he/she owns. To destroy a relation, the

QUEL statements "**destroy** relation-name" and **\q** are executed. When a relation is destroyed, its relation scheme is also destroyed. If we want to destroy only the tuples of a relation and to retain the relation scheme, then we can use the statement "**modify** relation-name **to truncated**" to produce an empty relation (which has only a scheme). However, after all relations in a database are destroyed, the underlying database name is still there, and the DBA can use the UNIX statement "**destroydb** database-name" to destroy the database. In addition to creating a relation by **create** and **copy** or by **create** and **append,** another way to create a new relation from one or more existing relations is to use the option **retrieve into,** which will be illustrated in example 8.16.

8.3.9 Displaying and Saving a Relation

To display a relation on the screen, the QUEL **print** statement

```
print relation-name
```

(followed by \g can be executed.

When a relation is created, it is temporarily saved (one week in INGRES version 7.7). To save a relation for a longer time, the QUEL **save** statement

```
save relation-name until month day year
```

(followed by **\g**) can be used where month, day, and year are represented, respectively, by two, two, and four digits such as 01 15 1986.

Example 8.10:

The relation supply is printed by executing the QUEL **print** command followed by **\g,** i.e.,

```
print supply /*request a printout of supply stored in the database */
\g /*request processing of the current query */
Executing . . .
supply relation
```

item	supplier
CALCULATOR	HP
CALCULATOR	TI
CAMERA	KODAK
FILM	KODAK
MICRO	HP
MICRO	IBM
PRINTER	IBM
RECORDER	ZENITH
TERMINAL	IBM
TERMINAL	ZENITH
TV	ZENITH

```
continue
```

8.3.10 Printing or Resetting the Query Buffer

To see the current contents of the work space at any time, we type **p** or **print**. To reset or erase the work space, we type **r** or **reset.** Both of these commands are executed immediately without requiring additional requests using the ''go'' commands (**g**). For example,

```
print supply
\p /* print the current contents of the work space */
print supply /* the most recently entered query is printed */
```

where ''print supply'' rather than the relation supply is printed. However, if the statement ''print supply'' is followed by the statement **g**, then INGRES offers the message ''Executing . . .'' and also prints the relation supply if it was previously created and stored in the database. Now, we reset the work space by typing

```
\r /* erase the work space */
go /* the work space becomes empty */
```

8.3.11 Storage Structures

INGRES supports various types of storage or file structures to improve the efficiency of storing and retrieving relations. When a relation is first created, it is always structured as a *heap* in which tuples are stored sequentially in accordance with the order of filling the tuples. The tuples in a heap are not sorted, and duplicates are not removed. Since a heap stores tuples independently of their values, all tuples must be examined to look for those tuples satisfying the qualification specified in a query when the query is processed. Whenever such a heap is not reasonably small, this exhaustive search is time-consuming. Thus, we need to modify the storage structure of a relation by using the QUEL **modify** command. However, only the owner of a relation can modify the storage structure of his/her relation. Note that heap is a kind of storage or file structure, but it has no connection with the data structure that is also called heap.

A heap does not need to have specified keyed domains that are not prime attributes defined in definition 7.2 (i.e., all specified keyed domains do not necessarily form a key for a relation), and can be classified as a nonkeyed storage structure. On the other hand, the keyed storage structures are known as *hash* and *isam,* and their compressed versions are called *chash* and *cisam.* A keyed storage structure does not store any duplicated tuples. The location of a tuple, or the locations of several tuples within a certain range of the values of their keyed domains within a keyed storage structure, can be determined by these values. When the keyed domains form a key for the corresponding relation, the locations of the tuples stored in the structure can be uniquely identified. On the other hand, when the keyed domains form only a proper subset of a key for the corresponding relation, the uniqueness property cannot be established. In a relation stored as a hash, the tuples are distributed randomly throughout the pages, according to a specific hashing function on the keyed domains (specified in the corresponding **modify** statement), and these keyed domains should form a key to possess the uniqueness property. In a relation stored as an isam, the tuples are placed approximately in their sorted positions. When a query is processed, only a portion of the isam structure is searched, since INGRES knows approximately where that portion is stored, based on the qualification specified in the query and the keyed domains as well. Since a portion of the isam structure may involve more than one tuple, the keyed domains might be only a proper subset of a key.

For hash and isam structures, there are two types of pages, known as *primary* and *overflow* pages. When a new tuple is appended to such a structure, INGRES first determines what page it belongs to based on the value of its keyed domains and then looks for room for it on that page. The tuple is stored on that page if a free space is available, and on a newly created page otherwise. The original page is called a *primary page,* and the newly created page is called an *overflow page.* When an overflow page becomes full, another overflow page is created. These pages are linked together.

A relation can be converted to any storage structure using a **modify** statement of the synopsis.

```
modify relation-name to storage-structure
[on keyed-domain [: sortorder]
[{, keyed-domain [: sortorder]}]]
[where [fillfactor = n][, minpages = n][, maxpages = n]]
```

where the keyed domains corresponding to column-names are distinct, and n has integer values. The **modify** command has many options, such as specifying how full to fill a primary page by setting a specific value (from 1 to 100) to the parameter **fillfactor,** and allocating a minimum or maximum number of primary pages by setting a specific number to the parameter **minpages** or **maxpages** when modifying a relation to hash or chash.

The compressed counterpart of each storage structure reduces the space size to accommodate each compressed tuple by suppressing all trailing blanks in each character domain. Although a compressed storage structure can save space, the price to pay for this advantage is the increased cost of updating, since the compressed tuples no longer have the same width. The DBA needs to consider the trade-off between saving space and increasing updating cost.

In addition to heap, hash, and isam, and their compressed versions, a relation can be modified to *heapsort* or *cheapsort* in which tuples are sorted (defaulted is ascending order) and duplicates are removed. Modification of a relation to **truncated** is equivalent to creation of an empty relation by removing all tuples from the relation being modified, releasing disk space, and making the relation a heap.

A relation is always initially created as a heap, since it is the most efficient structure for filling tuples by use of **copy, append,** or **retrieve into.** Hash has the advantage for locating a tuple by an exact match based on the value of its keyed domains. The primary page for a tuple with a definite value for the keyed domains can be easily computed by a specific hashing function. In addition to tuple matching by an exact value of its keyed domains, isam is useful for locating several tuples by matching a range of such values. However, isam is not so efficient as hash, since the isam index or directory must be searched first to locate its tuples. This directory is structured as a sparse index containing the value of the keyed domains of the first tuple on each page. Note that the keyed domains included in the **on** phrase of a **modify** statement may be only a part of a key for the relation being modified to isam. Adding extra keyed domains can increase the uniqueness, but the directory becomes larger. Consequently, it takes longer to search.

8.3.12 Secondary Indexes

A *secondary index* on an attribute A establishes a relation between ADOM(A) and the primary relation (whose scheme must contain A) from which the secondary index is defined. A primary relation with a secondary index on an attribute A is said to be an *inverted file* on A. A secondary index is an index on an attribute other than on the primary key for the primary relation. In other words, a secondary index on an attribute A is a relation that consists of the A-value of each tuple belonging to the primary relation together with the exact location of the tuple specified by the offset of the tuple in the primary location.

To create a secondary index, the QUEL **index** statement is of the synopsis

```
index on relation-name is index-name (attribute {, attribute})
```

where relation-name is the primary relation, index-name is the secondary index being created, and attributes belong to the primary relation and must be distinct. A secondary index can have at most six attributes. A secondary index is initially created as a heap and then automatically modified to an isam on all of its attributes.

Example 8.11:

To create the secondary index with the name itemtosales on the (primary) relation sales, we use

```
index on sales is itemtosales(ITEM)
```

We can use the **help** statement

```
help itemtosales
```

to see information concerning the relation itemtosales. When this statement is executed by \g, the following information is displayed.

```
Relation:             itemtosales
Owner:                yang
Tuple width:          16
Saved until:          day-of-the-week month day hour:minute:second year
Number of tuples      11
Storage structure:    ISAM file
Relation type:        secondary index on sales
attribute name        type      length      keyno.
item                  c         12          1
tidp                  i         4
```

where the column-name "tidp" is created by the system, has integer values, and can be viewed as a cursor or pointer. We can use the **print** statement

```
print itemtosales
```

to see the relation itemtosales.

itemtosales relation

item	tidp
CALCULATOR	0
CAMERA	7
FILM	8
MICRO	1
MICRO	4
PRINTER	2
PRINTER	5
RECORDER	9
TERMINAL	3
TERMINAL	6
TV	10

In this table, "tidp" has eleven integer values 0 through 10, each corresponding to the offset of a tuple in the primary relation sales, i.e., integer $i - 1$ is the offset of the i-th tuple in sales for $i = 1, \ldots, 11$. In this relation, each item-value is pointing to all tuples in sales having that item-value. Thus, the relation between ADOM(item) and sales is one-to-many (one-to-two as indicated by MICRO, PRINTER, and TERMINAL and one-to-one for the remaining items).

Secondary indexes have the advantage of increasing the processing efficiency of some queries. However, whenever a primary relation is updated because of the insertion, deletion, or modification of a tuple, all its secondary indexes must be accordingly updated. Is it worthwhile to pay this price? The DBA needs to consider the trade-off between improving efficiency and increasing update cost.

8.3.13 System Relations

For maintaining and organizing a database, INGRES provides system relations known as *relation, attribute, indexes, tree, protect,* and *integrities.* For each relation created by the system or a DBA in the underlying database, relation has one tuple. For each attribute in a system or user relation in the underlying database, attribute has one tuple. For each secondary index created by a user in the underlying database, indexes has one tuple. The DBA can use the UNIX statement "**sysmod** database-name" to modify system relations to hashes to achieve peak performance by removing most overflow pages.

To print the names of the system and user relations and their owners, we can use this statement

```
                         help \g
```

where the commands **help** and \ **g** need not be separated into two statements **help** and \ **g.**
Then the information displayed is

```
            Executing . . .
            relation name      relation owner
            relation           yang
            attribute          yang
            indexes            yang
            tree               yang
            protect            yang
            integrities        yang
            sales              yang
            supply             yang
            itemtosales        yang

            continue
```

We can use the statement "print relation" to get information about the system relation
named "relation." It contains one tuple for each relation created by the INGRES
superuser or a DBA. It has thirteen columns, among which the columns *reltups, relatts,*
and *relwid* indicate, respectively, the number of tuples per relation, the number of attributes per relation, and the number of bypes per tuple. The system relation named "attribute" has eight columns, among which the columns *attid, attoff, attfrmt,* and *attfrml* indicate, respectively, the column numbers per relation, the attribute offsets per relation
(starting from 0 for the first attribute of a relation), the data type per attribute, and the
number of bytes per attribute.

8.3.14 Editing the Work Space

After a query is processed, INGRES displays the message "continue", indicating that the
work space is nonempty. If we then type a new query, INGRES automatically erases the
previous query and saves the current query in the work space. When we need to modify or
correct the current query, we can avoid retyping the entire query by requesting the
INGRES monitor to write the work space to a temporary file and to call the UNIX **ed**
program. This is requested by typing \ **e** under the INGRES environment. Then the number of characters (including commas and/or blanks for separation) and lines in the work
space is printed on the screen. We can start to edit the query. For example, a few editor
commands used to create the UNIX file unixsale in example 8.8 were the commands **a,** to
append more information to the query; **w,** to write the query back to the work space; and
q, to quit the UNIX text editor. Note that we must precede a **q** with a **w** to pass the cor-
rected work space back to INGRES. The following commands are also useful for editing a
query.

j**p** means print the j-th line in the work space for j = 1, 2, . . .
s/i/j/**p** means substitute a j for an i on the current line and then print
that line.

Example 8.12:

We first enter the query

```
range of s is sale /*18 characters */
retrieve s.dept, s.item where s.dept = "COMPUTER" /* 49 characters */
```

Before executing this query by **g,** we discover two bugs in the first two lines (what are
they). Corrections proceed as follows:

```
\e /* INGRES monitor calls the UNIX ed program */
>>ed /*using the UNIX text editor */
"/tmp/file-name" 2 lines, 69 characters /*temporary file holds the query */
1p /*print first line */
range of s is sale /*first line*/
s/le/les/p /*substitute le by les and print the line */
range of s is sales /*corrected first line */
2p /*print second line */
retrieve s.dept, s.item where s.dept = "COMPUTER" /*second line */
s/s.dept, s.item /(s.dept, s.item) /p /*correct and then print second
line */
retrieve (s.dept, s.item) where s.dept = "COMPUTER" /*corrected second
line */
w /*writes the query back to the work space */
"/tmp/file-name" 2 lines, 72 characters /*temporary file holds the query */
q /*quit the UNIX text editor */
continue /*the work space is nonempty */
\a /*append more data to the query under the INGRES environment */
or s.dept = "DP"

\g

Executing . . .
```

dept	item
COMPUTER	CALCULATOR
COMPUTER	MICRO
COMPUTER	PRINTER
COMPUTER	TERMINAL
DP	MICRO
DP	PRINTER
DP	TERMINAL

(7 tuples)

continue

Note that the statement \a is essential in this example. Otherwise, INGRES considers the statement "or s.dept = ''DP'''' as the beginning of a new query and resets the work space before saving this statement. An alternative way to avoid resetting the work space is to use \p to print the current contents of the work space and then make additions to the qualification.

8.3.15 Query Processing

To process queries by QUEL and INGRES when a relation is involved, we must define a variable for the relation by a **range** statement as introduced in section 8.3.2.

We first consider the **retrieve** command for query processing. As already shown in example 8.12, involving the operation of selection, the variable s is declared in the **range** statement, the columns dept and item are given in the target list, and the condition for selecting tuples, prefixed by the key word **where,** is the formula formed by the disjunction of two atoms (i.e., s.dept = ''COMPUTER'' **or** s.dept = ''DP''), known as a *qualification* in QUEL. Qualifications in QUEL are more than formulas defined in the tuple calculus, since the former can contain built-in functions, aggregates, and so forth.

Note that INGRES does not check for duplicate tuples and does not eliminate duplications in the value (that is, a relation) of a tuple calculus expression being evaluated. When a variable ranges over a relation, the schemes of the variable and the relation are identical to the relation scheme previously created by a **create** command.

To append some condition for selecting tuples to the previous query, the next line should be such a command such as \p (print), \g (go), \a (append), among others, to save the previous query in the work space.

INGRES can do computations. In this case, an expression is evaluated to yield a value, and this value is assigned to a domain-variable whose name is used as a column-name on the printout. When no component of the underlying tuple-variable can be used as a domain-variable, we must use a new column-name (referred to as a "domain title" in INGRES) to accommodate each computed value. Otherwise INGRES does not know how to label or title the column on the printout. In addition to logical and comparison operators, an expression may involve arithmetic operators as shown in section 8.2.3. Suppose that the salary for each employee during the next year is increased by 8%. Then we can type

```
range of e is emp
retrive (e.name, e.salary = e.salary * 1.08, e.mgr, e.dept) \g
```

If we want to rename some column-name, such as renaming ''mgr'' as ''boss,'' we simply use ''boss = e.mg'' to replace ''e.mgr'' in the target list. Whenever a computation such as ''e.salary * 1.08'' is done, INGRES does not understand how to label the column on the printout. Thus, the prefixing part ''e.salary ='' is essential. We can use any name other than ''e.salary'' for this purpose.

In case we want to update the relation emp to reflect an 8% raise in salary, we can use the following **replace** statement.

```
replace e(salary = e.salary * 1.08) \g
```

where the tuple variable e, rather than the relation

```
emp, must be used. Similarly, we can use
```

```
delete e where qualification \g
```

to delete a number of tuples with some specified qualification.

Example 8.13:

Find the items supplied by both suppliers "IBM" and "HP." This query is similar to Q_2 in example 3.12 of chapter 3. The tuple calculus expression is

$$\{s1(item) \mid \exists s1(item\ supplier)\exists s2(item\ supplier)$$
$$(supply(s1) \cdot supply(s2) \cdot s1(item) = s2(item)$$
$$\cdot s1(supplier) = ``IBM'' \cdot s2(supplier) = ``HP'')\}$$

A QUEL solution to this query involves use of selection and projection and is shown in the following:

```
range of s1 is supply /* define variable s1 */
range of s2 is supply /* define variable s2 */
retrieve (s1.item) /* projection onto item */
where s1.item = s2.item and s1.supplier =
"IBM" and s2.supplier = "HP"
\g
Executing . . .
```

item
MICRO

```
(1 tuple)
```

In this example, the correspondence between the formula in the tuple calculus expression and the QUEL implementation is quite evident.

Example 8.14:

Find the departments selling one or more items supplied by "IBM." The tuple calculus expression for this query is

$$\{s(dept) \mid \exists s(dept\ item)\exists t(item\ supplier)$$
$$(sales(s) \cdot supply(t) \cdot s(item) = t(item) \cdot t(supplier) = ``IBM'')\}$$

A QUEL solution to this query is shown in the following:

```
range of s is sales /* define variable s */
range of t is supply /* define variable t */
retrieve unique (s.dept) /* projection onto dept and eliminate duplicates
*/
where s.item = t.item and t.supplier = "IBM" \g
Executing
```

dept
COMPUTER
DP

```
(2 tuples)
```

Note that if **unique** is omitted from the **retrieve** statement, then the departments COM-PUTER and DP each appear three times, since INGRES does not check and eliminate dupli-cates. The reason behind this approach is to achieve a better efficiency.

Example 8.15:

Find the join of sales and supply. The tuple calculus expression is

{d(dept item supplier) | ∃s(dept item) ∃t(item supplier)
(sales(s) · supply(t) · d(dept) = s(dept)
          · d(item) = s(item) · s(item) = t(item) · d(supplier) = t(supplier))}

A QUEL solution to this operation is as follows:

```
range of s is sales
range of t is supply
retrieve into dummy(dept = s.dept, item = s.item,
supplier = t.supplier)
where s.item = t.item
print dummy \g
Executing . . .
dummy relation
```

dept	item	supplier
COMPUTER	CALCULATOR	HP
COMPUTER	CALCULATOR	TI
COMPUTER	MICRO	HP
COMPUTER	MICRO	IBM
COMPUTER	PRINTER	IBM
COMPUTER	TERMINAL	IBM
COMPUTER	TERMINAL	ZENITH
DP	MICRO	HP
DP	MICRO	IBM
DP	PRINTER	IBM
DP	TERMINAL	IBM
DP	TERMINAL	ZENITH
PHOTO	CAMERA	KODAK
PHOTO	FILM	KODAK
VIDEO	RECORDER	ZENITH
VIDEO	TV	ZENITH

Example 8.16:

Find the departments selling all items supplied by IBM. This query is Q_1 and was solved in example 2.12 of chapter 2, in example 3.9 of chapter 3, and also in section 8.2.6 using ISBL. Shown in example 3.6 of chapter 3 is the tuple calculus expression. Since QUEL does not implement the universal quantifier, we do not need to use the tuple calculus expression. We can decompose the query Q_1 into subqueries by first forming a relation named "temp1" with scheme "department itemcount1" where an itemcount1-value is the number of items supplied by "IBM" and sold by a department-value that is a department in sales. The next relation named "temp2" with scheme "company itemcount2" where the itemcount2-value is the number of items supplied by company "IBM." The result is obtained by matching the same value of "itemcount1" and "itemcount2" and is stored in the relation "result." Then a QUEL solution is as follows:

```
range of x is sales
range of y is supply
retrieve into temp1(department = x.dept, itemcount1
= count(x.item by x.dept where x.item = y.item and y.supplier = "IBM"))
print temp1
retrieve into temp2(company = y.supplier, itemcount2
= count(y.item by y.supplier)) where y.supplier = "IBM"
print temp2
range of t1 is temp1
range of t2 is temp2
retrieve into result(dept = t1.department)
where t1.itemcount1 = t2.itemcount2
print result \g
Executing . . .
temp1 relation
```

department	itemcount1
COMPUTER	3
DP	3
PHOTO	0
VIDEO	0

temp2 relation

company	itemcount2
IBM	3

result relation

dept
COMPUTER
DP

In the first two **retrieve into** statements, the target lists also include qualifications for computations. When **retrieve into** is used, the corresponding relation-name must not already exist. In addition, if we want to print such a relation, the statement "**print** relation-name" must follow.

8.4 QUERY BY EXAMPLE AND QBE DBMS

8.4.1. Introduction

Query-By-Example (abbreviated as QBE) is a query language based on the domain calculus defined in chapter 3. QBE was proposed by pioneer Zloof [Zlo74, Zlo75a, Zlo75b], at IBM, as an attempt to develop an easy-to-learn and easy-to-use high level language for the nonprofessional user. It has been implemented by IBM, but the implementation does not completely follow Zloof's proposal. The examples, illustrated in subsequent sections, were tested using an implementation supported by IBM 3277 (Model 2) Display Station and a VM/370 CMS-based facility called the QBE Installed User Program [SH20-2077-0, SH20-2078-1].

A table in QBE may have at most 100 columns and any number of rows. Each table name or column name cannot exceed 32 characters in length, can contain blanks, but cannot include a period, an underscore, or an arithmetic operator. Unlike QUEL in INGRES, duplicated tuples in the result are detected and eliminated when a domain calculus expression is interpreted. Correspondence between the domain calculus and the QBE DBMS is shown in table 8-8. When **AND** or **OR** is used, there must be at least one blank or a parenthesis on each side of the logical operator **AND** or **OR**.

8.4.2 Entering QBE Environment

To use QBE and its DBMS, the user must be authorized. The user should consult the person responsible for the installation to become familiar with the login or sign-on procedure. The user should also become familiar with the following keys and terminology.

(1) The ENTER key is used to invoke the QBE system to process a request. After the ENTER key has been pressed, a single line appears at the bottom of the screen, and a single underscore character known as the *cursor* appears at the lower left of the

TABLE 8-8. CORRESPONDENCE OF TERMINOLOGY AND NOTATION

Domain calculus	QBE DBMS
prime attribute	key
secondary index	inversion or index
relation scheme	table definition
view	snapshot
column number	position
and	**&** or **AND**
or +	**|** or **OR**
not −	¬
≠	− =
≥	>= or =>
≤	<= or =<

screen. The characters CP READ, appearing at the lower right of the screen, indicate that the QBE system is waiting for instructions.

(2) To move the cursor to a desired position on the screen, the four positioning keys, labeled by the arrows pointing to east (forward right key), west (backward keys), north (up key), and south (down key), are used. Other cursor positioning keys are the New Line key, the TAB key, and the Back Tab key.

(3) The characters VM READ, appearing at the bottom right of the screen, indicate that the password has been accepted.

(4) The "read mode" is granted by entering QBE READ. The "write mode" is granted by entering only QBE. When a query is processed, it is in the "process mode."

Whenever a blank table skeleton appears on the screen, the user has entered the QBE environment. A blank table skeleton has four areas as shown in table 8-9.

TABLE 8-9. BLANK TABLE SKELETON

Table name area	Column name area
Row operator area	Data entry area

(1) Table name area—This area contains the name of a table. When the "print" operator **P.** (each operator must be followed by a period) is typed in this area, the operation is performed on the names of all data tables (including system tables if authorized) in the database. The system tables are TABLE(NAME, OWNER), DOMAIN(NAME, OWNER, DATA TYPE, IMAGE, MIN ICW, MAX ICW), PROGRAM(NAME, OWNER, COMMENTS), and AUTHORITY(TABLE NAME, USERID, PRT AUTH, UPD AUTH, DEL AUTH, INS AUTH) where the column names are separated by commas rather than blanks for avoiding confusion, since some column name is composed of two strings separated by a blank, such as DATA TYPE in DOMAIN. In these system tables, ICW, PRT, UPD, DEL, INS, and AUTH stand for, respectively, the input column width, print, update, delete, insert, and authority. The attribute NAME in TABLE, DOMAIN, or PROGRAM means, respectively, the table name, domain name, or program (including query) name. When the operator **P.** or **D.** ("delete") is typed with a specific table name following, the table is printed or deleted, respectively. When a specific table name followed by the operator **P.** is typed, the column names of the table are printed.

(2) Column name area—This area has a number of fields, each corresponding to a column. When an operator is typed in such a field and followed by a specific column name, the operation is performed on that column in the table.

(3) Row operator area—This area is used to perform operations on an entire row of the table. The system operators are: **P., D., I.** ("insert"), **U.** ("update"), **X.** ("execute"), **G.** ("group-by"), **AUTH.** ("authority"), **ALL.''** ("multiset set definition"), **AO.**(n) ("sort in an ascending order with sort priority n"), and **DO.**(n) ("sort in a descending order with sort priority n"). To sort tuples based only on one column uses **AO.** or **DO.** for an ascending or a descending order. To

sort tuples based on more than one column requires the use of **AO.**(n) or **DO.**(n) in each such column where n is an integer and specifies the sort priority of the column. When n = 1, the corresponding column is to be sorted first. There are other types of operators: aggregate (built-in functions), arithmetic comparison, arithmetic, and logical operators.

(4) Data entry area—This area has a number of fields equal to the number of columns. It contains the table data elements and query expressions being evaluated as values. There are two types of data elements: an *example element,* which is a term (variable) defined in the first-order logic and called a domain variable, denoted by a symbol prefixed by an underscore; and a *constant element,* which is a term (constant) defined in the first-order logic and called a value of a domain variable. When an operator is typed in any entry field, the operation is performed on all or some data elements of the corresponding column. When the operator **P.** is typed in a specific column, all values of the column are printed without duplicates.

If the user is familiar with the cursor positioning keys and the program function (PF) keys, he/she is ready to begin using QBE. When the IBM 3277 Display Station is used there are two screen boxes called the *condition box* and the *command box* and several PF keys. The PF10 key widens a column or box when more space is needed. PF7 adds a column (four columns by default) to a table or adds a row (two rows by default) to a table or box (command or condition). PF9 adds a continuation or folded row (indicated by colon boundaries). PF4 produces another table skeleton. PF1 erases a table skeleton, column, row, or column entry depending on the position of the cursor. When PF11 is pressed once (twice), one (two) condition box is (boxes are) given. When PF12 is pressed once (twice), one command box (plus another line) is given. The maximum number of table skeletons, along with the condition and command boxes, is twelve.

There are three states entailed in the following.

(1) Input state—This state represents the time interval during which a query is formulated or modified from the keyboard. This state is indicated by the message INPUT at the lower right of the screen.

(2) Processing state—This state represents the time interval during which the query is processed by the QBE system. The corresponding message is PROCESS. During this state, query processing can be interrupted by pressing the PF12 key.

(3) Output state—This state represents the time interval during which the results of a query are displayed on the screen. The corresponding message is OUTPUT.

In all three states, the first command in the command box is the next one to be processed by the QBE system.

8.4.3 Defining a Data Table

Definition of a data table can be accomplished either interactively during a QBE terminal session or with the bulk loader. Each table consists of a table name and the names of its columns. By the first method, creating a data table can only be accomplished in write mode. Values in domains must be characterized by declaring their data types. The data types are:

(1) **CHAR**(number)—Any value of this type is a character string of longest length declaring by ''number'' from 1 through 3200 characters.

(2) **FIXED**—This is for a numeric value in the range $-2,147,484,646$ to $2,147,483,647$ (a full word with 32 bits).

(3) **FLOAT**—This is for a numeric value that may be outside of the range for **FIXED** data.

(4) **DATE**—The default format for dates is of the form MM/DD/YY, meaning month/day/year.

(5) **TIME**—The default format for times is of the form HH:MM:SS, meaning hour:minutes:seconds.

When two distinct columns are compared, the columns must be compatible, i.e., their data types must be identical. Thus, compatible columns must be defined on the same domain. In addition to the data types, the column width on input or output can be defined by ''ICW number'' or ''OCW number,'' where ICW or OCW means input or output column width. A secondary index can be created by default or by declaring **INVERSION**. The order of entering columns is by default or is declared by **POSITION**. The prime attributes (i.e., attributes in a key for a table) are declared by **KEY**. We can use the ''insert'' operator **I.** to add the name of a new table, the column headings, and the tuples to create a tabular relation in the database. The ''insert'' operator **I.** is equivalent to the INGRES **append** command.

Example 8.17:

Create relation EMP with scheme NAME SALARY MGR DEPT.

I. EMP I.	NAME	SALARY	MGR	DEPT

To see the defaults of the values in columns, we can type **P.P.** in the row operator area. The defaults based on the column names are listed in the following table.

EMP	NAME	SALARY	MGR	DEPT
KEY	Y (DEF)	Y (DEF)	Y (DEF)	Y (DEF)
DOMAIN	-	-	-	-
TYPE	-	-	-	-
IMAGE	-	-	-	-
ICW	4 (DEF)	6 (DEF)	3 (DEF)	4 (DEF)
OCW	-	-	-	-
POSITION	1	2	3	4
INVERSION	Y (DEF)	Y (DEF)	Y (DEF)	Y (DEF)

In this table, a hyphen ''-'' stands for a null value, Y means yes, and (DEF) indicates a default. Each ICW value is equal to the length of its corresponding column name.

Suppose that NAME and MGR are defined on the domain called WORKER of **CHAR**(12), and SALARY and DEPT are, respectively, defined on the domains MONEY of **FIXED** and ADMINISTRATION of **CHAR**(14). Let NAME be the key for EMP. To complete the definition of EMP, we update the table as shown below.

EMP	NAME	SALARY	MGR	DEPT
KEY U.	Y (DEF)	N	N	N
DOMAIN I.	WORKER	MONEY	WORKER	ADMINISTRATION
TYPE I.	CHAR	FIXED	CHAR	CHAR
IMAGE I.	-	-	-	-
ICW U.	12	7	12	14
OCW	-	-	-	-
POSITION	1	2	3	4
INVERSION	Y (DEF)	Y (DEF)	Y (DEF)	Y (DEF)

where the letter N means no. When we change a defaulted field, we should erase the rest of the default indicator (DEF) by pressing the ERASE EOF key after we enter the appropriate symbol or value. The **IMAGE** entries define output editing formats for all types of data except character strings. The reader can follow this method to complete the table definitions of SALES and SUPPLY as already shown in tables 8-2 and 8-3.

To delete an existing column, we can type the "delete" operator **D.** preceding the name of the column to be deleted. To add a new column, we position the cursor in the last column, press the PF7 key to get a blank column on the end of the table, enter the "insert" operator **I.** followed by the name of the column to be added, and also add the other entries, such as **DOMAIN, TYPE,** and so forth for the new column.

To append tuples to the table EMP, we insert an entire tuple one at a time. For example, **I.** YANG 30000 JONES COMPUTER appends the first tuple to EMP. This is similar to the INGRES **append** statement. When inserting tuples into a table, single quotes enclosing constants are not required.

An alternative method, similar to the INGRES **copy** facility, uses the bulk loader without initiating a QBE session. The bulk loader is a utility program that is used to read an entire table definition along with its tuples into the database. This method is omitted here. The interested reader can refer to [SH20-2077-0].

8.4.4 Command and Condition Boxes

In addition to tables, there are two boxes: one is called the *command box*, in which a command can be issued for query processing, and the other is called the *condition box*, in which conditions can be entered for query retrieval.

To return from output state to input state for entering a query, we use the command box. When the PF12 key is pressed once, the answer of the previous query disappears, and the command box appears on the screen. We can widen the box by using the PF10 key, add rows to it by using the PF7 key, and erase it by using the PF1 key. To return to the previous query, type a special command **P.*** (redisplaying the original program or query), and press ENTER. Then we are in input state and can modify the previous query.

To get a complete list of the commands, we can type **P.** in the command box. The command **PRINTER** alone prints output (query and its results) with a hard copy after signing off or logout from the terminal session. The command **END** terminates the current QBE session. The command **CANCEL** stops current processing and redisplays the original program or query.

The condition box is used to enter retrieval conditions that are not in the table skeleton(s). Each such condition is entered on a separate line of the box and is similar to a formula. All conditions are conjuncted.

There are three types of conditions.

(1) Simple conditions—A simple condition is represented by ee ϑ c, whre ee is an example element used in a table skeleton and corresponds to a domain variable, ϑ is an arithmetic comparison operator, and c is a constant in some active domain. A simple condition corresponds to an atom as defined in (2) of definition 3.11.

(2) Compound condition—A compound condition is formed by at least two simple conditions. It corresponds to a formula composed of at least two atoms. For example, the compound 5000 < __ SALARY < 30000 corresponds to the formula 5000 <__ SALARY AND __ SALARY < 30000, where the order of precedence of the "less than" operator is higher than that of the "logical and" operator **AND**.

(3) Conditions with logical expressions—A logical expression is an expression composed of items separated by logical operators and enclosed by parentheses. The logical operators are **AND** (or **&**), **OR** (or **|**), and −. An item can be a constant element, an example element, an arithmetic expression, or a string expression, which can be preceded by −, or one of the comparison operators. For example, the condition __ SALARY = (> 5000 **AND** <30000) containing the logical expression on the right side of = is equivalent to the compound condition, shown in (2).

8.4.5 Single Table Processing

To process a query involving only a single table, programming a QBE solution is straightforward, since it is trivial to map a domain calculus expression to a QBE solution. A QBE solution may need to use a constant element, an example element, an arithmetic expression, a string expression, a logical expression, a condition box, and/or a command box. We consider several examples in the following. Whenever a row is interpreted, SALES(DEPT ITEM) of table 8-2 or SUPPLY(ITEM SUPPLIER) of table 8-8 is used. Whenever a negated row is involved, table 8-10 or 8-11 is used for a limited interpretation.

Example 8.18:

Find the items supplied by IBM (and also possibly supplied by other suppliers) in table 8-3. The domain calculus expression for this query is

$$\{y\,(\text{ITEM})\ \mid\ \text{SUPPLY}(y\ \text{"IBM"})\}$$

where y is a domain variable with scheme ITEM. A QBE solution is

SUPPLY	ITEM	SUPPLIER
	P. [___ A]	IBM

where IBM is a constant element and [___ A] is an optional example element corresponding to the domain variable y in the domain calculus expression. When a tuple in SUPPLY is examined, its ITEM-value is retrieved if its SUPPLIER-value is IBM. The answer is {MICRO, PRINTER, TERMINAL}. Note that MICRO and TERMINAL are also, respectively, supplied by HP and ZENITH. For the query, finding items that are only supplied by IBM, the answer is {PRINTER} (see example 8.21).

Example 8.19:

Find the items supplied by any supplier other than IBM (and also possibly supplied by IBM). The corresponding domain calculus expression is

$$\{y(\text{ITEM}) \mid \text{SUPPLY}(y\ \neg\ \text{``IBM''})\} \equiv$$
$$\{y(\text{ITEM}) \mid \exists z(\text{SUPPLIER})(\text{SUPPLY}(y\ z)\ \cdot$$
$$z \neq \text{``IBM''})\}$$

where $-$ IBM has four values, HP, TI, KODAK, and ZENITH. Hence, we have the following equivalence

$$\text{SUPPLY}(y - \text{``IBM''}) \equiv \text{SUPPLY}(y\ \text{``HP''}) + \text{SUPPLY}(y\ \text{``TI''})$$
$$+ \text{SUPPLY}(y\ \text{``KODAK''}) + \text{SUPPLY}(y\ \text{``ZENITH''}) \qquad (8.5)$$

where $+$ stands for the "logical or" operator. A QBE solution is

SUPPLY	ITEM	SUPPLIER
	P. [___ A]	¬IBM

The answer is {CALCULATOR, CAMERA, FILM, MICRO, RECORDER, TERMINAL, TV}. Note that MICRO and TERMINAL are also supplied by IBM. Note also that CALCULATOR is supplied by HP and TI, but it is printed only once in the answer since duplicates are eliminated. If we want to include the duplicates in the answer, we can use the multiset-oriented **ALL.** operator following **P.** and preceding ___ A (i.e., **P. ALL.___** A) in the SUPPLY table. For the query-finding items that are only supplied by suppliers other than IBM, the answer is {CALCULATOR, CAMERA, FILM, RECORDER, TV} (do exercise 8.15).

Example 8.20:

Find the items not supplied by IBM. The corresponding domain calculus expression is

$$\overline{\{y(\text{ITEM}) \mid \exists z(\text{SUPPLIER})(\text{SUPPLY}(y\ z)\ \cdot}$$
$$\text{SUPPLY}(y\ \text{``IBM''}))\} \equiv \{y(\text{ITEM}) \mid \overline{\text{SUPPLY}(y\ \text{``IBM''})}\}$$

where the equivalence is established by the fact that an item in the answer must be one that is not supplied by IBM but must be supplied by some other supplier. A QBE solution is

SUPPLY	ITEM	SUPPLIER
¬	___ A	IBM
	P. ___ A	

When the negated row in the table SUPPLY or the formula $\overline{SUPPLY(y\ ''IBM'')}$ in the domain calculus expression is interpreted, the formula is true for each tuple with number 1, 5, 9, 20, or 27, as shown in table 8-10 which contains the tuples that do not occur in SUPPLY since negated rows are interpreted. Thus, the answer is {CALCULATOR, CAMERA, FILM, RECORDER, TV} corresponding to the ITEM-values of the domain variable ___ A or y. Examples 8.18 and 8.20 are complementary to each other, i.e., the union of their disjoint answers is equal to ADOM(ITEM), or SUPPLY(y ''IBM'') + $\overline{SUPPLY(y\ ''IBM'')}$ is a tautology, and SUPPLY(y ''IBM'') · $\overline{SUPPLY(y\ ''IBM'')}$ is a contradiction. Note that when a row is negated, the ''print'' operator cannot be entered in any data entry field in the row. This is why we need to use two rows in this example. In addition, the two rows must be linked by the same example element, ___ A.

Example 8.21:

Find the items not supplied by all suppliers except IBM, i.e., supplied only by IBM. The corresponding domain calculus expression is

$$\{y(ITEM)\ |\ \exists z(SUPPLIER)(\overline{SUPPLY(y\ z)}\ \cdot$$
$$\overline{SUPPLY(y\ \neg''IBM'')})\} \equiv \{y(ITEM)\ |\ SUPPLY(y\ \neg''IBM'')\}$$

where the negated atom $\overline{SUPPLY(y\ \neg''IBM'')}$ is equivalent to the negation of (8.5), i.e.,

$$\overline{SUPPLY(y\ \neg''IBM'')} \equiv \overline{SUPPLY(y\ ''HP'')}\ \cdot$$
$$\overline{SUPPLY(y\ ''TI'')}\ \cdot\overline{SUPPLY(y\ ''KODAK'')}\ \cdot\ \overline{SUPPLY(y\ ''ZENITH'')} \qquad (8.6)$$

where the symbol · stands for the ''logical and'' operator. A QBE solution is

SUPPLY	ITEM	SUPPLIER
¬	___ A	¬IBM
	P. ___ A	

The answer is {PRINTER}. Examples 8.19 and 8.21 are complementary to each other as seen from their answers or domain calculus expressions.

8.4.6 Multiple Table Processing

To process a query involving more than one table, programming a QBE solution is still straightforward unless two or more rows are negated (do exercises 8.16 and 8.17).

Example 8.22:

Find the departments selling an item supplied by IBM (and also possibly supplied by other suppliers). From example 8.18, we found that IBM supplies MICRO, PRINTER, and TERMINAL where MICRO and TERMINAL are also supplied by HP and ZENITH, respectively. We can, based on the following domain calculus expression

{x(DEPT) | SALES(x "MICRO") + SALES(x "PRINTER") + SALES(x "TERMINAL")},

TABLE 8-10. ATUP(ITEM SUPPLIER) -
SUPPLY(ITEM SUPPLIER)

Tuple number j	ITEM	SUPPLIER
1	CALCULATOR	IBM
2	CALCULATOR	KODAK
3	CALCULATOR	ZENITH
4	CAMERA	HP
5	CAMERA	IBM
6	CAMERA	TI
7	CAMERA	ZENITH
8	FILM	HP
9	FILM	IBM
10	FILM	TI
11	FILM	ZENITH
12	MICRO	KODAK
13	MICRO	TI
14	MICRO	ZENITH
15	PRINTER	HP
16	PRINTER	KODAK
17	PRINTER	TI
18	PRINTER	ZENITH
19	RECORDER	HP
20	RECORDER	IBM
21	RECORDER	KODAK
22	RECORDER	TI
23	TERMINAL	HP
24	TERMINAL	KODAK
25	TERMINAL	TI
26	TV	HP
27	TV	IBM
28	TV	KODAK
29	TV	TI

provide a QBE solution

SALES	DEPT	ITEM
	P. ___ A	MICRO
	P. ___ B	PRINTER
	P. ___ C	TERMINAL

and obtain the answer {COMPUTER, DP}. To implement the ''logical or'' operations in the domain calculus expression by QBE, we must use different example elements, ___ A, ___ B, and ___ C each prefixed by a ''print'' command. Note that some department in the result may also sell an item not supplied by IBM. For example, COMPUTER also sells CALCULATOR supplied by HP or TI.

By this solution, we need to type three rows in the table SALES. Alternatively, we can type only one row in the table SALES and use the condition box as shown below.

SALES	DEPT	ITEM
	P.	___ITEM

CONDITIONS
___ITEM = (MICRO OR PRINTER OR TERMINAL)

where the condition contains the logical expression on the right side of =.

Another alternative method uses both tables SALES and SUPPLY linked by an example element of ITEM. The corresponding domain calculus expression is

$$\{x(DEPT) \mid \exists y(ITEM)(SALES(x\ y) \cdot SUPPLY(y\ ''IBM''))\}.$$

A QBE solution using the example element ___ RADIO to link SALES and SUPPLY is

SALES	DEPT	ITEM
	P.	___ RADIO

SUPPLY	ITEM	SUPPLIER
	___ RADIO	IBM

where the order of entering tables is arbitrary. This solution is equivalent to finding the join of SALES and SUPPLY and then performing a selection based on the constant element IBM and a projection onto DEPT.

We can create a view (snapshot in QBE terminology) with name DEPTSUPPLIER and print the view.

I. DEPTSUPPLIER I.	DEPT	SUPPLIER
I. P.	___ CLOTH	___ GE

SALES	DEPT	ITEM
	___ CLOTH	___ PEN

SUPPLY	ITEM	SUPPLIER
	___ PEN	___ GE

Then the table DEPTSUPPLIER is printed as

DEPTSUPPLIER	DEPT	SUPPLIER
	COMPUTER	HP
	COMPUTER	TI
	COMPUTER	IBM
	COMPUTER	ZENITH
	DP	HP
	DP	IBM
	PHOTO	ZENITH
	PHOTO	KODAK
	VIDEO	ZENITH

This view is stored in the database and can be used subsequently. From this view we see that the departments selling an item MICRO, PRINTER, and TERMINAL supplied by IBM are COMPUTER and DP. The corresponding domain calculus expression is

$$\{x(DEPT) \mid DEPTSUPPLIER(x \text{ ``IBM''})\}$$

and the corresponding QBE solution is

DEPTSUPPLIER	DEPT	SUPPLIER
	P.	IBM

Example 8.23

Find the departments selling all items supplied by IBM (and possibly other items supplied by other suppliers). This is the query Q_1 as solved by the relational algebra and the tuple calculus in chapters 1 and 3 and also in INGRES. Since the universal quantifier is not implemented in QBE, it is easier to take two steps, finding all items supplied by IBM as shown in example 8.18, and then solving this query by QBE as follows:

SALES	DEPT	ITEM
	__A	MICRO
	__A	PRINTER
	P. __A	TERMINAL

The answer is {COMPUTER, DP}. The corresponding domain calculus expression is

$$\{x(DEPT) \mid SALES(x\ ``MICRO") \cdot SALES(x\ ``PRINTER") \cdot$$
$$SALES(x\ ``TERMINAL")\}.$$

When "logical and" is involved, the example elements must be identical, and only one "print" operator can be entered. For the query-finding departments selling only all those items supplied by IBM, the answer becomes {DP} (do exercise 8.15). Similar to example 8.22, we can use the SALES table and the condition box to solve this problem where the condition is __ ITEM = (MICRO AND PRINTER AND TERMINAL).

Example 8.24:

Find the departments not selling any item supplied by IBM (and also possibly supplied by other suppliers). The corresponding domain calculus expression is

$$\{x(DEPT) \mid \exists y(ITEM)\ \exists y'(ITEM)(SALES(x\ y') \cdot \overline{SALES(x\ y)} \cdot$$
$$SUPPLY(y\ ``IBM"))\} \equiv \{x(DEPT) \mid \exists y(ITEM)(\overline{SALES(x\ y)} \cdot SUPPLY(y\ ``IBM"))\}.$$

A QBE solution is

SALES	DEPT	ITEM
¬	__A	__B
	P. __A	

SUPPLY	ITEM	SUPPLIER
	__B	IBM

When this query is processed, rows with tuple numbers 11, 12, 14, 19, 20, and 21, as shown in table 8-11, are used for a limited interpretation. Thus, the answer is {PHOTO, VIDEO} corresponding to the DEPT-values of the domain variable __ A or x. Examples 8.23 and 8.24 are complementary to each other.

Example 8.25:

Find the departments selling an item not supplied by IBM. The corresponding domain calculus expression is

$\{x(DEPT) \mid \exists y(ITEM)(SALES(x\ y) \cdot \overline{SUPPLY(y\ ``IBM'')}\ )\}.$

A QBE solution is

SUPPLY	ITEM	SUPPLIER
¬	___ PEN	IBM

SALES	DEPT	ITEM
	P.	___ PEN

The answer is {COMPUTER, PHOTO, VIDEO}, since the items not supplied by IBM, as found in example 8.20, are {CALCULATOR, CAMERA, FILM, RECORDER, TV} and each department in the answer sells at least one of such items.

Example 8.26:

Find the departments selling an item supplied by a supplier other than IBM. The corresponding domain calculus expression is

$$\{x(DEPT) \mid \exists y(ITEM)(SALES(x\ y) \cdot SUPPLY(y\ \neg``IBM''))\}$$

A QBE solution is

SALES	DEPT	ITEM
	P.	___INK

SUPPLY	ITEM	SUPPLIER
	___INK	¬ IBM

The answer is {COMPUTER, DP, PHOTO, VIDEO}, since the items supplied by suppliers other than IBM, as found in example 8.19, are {CALCULATOR, CAMERA, FILM, MICRO, RECORDER, TERMINAL, TV} and each department sells at least one of such items.

Example 8.27:

Find the departments selling an item not supplied by all suppliers except IBM. The corresponding domain calculus expression is

TABLE 8-11.   ATUP(DEPT ITEM) -
SALES(DEPT ITEM)

Tuple number j	DEPT	ITEM
1	COMPUTER	CAMERA
2	COMPUTER	FILM
3	COMPUTER	RECORDER
4	COMPUTER	TV
5	DP	CALCULATOR
6	DP	CAMERA
7	DP	FILM
8	DP	RECORDER
9	DP	TV
10	PHOTO	CALCULATOR
11	PHOTO	MICRO
12	PHOTO	PRINTER
13	PHOTO	RECORDER
14	PHOTO	TERMINAL
15	PHOTO	TV
16	VIDEO	CALCULATOR
17	VIDEO	CAMERA
18	VIDEO	FILM
19	VIDEO	MICRO
20	VIDEO	PRINTER
21	VIDEO	TERMINAL

$$\{x(DEPT) \mid \exists y(ITEM)(SALES(x\ y) \cdot \overline{SUPPLY(y\ \neg``IBM")})\}.$$

A QBE solution is

SALES	DEPT	ITEM
	P.	___ BOOK

SUPPLY	ITEM	SUPPLIER
	___ BOOK	IBM

The answer is {COMPUTER, DP}, since both departments in the answer sell PRINTER that is only supplied by IBM, as found in example 8.21.

Example 8.28:

Find the departments that do not sell an item supplied by a supplier other than IBM but may sell an item supplied by IBM. The corresponding domain calculus expression is

$$\{x(DEPT) \mid \exists y(ITEM)\, \exists y'(ITEM)(SALES(x\ y') \cdot \overline{SALES(x\ y)} \cdot$$
$$SUPPLY(y\ \neg\ ``IBM''))\} \equiv \{x(DEPT) \mid \exists y(ITEM)\overline{(SALES(x\ y) \cdot}$$
$$\overline{SUPPLY(y\ \neg``IBM''))}\}.$$

A QBE solution is

SALES	DEPT	ITEM
¬	__ A	__ B
	P. __ A	

SUPPLY	ITEM	SUPPLIER
	__ B	¬IBM

The answer is {COMPUTER, DP, PHOTO, VIDEO}, since the underlying items are all items in ADOM(ITEM) except PRINTER, as found in example 8.19 and each department sells at least one of such items. Note that examples 8.25 and 8.28 are not complementary to each other, as seen from their domain calculus expressions.

Example 8.29:

Find the union of the projections SALES[ITEM] and SUPPLY[ITEM]. The corresponding domain calculus expression is

$$\{y(ITEM) \mid \exists x(DEPT)\, \exists z(SUPPLIER)(SALES(x\ y)\ +\ SUPPLY(y\ z))\}$$

where DEPT and SUPPLIER are defined on the same domain. A QBE solution is

SALES	DEPT	ITEM
	__ DEPT	__ PEN

SUPPLY	ITEM	SUPPLIER
	__ INK	__ RCA

SALESUPPLY	ITEM
I.	⎯ PEN
I.	⎯ INK
	P.

The answer is

SALESUPPLY	ITEM
	CALCULATOR
	CAMERA
	FILM
	MICRO
	PRINTER
	RECORDER
	TERMINAL
	TV

Example 8.30:

Let RELA(A B) = {3 6, 2 5, 1 4} and RELB(B C) = {8 11, 5 10, 4 9} be relations. Find the difference RELB[B] − RELA[B]. The domain calculus expression is

$$\{b(B) \mid \forall a(A) \ \exists c(C)(\overline{RELA(a \ b) \cdot RELB(b \ c)})\}.$$

A QBE solution is

RELA	A	B
¬		⎯ B

RELB	B	C
	P. ⎯ B	

The answer is {8}.

8.4.7 Aggregates

In a QBE solution, we can use built-in functions to provide aggregation capabilities. These functions are: **CNT.**, to count the number of occurrences; **SUM.**, to compute the summation; **AVG.**, to find the average; **MAX.**, to choose the maximum; **MIN.**, to choose the minimum; and **UNQ.**, to use distinct objects only. The unique function **UNQ.** can be used with **CNT.**, **SUM.**, or **AVG.** such that **CNT.UNQ.** counts the number of distinct occurrences, **SUM.UNQ.** computes the summation of distinct values, and **AVG.UNQ.** stands for the division of **SUM.UNQ.** and **CNT.UNQ.** (i.e., **AVG.UNQ.** = **SUM.UNQ.** /**CNT.UNQ.**).

When any built-in function is used, it must be followed by the **ALL.** operator. For example, **CNT.ALL.__** ITEM and **CNT.UNQ.ALL.__** ITEM compute, respectively, the numbers of the elements in the multiset of items and in the set of items. When any built-in function is used in a data entry field, the corresponding column heading in the result table is modified by postfixing an additional word to the column name to reflect use of a built-in function. These words are **COUNT**, **SUM**, **MAX**, **MIN**, and **AVERAGE**.

In addition to the aggregate operators, there are aggregate functions. Similar to the "by"-list" in QUEL, QBE has the "group-by" operator **G.** to accomplish the same goal.

8.4.8 Renaming

To rename the name of a table or column, the owner simply types the old name followed by the "update" operator **U.** and the new name in the table name area or the corresponding column name field. The owner is responsible for updating the authority constraints, which are affected by renaming. This operation is performed in write mode.

8.4.9 Deleting a Relation Scheme

To destroy a relation scheme or table definition, the owner needs to delete all tuples in the table by typing the "delete" operator **D.** in the row operator area. Then the empty relation is yielded. The owner needs to type **D.** followed by the table name in the table name area to destroy its scheme.

8.5 PROLOG AND PROLOG DBMS

8.5.1 Introduction

PROLOG (PROgramming in LOGic) is a higher-level programming language, based on the clausal form of logic and developed in the seventies. It has been used for applications of symbolic computation in many areas, such as mathematical logic, artificial intelligence, and relational databases [Kow79, Clo81]. PROLOG exists in a number of implementations [Clo81]. The PROLOG with a database option (DATA-BASE PROLOG (in C) /UNIX version 7) composed of an interpreter and an input file is not as easy to use as we would like for processing queries; its extended version called PROLOG DBMS was used to test the examples in subsequent sections. This extended version was developed by Salah at UAB and is described in the Appendix. A PROLOG session is initiated by use of the command that is composed of the file names of the extended versions of the interpreter and the input file. These files are maintained in the user's home directory under the UNIX environment. The user can further extend the input file with his/her own programs. The user should consult the person responsible for the installation to start a session.

The PROLOG DBMS matches tuples and pushes them onto a stack. The interpreter reads the top element of the stack. Whenever the interpreter backtracks to obtain another tuple, it pops the top element from the stack.

8.5.2 Clausal Form of Logic and Horn Clauses

In section 0.4.4 of chapter 0, we mentioned two types of Horn clauses. In many applications of logic, it is sufficient to restrict the form of clauses to Horn clauses. In addition, any problem that can be represented in logic can be transformed into Horn clauses. In section 0.5 on the first-order logic, we defined terms, n-place predicates, atoms, and formulas.

Let $A_1, \ldots, A_n, B_1, \ldots, B_{m-1}$, and B_m be atoms. A *clause* is a formula of the clausal form of logic

$$B_1 + \ldots + B_m <- A_1 \cdot \ldots \cdot A_n$$

where the implication symbol $<-$ can be pronounced ''if'' and $+$ stands for the ''logical or'' or ''disjunction'' operator and $\cdot$ for the ''logical and'' or ''conjunction'' operator. The atoms $A_1, \ldots, A_{n-1}$, and A_n are the *(joint) conditions* of the clause and the atoms $B_1, \ldots, B_{m-1}$, and B_m are the *(alternative) conclusions* of the clause. The clausal form of logic has the two basic cases.

(1) No conditions—In this case, a clause has no conditions and is of the form

$$B_1 + B_2 + \ldots + B_m <-$$

This clause can be interpreted as stating unconditionally that ''B_1 or $\ldots$ or B_m'' for all variables $x_1, \ldots, x_k$ contained in the clause.

(2) At most one conclusion—In this case, a clause has at most one conclusion and is called a *Horn clause*. There are two types of Horn clauses, which are supported by the PROLOG DBMS. A Horn clause containing one conclusion, denoted by an unnegated atom, is called *headed*, since the conclusion can be viewed as the *head*. In the PROLOG DBMS, it is written as

$$+B_1 \; -A_1 \; -A_2 \; \ldots \; -A_n;$$

where B_1 is the head and is prefixed by $+$ and the conjunction of A_1 through A_n is the *body* in which each A_j for $1 \leq j \leq n$ is prefixed by $-$. The head of a Horn clause describes what conclusion the clause is intended to define, and the body describes all conditions that must be satisfied, one after another, for the head to be true. As shown in the Appendix, this type of clause is used to provide the definition of a new predicate in the extended input file. A Horn clause that has no conclusions is called **headless** and is written, in PROLOG DBMS as

$$-A_1 \ -A_2 \ \ldots \ -A_n;,$$

which will be used to write a PROLOG solution for processing a query.

8.5.3 UNIX and PROLOG Environments

There are two environments involved when a query is processed by the PROLOG DBMS.

(1) *UNIX environment*—The UNIX environment is indicated by the symbol % appearing on the beginning of each line. Under this environment we can create a relation scheme or relation; rename a relation or attribute name; permute attributes, edit tuples including insertion, deletion, and update; and invoke system programs **DB_MAKE**, **DB_INIT**, **DB_SCAN**, and the PROLOG DBMS for managing database. Under the UNIX environment %, we can initialize a database by executing **DB_INIT**. Then the message indicating the number of entries in a system file called *H_tab* is displayed on the screen. In subsequent examples, this message is not included for simplicity.

(2) *PROLOG environment*—This environment is indicated by ? instead of %. Under this environment we can fill tuples; edit tuples including insertion, deletion, and update; rename and permute nonprime attributes; permute tuple components; create temporary relations; define predicates; disengage relations in the underlying database; call UNIX; and perform other tasks of a similar nature. To terminate a PROLOG session type −**stop**· Then a message is displayed on the screen indicating the end of a PROLOG session and the number of entries left in the H_tab file. This message is omitted in subsequent examples. Whenever a PROLOG session is terminated, a UNIX session resumes.

8.5.4 Correspondence of Terminology and Notation

The correspondence of terminology and notation used in this book and PROLOG is listed in table 8-12.

TABLE 8-12. CORRESPONDENCE
OF TERMINOLOGY AND NOTATION

Relational database	PROLOG
relation	indexfile
domain variable a	*a
conjunction .	−
negation −	**not**
equality =	**$$$$eq**
less than <	**lt**
addition +	**plus**
subtraction −	**plus**
multiplicaton ×	**multiply**
division /	**divide**
multi-set [ ]	list
set { }	list

A multiset or set is denoted by a list derived, respectively, by **bag** or **uniquebag,** which will be explained in section 8.5.7. A − B is viewed as A + (−B).

8.5.5 Scripting a Session

A hard copy of the programming activities done in a session on a video terminal can be obtained by scripting the session. The method is entailed in the following.

(1) Start the script by typing ''**script** file-name'' under the UNIX environment. While the script is active, all terminal input and output is copied into the designated file.

(2) Proceed with the UNIX and/or PROLOG programming activities.

(3) Press ''Control'' and ''D'' keys to terminate the script.

(4) Print the scripted file by typing ''**lpr** file-name'' under the UNIX environment.

When a session is scripted, creating or updating a UNIX file must be done using the interactive or open mode (i.e., use the UNIX text editor **ed** as already demonstrated in example 8.8 of section 8.3.8). It is also important to be aware that when a session is scripted the output being sent to the terminal screen is not actually displayed there until the buffer for the disk file either has been filled or is being forced out due to execution of the PROLOG –**stop;** statement.

8.5.6 Textfiles and Indexfiles

In the PROLOG DBMS, there are two types of files, referred to as textfiles and indexfiles. In subsequent examples, we will arbitrarily use lowercase or uppercase identifiers as the names of textfiles or indexfiles respectively. By lowercase and uppercase names, both types of files are easily identified and associated.

(1) *textfile*—A textfile is a file created under the UNIX environment. A textfile is in a user-friendly form, and its name is unrestricted (except using lowercase names in this chapter). The format of a textfile is shown below.

#RELATION indexfile-name arity

#KEYS permutation of argument numbers followed by key specification

#ARGS argument number followed by description of argument for each argument

each tuple (one at a line)

The lines beginning with the symbol # form the heading, which defines scheme (including name and attributes), arity, primary key, and order of attributes of its corresponding indexfile. A (possibly empty) body of tuples follows. When the body is empty, the textfile is the empty relation. Note that a heading contains more information than a relation scheme.

(2) *indexfile*—An indexfile is a relation of the underlying database used for query processing under the PROLOG environment. It is converted from a textfile by UNIX command ''**DB_MAKE** textfile-name.'' An indexfile is in a form structured as a multilevel balanced tree (B-tree) determined by the contents of the heading of its

corresponding textfile. The name and arity of an indexfile are the name and positive integer following the keyword **#RELATION.** The (primary) key and the argument numbers defined in the heading determine the structure of the corresponding indexfile such that a B-tree has one level for each prime attribute. Note that the keywords **#RELATION, #KEYS,** and **#ARGS** must be in uppercase letters and # can not be followed by any blanks. In addition, the last line of a textfile must be the last **#ARGS** line if the body is empty, and the last tuple otherwise. If the last line of such a file is a blank line, then it is considered as a part of the file, and a subsequent **DB_MAKE** operation cannot be successfully performed.

8.5.7 Knowledge Representations

In this section we discuss the PROLOG equivalent of the following representations.

In section 0.4 of chapter 0, a symbol denoting a proposition is called an atom. In section 0.5 of chapter 0, an n-place predicate $p(t_1, \ldots, t_n)$ is also an atom where the predicate symbol p is a term and each argument t_j for $1 \leq j \leq n$ is a term, and a term is a constant, variable, or n-place function symbol. In PROLOG, a constant does not need to be quoted and a variable must be prefixed by an asterisk *. Since an attribute defined as an argument of a tuple in a relational database is only a constant and an argument used in PROLOG is a term, the term *argument* is more inclusive than *attribute*. A predicate such as a relation SALES(*dept, MICRO) indicating a department selling MICRO and a command such as **line** to skip a line are atoms in logic and are referred to as *functors* in PROLOG.

A component of a tuple or equivalently a value of a domain variable is represented either by a character string enclosed in a pair of double quotation marks or a nonspace (nonblank) character other than quote followed by a character string not containing a comma. A tuple of n elements is composed of n components separated by commas or blanks. Thus, a tuple can be denoted by a sequence of length n (i.e., elements are separated by commas), a string of length n (i.e., elements are concatenated and separated by blanks), or even n elements separated by commas and blanks. A tuple can be converted into a list by **bag** or **uniquebag.** Suppose that a tuple is $a_1 a_2 \ldots a_n$. The list representation is

$$.(a_1,.(a_2,.(\ldots ,.(a_n,nil) \ldots)))$$

where **nil** is the empty list. A relation (indexfile) has a heading defining its scheme, arity, key, and order of attributes, and a body containing its tuples.

8.5.8 Initialization and Maintenance of System Relations

In this section, we introduce the two system relations, **relation** and **argument** (by which a database scheme is represented) and three system programs **DB_INIT, DB_MAKE,** and **DB_SCAN**.

The **DB_INIT** system program initializes the system relations **relation** and **argu-**

ment. These relations are automatically defined as indexfiles by the system and cannot be used as textfiles. During the initialization, two tuples of the form: "name of relation", "arity", i.e.,

```
"relation", "2"
"argument", "3"
```

are automatically stored in **relation** and five tuples of the form "name of relation", "argumentnumber", "description of argument", i.e.,

```
"relation", "1", "name of relation"
"relation", "2", "number of arguments"
"argument", "1", "name of relation"
"argument", "2", "argumentnumber"
"argument", "3", "description of argument"
```

are automatically stored in **argument**. When a **DB_MAKE** is performed on a textfile, the name and arity of the corresponding indexfile are stored as a tuple in the system relation **relation,** and the three elements (i.e., indexfile-name, argument-number, and attribute) of each argument of the indexfile are stored as a tuple in the system relation **argument**. When a tuple that was initialized by **DB_INIT** has been deleted from a system relation, it can be recovered only by another **DB_INIT**. When a tuple that was filled by **DB_MAKE** has been deleted from a system relation, it can be recovered by **DB_MAKE**.

The key for **relation** is the first attribute (i.e., indexfile-name). We can never rename an indexfile-name by use of the PROLOG predicate **update**, since a key-value is used to match the tuple containing this key value, and therefore, it cannot be changed by **update**. The key for **argument** is the first two attributes ("indexfile-name" and "argument-number"). We can rename a nonprime attribute by **update** under the PROLOG environment. Although we can permute all nonprime attributes by updating their argument-numbers under the PROLOG environment, the corresponding attribute values of the tuples are not accordingly permuted.

A textfile is converted into an indexfile by UNIX command

```
DB ___ MAKE[-p]textfile-name
```

where −**p** is the option to copy the contents of the filename to **stdout,** the standard output file. **DB_MAKE** creates the indexfile and engages the indexfile with the underlying database scheme by storing the tuple "indexfile-name", "arity" in **relation** and the tuples "indexfile-name", "argument-number", "attribute" for each argument in **argument**. After **DB_MAKE** is executed, a message indicating the number of entries left in the file H_tab is displayed. We omit this type of message in subsequent examples.

The UNIX command to execute the program called **DB_SCAN** is of the form

```
DB_SCAN indexfile-name [> textfile-name]
```

This program reads an indexfile and converts it into the format of its corresponding textfile based on its heading. The primary key defined in its textfile determines its structure such that a B-tree has one level for each prime attribute. For example, when **DB_SCAN** SUPPLY is executed, the displayed relation SUPPLY is similar to the textfile supply except that the relation name, argument names, or each component of a tuple is enclosed in a pair of double quotation marks and the order of the **#ARGS** lines in the heading may be rearranged. The option [> textfile-name] makes a backup copy of the indexfile (i.e., the textfile becomes a copy of the indexfile but retains its original name).

8.5.9 Creating a Relation

A relation for query processing can be an indexfile engaged in the underlying database or a temporary file whose definition of scheme is not required.

To create a temporary relation, each tuple is defined by a headed Horn clause without any conditions, considered as a fact. More specifically, each tuple is created by typing the symbol + (can be viewed as definition), followed by the relation name to be created, a mathematical tuple of attribute-values (i.e., attribute-values separated by commas and enclosed by parentheses), and delimited by a semicolon.

Example 8.31:

Create the relation SALES(DEPT ITEM) as shown in table 8-2. To create SALES, we need first to initialize the database by use of **DB_INIT**, to enter the PROLOG environment by means of an invocation, and then to type tuples one after another. The environment indicators % for UNIX and ? for PROLOG are displayed by the systems and are included here to differentiate environments.

```
% DB_INIT /*initialize the database */
% /*invoke PROLOG DBMS */
? +SALES (COMPUTER, CALCULATOR); /*first tuple of relation SALES */
? +SALES (COMPUTER, MICRO) ;
? +SALES (COMPUTER, PRINTER) ;
? +SALES (COMPUTER, TERMINAL) ;
? +SALES (DP, MICRO) ;
? +SALES (DP, PRINTER) ;
? +SALES (DP, TERMINAL) ;
? +SALES (PHOTO, CAMERA) ;
? +SALES (PHOTO, FILM) ;
? +SALES (VIDEO, RECORDER) ;
? +SALES (VIDEO, TV) ; /*last tuple of relation SALES */
? /*PROLOG is ready to accept input */
```

where each comment enclosed by a pair of /* and */ is provided for the reader of this example and cannot be included as a part of the code. After the relation SALES has been created, we can process queries related to this relation. However, SALES is only temporary and is erased when the session is terminated by −**stop**.

Example 8.32:

Find the items sold by DP. A PROLOG solution, assuming the relation SALES has been created as in example 8.31, is

```
? -SALES(DP, *item) -line -w(*item) -line; /*headless Horn clause */
MICRO
PRINTER
TERMINAL
```

where the last three lines form the answer. In the 2-place predicate SALES(DP, *item), DP and *item are arguments corresponding, respectively, to a constant and a variable defined as terms in the first-order logic. A variable, such as *item, can be viewed as a domain variable, and any such variable must be prefixed by an asterisk *. The command **w**(*item) writes the values of *item on the output file. The command **line** means that the current line of the output file is terminated or simply that a line is skipped. Both **w**(argument) and **line** provide communications with the outside world, and a call on either one never creates any backtracking points.

This method is simple to use, since we simply create temporary relations and process queries and never involve **DB_MAKE** and **DB_SCAN**. However, the created relations are not stored in the underlying database and are erased when the session is terminated.

Example 8.33:

The format of the textfile, supply, corresponding to the relation SUPPLY as shown in table 8-3, is created in a batch mode under the UNIX environment as shown below.

```
% vi supply /* initiate creation of textfile supply */
#RELATION SUPPLY 2 /* indexfile SUPPLY with arity 2 */
#KEYS 1 2 2 /* both attributes form the all-key */
#ARGS 1 ITEM /* first attribute ITEM */
#ARGS 2 SUPPLIER /* second attribute SUPPLIER */
CALCULATOR,HP /* first tuple */
CALCULATOR,TI
CAMERA,KODAK
FILM,KODAK
MICRO,HP
MICRO,IBM
PRINTER,IBM
RECORDER,ZENITH
TERMINAL,IBM
TERMINAL,ZENITH
TV,ZENITH /* last tuple */
/* press key ESC to quit editing */
:wq /* store supply */
% DB_MAKE supply /*create indexfile SUPPLY */
```

where the first four lines after the call to the **vi** editor form the heading, and the tuples form the body. The second line, which begins with the key word **#KEYS**, needs more explanation. The permutation of the argument numbers is 1 2 (corresponding to ITEM SUPPLIER), and the integer 2 indicates that ITEM SUPPLIER is the all-key. The relation SALES can be similarly created and stored in the underlying database (do exercise 8.18) for subsequent uses.

8.5.10 Query Processing

When the relations have been created, queries concerning these relations can be processed under the PROLOG environment. A PROLOG solution can be written as a headless Horn clause.

Example 8.34:

> For the query-finding the items supplied by IBM (and also possibly supplied by other suppliers) as given in example 8.18, a PROLOG solution is typed on the first line, and the answer is then printed as shown in the following:

```
? -SUPPLY(*item,IBM) -line -w(*item) -line;
TERMINAL
MICRO
PRINTER
```

Example 8.35:

> For the query-finding the items supplied by any supplier other than IBM (and also possibly supplied by IBM) as given in example 8.19, a PROLOG solution and its answer are

```
? -SUPPLY(*item, *suplier) -not($$$$eq(*supplier,IBM))
-line -w(*item) -line;
TV
TERMINAL
CAMERA
FILM
MICRO
RECORDER
CALCULATOR
CALCULATOR
```

where duplicates such as CALCULATOR are not eliminated. The predicate **not($$$$eq**(*supplier, IBM)) implements the atom *supplier $\neq$ IBM where **not** must use lowercase letters. A constant, such as IBM, cannot be negated (i.e., we cannot say **not**(IBM)) and needs not be enclosed in a pair of double quotation marks (even it is nonnumeric). The predicate **$$$$eq**(*x, *y) is supported by the PROLOG.

To eliminate duplicates, we need to create an indexfile to hold the answers by **storetuple,** then print the answers from the indexfile. To store tuples into an indexfile by use of **storetuple** automatically eliminates duplicated tuples. For the query in this example, a PROLOG solution is

(1) Create a textfile called answer under the UNIX environment:

```
% vi answer /* to be used to hold answer in its indexfile */
#RELATION ANSWER 1
#KEYS 1 1
#ARGS 1 RESULT
where :wq following the last line is omitted here and will be omitted
in subsequent examples.
```

(2) Create the indexfile of answer by

% DB_MAKE answer

(3) Change environment by invoking the PROLOG DBMS

(4) Process the query as follows:

```
? -SUPPLY(*item, *supplier) -not($$$$eq(*supplier, IBM))
  -storetuple(ANSWER(*item));
? -ANSWER(*item) -line -w(*item) -line;
```

where the database function **storetuple** fills distinct tuples into the indexfile ANSWER.

Example 8.36:

Find the join of the relations SALES and SUPPLY. A PROLOG solution and its answer are as follows:

```
? -SALES(*dept, *item) -SUPPLY(*item, *supplier)
  -line-w(*dept) -w(",") -w(*item) -w(",") -w(*supplier) -line;
DP,TERMINAL,ZENITH
DP,TERMINAL,IBM
DP,MICRO,HP
DP,MICRO,IBM
DP,PRINTER,IBM
VIDEO,TV,ZENITH
VIDEO,RECORDER,ZENITH
COMPUTER,TERMINAL,ZENITH
COMPUTER,TERMINAL,IBM
COMPUTER,MICRO,HP
COMPUTER,MICRO,IBM
COMPUTER,PRINTER,IBM
COMPUTER,CALCULATOR,TI
COMPUTER,CALCULATOR,HP
PHOTO,CAMERA,KODAK
PHOTO,FILM,KODAK
```

If we want to use blanks for separation, we can use the atom **w**(" ") to replace **w**(",") where one or more blanks can be used in **w**(" "). Similar to example 8.31, the join created here is not stored in the underlying database. If we want to store a relation created under the PROLOG environment, we must follow the process used in example 8.35 to store each resulting tuple.

In this example, we can use the **wr** command with three arguments to replace the five **w** commands, i.e., use −**wr**(*dept, *item, *supplier) to replace −**w**(*item) −**w**("‚") −**w**(*item) −**w**("‚") −**w**(*supplier) where **wr** is defined in the Appendix, and the output format is predetermined in the definition of **wr** (i.e., the components of each tuple start at position numbers 1, 16, and 31, respectively).

Example 8.37:

Create the join of SALES and SUPPLY and store it in the database.

```
% vi salesupply
#RELATION SALESUPPLY 3
#KEYS 1 2 3 3
#ARGS 1 DEPT
#ARGS 2 ITEM
#ARGS 3 SUPPLIER
% DB_MAKE salesupply
/* Invoke PROLOG DBMS */
? -SALES(*dept, *item) -SUPPLY(*item, *supplier)
  -line -w(*dept) -w(" ") -w(*item) -w(" ") -w(*supplier) -line
  -storetuple(SALESUPPLY(*dept, *item, *supplier));
```

Then the relation SALESUPPLY is displayed on the screen and also stored in the underlying database.

Based on the join SALESUPPLY, we can find the departments selling an item supplied by IBM (and also possibly supplied by other suppliers) as solved by QBE in example 8.22. A PROLOG solution and its answer are

```
? -SALESUPPLY(*dept, *item, IBM) -line -w(*dept) -line;
DP /* displayed three times */
COMPUTER /*displayed three times */
```

where duplicates are not eliminated as indicated in the comments.

For eliminating duplicates in the answer a solution is

```
? -ANSWER(*x) -delete(ANSWER(*x)); /* delete old tuples */
? -SALESUPPLY(*dept, *item, IBM) -storetuple(ANSWER(*dept));
? -ANSWER(*dept) -line -w(*dept) -line;
```

Example 8.38:

For the query, shown in example 8.26, finding the departments selling an item supplied by a supplier other than IBM, a PROLOG solution and its answer are

```
? -SALES(*dept, *item)-SUPPLY(*item, *supplier)
-not($$$$eq(*supplier, IBM))
  -line -w(*dept) -line;
DP /* twice */
VIDEO /* twice */
COMPUTER /* four times */
PHOTO /* twice */
```

For those queries, which are given in examples 8.20, 8.21, 8.25, 8.27, and 8.28, and require use of the active complements of the relations SALES and SUPPLY for limited interpretations, we need to create the active complex product of the active domains ADOM(DEPT) and ADOM(ITEM) and that of ADOM(ITEM) and ADOM(SUPPLIER) and then to define these complements.

Example 8.39:

Find the active complement of the relation SALES, call it NOTSALES, and store it in the database. A PROLOG solution is as follows:

(1) Create the active domains called ADOMDEPT and ADOMITEM under the UNIX environment.

```
% vi adomdept
#RELATION ADOMDEPT 1
#KEYS 1 1
#ARGS 1 DEPT
COMPUTER
DP
PHOTO
VIDEO
% vi adomitem
#RELATION ADOMITEM 1
#KEYS 1 1
#ARGS 1 ITEM
CALCULATOR
CAMERA
FILM
MICRO
PRINTER
RECORDER
TERMINAL
TV
```

(2) Create the relation scheme for the active complex product of ADOMDEPT and ADOMITEM, and call it ATUPDEPTITEM.

```
% vi atupdeptitem
#RELATION ATUPDEPTITEM 2
#KEYS 1 2 2
#ARGS 1 DEPT
#ARGS 2 ITEM
```

(3) Create the relation scheme for the complement of SALES, and call it NOTSALES.

```
% vi notsales
#RELATION NOTSALES 2
#KEYS 1 2 2
#ARGS 1 DEPT
#ARGS 2 ITEM
```

(4) Perform **DB_MAKE** on all four UNIX files created in (1) through (3).

```
% DB_MAKE adomdept
% DB_MAKE adomitem
% DB_MAKE atupdeptitem
% DB_MAKE notsales
```

(5) Generate and store the relations ATUPDEPTITEM and NOTSALES under the PROLOG environment.

```
/* Invoke PROLOG DBMS */
? -ADOMDEPT(*dept)-ADOMITEM(*item)
-storetuple(ATUPDEPTITEM(*dept, *item));
? -ATUPDEPTITEM(*dept, *item)-not(SALES(*dept, *item))
  -storetuple(NOTSALES(*dept, *item));
? -stop;
```

(6) Perform **DB_SCAN** on all indexfiles created under the UNIX environment.

```
% DB_SCAN ADOMDEPT
```

where the displayed relation is the indexfile ADOMDEPT, and is omitted here.

```
% DB_SCAN ADOMITEM
```

where the displayed relation is the indexfile ADOMITEM, and is omitted here.

```
% DB_SCAN ATUPDEPTITEM > atupdeptitem
```

where the displayed relation denotes the indexfile ATUPDEPTITEM, which contains 32 tuples corresponding to those tuples of table 3-1 in chapter 3, and the textfile atupdeptitem is a copy of ATUPDEPTITEM.

```
% DB_SCAN NOTSALES > notsales
```

where the relation displayed is the indexfile NOTSALES, which contains 21 tuples corresponding to those tuples of table 8-11 of section 8.4.6, and the textfile notsales is a copy of NOTSALES.

The tuples in the indexfiles ATUPDEPTITEM and NOTSALES are copied into the textfiles atupdeptitem and notsales, respectively. However, the textfiles atomdept and adomitem are still in their original forms, since the copying option is not used in their corresponding **DB_SCAN** statements. Following this method, we can create the active complex product ATUPITEMSUPPLIER of ADOM(ITEM) and ADOM(SUPPLIER) and the active complement NOTSUPPLY of the relation SUPPLY (do exercise 8.18). When NOTSALES and NOTSUPPLY have been stored in the underlying database, we can solve queries involving either active complement.

Example 8.40:

For the query finding the items not supplied by IBM, as given in example 8.20, a PROLOG solution is

```
? -NOTSUPPLY(*item, IBM) -line -w(*line) -line;
```

and its answer is

```
                    TV
                    CAMERA
                    FILM
                    RECORDER
                    CALCULATOR
```

Example 8.41

For the query finding the departments not selling any item supplied by IBM, as given in example 8.24, a PROLOG solution is

```
? -NOTSALES(*dept, *item) -SUPPLY(*item, IBM) -line -w(*dept -line;
```

and its answer is

```
                    VIDEO /* three times */
                    PHOTO /* three times */
```

Example 8.42:

For the query finding the departments selling an item not supplied by IBM, as given in example 8.25, a PROLOG solution is

```
? -SALES(*dept, *item) -NOTSUPPLY(*item, IBM) -line -w(*dept) -line;
```

and its answer is

```
                    VIDEO /* twice */
                    COMPUTER
                    PHOTO /* twice */
```

Example 8.43:

For the query-finding the items supplied only by IBM, as given in example 8.21, a PROLOG solution not based on the right side of (8.6) is still straightforward since the formula $\overline{(SUPPLY(y \neg ``IBM'')}$ is also equivalent to

$$\forall(SUPPLIER)\overline{(SUPPLY(y\ z)} \cdot z \neq ``IBM''),$$

and a universal quantifier can be implemented in PROLOG.

Implementing a universal quantifier requires use of the extended predicates **uniquebag** and **member** and a temporary relation such as ANSWER used in example 8.35. Before using ANSWER, we have to check whether ANSWER is an empty relation. If ANSWER is not empty, then we must delete all of its tuples. When ANSWER is empty, we proceed as follows:

```
? -SUPPLY(*item, *supplier) -not($$$$eq(*supplier, IBM))
  -storetuple(ANSWER(*item));
? -uniquebag(ANSWER(*item1), *item 1, *item1) -SUPPLY(*item2, IBM)
  -not(member(*item2, *item1)) -line -w(*item2) -line·
```

The answer is PRINTER.

Example 8.44:

For the query-finding the departments selling an item supplied by a supplier other than IBM, as given in example 8.26, a PROLOG solution is

```
    ? -SALES(*dept, *item) -SUPPLY(*item, *supplier)
      -not($$$$eq(*supplier, IBM)) -line -w(*dept) -line;
```

and the answer is

```
DP /* twice */
VIDEO /* twice */
COMPUTER /* four times */
PHOTO /* twice */
```

Example 8.45:

For the query-finding the departments selling an item not supplied by all suppliers except IBM, as given in example 8.27, a PROLOG solution is

```
? −SALES(*dept,*item) −NOTSUPPLY(*item, HP) −NOTSUPPLY(*item,TI)
−NOTSUPPLY(*item,KODAK) −NOTSUPPLY(*item,ZENITH) −line−w(*dept) −line;
```

and the answer is

```
DP
COMPUTER
```

Example 8.46:

For the query-finding the departments not selling an item supplied by a supplier other than IBM, as given in example 8.28, a PROLOG solution is

```
? −NOTSALES(*dept, *item) −SUPPLY(*item, *supplier)
  −not($$$$eq(*supplier, IBM)) −line −w(*dept) −line;
```

and the answer is

```
DP /* six times */
VIDEO /* six times */
COMPUTER /* four times */
PHOTO /* six times */
```

Example 8.47:

Given the relations RELA(A B) = {3 6, 2 5, 1 4} and RELB(B C) = {8 11, 5 10, 4 9}, as shown in example 8.30, finding the difference RELB[B] − RELA[B] can be accomplished by the following PROLOG solution.

(1) Create the textfiles rela(A B), relb(B C), adomb(B), inter(B), and difference(B) where the first two correspond to RELA and RELB and the remaining three correspond to the active domain of B, the intersection of RELA[B] and RELB[B], and the difference to be found.

(2) Use **DB_MAKE** to convert the textfiles into the indexfiles RELA, RELB, ADOMB, INTER, and DIFFERENCE.

(3) ? −RELA(*a, *b) −storetuple(ADOMB(*b));
    ? −RELB(*b, *c) −storetuple(ADOMB(*b));

```
? -RELA(*a, *b) -RELB(*b, *c) -storetuple(INTER(*b));
? -RELB(*b, *c) -not(INTER(*b)) -storetuple(DIFFERENCE(*b)) -line
  -w(*b) -line;
```

The answer is 8. The relation ADOMB(B) is also the union of RELA[B] and RELB[B].

Example 8.48:

Find the union and intersection of the projections RELA[B] and RELA[B] of the relation RELA and RELB as given in example 8.47. Using the extended predicates **union** and **intersect,** as shown in the Appendix, PROLOG solutions are:

```
? -uniquebag(RELA(*a, *b1), *b1, *b1)
-uniquebag(RELB(*b2, *c), *b2, *b2)
  -union(*b1, *b2, *u) -wflist(*u, 4);
? -uniquebag(RELA(*a, *b1), *b1, *b1)
-uniquebag(RELB(*b2, *c), *b2, *b2)
  -intersect(*b1, *b2, *i) -wflist(*i, 4);
```

In **uniquebag**(RELA(*a, *b1), *b1, *b1), each one of the left two variables *b1 denotes a single b1-value in the relation RELA one at a time, whereas the third variable *b1 is a list of distinct b1-values.

When two relations are union-compatible and their arities are greater than 1, we must transform their tuples into lists by **bag** or **uniquebag** before performing an operation of **union** or **intersect.**

Example 8.49:

Suppose that the attributes A and C in RELA(A B) and RELB(B C) are compatible. Find the union of RELA(A B) and RNB(C B) where RNB(C B) is permuted from RELB(B C). A PROLOG solution is

```
? +RNB(*c,*b) -RELB(*b,*c); /* permute columns */
? +wtuple(nil) -line;
? +wtuple(.(*head,*tail)) -w(*head)-line-wtuple(*tail);
? -uniquebag(RELA(*a,*b),.(*a,*b), *list1)
-uniquebag(RNB(*c,*d),.(*c,*d), *list2) -union(*list1, *list2, *u)
-wtuple(*u);
.(1,4)
.(2,5)
.(3,6)
.(9,4)
.(10,5)
.(11,8)
```

The relation RNB is a temporary file to hold the permuted tuples of RELB, and the command **wtuple** is defined to write tuples one on a line. An alternative PROLOG solution that uses an indexfile is shown in the following:

```
% vi unions /* define an empty textfile */
#RELATION UNIONS 2
#KEYS 1 2 2
#ARGS 1 A
#ARGS 2 B
% :wq
% DB:_MAKE unions /* define an empty indexfile */
/* Invoke PROLOG DBMS */
? -RELA(*a, *b) -storetuple(UNIONS(*a, *b));
? -RELB(*b, *c) -storetuple(UNIONS(*c, *b));
? -UNIONS(*a, *b) -line -wr(*a, *b) -line;
```

Each tuple in the union UNIONS is printed as a string rather than a list.

8.5.11 Updating and Deleting Tuples

In previous examples, we have used a PROLOG database function called **storetuple** to fill tuples, one at a time, into an indexfile. We now consider two functions known as **update** and **delete**.

To update any component of a tuple except a value of the primary key in an indexfile, we can use the statement

```
?-update(indexfile-name(a new tuple whose components are separated by
commas));
```

where the new tuple is used to replace the tuple with the same key value.

Example 8:50:

Suppose that we want to update the tuple "YANG 30000 COMPUTER JONES" in the relation EMP where NAME is the key, to change his salary to 33000 and his dept to ELECTRONICS. A PROLOG solution is

```
? -update(EMP(YANG, 33000, ELECTRONICS, JONES));
```

Note that a key value such as YANG in EMP cannot be updated by this function. If we want also to replace the original textfile emp by a copy of the updated indexfile EMP, we perform

```
% DB_SCAN EMP > emp
```

To delete a single tuple or a number of tuples one at a time, we can use the **delete** function.

Example 8.50:

To delete the tuple "YANG 33000 ELECTRONICS JONES" from EMP we execute

```
? -delete(EMP(YANG, 33000, ELECTRONICS, JONES));
```

Deleting all tuples in the indexfile SUPPLY such that the supplier is IBM is done by

```
?  -SUPPLY(*item, IBM) -delete(SUPPLY(*item, IBM));
```

By this method only tuples in an indexfile are deleted. Thus, indexfiles can be considered as views created from textfiles for the convenience of query processing. If all arguments are variables, then all tuples are deleted. However, its scheme is still engaged in the underlying database scheme. To disengage an indexfile we must delete the tuples concerning the scheme of this relation from **relation** and **argument** by **deleterel**(indexfile-name, arity).

As an alternative method for updating or deleting tuples of an indexfile, we can copy its tuples into its textfile by ''**DB_SCAN** indexfile-name > textfile-name,'' update or delete tuples in the textfile under the UNIX environment, and convert the textfile into its indexfile by ''**DB_MAKE** textfile-name.'' Renaming or permuting attributes of an indexfile would be more easily accomplished by destroying the original indexfile and updating the corresponding textfile as just discussed.

EXERCISES

The following exercises are based on a part of the department store database, as shown in tables 8-2 (SALES(DEPT ITEM)), 8-3 (SUPPLY(ITEM SUPPLIER)), and 8-13.

TABLE 8-13. EMP(NAME SALARY MGR DEPT)

EMP	NAME	SALARY	MGR	DEPT
	DEAN	36000	–	–
	HOPE	26000	LONGSHORE	PHOTO
	JONES	35000	DEAN	COMPUTER
	LONGSHORE	255000	DEAN	PHOTO
	REGAN	31000	SMITH	DP
	ROBERTA	25900	WANG	VIDEO
	SMITH	28000	DEAN	DP
	WANG	34000	DEAN	VIDEO
	YANG	30000	JONES	COMPUTER

where NAME is the primary key and − denotes a null value. Note that lowercase names for relations and attributes are still used in INGRES.

8.1 After the QUEL statement \r is executed, what would be the message displayed on the screen? When the statement \p is then followed, what would be the message?

8.2 Assume that the relation supply has been created and stored in the underlying INGRES database. Find a QUEL solution to select tuples from supply such that each tuple selected has its supplier-value other than "IBM."

8.3 Create the relation scheme emp(name salary mgr dept) by a QUEL code, and fill its tuples as given in table 8-13.

8.4 Find a QUEL solution to print the names, the salaries, and each average salary per department using the aggregate function "**avg**(e.salary **by** e.dept)" where e is the tuple variable defined in "**range of** e **is** emp".

8.5 Find a QUEL solution to print the names and the salaries such that each salary is more than the average salary in the underlying department store database.

8.6 Find a QUEL solution to print the names and the salaries such that an employee's salary is more than his/her manager's salary.

8.7 Let R = A1 . . . An and S = B1 . . . Bn be union-compatible relation schemes. Find a QUEL solution to rename a relation s(S) to s(R).

8.8 Find a QUEL solution to compute the union t(R) = r(R) $\cup$ s(R).

8.9 Find a QUEL solution to compute the difference t(R) = r(R) $-$ s(R).

8.10 Find a QUEL solution to compute the complex product t(R S) = r(R) * s(S).

8.11 Find a QUEL solution to compute the intersection t(R) = r(R) $\cap$ s(R).

8.12 When the relation schemes for sales and supply were created in the text, the formats of dept and supplier were declared the same. We can assume that dept and supplier are compatible so that sales and supply are union-compatible. Using the QUEL solutions to exercise 8.6 through 8.11, find supply(dept item) (renaming and permutation), sales $\cup$ supply, sales $-$ supply, sales * supply, and sales $\cap$ supply.

8.13 Formulate a projection by a QUEL code with the capabilities of column permutation and renaming.

8.14 Provide a QBE solution to find all items supplied by suppliers other than IBM. The corresponding domain calculus expression is

$$\{y(ITEM) \mid SUPPLY(y \neg \text{ "IBM"}) \cdot \overline{SUPPLY(y \text{ "IBM"})}\}.$$

8.15 Assume that the relation sales has been created and stored in the underlying INGRES database. Provide a QBE solution to find the departments selling only all those items supplied by IBM. The corresponding domain calculus expression is

$$\{x(DEPT) \mid \forall y(ITEM) \ \forall \ z(ITEM)$$
$$(SALES(x \ y) \cdot \overline{SUPPLY(y \text{ "IBM"})} \cdot \overline{SALES(x \ z)} \cdot SUPPLY(z \text{ "IBM"}))\}.$$

*8.16 Suppose that a QBE solution to a query is shown below:

SALES	DEPT	ITEM
¬	_DEPT P. _DEPT	_ITEM

SUPPLY	ITEM	SUPPLIER
¬	_ITEM	IBM

What would be the query, the corresponding domain calculus expression, and the expected answer? Execute this QBE code on the underlying database to obtain an answer. Is this answer consistent with the expected answer?

*8.17 Suppose that a QBE solution to a query is shown below:

SUPPLY	ITEM	SUPPLIER
¬	_ITEM	-IBM

SALES	DEPT	ITEM
¬	_DEPT P._DEPT	_ITEM

What would be the query, the corresponding domain calculus expression, and the expected answer? Execute this QBE code on the underlying database to obtain an answer. Is this answer consistent to the expected answer?

8.18 Create and store the relations SUPPLY and SALES for PROLOG query processing.

8.19 Find a PROLOG solution to create the active complement NOTSUPPLY of the relation SUPPLY with respect to the active complex produce ATUPITEMSUPPLIER, and store it in the underlying database.

8.20 Find a PROLOG solution to solve the query Q_1, as given in example 8.23.

8.21 For the query finding the departments not selling an item that is not supplied by IBM, the corresponding domain calculus expression is

$$\{x(DEPT) \mid \exists y(ITEM)(\overline{SALES(x \ y)} \cdot \overline{SUPPLY(y \ ``IBM'')})\}.$$

Find a PROLOG solution and its answer. The expected answer is

```
DP /* five times */
VIDEO /* three times */
COMPUTER /* four times */
PHOTO /* three times */
```

8.22 For the query finding the departments not selling an item that is supplied only by IBM, the corresponding domain calculus expression is

$$\{x(DEPT) \mid \exists y(ITEM)(\overline{SALES(x \ y)} \cdot \overline{SUPPLY(y \ \neg \ ``IBM'')})\}.$$

Find a PROLOG solution and its answer. The expected answer is

```
VIDEO /* twice */
PHOTO /* twice */
```

8.23 Find a PROLOG solution for the query in example 8.38 such that the answer contains no duplicates.

8.24 For the query in example 8.45 find an alternative PROLOG solution by means of a universal quantifier as similarly implemented in example 8.43.

8.25 Provide a PROLOG solution to find the union of two union-compatible relations with arities greater than two and to represent each tuple by a sequence of components (i.e., elements separated by commas).

*8.26 Find PROLOG solutions to compute simple aggregates, such as "average," and aggregate functions, such as "average salary by department," similar to those introduced in QUEL (section 8.3.2) or in QBE (section 8.4.7). Note that PROLOG does not support floating point arithmetic.

APPENDIX: AN EXTENSION OF PROLOG WITH A DATABASE OPTION

Akram Salah

This Appendix contains some functors (commands and predicates) defined in an extended version, written at UAB, of the PROLOG with a database option, which was written in programming language C by Bruynooge at the Katholieke University, Belgium, in 1980 [Bru80]. The Appendix shows only the provisions that are not available in the original version. Some changes were necessary so that the PROLOG interpreter could be run under VAX/UNIX version 7. Other extensions were designed to simplify the use of PROLOG in general and the PROLOG with a database option in particular.

The changes in the source code of the interpreter are primarily in the type declarations of variables and are transparent to the user. The change that is not transparent to the user is in the PROLOG command called **list,** which displays all PROLOG relations defined in a session. This command originally displayed each relation (including its name and arity) on a line, but its modified version displays four relations (including their names and arities) on a single line. Thus, the user is usually able to see all relations on a single screen. This change is made in a source module called "listfunctors."

The other extensions were written in PROLOG and are included in the file **input** (which is an extended version of the original input file also called **input**). The definitions of the added PROLOG clauses are as follows:

(1) The original version needs to execute a PROLOG command **file**(indexfilename, arity) for each indexfile converted from its corresponding textfile by means of UNIX command "**DB_MAKE** textfile-name," so that the indexfile-name and its arity can be registered in the system relation called **relation** to establish the directory of the database in a PROLOG session. For the purpose that the user will not have to enter these **file** commands in each PROLOG session, we have defined

```
-file(relation, 2); /*system relation relation and its arity 2 */
-relation(*indexfile_name, *arity)-not($$$$eq(*indexfile_name, relation))
-file(*indexfile_name, *arity);
```

Both of these clauses are included in input. When the PROLOG is invoked, the first clause automatically calls **file** to activate or engage the name and arity of the system relation **relation** itself within the session. The second clause automatically calls **file** to activate or engage the indexfile (including its name and arity) of each relation or relation scheme defined in **relation.** The purpose of these clauses is to create the directory of the database for the current session.

(2) The new command **listrels** is defined as:

```
    + listrels-w(RELATION, 18) -w(ARITY) -line(2)
    -relation(*name, *arity) -w(*name, 20) -w(*arity) -line;
```

The first line of the code writes the heading ''RELATION followed by 10 blanks ARITY'' and skips two lines by **line**(2), which is an extension of **line.** The second line of the code writes the name and arity of each relation stored in **relation** on a single line. This command is automatically called whenever the PROLOG session is entered. We can also call it to list the names and arities of all relations at any time during the session.

(3) The new command **deleterel** is defined as:

```
+deleterel(*indexfile_name,*arity)-delete(relation (*indexfile_name,*arity))
-argument(*argument_name, *argument_no, *description)
-delete(argument(*argument_name, *argument_no, *description));
```

This command deletes an indexfile from both system relations **relation** and **argument** under the PROLOG environment. This is equivalent to deleting or disengaging an indexfile from the current database. However, it does not delete the indexfile itself or its textfile. Recovery of a deleted indexfile into a database can be only done by executing ''**DB_MAKE** textfile-name'' under the UNIX environment.

(4) The new command **uniquebag**(predicate, answer, list _ of _ answers) is defined as

```
+member(*element,.(*element,*tail));
+member(*element,.(*head, *tail))-member(*element,*tail);
+set(nil, nil) -/; /* The cut "/" terminates backtracking */
+set(.(*head,*tail),*setform)  -member(*head,*tail)-set(*tail, *setform)
-/;
+set(.(*head, *tail),.(*head, *setform))-set(*tail, *setform) -/;
+uniquebag(*predicate,*answer,*set) -bag(*predicate,*answer, *listform)
-set(*listform, *set);
```

The **member** determines whether a given element is a member of a given list of (not necessarily distinct) elements. The **set** transforms a given list of (not necessarily distinct) elements into a list of distinct elements by eliminating duplicates. The **uniquebag** transforms a **bag** such that a list of (not necessarily distinct) answers of a predicate becomes a list of distinct answers.

(5) The command **wlist**(list) writes the elements of a list on separate lines. Its definition is

```
+ wlist(nil);
+wlist(.(*head,*tail))-w(*head)-line-wlist(*tail);
```

(6) The command **help** displays a summary of the PROLOG built-in commands in seven categories. When a positive integer i in {1, 2, . . ., 7} is specified while **help** is called, the i-th category is displayed. The definition of **help** is rather long and is not included in this Appendix.

(7) The command **line**(i) skips i lines. Its definition is

```
+line(0);
+line(*n)-line-plus(*n, -1, *m) line(*m);
```

where **plus**(*n, -1, *m) implements the subtraction "*m = *n - 1."

(8) The command **tab**(i) skips i blanks. Its definition is

```
+tab(0);
+tab(*n) -w(" ")-plus(*n, -1, *m) -tab(*m); /*" " in w(" ") contains one
blank */
```

(9) The command **wflist**(list, width) writes the elements of a list such that each element is written within **width** character positions. Its definition is

```
+wflist(nil,*)-line;
+flist(.(*head, *tail),*width) -w(*head,*width) -wflist(*tail,*width);
```

(10) The four write commands **wr** with 2, 3, 4, or 5 arguments are added. Each one of them is defined separately and writes its arguments at predetermined positions on one line. Their definitions are

```
+ wr(*arg1,*arg2)-w(*arg1,15)-w(*arg2,15)-line;
+ wr(*arg1,*arg2,*arg3) -w(*arg1,15) -w(*arg2,15)-w(arg3,15)-line;
+ wr(*arg1,*arg2,*arg3,*arg4) -w(*arg1,15) -w(*arg2,15)-w(*arg3,15)
-w(*arg4,15)-line;
+ wr(*arg1,*arg2,*arg3,*arg4,*arg5) -w(*arg1,15)
-w(*arg2,15) -w(*arg3,15)
-w(*arg4,15)-w(*arg5,15)-line;
```

(11) The following clauses perform the intersection of two lists with values. These lists are assumed to contain values resulting from previous queries. The command **intersect**(list1, list2, result_list) is defined as:

```
+ intersect(nil,*, nil)-/;
+ intersect(.(*head1, *tail1),*list2,.(*head1,*tail3))
-member(*head1,*list2)
-intersect(*tail1,*list2,*tail3)-/;
+ intersect(.(*head1,*tail1),*list2,*tail3)
-intersect(*tail1,*list2,*tail3)-/;
```

(12) The following clause performs the union of two lists with compatible values. As in the previous case, these two lists are assumed to contain values resulting from previous queries. The command **union**(list1, list2, result_list) is defined as:

```
+union(*list1,*list2,*union_list)-append(*list1, *list2,*list)
-set(*list,*union_list);
```

This clause performs the union by appending the two input lists, using the program **append** (its definition follows), and calls **set** (defined in (4)) to delete the duplicates from the appended list. The definition of **append** is

```
+append(nil,*list,*list);
+append(. (*head1,*tail1),*list2,. (*head1,*tail3))
-append(*tail1,*list2,*tail3);
```

(13) The predicate **length** counts the number of elements in a list. The command "**length**(list, n)", where n is the length of list, is defined as:

```
+length(. (*head,*tail),*n)-length(*tail,*m)-plus(*m,1,*n);
+length(nil,0)-/;
```

BIBLIOGRAPHY

Aho, A. V., C. Berri, and J. D. Ullman. "The Theory of Joins in Relational Databases," *ACM Trans. on Database Systems*, 4, 3 (Sept. 1979), 297–314.

Armstrong, W. W. "Dependency Structures of Database Relationships," *1974 IFIP Cong.*, Geneva, Switzerland, 580–83.

Armstrong, W. W., and C. Delobel. "Decompositions and Functional Dependencies in Relations," *ACM Trans. on Database Systems*, 5, 4 (Dec. 1980), 404–30.

Arora, A. K., and C. R. Carlson. "The Information Preserving Properties of Relational Databases Transformations," *VLDB IV*, West Berlin, Germany, ACM, IEEE, 1978, 352–59.

Astrahan, M. M., et al. "System R: Relational Approach to Database Management," *ACM Trans. on Database Systems*, 1, 2 (June 1976), 97–137.

———— "A History and Evaluation of System R," *IBM Report RJ2843*, San Jose, CA, June, 1980.

Atzeni, P., and N. M. Morfuni. "Functional Dependencies in Relations with Null Values," *Information Processing Letters*, 18, (May 1984), 233–38.

Atzeni, P., and D. S. Parker. "Properties of Acyclic Database Schemes: an Analysis," *XP2 Workshop on Relational Database Theory*, Pennsylvania State Univ., Univ. Park, PA, June, 1981.

Ausiello, G., A. D'Atri, and D. Sacca. "Graph Algorithms for Functional Dependency Manipulation," *JACM*, 30, 4 (Oct. 1983), 752–66.

Babb, E. "Joined Normal Form: a Storage Encoding for Relational Databases," *ACM Trans. on Database Systems*, 7, 4 (Dec. 1982), 588–614.

Banchilon, F. "On the Completeness of Query Languages for Relational Databases," *Seventh Symp. on Math Found. of Computing*, Springer-Verlag, NY, 1978, 112–23.

Batory, D. S., and C. C. Gotlieb. "A Unifying Model of Physical Databases," *ACM Trans. on Database Systems*, 7, 4 (Dec. 1982), 509–39.

BEERI, C., AND P. A. BERNSTEIN. "Computational Problems Related to the Design of Normal Form Relational Schemas," *ACM Trans. on Database Systems,* 4, 1 (March 1979), 30, 59.

BEERI, C., R. FAGIN, AND J. H. HOWARD. "A Complete Axiomatization for Functional and Multivalued Dependencies in Database Relations," *ACM SIGMOD Conf.,* 1977, 47–61.

BEERI, C., P. A. BERNSTEIN, AND N. GOODMAN. "A Sophisticate's Introduction to Database Normalization Theory," *VLDB IV,* West Berlin, Germany, ACM, IEEE, 1978, 113–24.

BEERI, C., AND P., HONEYMAN. "Preserving Functional Dependencies," *SIAM J. on Computing,* 10, 3, (August 1981), 647–56.

BEERI, C., D. MAIER, AND J. D. ULLMAN. "Properties of Acyclic Database Schemes," *ACM Symp. on Theory of Computing,* 1981, 355–62.

BEERI, C., AND M. Y. VARDI. "The Implication Problem for Data Dependencies," *Computer Science Report,* Hebrew Univ. Jerusalem, Israel, May, 1980.

————— . "Formal Systems for Tuple and Equality Generating Dependencies," *SIAM J. on Computing,* 13, 1, (Feb. 1984), 76–98.

————— . "A Proof Procedure for Data Dependencies," *JACM,* 31, 4 (Oct. 1984), 718–41.

BEERI, C., ET AL. "Equivalence of Relational Database Schemes," *SIAM J. on Computing,* 10, 2 (May 1981), 352–70.

BEERI, C., ET AL. "On the Desirability of Acyclic Database Schemes," *IBM Report RJ3131,* Yorktown Heights, NY, May 22, 1981.

BEERI C., ET AL. "On the Desirability of Acyclic Database Schemes," *JACM,* 30, 3 (July 1983), 479–513.

BEKESSY, A., AND J. DEMETROVICS. "Contribution to the Theory of Database Relations," *Discrete Math.,* 27, North-Holland, Amsterdam, Netherland, (1979), 1–10.

BERNSTEIN, P. A. "Synthesizing Third Normal Form Relations from Functional Dependencies," *ACM Trans. on Database Systems,* 1, 4 (Dec. 1976), 277–98.

BERNSTEIN, P. A., AND D. M. CHIU. "Using Semi-joins to Solve Relational Queries," *JACM,* 28, 1 (Jan. 1981), 25–40.

BERNSTEIN, P. A., AND N. GOODMAN. "Full Reduces for Relational Queries Using Multi-attribute Semi-joins," *IEEE Computer Network Symp.* 1979.

————— . "What Does Boyce-Codd Normal Form Do?," *VLDB VI,* Montreal, Canada, ACM. IEEE, 1980, 145–59.

BISKUP, J. "On the Complementation Rule for Multivalued Dependencies on Database Relations," *Acta Informatica,* Springer-Verlag, NY, 10, 3 (1978), 297–305.

————— . "A Formal Approach to Null Values in Database Relations," *Advances in Database Theory,* (1980), 299–342.

————— . "Inferences of Multivalued Dependencies in Fixed and Undetermined Universes," *Theoretical Computer Science,* North-Holland, Amsterdam, Netherland, 10, 1 (Jan. 1981), 93–106.

————— . "A Foundation of Codd's Relational Maybe-Operations," *ACM Trans. on Database Systems,* 8, 4 (Dec. 1983), 608–36.

BISKUP, J., U. DAYAL, AND P. A. BERSTEIN. "Synthesizing Independent Database Schemes," *ACM SIGMOD Conf.,* 1979, 143–52.

BITTON, D., ET AL. "Parallel Algorithms for the Execution of Relational Database Operations," *ACM Trans. on Database Systems,* 8, 3 (Sept. 1983), 423–53.

BLASGEN, M. W., ET AL. "System R: An Architectural Overview," *IBM Systems J.,* 20, 1 (Feb. 1981), 41–62.

BOURNE, S. R. "The UNIX Shell," *The Bell System Technical J.,* 57, 6, 2 (July-August 1978), 1971–90.

BRUYNOOGHE, M. PROLOG in C for UNIX Version 7, *Applied Mathematics and Programming Division*, Katholieke Universiteit, Louven, Belgium, 1980.

CHAMBERLIN, D. D. "Relational Database Management Systems," *ACM Computing Surveys*, 8, 1 (March 1976), 43–66.

CHAMBERLIN, D. D., AND R. F. BOYCE. "SEQUEL: a Structured English Query Language," *ACM SIGMOD Workshop on Data Description, Access, and Control*, 1974, 249–64.

CHAMBERLIN, D. D., ET AL. "SEQUEL 2: a Unified Approach to Data Definition, Manipulation, and Control," *IBM J. Research Development.*, 20, 6 (Nov. 1976), 560–75.

CHANDRA, A. K., H. R. LEWIS, AND J. A. MAKOSKY. "Embedded Implication Dependencies and Their Inference Problem," *ACM Symp. on Theory of Computing*, 1981, 342–54.

CHEN, P. P. "The Entity-Relationship Model—Toward a Unified View of Data," *ACM Trans. on Database Systems*, 1, 1 (March 1976), 9–36.

CLOCKSIN, W. F., AND C. S. MELLISH. *Programming in Prolog*, Springer-Verlag, NY, 1981.

CODASYL Data Base Task Group April 71 Report, ACM, New York.

CODD, E. F. "A Relational Model of Data for Large Shared Data Banks," *CACM*, 13, 6 (June 1970), 377–87.

——————. "A Data Sublanguage Founded on the Relational Calculus," *ACM SIGFIDET Workshop on Data Description, Access and Control*, Nov. 1971, 35–61.

——————. "Normalized Database Structure: a Brief Tutorial," *ACM SIGFIDET Workshop on Data Description, Access and Control*, Nov. 1971, 1–17.

——————. "Further Normalization of the Data Base Relational Model," *Data Base Systems*, ed. Randall Rustin. Englewood Cliffs: Prentice-Hall, 1972.

——————. "Relational Completeness of Data Base Sublanguages," *Data Base Systems*, ed. Randall Rustin. Englewood Cliffs: Prentice-Hall, 1972.

——————. "Recent Investigations in Relational Database Systems," *1974 IFIP Conf.*, 1017–21.

——————. "Extending the Database Relational Model to Capture More Meaning," *ACM Trans. on Database Systems*, 4, 4 (Dec. 1979), 397–434.

COOK, S. A. "The Complexity of Theorem-proving Procedures," *ACM Symp. on Theory of Computing*, 1971, 151–8.

COSMADAKIS, S. S., AND C. H. PAPADIMITRIOU. "Updates of Relational Views," *JACM*, 31, 4 (Oct. 1984), 742–60.

DATE, C. J. *An Introduction to Database Systems*, 3rd ed., Addison-Wesley Publishing Co., 1981.

DE BRA, P., AND J. PAREDAENS. "Horizontal Decompositions and Their Impact on Query Solving," *ACM SIGMOD Record*, 13, 1 (Sept. 1982), 46–50.

DELOBEL, C. "Normalization and Hierarchical Dependencies in the Relational Data Model," *ACM Trans. on Database Systems*, 3, 3 (Sept. 1978), 201–22.

DELOBEL, C., AND R. G. CASEY. "Decomposition of a Data Base and the Theory of Boolean Switching Functions," *IBM J. Research Develop.*, 17, 5 (Dec. 1973), 374–86.

DELOBEL, C., R. G. CASEY, AND P. A. BERNSTEIN. "Comment on Decomposition of a Data Base and the Theory of Boolean Switching Functions," *IBM J. Research Develop.*, 21, 5 (Sept. 1977), 484–85.

DEMETROVICS, J. "On the Number of Candidate Keys," *Information Processing Letters*, 7, 6 (Oct. 1976), 226–69.

DEMOLOMBE, R. "Generalized Division for Relational Algebraic Language," *Information Processing Letters*, 14, 4 (June 13, 1982), 174–78.

EPSTEIN, R. A TUTORIAL on INGRES, *Memo No. ERL-M77-25*, Electronics Research Lab., University of California, Berkeley 94720, Dec. 25, 1977.

——————. Creating and Maintaining a Database Using INGRES, *Memo No. ERL-M77-71*, Electronics Research Lab., University of California, Berkeley 94720, Dec. 16, 1977.

FAGIN, R., "The Decomposition Versas the Synthetic Approach to Relational Database Design," *VLDB III,* Tokyo, Japan, ACM, IEEE, 1977, 441–46.

_____ . "Functional Dependencies in a Relational Database and Propositional Logic," *IBM J. Research Develop.,* 21, 6 (Nov. 1977), 534–44.

_____ . "Multivalued Dependencies and a New Normal Form for Relational Databases," *ACM Trans. on Database Systems,* 2, 3 (Sept. 1977), 262–78.

_____ . "Normal Form and Relational Database Operators," *ACM SIGMOD Conf.,* 1979, 153–60.

_____ . "Horn Clauses and Database Dependencies," *ACM Symp. on Theory of Computing,* 1980, 123–34.

_____ . "A Normal Form for Relational Databases that is Based on Domains and Keys," *ACM Trans. on Database Systems,* 6, 3 (Sept. 1981), 387–415.

_____ . "Types of Acyclicity for Hypergraphs and Relational Database Schemes," *IBM Report RJ3330,* Yorktown Heights, NY, Nov. 25, 1981.

_____ . "Degrees of Acyclicity for Hypergraphs and Relational Database Schemes," *JACM,* 30, 3 (July 1983), 514–40.

FAGIN, R., A. O. MENDELZON, AND J. D. ULLMAN. "A Simplified Universal Relation Assumption and Its Properties," *ACM Trans. on Database Systems,* 7, 3 (Sept. 1982), 343–60.

FAGIN, R., J. D. ULLMAN, AND M. Y. VARDI. "On the Semantics of Updates in Databases," *ACM SIGACT-SIGMOD Symp. on Principles of Database Systems,* March 1983, 352–365.

FORSYTH, J., AND R. FADOUS. "Finding Candidate Keys for Relational Databases," *ACM SIGMOD Conf.,* 1975, 203–10.

FRY, J. P., AND E. H. SIBLEY. "Evolution of Data Base Management Systems," *ACM Computing Surveys,* 8, 1 (March 1976), 7–42.

GALIL, Z. "An Almost Linear-time Algorithm for Computing a Dependency Basis in a Relational Database," *JACM,* 29, 1 (Jan. 1982), 96–102.

GALLAIRE, H., AND J. MINKER, EDS. *Logic and Databases.* NY: Plenum Publishing Co., 1979.

GALLAIRE, H., J. MINKER, AND J. M. NICOLAS, EDS. *Advances in Data Base Theory,* Vol. 1, NY: Plenum Publishing Co., 1980.

GALLAIRE, H., J. MINKER, AND J. NICOLAS. "Logic and Databases: A Deductive Approach," *ACM Computing Surveys,* 16, 2 (June 1984), 153–86.

GAREY, M. R., AND D. S. JOHNSON. *Computers and Intractability: A Guide to the Theory of NP-completeness,* San Francisco CA: Freeman, 1979.

GINSBURG, S., AND R. HULL. "Sort Sets in the Relational Model," *ACM SIGACT-SIGMOD Symp.,* March 1983, 332–39.

GINSBURG, S., AND S. M. ZAIDDAN. "Properties of Functional-dependency Families," *JACM,* 29, 3 (July 1982), 678–98.

GRAHAM, M. H. "Functions in Databases," *ACM Trans. on Database Systems,* 8, 1 (March 1983), 81–109.

GRAHAM, M. H., AND A. O. MENDELZON. "Strong Equivalence of Relational Expressions under Dependencies," *Information Processing Letters,* 14, 2 (April 20, 1982), 57–62.

GRISWOLD, R. E., J. F. POAGE, AND I. P. POLONSKY. *The SNOBOL4 Programming Language,* 2nd ed., Englewood Cliffs: Prentice-Hall, 1971.

HEGNER, S. J. "Algebraic Aspects of Relational Database Decomposition," *ACM SIGACT-SIGMOD Symp.,* March 1983, 400–13.

HELD, G. D., M. R. STONEBRAKER, AND E. WONG. "INGRES–a Relational Database System," *In NCC 1975,* AFIPS Press, Arlington, Va., 1975.

HONEYMAN, P. "Testing Satisfaction of Functional Dependencies," *JACM,* 29, 3 (July 1982), 668–77.

HSIAO, D. K. ED. *Advanced Database Machine Architecture,* Englewood Cliffs: Prentice-Hall, 1983.

HULL, R. "Finitely Specifiable Implicational Dependency Families," *JACM,* 31, 2 (April 1984), 210–26.

IMIELINSKI, T., AND W. L. LIPSKI, JR. "Incomplete Information in Relational Databases," *JACM,* 31, 4 (Oct. 1984), 761–91.

IMS/VS Publications: General Information, GH-20-1260; System/Application Design Guide, SH-20-9025; Application Programming Reference Manual, SH-20-9026; Systems Programming Reference Manual, SH-20-9027; (1978), IBM Corp., White Plains, New York 10604.

JACOBS, B. E. "On Database Logic," *JACM,* 19, 2 (April 1982), 310–32.

KENT, W. "Consequences of Assuming a Universal Relation," *ACM Trans. on Database Systems,* 6, 4 (Dec. 1981), 539–56.

——— . "The Univeral Relation Revisited," *ACM Trans. on Database Systems,* 8, 4 (Dec. 1983), 644–48.

KIM, W. "Relational Database Systems," *ACM Computing Surveys,* 11, 3 (Sept. 1979), 185–212.

——— . "A New Way to Compute the Product and Join of Relations," *ACM SIGMOD Conf.,* 1980, 178–87.

KLUG, A. "Calculating Constraints of Relational Expressions," *ACM Trans. on Database Systems,* 5, 3 (Sept. 1980), 260–90.

——— . "Equivalence of Relational Algebra and Relational Calculus Query Languages Having Aggregate Functions," *JACM,* 29, 3 (July 1982), 699–717.

KLUG A., AND R. PRICE. "Determining View Dependencies Using Tableaux," *ACM Trans. on Database Systems,* 7, 3 (Sept. 1982), 361–80.

KOWALSKI, R. *Logic for Problem Solving,* North-Holland, NY, 1979.

LaCROIX, M. AND A. PIROTTE. "Generalized Joins," *ACM SIGMOD Record,* 8, 3 (Sept. 1976), 14–5.

LARSON, P. A. "Analysis of Index-sequential File with Overflow Chaining," *ACM Trans. on Database Systems,* 6, 4 (Dec. 1981), 671–80.

LEWIS, E. A., L. C. SEKINO, AND P. D. TING. "A Canonical Representation for the Relational Schema and Logical Data Independence," *IEEE Computer Software and Applications Conf.,* 1977, 276–80.

LI, D. A PROLOG Database System, *Research Studies Press Ltd.,* John Wiley & Sons, Inc., NY, 1984.

LIEN, Y. E. "Multivalued Dependencies with Null Values in Relational Databases," *VLDB V,* Rio de Janeiro, Brazil, ACM, IEEE, 1979, 61–66.

——— . "Hierarchical Schemata for Relational Database Schemata," *ACM Trans. on Database Systems,* 6, 1 (March 1981), 48–69.

——— . "On the Equivalence of Database Models," *JACM,* 29, 2 (April 1982), 333–62.

LING, T. W., F. W. TOMPA, AND T. KAMEDA. "An Improved Third Normal Form for Relational Databases," *ACM Trans. on Database Systems,* 6, 2 (June 1981), 329–46.

LIPSKI, W. JR., "On Semantic Issues Connected with Incomplete Databases," *ACM Trans. on Database Systems,* 4, 3 (Sept. 1979), 262–96.

——— . "On Databases with Incomplete Information," *JACM,* 28, 1 (Jan. 1981), 41–47.

LOZINSKII, E. L. "Construction of Relationals in Relational Databases," *ACM Trans. on Database Systems,* 5, 2 (June 1980), 208–24.

LUCCHESI, C. L., AND S. L. OSBORN. "Candidate Keys for Relations," *J. Computer and System Sciences*, 17, 2 (Oct. 1978), 270–9.

MAIER, D. "Minimum Covers in the Relational Database," *JACM*, 27, 4 (Oct. 1980), 664–74.

——— . *The Theory of Relational Databases*, Potomac, MD: Computer Science Press, 1983.

MAIER, D., A. O. MENDELZON, AND Y. SAGIV. "Testing Implications of Data Dependencies," *ACM Trans. on Database Systems*, 4, 4 (Dec. 1979), 455–69.

MAIER, D., Y. SAGIV, AND M. YANNAKAKIS. "On the Complexity of Testing Implications of Functional and Join Dependencies," *JACM*, 28, 4 (Oct. 1981), 680–95.

MAIER, D., AND J. D. ULLMAN. "Connections in Acyclic Hypergraphs," *Research Report No. STAN-CS-81-853*, Department of Computer Science, Stanford University, Stanford, CA 94305, May 1981.

——— . "Maximal Objects and the Semantics of Universal Relation Databases," *ACM Trans. on Database Systems*, 8, 1 (March 1983), 1–14.

——— . "Fragments of Relations," *ACM SIGMOD Record*, 13, 4 (May 1983), 15–22.

MAIER, D., AND D. S. WARREN. "Incorporating Computed Relations in Relational Databases," *ACM SIGMOD Conf.*, 1981, 176–87.

MENDOLZON, A. O. "On Axiomatizing Multivalued Dependencies and the Decomposition of Database Relations," *JACM*, 26, 1 (Jan. 1979), 37–44.

——— . "Generalized Mutual Dependencies and the Decomposition of Database Relations," *VLDB V*, Rio de Janeiro, Brazil, ACM, IEEE, (1979) 75–82.

MICHAELS, A. S., B. MITTMAN, AND C. R. CARLSON. "A Comparison of Relational and CODASYL Approaches to Data-base Management," *ACM Computing Surveys*, 8, 1 (March 1976), 125–51.

MINKER, J. "Performing Inferences over Relational Databases," *ACM SIGMOD Conf.*, 1975, 79–91.

——— . "Search Strategy and Selection Function for an Inferential Relation System," *ACM Trans. on Database Systems*, 3, 1 (March 1978), 1–31.

MITCHELL, J. C. "Inference Rules for Functional and Inclusion Dependencies," *ACM SIGACT-SIGMOD Symp.*, March 1983, 53–69.

NAMIBAR, K. K. "Some Analytic Tools for the Design of Relational Database Systems," *VLDB V*, Rio de Janeiro, Brazil, ACM, IEEE, 1979, 417–28.

NICOLAS, J. M. "First Order Logic Formalization for Functional, Multivalued and Mutual Dependencies," *ACM SIGMOD Conf. on Management of Data*, 1978, 40–46.

OSBORN, S. L. "Testing for Existence of a Covering Boyce-Codd Normal Form," *Information Processing Letters*, 8, 1 (Jan. 1979), 11–14.

PAREDAENS, J. "On the Expressive Power of Relational Algebra," *Information Processing Letters*, 7, 2 (Feb. 1978), 44–49.

——— . "Horizontal and Vertical Decompositions," *XP1 Workshop on Database Theory*, SUNY at Stony Brook, NY, June-July, 1980.

PAREDAENS, J., AND P. DE BRA. "On Horizontal Decompositions," *XP2 Workshop on Relational Database Theory*, Pennsylvania State Univ., Univ. Park, PA, June, 1981.

PAREDAENS, J. AND D. JANSSENS. "Decompositions of Relations: A Comprehensive Approach," *Advances in Database Theory* (1980), 73–100.

Query-by-Example Program Description/Operations Manual, *Program Number: 5796-PKT, SH20-2077-0*, 1st ed. (September 1978), IBM Corp., White Plains, New York 10604.

Query-by-Example Terminal User's Guide, *Program Number: 5796-PKT, SH-20-2078-1*, 2nd ed. (June 1980), IBM Corp., White Plains, New York 10604.

REITER, R. "Equality and Domain Closure for First-order Databases," *JACM*, 27, 2 (April 1980), 235–49.

RISSANEN, J. "Independent Components of Relations," *ACM Trans. on Database Systems*, 2, 4 (Dec. 1977), 317–25.

RITCHIE, D. M. "A Retrospective," *The Bell System Technical J.*, 57, 6, 2 (July-August 1978), 1947–70.

RITCHIE, D. M., AND K. THOMPSON. "The UNIX Time-sharing System," *The Bell System Technical J.*, 57, 6, 2 (July-August 1978), 1905–30.

RITCHIE, D. M., ET AL. "The C Programming Language," *The Bell System Technical J.*, 57, 6, 2 (July-August 1978), 1991–2020.

SACCA, D. "Closure of Database Hypergraphs," *IBM Report RJ 3723*, Yorktown Heights, NY, Dec. 17, 1982.

SADRI, F., AND J. D. ULLMAN. "Template Dependencies: a Large Class of Dependencies in Relational Databases and Its Complete Axiomatization," *JACM*, 29, 2 (April 1982), 363–72.

SAGIV, Y. "An Algorithm for Inferring Multivalued Dependencies with an Application to Propositional Logic," *JACM*, 27, 2 (April 1980), 250–62.

SAGIV, Y., AND S. F. WALECKA. "Subset Dependencies and a Completeness Result for a Subclass of Embedded Multivalued Dependencies, " *JACM*, 29, 1 (Jan. 1982), 103–17.

SAGIV, Y., AND M. YANNAKAKIS. "Equivalence Among Relational Expressions with the Union and Difference Operators," *JACM*, 27, 4 (Oct. 1980), 633–54.

SAGIV, Y., ET AL. "An Equivalence Between Relational Database Dependencies and a Fragment of Propositional Logic," *JACM*, 28, 3 (July 1981), 435–53.

SCIORE, E., "A Complete Axiomatization of Full Join Dependencies," *JACM*, 29, 2 (April 1982), 373–93.

———. "Inclusion Dependencies and the Universal Instance," *ACM SIGACT-SIGMOD Symp. on Principles of Database Systems*, March 1983, 48–57.

SIBLEY, E. H. "The Development of Data-base Technology," *ACM Computing Surveys*, 8, 1 (March 1976), 1–6.

STOCKMEYER, L. H., AND C. K. WONG. "On the Number of Comparisons to Find the Intersection of Two Relations," *SIAM J. on Computing*, 8, 3, (August 1979), 388–404.

STONEBRAKER, M., ET AL.. "The Design and Implementation of INGRES," *ACM Trans. on Database Systems*, 1, 3 (Sept. 1976), 189–222.

TAYLOR, R. W., AND R. L. FRANK. "CODASYL Data-base Management System," *ACM Computing Surveys*, 8, 1 (March 1976), 67–104.

THOMPSON, K. "UNIX Implementation," *The Bell System Technical J.*, 57, 6, 2 (July-August 1978), 1931–46.

TODD, S. "PRTV, an Efficient Implementation for Large Relational Data Bases," *VLDB I*, Framingham, MA, ACM, Sept 22-24, 1975, 554–56.

———. "The Peterlee Relational Test Vehicle—A System Overview," *IBM Systems J.*, 15, 4 (Dec. 1976), 285–308.

TSICHRITZIS, D. C., AND A. KLUG, EDS. "The ANSI/X3/SPARC DBMS Framework: Report of the Study Group on Data Base Management Systems," *Information Systems*, 3 (1978).

TSICHRITZIS, D. C., AND F. H. LOCHOVSKY. "Hierarchical Data-base Management," *ACM Computing Surveys*, 8, 1 (March 1976), 105–24.

———. *Data Models*, Englewood Cliffs: Prentice-Hall, 1982.

ULLMAN, J. D. *Principles of Database Systems*, 2nd ed., Potomac, MD: Computer Science Press, 1982.

_____ . "On Kent's Consequences of Assuming a Universal Relation," *ACM Trans. on Database Systems,* 8, 4 (Dec. 1983), 637–43.

VARDI, M. Y. "The Implication and Finite Implication Problems for Typed Template Dependencies," *Report No. STAN-CS-82-912,* Department of Computer Science, Stanford University, Stanford, CA 94305, May 1982.

_____ . "A Note on Lossless Database Decompositions," *Information Processing Letters,* 18 (June 18, 1984), 257–60.

VASSILIOU, Y. "Null Values in Database Management: a Denotational Semantics Approach," *ACM SIGMOD Conf.,* 1979, 162–69.

_____ . "Functional Dependencies and Incomplete Information," *VLDB VI,* Montreal, Canada, ACM, IEEE, (1980), 260–69.

_____ . "Testing Satisfaction of FDs on a Multi-relation Database 'Fast'," *XP1 Workshop on Relational Database Theory,* SUNY at Stony Brook, NY, June-July, 1980.

WONG, E. "A Statistical Approach to Incomplete Information in Database Systems," *ACM Trans. on Database Systems,* 7, 3 (Sept. 1982), 470–88.

WOODFILL, J., ET AL. INGRES VERSION 7, *Reference Manual,* April 18, 1981.

YANG, C. C. "Comments on Graph Algorithms for Functional Dependency Manipulation," submitted for publication.

YANG, C. C., AND C. P. MAY. "Algorithms for Finding Directed Graph Isomorphisms by Finite Automata," *Intern. J. of Computer and Information Sciences,* 9, 2 (1980), 117–40.

YANNAKAKIS, M. "Algorithms for Acyclic Database Schemes," *VLDB VII,* Cannes, France, ACM, IEEE, 1981, 328–32.

ZANIOLO, C. Analysis and Design of Relational Schemata for Database Systems, *Doctoral diss.,* UCLA, Los Angeles, CA, July, 1976.

_____ . "Mixed Transitivity for Functional and Multivalued Dependencies in Database Relations," *Information Processing Letters,* 8, 1 (Jan. 1979), 11–14.

_____ . "Database Relations with Null Values," (extended abstract), *ACM Symp. on Principles of Database Systems,* 1982, 27–33.

_____ . "A New Normal form the Design of Relational Database Schemata," *ACM Trans. on Database Systems,* 7, 3 (Sept. 1982), 489–99.

ZANIOLO, C., AND M. A. MELKANOFF. "A Formal Approach to the Definition and the Design of Conceptual Schemata for Database Systems," *ACM Trans. on Database Systems,* 7, 1 (March 1982), 24–59.

ZLOOF, M. M. "Query by Example," *IBM Report RC4917,* Yorktown Heights, NY, July 2, 1974.

_____ . "Query-by-Example: the Invocation and Definition of Tables and Forms," *IBM Report RC5115,* Yorktown Heights, NY, Feb. 1975.

_____ . "Query by Example," *National Computer Conference,* 1975, 431–38.

INDEX

A

Active domain
    in relational model, 15
Active domains, extended
    in relational model, 15
    in tuple calculus expressions, 58–59
Additivity
    of functional dependencies, 86
    of multivalued dependencies, 122
Afunctional dependencies, 84
Aggregate functions, in QUEL (QUEry
        Language), 192
Aggregate operations, in QUEL (QUEry
        Language), 191–92
Aggregation functions, in QBE, 225–26
Algebra, relational. *See* Relational algebra
All-key, 25, 93–94
Antisymmetric relation, 4
Arcs, in graph theory, 10
Arc-sequence, 10
Arithmetic operators, in QUEL (QUEry
        Language), 192–93

Arity, 3
Articulation point, 10
Articulation set, 10
Asymmetric relation, 4
Atomic formulas (atoms)
    in domain calculus, 69–70
    in functional dependencies, 81–82
    in propositional logic, 5
    in tuple calculus, 50–51
Attributes
    constraints of, 22
    extraneous, 95
    in ISBL (Information System Base
        Language), 184
    in QUEL (QUEry Language), 190–91
    in relational model, 13–16
Augmentation
    of functional dependencies, 84
    of multivalued dependencies, 120–21

B

Base relations, 20–21

Binary operations. *See also specific operations*
  in relational algebra, 32
  in set theory, 2–3
Binary relation, 4
Binding, in ISBL (Information System Base Language), 188
Boundedness of variables, 8
  domain variables, 70
  tuple variables, 51–53
Boyce-Codd normal form, 169–72

C

Calculus, relational. *See* Relational calculus
Candidate keys. *See* Keys
Cardinality (or cardinal number) of a set, 1
Cartesian product of two sets, 2, 3
CAZ-graphs, 28
Closed formula, in first-order logic, 8, 9
Closure
  of an FD-graph, 104–9
  of a set of functional dependencies, 87–91
  redundant and nonredundant, 89–90
  subset closure, 90–91
Coalescence, of functional and multivalued dependencies, 124–25
Co-domain, 4
Command box, in QBE, 212, 214–15
Comparison operators, in QUEL (QUEry Language), 192
Compatibility, union, 32
Complement, in relational model, 14–15
Complementation, of multivalued dependencies, 120
Completeness of inference rules, 92–93
Complex product
  definition of, 37–39
  extended active, in tuple calculus expressions, 59
  reduction to tuple calculus, 69
  of two sets, 2

Component, in graph theory, 10
Composition, 4
Compound nodes, implication graphs with, 100–102, 110
Conceptual (logical) database, 12
Condition box, in QBE, 212, 214–15
Conflict-free virtual keys, of multivalued dependencies, 128–29
Conjunction, in propositional logic, 5
Conjunctive normal form, 6
Consistent formula, in propositional logic, 5
Constant relations, 21
Constants, in QUEL (QUEry Language), 191
Constraints, 22–28
Contradiction
  in functional dependencies, 82–83
  in propositional logic, 5
Coverings
  of FD-graphs, 107
  of a set of functional dependencies, 94–97
Cycles, in graph theory, 10

D

Database management systems (DBMSs)
  architecture (levels) of, 12
  models of, 12–13. *See also* Relational model of databases
Database schemes
  full, 133–34
  normalization of. *See* Normalization
  synthesis algorithm for finding, 167–69
Data dependencies. *See also* Join dependencies; Key dependencies; Multivalued dependencies
  afunctional, 84
  transitive, third normal form and, 150–55
Data models, 12–13. *See also* Relational model of databases
Decomposition

of functional dependencies, 86–87
of multivalued dependencies, 122–24
Decomposition trees, 28
Degenerate tree, in graph theory, 11
Degree of a vertex, 10
Dependencies. *See* Data dependencies
Dependency basis, of multivalued
    dependencies, 125–27
Derived relation (or view), 20–21
Difference
    definition of, 36–37
    in functional dependencies, 82
    in ISBL (Information System Base
        Language), 186
    reduction to tuple calculus, 68–69
    of two sets, 2
Directed graphs (or digraphs), 10–11
Disjoint (or mutually exclusive) sets, 2
Disjunction, in propositional logic, 5
Disjunctive normal form, 6
Distinguished variables, lossless join
    dependencies and, 136
Division, definition of, 45–46
Domain calculus, 69–78
    atoms in, 69–70
    reduction of tuple calculus to, 72
    reduction to relational algebra, 72–78
Domain calculus expression, 71–72
Domains
    of attributes, 13–16
    of functions, 3
    primary, 23

E

Edges, in graph theory, 10
Edge sequence, 10
Elementary key normal form, 155–57,
    171–72
Element of a set, 1
Embedded join dependencies, 133
Embedded multivalued dependencies,
    127–28

Empty relations, 20
Empty set, 1
EQUEL (Embedded QUEL), 194, 195
Equi-join, 44
Equivalence, 4
    of FD-graphs, 107–9
    between formulas, 5–6
    logical. *See* Logical equivalence
Existence theorem
    for join dependencies, 139–40
Existential quantifiers, 7
Expressions, in QUEL (QUEry Language),
    192–93
Extended active complex product, 59
Extended active domains
    in relational model, 15
    in tuple calculus expressions, 58–59
Extension(s), 19
    user, in PRTV (Peterlee Relational Test
        Vehicle), 187–88
External database, 12
Extraneous attributes, 95

F

FD-closure, 87–91
    redundant and nonredundant, 89–90
FD-coverings, 94–97
FD-graphs, 28. *See also* Implication graphs
    closure of, 104–9
    covering of, 107
    definiton of, 97–98
    equivalence of, 107–9
    LR-minimal, 111–12
    minimal, 111–12
    nonredundant, 106–7
    optimal, 112
    redundant, 106
    synthesis algorithm based on, 157–69
        database scheme, finding a, 167–69
        LR-minimal graph covering,
            algorithm for finding an,
            163–67

FD-graphs (*cont.*)
    minimal graph covering, algorithm
        for finding a, 159–63
    nonredundant graph covering,
        algorithm for finding a, 158–59
FD satisfaction problem, 87
Field, 13
First normal form, 145–46
First-order logic, 7–10
Floating point constants, in QUEL (QUEry
    Language), 191
Forest, in graph theory, 11
Formulas (well-formed formulas)
    atomic. *See* Atomic formulas (atoms)
    equivalence between, 5–6
    in first-order logic, 8
    interpretations of, 5, 8–9
    in propositional logic, 5
Fourth normal form, 172–74
Freedom
    of domain variables, 70
    of tuple variables, 51–53
Free variable, 8
F-rule, 136
Full database schemes, 133–34
Full quadratic join, 37
    in ISBL (Information System Base
        Language), 186
Functional dependencies, 22, 80–114
    closure of a set of, 87–91
    coverings of a set of, 94–97
    definition of, 80–81
    graphical representations of, 97–113
        closure of an FD-graph, 104–9
        definition of, 97–98
        equivalence of FD-graphs, 107–9
        implication graphs, 98–107
        LR-minimal FD-graphs, 111–12
        minimal FD-graphs, 111–12
        nonredundant FD-graphs, 106–7
        optimal FD-graphs, 112
        redundant FD-graphs, 106
        redundant full arcs, 112
        superfluous compound nodes, 110–11
    inference rules for, 83–87
        augmentation, 84
        coalescence, 124–25
        independent, 83–84
        multivalued dependencies and,
            124–25
        pseudo-transitivity, 84–86
        reflexivity, 83–84
        replication, 124
        soundness and completeness of,
            91–92
        transitivity, 84
    key dependencies and, 93–94
    logical equivalences of, 81–83
    MVD counterpart of, 124
Functions, 3–4

G

Global variable, 7
Graham-reduction of a hypergraph, 11
Graph closure, of FD-graphs, 104–9
Graph covering, algorithm for finding a
    LR-minimal, 163–67
    minimal, 159–63
    nonredundant, 158–59
Graphical representations of functional
    dependencies. *See* Functional
    dependencies–graphical
    representations of
Graphs
    directed, 10–11
    hypergraphs, 11, 27
    implication. *See* Implication graphs
    undirected, 10–11
Graph theory, 10–11

H

Hamiltonian cycle, 10
Horizontal normalization, 179–80
Horn clauses, 7
    in PROLOG, 227–28
Hyperedges, 11

I

Identity function, 4
Implication graphs, 88, 98–107
    with compound nodes, 100–102
        superfluous, 110
    definition of, 98–101
    dotted, 99–101
    full, 99
    with intermediate nodes, 100–102
Inconsistent formula, in propositional
        logic, 5
In-degree of a vertex, 10
Independent inference rules
    for functional dependencies, 83–84
    for multivalued dependencies, 120–21
Indexes, secondary: in QUEL, 202–3
Induction: reduction to tuple calculus, 68
Inference rules
    for functional dependencies, 83–87
        augmentation, 84
        closure of a set of functional
            dependencies, 87–91
        decomposition or projecivity, 86–87
        independent, 83–84
        multivalued dependencies and,
            124–25
        pseudo-transitivity, 84–86
        reflexivity, 83–84
        soundness and completeness of,
            91–92
        transitivity, 84
        union or additivity, 86
    for join dependencies, 141–43
    for multivalued dependencies, 120–25
        augmentation, 120–21
        coalescence, 124–25
        complementation or symmetry, 120
        decomposition or projectivity,
            122–24
        functional dependencies and, 124–25
        independent, 120–21
        pseudo-transitivity, 122
        reflexivity, 120

replication, 124
transitivity, 121
union or additivity, 122
INGRES (INteractive Graphics and
        REtrieval System), 190–209. *See
        also QUEL*
    creating a relation scheme in, 196
    creating or destroying a database in, 195
    editing the work space in, 204–6
    entering or leaving, 196
    environments involved in, 194
    EQUEL (Embedded QUEL) and, 194,
        195
    pattern matching in, 193
    primary and overflow pages in, 201
    printing or resetting the query buffer in,
        200
    query processing by, 206–9
    storage structures in, 200–202
    system relations in, 203–4
Insert-update-delete rules, 24–25
Instance, 19
Integer constants, in QUEL (QUEry
        Language), 191
Intention, 19
Intermediate nodes, implication graphs
        with, 100–102
Internal (physical) database, 12
Interpretations
    of formulas
        in first-order logic, 8–9
        in propositional logic, 5
    limited
        of closed domain calculus formulas,
            71
        of tuple calculus expressions, 59–60
    of tuple calculus expressions, 58–64
Intersection
    definition of, 42–43
    in ISBL (Information System Base
        Language), 186
    of two sets, 2
Invalid formula, in propositional logic, 5
ISBL (Information System Base

ISBL (*cont.*)
      Language),183–86, 188
    algebraic operations in, 185–86
    attributes in, 184
    binding in, 188
    difference in, 37
    named variables in, 185
    objects in, 184
    query processing in, 188–90
    selector in, 184–85
Isolated vertex, in graph theory, 11

J

Join
    definition of, 44–45
    in ISBL (Information System Base
        Language), 186
    natural, 44–45
Join dependencies, 132–43
    definition of, 132–33
    embedded, 133
    existence theorem for, 139–40
    full, 133
        membership problem for, 140–41
    inference rules for, 141–43
    losslessness of, 134–35
        testing of, 136–38
J-rule, 138

K

K-ary operations, 3
Key dependencies, 22, 23, 93–94
Keys
    definition of, 23, 93–94
    primary, 23
K-tuples, *See* Tuples

L

Leaf, in graph theory, 11
Left-reduction, 95

Legal formulas, in tuple calculus, 53–56
Limited interpretations
    of closed domain calculus formulas,
        71
    of tuple calculus expressions, 59–60
Literals, 6
Local variable, 7
Logic
    first-order, 7–10
    propositional, 4–7
Logical (conceptual) database, 12
Logical consequence, in propositional
        logic, 6–7
Logical equivalence
    of functional dependencies, 81–83
    of multivalued dependencies, 116–19,
        130
Logical operators, in QUEL (QUEry
        Language), 192
Losslessness of join dependencies, 134–35
    testing of, 136–38
LR-minimal FD-graphs, 111–12
LR-minimal graph covering, algorithm for
        finding an, 163–67

M

Maps, 3. *See also* Functions
Mathematical tuples, 16
Member of a set, 1
Membership problem, for full join
        dependencies, 140–41
Minimal FD-graphs, 111–12
Minimal graph covering, algorithm for
        finding, 159–63
Minimal set of functional dependencies,
        95–96
Multiset, 1
Multivalued dependencies, 115–30
    conflict-free virtual keys and, 128–29
    definition of, 115–16
    dependency basis of, 125–27
    embedded, 127–28

inference rules for, 120–25
    augmentation, 120–21
    coalescence, 124–25
    complementation or symmetry, 120
    decomposition or projectivity,
        122–24
    functional dependencies and, 124–25
    independent, 120–21
    pseudo-transitivity, 122
    reflexivity, 120
    replication, 124
    transitivity, 121
    union or additivity, 122
logical equivalence of, 116–19, 130
nontrivial, 125
trivial, 125
Mutually exclusive (or disjoint) sets, 2

N

Named variables, in ISBL (Information
        System Base Language), 185
Natural join, 44–45
Negation
    in functional dependencies, 82–83
    in propositional logic, 5
Nodes (or vertices), 10–11
Nonredundant FD-graphs, 106–7
Nonredundant graph covering, algorithm
        for finding, 158–59
Non-reflexive relation, 4, 5
Nontrivial multivalued dependencies, 125
Normal forms
    Boyce-Codd, 169–72
    elementary key, 155–57, 171–72
    first, 145–46
    in first-order logic, 9
    fourth, 172–74
    project-join, 174–79
    in propositional logic, 6
    second, 146–50
    third, 150–55, 171–72
Normalization, 145–81

horizontal, 179–80
vertical. *See* Vertical normalization
NP-completeness, 11
NP-hardness, 11
n-place (or n-ary) function, 3
n-place (or n-ary) predicate, 7
n-place (or n-ary) relation, 4
Nulls, 21
Numeric operators, in QUEL (QUEry
        Language), 192–93

O

Objects, in ISBL (Information System
        Base Language), 184
One-to-one correspondence, 4
One-to-one function, 4
Onto function, 4
Optimal FD-graphs, 112
Optimal set of functional dependencies,
        96–97
Out-degree of a vertex, 10

P

Partial function, 4
Partition, 4
Path, in graph theory, 10, 11
Pattern matching, in INGRES, 193
Physical (internal) database, 12
Power set, 2
Predicates, in first-order logic, 7
Prenex normal form, 9
Primary domains, 23
Primary keys, 23
Projection, 25, 34
    definition of, 39–40
    in ISBL (Information System Base
        Language), 185–86
    reduction to tuple calculus, 69
Projectivity
    of functional dependencies, 86–87
    of multivalued dependencies, 122–24

Project-join normal form, 174–79
PROLOG (PROgramming in LOGic and
    PROLOG DBMS, 226–43
  clausal form of logic in, 227
  correspondence of terminology and
      notation in, 228–29
  extension of, with a database option, 247
  Horn clauses in, 227–28
  initialization and maintenance of system
      relations in, 230–32
  knowledge representations in, 230
  query processing in, 234–42
  scripting a session in, 229
  textfiles and indexfiles in, 229–30
  UNIX environment and, 228
  updating and deleting tuples in, 242–43
Proposition, 5
Propositional logic, 4–7
PRTV (Peterlee Relational Test Vehicle),
    183–84
  query processing in, 188–90
  user extensions in, 187–88
  value of a named variable in, 188
Pseudo-transitivity
  of functional dependencies, 84–86
  of multivalued dependencies, 122

Q

QBE (Query-by-Example) and QBE
    DBMS, 210–26
  aggregates in, 225–26
  blank table skeleton in, 211–12
  condition and command boxes in, 212,
      214–15
  creating a relation in, 232–33
  definition of a data table in, 212–14
  deleting a relation scheme in, 226
  entering the environment of, 210–12
  ENTER key in, 210
  multiple table processing in, 218–25
  renaming in, 226
  single table processing in, 215–18
Qualifications, in QUEL, 206

Quantification, in first-order logic, 7–8
QUEL (QUEry Language), 190–209. *See
    also* INGRES (INteractive
    Graphics and REtrieval System)
  aggregate functions in, 192
  aggregate operations in, 191–92
  attributes in, 190–91
  constants in, 191
  correspondence between tuple calculus
      and, 193–94
  creating a relation scheme in, 196
  creating or destroying a relation in,
      197–99
  displaying and saving a relation with,
      199
  Embedded (EQUEL), 195
  expressions in, 192–93
  printing or resetting the query buffer
      with, 200
  qualifications in, 206
  query processing by, 206–9
  secondary indexes in, 202–3
  storage structures in, 200–202
  variables in, 191
Query languages. *See also* ISBL
    (Information System Base
    Language); PROLOG
    (PROgramming in LOGic) and
    PROLOG DBMS; PRTV (Peterlee
    Relational Test Vehicle); QBE
    (Query-by-Example) and QBE
    DBMS
  classes of, 31
Query processing
  in ISBL (Information System Base
      Language) and PRTV (Peterlee
      Relational Test Vehicle), 188–90
  in PROLOG, 234–42
  by QUEL and INGRES, 206–9
Quotient, definition of, 45–46

R

Range of a function, 3–4

Record, 16
Redundant FD-graphs, 106
Redundant full arcs, 112
Reflexive FD-graphs, 107
Reflexive relation, 4
Reflexivity
    of functional dependencies, 83–84
    of multivalued dependencies, 120
Relational algebra, 31–48
    additional operations for query
        languages based on, 46
    complex product in, 37–39
    difference in, 36–37
    intersection in, 42–43
    in ISBL (Information System Base
        Language), 185–86
    natural join in, 44–45
    projection in, 39–40
    quotient or division in, 45–56
    reduction of domain calculus to, 72–78
    reduction to tuple calculus, 68–69
    renaming in, 33–35
    selection in, 40–41
    theta-join in, 43–44
    union-compatibility in, 32
    union in, 35–36
Relational calculus, 49–78. *See also*
        Domain calculus; Tuple calculus
Relational model of databases
    attributes and domains in, 13–16
    constraints in, 22–28
    definition of, 28–29
    relations and databases in, 19–22
    tables in, 14
    tuples in, 16–19
        algebra of, 4 (*See also* Relational
            algebra)
        base, 20–21
        constant, 21
        empty, 20
        in relational model, 19–22
        tabular representation of, 20
        universal, 21–22
        unnamed, 21

Relation schemes, 19–22
    adding attributes to, 26
    graphic representation of, 27–28
    horizontal normalizaton of, 179–80
    in INGRES and QUEL, 196
    vertical normalization of. *See* Vertical
        normalization
Renaming
    definition of, 33–35
    reduction to tuple calculus, 68
Replication, of functional and multivalued
        dependencies, 124
Restriction of a function, 3
Right-reduction, 95
Rooted tree, in graph theory, 11

S

Secondary indexes, in QUEL (QUEry
        Language), 202–3
Second normal form, 146–50
Selection
    definition of, 40–41
    in ISBL (Information System Base
        Language), 185
    reduction to tuple calculus, 69
Selector, in ISBL (Information System
        Base Language), 184–85
Self-loop, 10
Set operations, 2
Set theory, 1–3
Singleton set, 1
Soundness of inference rules, 92
Storage structures, INGRES, 200–202
String, 3
String constants, in QUEL (QUEry
        Language), 191
Subset closure, 90–91
Superfluous compound nodes, 110–11
Superkeys, definition of, 93–94
Superset, 2
Symmetric relation, 4
Symmetry of multivalued dependencies,
        120

Synthesis algorithm, based on FD-graphs.
    See FD-graphs–synthesis algorithm
    based on

T

Tables, in relational model, 14
Target list, 196
Target row, 136
Tautology
    in functional dependencies, 82–83
    in propositional logic, 5
Terms, in first-order logic, 7
Theta-join, definition of, 43–44
Theta-selection (or restriction), 41–42
Third normal form, 150–55, 171–72
Trail, in graph theory, 10
Transitive dependency, third normal form
    and, 150–55
Transitive relation, 4
Transitivity
    of functional dependencies, 84
    of multivalued dependencies, 121
Trees
    in graph theory, 11
    decomposition, 28
Trivial multivalued dependencies, 125
Tuple calculus, 49–69
    atoms in, 50–51
    correspondence between QUEL (QUEry
        Language) and, 193–94
    definition of, 50
    formulas in, 50–56
        legal, 53–56
    reduction of relational algebra to,
        68–69
    reduction to domain calculus, 72
Tuple calculus expression, 56–67
    definition of, 56–57
    interpretations of, 58–64
    safe, 64–67
Tuples, 3, 16–19
    mathematical, 16

U

Unary operations, in relational algebra, 32
Undirected graphs, 10–11
Union
    definition of, 35–36
    of functional dependencies, 86
    in ISBL (Information System Base
        Language), 186
    of multivalued dependencies, 122
    reduction to tuple calculus, 68
Union-compatibility, definition of, 32
Union of two sets, 2
Universal key, project-join normal form
    and, 176–77
Universal quantifiers, 7
Universal relation assumption, 21–22
UNIX environment
    in INGRES (INteractive Graphics and
        REtrieval System), 194, 195
    PROLOG DBMS and, 228
Unnamed relations, 21
User extensions, in PRTV (Peterlee
    Relational test Vehicle), 187–88

V

Value-sets of attributes, 13–16
Variables, in QUEL (QUEry Language),
    191
Venn diagrams, multivalued dependencies
    and, 117–18, 124
Vertex-sequence, 10
Vertical normalization, 145–79, 180–81
    Boyce-Codd normal form and, 169–72
    elementary key normal form and,
        155–57
    first normal form and, 145–46
    fourth normal form and, 172–74
    project-join normal form and, 174–79
    relationship among 3NF, EKNF, and
        BCNF relation schemes and,
        171–72

second normal form and, 146–50
synthesis algorithm for. *See* FD-
    graphs–synthesis algorithm based
    on
third normal form and, 150–55, 171–72
Vertices (or nodes), 10–11
Virtual keys, conflict-free: of multivalued

dependencies, 128–29

W

Well-formed formulas. *See* Formula

FD-graphs (*cont.*)